Chpte 1

1-16

3, 45,

w/knd Lease vs. Purchase Decisions

Case A, G, Crawford Industries

showed asset up $$$ in Bigsher

FINANCIAL STRATEGY

FINANCIAL STRATEGY

Studies in the creation, transfer, and destruction of shareholder value

WILLIAM E. FRUHAN, JR.

Graduate School
of Business Administration
Harvard University

1979

IRWIN

Homewood, Illinois 60430

ISBN 0-256-02228-3
Library of Congress Catalog Card No. 78–70005

Printed in the United States of America

9 10 11 12 13 14 MP 4 3 2 1 0 9 8

To Ginny, Matt, and Billy

Preface

This book is part of an ongoing effort to raise issues in the area of financial strategy that have relevance for both senior financial executives and students of business administration. In this effort I have enjoyed a great deal of help from many professional colleagues involved in the field of business education. Major contributions to the book both in its formative stages and throughout its development were made by Gordon Donaldson, Robert R. Glauber, John Lintner, John H. McArthur, and William L. White.

As draft chapters of the book were completed, Derek F. Abell, William J. Abernathy, Norman A Berg, J. Keith Butters, Robert D. Buzzell, Jesse W. Markham, David W. Mullins, Jr., Michael E. Porter, Richard S. Rosenbloom, W. Earl Sasser, Jr., Eli Shapiro, A. Michael Spence, Howard H. Stevenson, and Richard F. Vancil all contributed valuable insights which helped significantly to improve the final product. Max R. Hall provided invaluable editorial assistance.

Numerous colleagues from industry were extremely generous with their time in reviewing the seven chapters in the book which deal with individual firms. Drafts of each of these seven chapters benefitted from the comments of as many as four different individuals with specific expertise about each of the businesses in question.

The financial support for this book came from the Harvard Business School. I wish to thank the Division of Research, and especially its director, Associate Dean Richard S. Rosenbloom for providing the resources needed to underwrite the research effort.

I am indebted to Anne S. Mundo for much of the computer programming utilized in Chapter 1. Rita Colella and H. E. Pocius provided invaluable support through their tireless efforts in typing the manuscript through a seemingly endless series of revisions.

Finally, any errors in the book remain uniquely my own.

January 1979   *William E. Fruhan, Jr.*

Contents

INTRODUCTION, 1

PART ONE: GAINING ENTRY INTO THE BUSINESS HALL
OF FAME

Chapter 1. Hall of Fame firms, 7

PART TWO: PROCESSES BY WHICH SHAREHOLDER VALUES
ARE CREATED, TRANSFERRED, AND DESTROYED

Chapter 2. The levers that managers can utilize to enhance shareholder
values, 65

PART THREE: EXAMPLES OF FIRMS CREATING, TRANSFERRING,
AND DESTROYING SHAREHOLDER VALUES

Value creation

Chapter 3. Avon Products, Inc., 93

Chapter 4. The grocery retailing industry, 115

Chapter 5. Freeport Minerals Company, 129

Chapter 6. General Electric Company, 149

Value transfer

Chapter 7. The computer leasing industry, 180

Value destruction

Chapter 8. The Great Atlantic & Pacific Tea Company, Inc., 209

Value creation, transfer, and destruction

Chapter 9. The Levitz Furniture Corporation, 237

PART FOUR: SUMMARY AND CONCLUSIONS

Chapter 10. The scope and the ethics of value transformation opportunity, 277

BIBLIOGRAPHY, 287

INDEX, 297

Introduction

This book describes how firms achieve entry into the Hall of Fame of American business. Not many firms make it. Some get there on pure luck. Most get there because extremely able managers pulled critical levers at important points in the evolutionary development of their companies. For these managers the trick was knowing which levers to pull, and when pulling these levers would produce significant results in terms of profitability and security valuations.

A detailed examination of how a particular firm "made it" may produce some insight as to how others might achieve similar results. That is one of the purposes of this book. A well-marked path designed to enhance the performance of each and every firm will obviously not emerge from this book. Life is not that simple. Instead, the broader objective of this book is to demonstrate that systematic thinking about methods for creating, transferring, and destroying[1] shareholder wealth can have a significant financial payoff for a firm's shareholders. Such thinking may help to identify which levers to pull, and when the time is right to pull them.

Managerial efforts aimed at enhancing shareholder wealth are a central concern in this book. Management motivations are not. I will not attempt to demonstrate that the pursuit of enhanced security valuations is, or ought[2] to be, the driving force, or even a highly important force, in

---

[1] A firm can sometimes enhance the wealth of its own shareholders by eroding the profitability of its competitors. Erosion in the profitability of competing firms may cause a critical source of financing to be cut off for these firms, thereby crippling their growth and eroding the wealth of their shareholders.

[2] The objective of shareholder wealth maximization is a necessary condition for the efficient allocation of economic resources. In addition, managers have a legal obligation to serve the economic interests of their shareholders. Finally, senior corporate officers receive ownership income (dividends plus capital gains) from stock in

1

motivating management action. Our explorations will be limited to gaining an understanding of the effect of management actions on security valuations, regardless of the motivations prompting these actions. As the title of the book suggests, the management choices we will examine have both financial and strategic significance.

The book is divided into four parts. The first part, Chapter 1, explores the economic factors that influence the valuation of common stocks. A present-value model is utilized. It permits us to value a firm's common stock, in a rational economic framework, by examining the firm's product-market investment opportunities. The model shows what it takes to make it into the Hall of Fame of American business. Chapter 1 then identifies those firms that actually have made it. These are firms that consistently earn rates of return on equity that exceed their equity capital costs.

The second part of the book, Chapter 2, explores the general processes by which shareholder values can be (1) created, (2) transferred, or (3) destroyed. Because value creation appears to have the greatest dollar significance of the three value-enhancing activities, value creation techniques are explored most fully in the book.

The *creation of value* for shareholders occurs in several ways. Entry barriers can be developed. Entry barriers make it possible for a firm to increase operating revenues above (or reduce operating cost below) levels that would otherwise exist in a fully competitive situation. Success in capitalizing upon entry barriers permits a firm to generate larger cash flows on a given capital base than would be possible absent the entry barrier. Higher cash flows then translate into higher equity values, given a specific level of capital costs. Another way to create value for shareholders relates to the reduction of capital costs. A firm can sometimes (*a*) design securities to attract capital at rates lower than those available to less resourceful competitors, or (*b*) reduce its business risk below that experienced by less imaginative competitors, or (*c*) achieve a capital structure that produces a lower overall capital cost than its less resourceful competitors. Success in any one of these areas will translate into higher equity values for the firm's shareholders at any given level of operating cash-flow generation.

Value transfer, another broad area of value-enhancing activity, can occur when the value of a specific security is temporarily detached from the underlying economic reality of the issuing firm's real investment opportunities. Value transfers arise primarily because of imperfections in the pricing efficiency of the capital markets. In contrast to value creation,

---

the firms they manage that, on average, frequently exceeds their direct compensation. (See Wilbur G. Lewellen, *The Ownership Income of Management,* National Bureau of Economic Research, 1971, pp. 102–3. Market efficiency, legal obligation, and personal interest thus often converge for senior managers on the issue of shareholder wealth maximization.

the transfer of value among security holders is a zero-sum game. What one group of security owners wins, a second group of security holders loses. Firms that successfully achieve value transfers generally do so by acquiring assets (cash or the ownership of another firm) in exchange for their own "overvalued"[3] securities. Other forms of value transfer are possible, and they will be explored, but the type noted above is the most common. Viewed as a management tool, value-*transfer* appears to be less important in aggregate dollar significance than value-*creation*. Nevertheless, it is not hard to find examples of value-*transfers* amounting to hundreds of millions of dollars, particularly during times when the securities markets seem to be guided more by the phases of the moon than by rational economics.

Value destruction is the third and final area of value-enhancing activity that is explored in this book. Value destruction occurs relatively infrequently in the competitive environment. Nevertheless, financially oriented business strategies that ultimately weaken or eliminate competition do emerge. A price war is the clearest example. Obviously, destroying the value of a competitor's common stock must be an *incidental result* of a broader strategy, rather than the *principal objective* of that strategy. Some quite unpleasant legal problems can arise for practitioners of the value-destruction art if this fact is not clearly understood.

Part III of this book moves from general principles to specific examples of value enhancement. The individual firms examined in Part III are actively creating, transferring, and destroying shareholder values. The value creation segment of Part III includes four clinical examples. At the top of the pyramid stands a firm that enjoys a unique market position and a unique level of profitability. Chapter 3 describes the economics of Avon Products' remarkable success.

Chapter 4 looks at some stellar performers in a mundane industry. The stars of this chapter are the grocery retailers Winn-Dixie, Weis Markets, Lucky Stores, and the Dillon Companies, all of which appear in the Chapter 1 list of firms earning high rates of return on equity. While large, these firms rank only 6, 31, 5, and 16, respectively, in terms of 1976 national grocery sales.[4] Chapter 4 shows why these otherwise undistinguished firms show up in the Hall of Fame as a result of value creation for their shareholders.

Chapter 5 departs from the pattern of looking at an *entire firm* in the

---

[3] The term "overvalued" is used here in a special context. Chapter 1 describes a method for valuing a firm's equity securities where this value is a function of the firm's investment opportunities, and the discounted value of the cash flows streaming from these investment opportunities. In those situations where the *market* value of a firm's equity securities exceeds the rational *economic* value of those securities (as defined above), the securities are deemed to be overvalued.

[4] *Progressive Grocer*, April 1977, pp. 126, 130.

value creation context, and looks at an individual capital investment *project*. Here the focus of attention is on how a business architect enhances the expected rate of return on an otherwise marginal investment opportunity. The firm is Freeport Minerals, and the investment project is a copper mine in Indonesia.

Chapter 6 is a study in making a silk purse out of a sow's ear. The industry is computers, and the problem is how to generate value from a hopelessly inadequate market position. This chapter shows how General Electric creates value via the financial design of the sale of its computer division.

The value-transfer segment of Part III consists primarily of Chapter 7. This chapter examines the third-party computer leasing industry that blossomed in the United States in the late 1960s. Firms in this industry capitalized on an overvaluation of their securities first by raising enormous amounts of equity capital, and later by acquiring other firms (or being acquired by other firms) in exchange for stock. By the time security valuations in this industry became linked to economic reality, value transfers across the various investor groups participating in the industry amounted to close to $1 billion.

Chapter 8 examines value destruction. The chapter focuses on the efforts of the largest national supermarket chain, A&P, to improve its competitive posture. Part of the firm's strategy is to cut price. The chapter explores both the economics and the competitive consequences of a price war.

Chapter 9 is the final clinical example. This chapter shows one firm *simultaneously* exploiting all three areas of value-enhancing opportunity. The firm, Levitz Furniture, *creates* value via scale economies and local market dominance (as in the supermarket example of Chapter 4). It *transfers* value via large and frequent equity offerings at prices that are demonstrably detached from economic reality. Finally Levitz's pricing and store location strategies produce enormous start-up losses for retailers who copy the Levitz retailing approach. These losses produce, as one effect, value *destruction* for the shareholders of Levitz's competitors.

Part IV, the final section of the book, examines the aggregate economic significance of value creation, transfer, and destruction. It also touches upon the social consequences and the ethics of creating, transferring, and destroying shareholder value.

PART ONE

Gaining entry into the
business Hall of Fame

1

Hall of Fame firms

Managers create economic value for their firm's shareholders whenever they undertake investments that produce returns that exceed capital costs. This chapter will focus first on developing a mathematical model that places a specific economic value on the opportunity to invest capital in a particular business at returns that vary from (and, more specifically, exceed) capital costs.

A simple but powerful link exists between a firm's decisions on capital investments and a rational investor's valuation of that firm's equity securities. Early explorations into this link partitioned the value of a firm's equity securities into two different components.[1] The first component of value arose from the future cash flows streaming from the assets the firm *already* had in place. The second component of value arose from the cash flows investors anticipated from investments that the firm would have the opportunity to make some time in the *future*. For firms facing a large volume of future investment opportunities promising returns substantially in excess of capital costs for a long time period, this second component of value is quite important.

ASSUMPTIONS FOR A SAMPLE CALCULATION

A security valuation model (that takes into account the cash flows streaming from a firm's existing as well as future capital investments) can be made explicit in an operationally useful way as follows:

---

[1] The most prominent of the earliest works explicitly dealing with this issue is Merton H. Miller and Franco Modigliani, "Dividend Policy, Growth, and the Valuation of Shares," *The Journal of Business,* October 1961.

1. Assume that Firm A has a net worth of $100, and that it earns an annual after-tax profit of $30 on that equity base. The firm has either a fixed proportion of debt in its capital structure, or, as in the following example, an all-equity capital structure. Assume further that a business facing similar risk in a perfectly competitive market[2] could be expected to earn only a 10 percent profit on its equity, and that the appropriate cost of equity capital for Firm A is therefore 10 percent.

2. Assume that Firm A's ability to earn the abnormally high 30 percent return on equity will last (for example, until the expiration of a patent) only for the next ten years, and that at the end of ten years its rate of return will immediately fall to the level of 10 percent.

3. Finally, assume that the portfolio of abnormally high return investment opportunities (averaging 30 percent[3]) facing Firm A is growing sufficiently fast so as to exhaust only 50 percent of the firm's earnings each year, and that the remainder of the earnings are returned to the shareholders as dividends.

Given these assumptions the question of interest to us is, "What is the economic value, today, of Firm A's equity to a rational investor?" By discounting the expected cash flows produced according to the specified assumptions, we arrive at an answer of $324.08 (Table 1–1). Since the original investment by Firm A's shareholders was only $100.00, Firm A's management has succeeded in creating value equal to $324.08 — $100.00 = $224.08. What is the source of this value creation?

THE SOURCE OF VALUE CREATION: THE PROFILE OF INVESTMENT OPPORTUNITY

Absent new[4] capital-investment opportunities offering rates of return exceeding 10 percent, the cash flows produced by Firm A's existing equity would be worth $222.92 (Table 1–2). Had Firm A earned only 10 percent on its equity base at the outset, and had it enjoyed future investment

---

[2] This refers to perfectly competitive financial markets (that is, the markets for securities).

[3] This *average* rate could imply some investment opportunities promising returns on equity substantially in excess of 30 percent, and others at returns all the way down to 10 percent. In addition, these investment opportunities would not necessarily earn average returns on equity of 30 percent over their *entire* projected lives. Indeed, average returns on equity of 30 percent would be earned only during the time period (ten years in the example above) during which returns in excess of capital costs were anticipated.

[4] "New" investments relate only to those investments that would actually expand the firm's investment base. It is assumed, implicitly, that cash flow resulting from depreciation is reinvested annually to maintain both the capital investment base and the 30 percent ROE figure.

TABLE 1-1
Calculation of the economic value of a firm's equity (versus its book value)

Start of year	(1) Book value of shareholder's investment	(2) ROE achieved	(3) Profit after tax	(4) Retained earnings	(5) Cash return to shareholders from dividends and/or sale of stock at book value	(6) Present value factor at 10% discount rate	(7) Present value of (5)
1	$100.00	30%	$ 30.00	$15.00	$ 15.00	0.909	$ 13.64
2	115.00	30	34.50	17.25	17.25	0.826	14.25
3	132.25	30	39.68	19.84	19.84	0.751	14.90
4	152.09	30	45.62	22.81	22.81	0.683	15.58
5	174.90	30	52.46	26.23	26.23	0.621	16.29
6	201.13	30	60.34	30.17	30.17	0.564	17.02
7	231.30	30	69.38	34.69	34.69	0.513	17.80
8	265.99	30	79.78	39.89	39.89	0.467	18.63
9	305.88	30	91.76	45.88	45.88	0.424	19.45
10	351.76	30	105.54	52.77	52.77	0.386	20.37
11	404.53	10			404.53*	0.386	156.15
							$324.08

$$\text{Economic value} = 3.24$$
$$\text{Book value}$$

Where the firm faces (a) Investment opportunities with 30% returns to equity in (b) amounts sufficient to exhaust 50% of each year's earnings for (c) 10 years, and (d) where the firm has a 10% cost of equity.

*It is assumed here that the stock will be sold at book value at the end of year 10, once it is clear that future ROEs will equal only the firm's assumed cost of equity of 10%. The model also assumes that there is no *uncertainty* about the price of the stock at the end of year 10. The stock at that point (and at all points during the ten intervening years) is assumed to be rationally valued such that a sale at any *intervening* point in time would also produce a 10% return to the shareholder. This 10% return would be made up of dividends plus capital gains as indicated below.

Year	Economic value of stock		Capital gain in year	Dividend in year	Total return in year	Rate of return in year
	Start of year	End of year				
1	$324.08	$341.36	$17.28	$15.00	$32.28	10.0%
2	341.36	358.15	16.79	17.25	34.04	10.0
3	358.15	374.12	15.97	19.84	35.81	10.0
4	374.12	388.72	14.60	22.81	37.41	10.0
5	388.72	401.36	12.64	26.23	38.87	10.0
6	401.36	411.32	9.96	30.17	40.13	10.0
7	411.32	417.76	6.44	34.69	41.13	10.0
8	417.76	419.64	1.88	39.89	41.77	10.0
9	419.64	415.72	(3.92)	45.88	41.96	10.0
10	415.72	404.53	(11.19)	52.77	41.58	10.0

TABLE 1-2
Calculation of the economic value of a firm's equity (versus its book value)

Start of year	(1) Book value of shareholder's investment	(2) ROE achieved	(3) Profit after tax	(4) Retained earnings	(5) Cash return to shareholders from dividends and/or sale of stock at book value	(6) Present value factor at 10% discount rate	(7) Present value of (5)
1	$100.00	30%	$30.00	0	$ 30.00	0.909	$ 27.27
2	100.00	30	30.00	0	30.00	0.826	24.78
3	100.00	30	30.00	0	30.00	0.751	22.53
4	100.00	30	30.00	0	30.00	0.683	20.49
5	100.00	30	30.00	0	30.00	0.621	18.63
6	100.00	30	30.00	0	30.00	0.564	16.92
7	100.00	30	30.00	0	30.00	0.513	15.39
8	100.00	30	30.00	0	30.00	0.467	14.01
9	100.00	30	30.00	0	30.00	0.424	12.72
10	100.00	30	30.00	0	30.00	0.386	11.58
11	100.00	30	30.00	0	100.00*	0.386	38.60
							$222.92

$$\frac{\text{Economic value}}{\text{Book value}} = 2.22$$

Where the firm faces (a) no new capital investment opportunities with returns exceeding 10%, although the firm earns 30% on equity at the outset; (b) returns on equity will collapse from 30% to 10% at the end of 10 years; (c) the cost of equity to the firm is 10%.

*It is assumed that the stock will be sold at book value at the end of year 10, once it is clear that future ROEs will equal only the firm's assumed cost of equity of 10%. The model also assumes that there is no *uncertainty* about the price of the stock at the end of year 10, or at any point during the ten intervening years. The stock is assumed to be rationally valued such that a sale at any point in time would produce a 10% return to shareholders.

opportunities offering only 10 percent returns, the discounted value of its future cash flows would, of course, equal only $100.

The $324.08 value for Firm A's equity securities calculated in Table 1–1 can thus be allocated as follows:

1. $100.00 can be attributed to the original investment (assuming it had been able to produce only the competitively demanded 10 percent rate of return).
2. $122.92[5] can be attributed to the fact that the original $100.00 investment was expected to produce returns on equity for a ten-year period that exceeded equity costs by some 20 percentage points.
3. $101.16[6] can be attributed to the fact that investors in Firm A anticipated that the firm would have, annually over the next ten years, investment opportunities sufficient to utilize 50 percent of the firm's profits. These investment opportunities promised, on average, to return 30 percent on equity until the end of the tenth year. Profits not reinvested would be returned to shareholders as dividends, but cash flow resulting from depreciation charges would be reinvested.

The sample calculations carried out above are entirely hypothetical. The specific assumptions describing Firm A's existing and future investment opportunities are probably realistic for only a handful of U.S. nonfinancial corporations (NFCs). The example clearly needs to be extended to cover a wider spectrum of investment opportunity profiles characteristic of U.S. firms. Happily this is a rather straightforward task. Table 1–3 accomplishes this goal. Table 1–3 represents the link between investment opportunity and security valuations.

THE ECONOMIC VALUE/BOOK VALUE MATRICES

Table 1–3 displays the *multiple of book value* at which a firm's equity security should be economically valued as a function of three factors. The three factors were introduced in Table 1–1. They are:

1. The *size of the percentage point spread* projected to be earned on common equity over the cost of the firm's common equity.
2. The *volume* of future capital investment opportunities promising average rates of return equal to the level indicated in (1) above. This is expressed in terms of the common equity increase each year in relation to net profits available for common stock.[7]

---

[5] This equals $222.92 − $100.00 (i.e., the Table 1–2 result minus the original equity investment valued at book value).

[6] This equals $324.08 − $222.92 (i.e., the Table 1–1 result minus the Table 1–2 result).

[7] This is equal to net profits after taxes (less preferred stock dividends, if any).

TABLE 1-3
Matrices of projected economic value/book value ratios*

Percentage point spread projected to be earned on common stock equity over and above the firm's cost of equity capital[†]

Projected number of years during which the extraordinary returns on common stock equity noted at the top of each matrix will be earned in the future

Projected level of extraordinary return reinvestment opportunity anticipated in the future expressed as ($ annual growth in common stock equity)/($ annual profit after tax)

0.3

	-5	0	+5	+10	+20
5	0.8	1.0	1.2	1.4	1.9
10	0.7	1.0	1.3	1.8	2.7
15	0.6	1.0	1.5	2.1	3.6
30	0.5	1.0	1.7	2.7	5.8

0.5

	-5	0	+5	+10	+20
5	0.8	1.0	1.2	1.5	2.0
10	0.7	1.0	1.4	1.9	3.2
15	0.6	1.0	1.6	2.4	4.8
30	0.4	1.0	2.0	3.7	12.2

0.7

	-5	0	+5	+10	+20
5	0.8	1.0	1.2	1.5	2.1
10	0.6	1.0	1.5	2.1	3.9
15	0.5	1.0	1.7	2.8	6.8
30	0.4	1.0	2.5	5.8	30.8

1.0

	-5	0	+5	+10	+20
5	0.8	1.0	1.2	1.5	2.3
10	0.6	1.0	1.6	2.4	5.3
15	0.5	1.0	1.9	3.7	12.2
30	0.2	1.0	3.8	13.5	149.3

2.0‡

	-5	0	+5	+10	+20
5	0.8	1.0	1.3	1.8	3.2
10	0.5	1.0	2.1	4.4	22.3
15	0.3	1.0	3.8	13.0	161.6

*For use in valuing the common stocks of firms facing different portfolios of real (i.e., nonfinancial) investment opportunities. The economic value/book value ratios produced in this table can be calculated from the following equation:

$$\frac{\text{Economic value}}{\text{Book value}} = \left(\frac{1 + (\text{ROE})\,(\text{RET})}{1 + K_e}\right)^n + \frac{\text{ROE}(1-\text{RET})}{K_e - (\text{ROE})\,(\text{RET})}\left[1 - \left(\frac{1 + (\text{ROE})\,(\text{RET})}{1 + K_e}\right)^n\right]$$

where ROE = the anticipated rate of return on common stock equity;

K_e = the cost of common stock equity;

RET = the projected level of extraordinary return reinvestment opportunities anticipated each year in the future, expressed as a fraction of the anticipated profit after taxes for that year;

n = The projected number of years during which extraordinary returns on common stock equity are expected to be earned.

†The firm's cost of equity capital in each case is assumed to be 10% for purposes of this example.

‡A firm can grow its equity base by more than 100% annually by either selling stock for cash or issuing stock in acquisitions.

3. The *number of years* during which the exceptional returns noted in (1) and (2) above will continue to be available before these returns are forced to the level of the firm's cost of common equity by, for example, competitive pressures.[8]

The single calculation of Table 1–1 can be easily traced to Table 1–3. The circled value in Table 1–1 is the circled value in the more fully described universe of corporate investment opportunity profiles captured in Table 1–3. The calculations of Table 1–3 span, for firms, the range of possible rates of return on common equity from 5 percent to 30 percent. Assuming a 10 percent cost of common equity, this is equivalent to a percentage point spread earned above the cost of equity equal to −5 percentage points to +20 percentage points as shown across the top of the matrices in Table 1–3.

The matrices of Table 1–3 also span annual reinvestment rates ranging from 30 percent of profits to 200 percent of profits.[9] Variations in this variable are expressed along the right-hand side of Table 1–3.

Finally, Table 1–3 assumes that competitive forces will force a firm's return on equity back to a rate that is consistent with its capital costs at a specific point in time ranging from 5 to 30 years in the future. Variations in this variable are captured along the left-hand side of the exhibit.

Within the parameters outlined above, the matrices of Table 1–3 indicate the economic value (measured in relation to book value) for any firm's common equity security.[10] That value is, of course, a function of the attractiveness of the investment opportunity posture of the firm.

THE HISTORIC INVESTMENT OPPORTUNITY PROFILE OF U.S. NFCs

Table 1–4 confirms that the Table 1–3 categorization in fact captures the broad range of actual performance historically achieved by U.S. NFCs

---

[8] Table 1–3 assumes that ROEs in excess of equity capital costs will end abruptly at the conclusion of the time frame chosen. If these returns are assumed to decay linearly over the last five years of the time frame chosen, the effect of this change in assumptions on the present value of the cash flows is not usually very significant. The greatest effect occurs when the point spread between ROEs and equity capital costs is high, and the time period over which this differential is sustained is short.

[9] The definition of "reinvestment" here encompasses both net worth increases generated as a result of the sale of new shares for cash, as well as net worth increases generated by the issuance of new shares for corporate acquisitions. Thus, reinvestment can (and for some firms does) exceed 100 percent of profits earned.

[10] Implicit in Table 1–3 is the assumption that each firm's cost of equity capital is 10 percent. This is obviously a highly simplified assumption, which is used only for illustrative purposes. The limitations of this assumption can be easily overcome by simply recalculating Table 1–3 for equity capital costs in 1 percent increments ranging, for example, from 5 percent to 25 percent. This is a computationally trivial but physically bulky undertaking.

TABLE 1-4

Percentage of 1,448 firms with average rates of return on common equity as indicated across the top of the matrix, and average increase in common equity (measured as a fraction of net profits) as indicated along the left side of the matrix

		Average rate of return on common equity, 1966-1975*					
		1.9% or less	2.0% to 7.9%	8.0% to 11.9%	12.0% to 17.9%	18.0% to 24.9%	25.0% and over	Row totals
	0.19 or less	2.7%	2.4%	0.6%	0.5%	0.3%	0.1%	6.6%
Level of reinvestment of firms expressed as average annual increase in common equity/average annual profit after tax†	0.20 to 0.39	0.4	1.9	1.9	1.3	0.2	0.3	6.0
	0.40 to 0.59	0.3	2.8	6.4	5.2	1.2	0.5	16.4
	0.60 to 0.79	0.3	3.0	8.2	9.2	2.4	0.2	23.3
	0.80 to 1.19	0.4	4.3	9.9	10.6	2.0	0.1	27.3
	1.20 to 1.59	0.6	3.8	4.8	2.8	0.5	0.0	12.5
	1.60 and over	1.7	4.8	0.9	0.4	0.0	0.0	7.8
	Column totals	6.4%	23.0%	32.7%	30.0%	6.6%	1.2%	100.0%

*Average rate of return on common equity is measured for an individual firm as:

$$\left[\sum_{n=1966}^{1975} (\text{Profit to common equity})_n \right] \div \left[\sum_{n=1966}^{1975} (\text{Common equity})_n \right].$$

The ratio of sums is used in this definition rather than the average of yearly ratios in order to reduce distortions caused by some extreme values produced in individual years. A one-year loss that was substantial in relation to net worth could, for example, produce a significant distortion of the data if the average of yearly ratios were utilized.

†(Average annual growth of common equity)/(Average annual profit after tax) is measured for an individual firm as:

$$\left[(\text{Common equity})_{1975} - (\text{Common equity})_{1966} \right] \div \left[\sum_{n=1967}^{1975} (\text{Profit to common equity})_n \right].$$

Note: The characteristics of the 1,448 firms included in this table are described in Footnote 11.

regarding rates of return and reinvestment rates. This exhibit shows that a large sample of U.S. NFCs exhibited the following characteristics.[11]

1. For 92.4 percent of the sample firms, the average rate of return on common equity ranged between 2 percent and 24.9 percent. This would correspond to a —8 percentage point to +15 percentage point spread over the assumed equity cost of 10 percent noted in Table 1–3. Just 6.4 percent of the sample firms achieved an average ROE below 2.0 percent during the ten-year period, while 7.8 percent of the firms achieved an average ROE of 18.0 percent or higher.

2. For 67 percent of the sample firms, the average annual increase in common equity ranged from 40 percent to 119 percent of average annual profits. For 12.6 percent of the sample firms, the average annual increase in common equity was below 39 percent of annual profits. For 20.3 percent of the sample firms, the average increase in common equity exceeded 119 percent of average annual profits. This latter result was somewhat surprising. It is explained largely by major acquisitions that were accomplished via exchanges of stock.

3. Another somewhat surprising empirical observation relates to the fraction of firms that expanded their equity bases quite rapidly in relation to their earnings, while averaging rather low ROEs. About 9.6 percent of the sample firms expanded their equity bases over the ten-year period at the rate of 120 percent or more of average annual earnings, while producing average ROEs of only 2.0 percent to 7.9 percent over the period.[12] The rapid expansion and low ROEs of many of these firms can be explained as follows. The firms made

---

[11] The 1,448 firms in this sample include all of the firms that satisfied the following constraints:

a. They were included in the Compustat "Primary, Supplementary, and Tertiary Industrial Files." (These include, among others, all of the NYSE and AMEX industrials, the Fortune 500, and the S&P 425 industrials.) A few non-U.S. firms are included in the above totals, where the firms' equity securities are actively traded in U.S. markets.

b. They were firms for which data on profit to common equity, common equity, common stock price, and number of common shares outstanding were available for every year from 1966 to 1975.

c. They were firms that never had a negative value for common equity between 1966 and 1975.

[12] About 2.3 percent of the sample firms altered their equity bases over the ten-year period at the rate of 120 percent or more of average annual earnings, while producing average ROEs of *less than 2.0 percent*. Most of the firms in this category actually suffered an *erosion* in their equity bases because of cumulative losses over the period. The combined effects of dividend payments, cumulative losses, and reduced net worth produces an anomalous result according to the definition of the reinvestment rate utilized in Table 1–4. Such firms appear to have high reinvestment rates when, in fact, they are contracting.

major acquisitions[13] via exchanges of stock during the conglomerate merger movement of 1967–69, and later suffered major profit problems. Obviously not all of the firms in this category followed the pattern noted above, but it was a clearly observable general characteristic for this group of firms.

4. At the other end of the spectrum we find very few firms that are both earning very high ROEs and expanding their equity bases significantly faster than their annual profits. Only 0.5 percent of the sample firms earned an ROE exceeding 18.0 percent while simultaneously expanding their equity bases by more than 120 percent of annual earnings. This empirical observation is not surprising since a firm increasing its equity base at 50 percent per year for ten years would experience a 58-fold increase in net worth over this time period.[14]

5. Finally, it should be noted that a surprisingly large number of firms seem able to survive and continue as independent entities for quite long time periods while earning abysmal rates of return on equity. Some 29.4 percent of the sample firms earned an average ROE of less than 8 percent over the ten-year time period.

THE RESULTS OF THE ECONOMIC VALUE/BOOK VALUE MODEL

Table 1–3 presents some quite interesting observations on the value-creation potential inherent in a firm's profile of investment opportunity. A move from left to right along the horizontally circled line of data in the exhibit shows the valuation impact associated with business investment opportunities promising *successively increasing* rates of return. A move from the top down along the vertically circled column of data in the exhibit shows the equity-valuation impact associated with success in *extending the time frame* of any competitive advantage a firm might enjoy before competitive pressures force the rate of return back to purely competitive levels. Finally, the dotted arrow demonstrates the enormous valuation associated with the equity securities of *rapidly growing* high-return businesses. Broadly speaking, the upper left-hand corner of Table 1–3 represents the investment opportunity profile of U.S. firms in mature industries that are noncompetitive in world markets.[15] As we

---

13 Of the 124 firms in this category (9.6 percent of the 1,448-firm sample), 83 firms experienced a growth in book value of total common equity exceeding 50 percent in at least one year of the period 1966–75. In almost all cases this growth came as a result of one or more acquisitions for stock.

14 A firm earning a 25 percent ROE and expanding its equity base by 200 percent of earnings each year would expand its net worth by a factor of 58 over ten years.

15 Also included in this category are firms that occupy uneconomic market positions in otherwise healthy industries, and firms with other debilitating characteristics such as poor management.

move to the bottom right-hand corner of Table 1–3, we find the firms that investors perceive to be the embryonic IBMs, Xeroxes, and Avons of the future. Obviously, economic value soars as we move along this diagonal in the exhibit.

REAL INVESTMENT VERSUS FINANCIAL INVESTMENT DECISIONS

All of the analysis developed to this point has related to the viewpoint of an investor making a rational economic valuation of an equity security. Exactly the same analysis can be used by a firm in its capital budgeting decisions regarding real asset acquisitions. In such situations the multiples of economic value in relation to book value drawn from Table 1–3 can be viewed as the present value of the maximum cash losses that a firm ought to be willing to sustain in order to achieve the investment opportunity posture corresponding to the appropriate matrix element in Table 1–3. Thus, in order to buy into a market area with future investment opportunities similar to Firm A (Table 1–1), a firm ought to be willing to invest[16] (in present value entry-costs or start-up losses) up to a maximum of $224.08 for every $100 of earning assets established in this business.[17]

The above approach to strategic capital budgeting explains to some degree why firms such as GE and RCA were willing to invest very large sums of money at a substantial loss year after year in the 1960s in an effort to gain a share of the highly profitable (to IBM) computer manufacturing business.[18] It similarly helps to explain why drug firms "invest" in research, and why consumer products firms "invest" in heavy advertising in order to build a market franchise for their products.

The preceding discussion has produced a simplified model for valuing a firm's equity securities (or its real asset investment choices) that is

---

[16] While funds would be invested in establishing a market position, this "investment" would not be reflected in any balance-sheet asset account. Instead, both cash and net worth would decline by the amount of the after-tax loss sustained in establishing the market position.

[17] In this example investors would receive their required 10 percent return on equity (thus making the investment entirely rational) if the firm were to:

a. invest $224.08 that was to be absorbed in after-tax start-up losses, and
b. invest $100 that was to produce a 30 percent ROE for ten years, and 10 percent ROE thereafter as shown in Table 1–1, and
c. invest 50 percent of its earnings each year in investment opportunities that promised to produce, on average, 30 percent ROEs until the end of the ten-year period.

This calculation again assumes that the new business being entered has risk characteristics consistent with a 10 percent cost of equity capital.

[18] We shall explore this concept at greater length in Chapter 10.

based upon the attractiveness of the firm's investment opportunities.[19] Our focus has been on the determination of *economic*[20] value. In Table 1–3 this economic value is related to book values as determined through the application of historical cost accounting principles (GAAP).[21]

The creation of *economic* value ought to be important to managers and shareholders only to the extent that economic value ultimately translates into *market* value. I thus need to demonstrate that the economic model developed in Table 1–3 represents a useful concept that can assist managers in measuring the long-run success of their stewardship. This can be done by showing a long-run correspondence between the observed market-value/book-value ratio for firms and the economic-value/book-value ratio data generated by the economic model.

AGGREGATE MARKET-VALUE/BOOK-VALUE DATA—UNADJUSTED

Table 1–5 presents a historical overview of market-value/book-value ratios of the common stocks of specific groups of U.S. nonfinancial corporations (NFCs). There are two facts about Table 1–5 that deserve close attention. In the first three columns of Table 1–5, the market-value/book-value ratios substantially exceed 1.0 in almost every year.[22] If "market" value were an accurate reflection of "economic" value over the long run, this phenomenon could not occur unless:

1. Book values as calculated according to historical cost accounting substantially understate the economic definition of book value,[23] and/or
2. At least some U.S. NFCs in each of the subgroupings of Table 1–5 were consistently earning profits well above the levels possible in a perfectly competitive environment. A perfectly competitive product

---

[19] At this point the model (*a*) ignores the effects of inflation and general product price level changes; (*b*) assumes a synchronized age distribution of capital equipment, and that the depreciation policies of firms reflect true economic depreciation; and (*c*) ignores the income tax effects created by any deviations from the assumptions stated in (*b*). Later in the chapter we will improve the model by incorporating some adjustments for the effects of inflation. Finally, Table 1–3 assumes that the firm's risk (as reflected in its cost of equity capital) does not change over time as new investments are undertaken, nor as the horizon during which monopoly rents may be earned is shortened.

[20] By the term *economic* value we mean value as defined by a rational investor who values an asset by discounting the cash flows received as a result of the ownership of that asset at the appropriate cost for the capital at risk.

[21] GAAP: "generally accepted accounting principles."

[22] As suggested by the second column of data in Table 1–3, if all firms earned returns on equity equal to their respective costs of equity capital, the market-value/book-value ratio for each and every firm would equal exactly 1.0.

[23] This problem is explored in considerable detail in the appendix to this chapter.

TABLE 1-5
Historic cost market-value/book-value ratios for selected U.S. firms, and estimated
replacement cost market-value/book-value ratios for all U.S. nonfinancial corporations,
1951–1975

	(1) Dow Jones 30 Industrials*	(2) Standard & Poor's 425 Industrials*	(3) 1,448 Compustat Companies*	(4) All U.S. Nonfinancial Corporations[†]
1951. . . . . . 1.3		1.3	—	—
1952. . . . . . 1.4		1.3	—	—
1953. . . . . . 1.3		1.2	—	—
1954. . . . . . 1.6		1.7	—	—
1955. . . . . . 1.8		1.9	—	—
1956. . . . . . 1.8		1.9	—	—
1957. . . . . . 1.5		1.5	—	—
1958. . . . . . 1.9		1.9	—	—
1959. . . . . . 2.4		2.0	—	—
1960. . . . . . 1.7		1.8	—	0.9
1961. . . . . . 1.9		2.2	—	1.2
1962. . . . . . 1.6		1.8	—	1.0
1963. . . . . . 1.8		2.1	—	1.2
1964. . . . . . 2.1		2.2	—	1.3
1965. . . . . . 2.1		2.3	—	1.5
1966. . . . . . 1.7		1.9	1.8	1.1
1967. . . . . . 1.9		2.2	2.2	1.2
1968. . . . . . 1.8		2.3	2.3	1.4
1969. . . . . . 1.5		2.0	1.9	1.1
1970. . . . . . 1.5		1.9	1.8	0.8
1971. . . . . . 1.5		2.0	1.9	0.9
1972. . . . . . 1.6		2.3	2.1	1.1
1973. . . . . . 1.2		1.7	1.6	0.9
1974. . . . . . 0.8		1.1	1.0	0.6
1975. . . . . . 1.1		1.4	1.3	0.6

*Ratios calculated using book values at historic cost.
[†]Ratios calculated using book values at replacement cost.
Sources: Column 1 — *Barron's,* April 23, 1973, and October 25, 1976, for market values,
and March 14, 1977, for book values.
Column 2 — Standard & Poor's *Trade and Securities Statistics, Security Price
Index Record,* 1976 ed.; p. 5 for market value, and p. 32 for
book value.
Column 3 — Compustat data from firms selected according to criteria specified
in footnote 11.
Column 4 — D. M. Holland and S. C. Myers, "Trends in Corporate Profitability
and Capital Costs" (Mimeo), August 1977, Table A-1 for market
values; book values were calculated from data found in *Statistics
of Income, Corporation Income Tax Returns,* U.S. Government
Printing Office, adjusted with replacement-cost data for inventories and net capital stock found in Table A-2a of the Holland
and Myers paper noted above.

market environment would be one in which each firm earned a return on equity equal to its cost of equity.

As I hope to demonstrate, *both* of these possible explanations contribute to the unexpectedly high values observed in the first three columns of Table 1–5.

AGGREGATE MARKET-VALUE/BOOK-VALUE DATA—ADJUSTED

The fourth column of Table 1–5 partially adjusts the market-value/book-value results of Columns 1–3 for the problem noted in (1) above. If the GAAP-defined common equity of all U.S. NFCs is adjusted to take into account the replacement cost of *inventory* and *net fixed assets* (excluding land), the historical market-value/book-value relationship for U.S. NFCs declines quite sharply.[24] If the appropriate computational adjustments are made at the aggregate level to capitalize and then amortize (over an appropriate period) expenditures for both advertising and research and development, the market-value/book-value data of Column 4, Table 1–5, would decline even further.[25] Such adjustments are appropriate since expensing advertising and research and development charges immediately (as required by GAAP) can seriously distort both profits and book value as noted in the appendix. Indeed, it would appear that the market-value/book-value ratios for U.S. NFCs (corrected for replacement cost accounting and the capitalization and amortization of advertis-

---

[24] Much of the data utilized in calculating Column 4 of Table 1–5 was taken from D. M. Holland and S. C. Myers, "Trends in Corporate Profitability and Capital Costs" (mimeographed), August 1977. In the Holland and Myers paper a ratio is derived that links the market value of NFC debt and equity to the replacement cost of NFC net assets. Net assets are defined by Holland and Myers as total assets valued at replacement cost (except for land, which is valued at historical cost, and "investments," which are omitted entirely) less all non-interest-bearing liabilities. This ratio, called "augmented q" by Holland and Myers, differs conceptually in definition from the data in Column 4 of Table 1–5 in the following ways. First, the "augmented q" concept relates to NFC total capital, not just equity capital. Second, in "augmented q," NFC debt is valued at current market prices (i.e., replacement cost). Column 4 of Table 1–5 implicitly values NFC debt at historical (i.e., book) value. The logic for valuing NFC debt at book rather than market value in the Table 1–5 calculations is as follows. In linking the assumed *future* profitability of real (i.e., product-market) investments to the *historical* profitability of real investments, it is unreasonable either to enhance or burden the assumed future profitability of real investments with market gains or losses associated with past debt-financing decisions. This approach to measuring the future profitability of investment based on historical profitability also assumes a constant level of future interest rates (and implicitly assumes an expectation of a constant level of future inflation rates). The above facts notwithstanding, the data of column 4 of Table 1–5 differ very modestly from "augmented q" as defined by Holland and Myers.

[25] Adjustments will be made at the individual firm level later in this chapter in order to demonstrate this effect.

ing and research and development expenditures) would not stray significantly above 1.0 during most of the years 1960–73. This suggests that at the *aggregate* level of analysis, market-value/book-value ratios for the common stocks of U.S. NFCs seem to be reasonably consistent with both a broadly competitive product-market economy, and a rational economic model of security valuation. Both of these conclusions flow from the following fact. To the extent that the *market* value of a firm's equity exceeds the *book* value of that equity (adjusted for replacement cost accounting and the capitalization and amortization of advertising and research and development expenditures), the difference between these two values can be attributed to the capitalized value of monopoly rents and/or imperfections in the securities markets that reflect investor valuation errors.

Considerable care must be exercised in drawing further conclusions from the evidence suggesting that market-value/book-value ratios at the *aggregate* level appear to be reasonably consistent with a broadly competitive product-market economy and a rational economic model of security valuation. In particular, the evidence does not suggest that monopoly rents and securities valuation errors are either nonexistent or unimportant at the level of *individual* firms. Indeed, demonstrating that monopoly rents and securities valuation errors can be extremely significant to individual firms represents an important objective of this book.

RECENT DECLINE IN CAPITAL PRODUCTIVITY

Table 1–5 portrays one other fact that is clearly worth noting. Market-value/book-value ratios for the common stocks of U.S. NFCs have eroded sharply in the mid-1970s. As Holland and Myers[26] and others[27] have pointed out, following an extraordinary crest in the 1963–68 period there has been a very significant decline in "real" (inflation-adjusted) profitability for U.S. NFCs in recent years. The valuation implications of this phenomenon are clear from Table 1–3. If new investments by U.S. NFCs cannot produce real (inflation-adjusted) returns to equity that are at least equivalent to real (inflation-adjusted) equity costs, managers choosing to make these marginal investments destroy economic value (and, by implication, market value). The potential impact of eroded profit opportunity upon the level of future capital investment for U.S. NFCs is obvious if this profitability trend turns out to be more than just a transitory phenomenon.[28]

---

[26] Holland and Myers, "Trends in Corporate Profitability and Capital Costs."

[27] *Economic Report of the President,* January 1977, U.S. Government Printing Office, pp. 27–31.

[28] In a paper entitled, "Is the Rate of Profit Falling?", which was presented at the Brookings Panel on Economic Activity, April 1977, Martin Feldstein and Law-

THE GENERAL CONGRUENCE OF "ECONOMIC" VALUE AND "MARKET" VALUE DATA

Table 1-5 shows aggregate market-value/book-value data for U.S. NFCs for time periods extending up to 25 years. These data provide an opportunity to validate, at the *aggregate* level, the comparability between actual market valuations and the value ranges predicted by the rational economic model. Table 1-5 offers no insight into this fit at a much lower level of firm aggregation, however, and this task is reserved for Table 1-6. Table 1-6 stratifies the U.S. NFCs according to performance measures originally detailed in Table 1-3. The data on market-value/book-value ratios are presented for a single point in time (December 31, 1975). The data of Table 1-6 (when overlaid on the expected ranges of market-value/book-value ratios calculated in Table 1-3) corroborate, at a greatly reduced level of aggregation, the general congruence between economic value and market value. Market-value/book-value ratio results (for categories of firms with similar historic investment opportunity profiles as reflected in their ROEs and equity expansion rates) seem to be consistent with the ranges shown in the Table 1-3 economic model.[29] It is worth recalling that this corroboration comes in *spite* of the quite rigid and extremely simplistic assumption of Table 1-3 that the cost of equity capital for each and every firm is 10 percent. In comparing Table 1-3 and Table 1-6, one needs to keep in mind the results of Column 4, Table 1-5. *Real* profitability was quite depressed in 1975, in contrast to *nominal* profitability for the year, which was only slightly below the average for the prior decade. In 1975 a firm earning a *nominal* ROE of 8 percent to 11.9 percent (Table 1-6) was almost certainly earning a *real* ROE several points below its real cost of equity. Thus, in Column 4 of Table 1-5, we

---

rence Summers argue that the recent decline in rates of return can be explained largely in terms of (*a*) unusually low utilization of productive capacity and (*b*) random year-to-year fluctuations in profitability of a type often observed previously. They argue that the factors contributing to the fall in return during the early 1970s were transitory, so that the decline in returns is also a short-run phenomenon. Holland and Myers reach a similar conclusion in their paper noted previously. They conclude (p. 47) "that the after tax [return on capital] shows neither a downward nor upward trend. Variations around its central tendency can be explained, in large part, by changes in the level of economic activity and in the rate of inflation. In particular, the poor profitability record of the last half dozen years can be explained by the combination of a slack economy and a brisk inflation."

[29] The one column of data in Table 1-6 that seems to be least consistent with the Table 1-3 data is the "1.9 percent or less" return-on-equity column. The absolute *level* of the market-value/book-value ratios in this column appear to be higher than one would expect given the level of the data in adjoining columns. A number of high-technology firms (with significant research and development expenses) and natural resource–based firms (with valuable assets not reflected on their balance sheets) may account, at least in part, for this apparent aberration.

TABLE 1-6

Median market-value/book-value ratios as of December 31, 1975, for the common stocks of 1,448 firms with average rates of return on common equity as indicated across the top of the matrix, and average annual increase in common equity (measured as a fraction of net profits) as indicated along the right side of the matrix.

Level of reinvestment of firms expressed as average annual increase in common equity[†]/average annual profit after tax	Average rate of return[*] on common equity, 1966–1975					
	1.9% or less	2.0% to 7.9%	8.0% to 11.9%	12.0% to 17.9%	18.0% to 24.9%	25.0% and over
0.19% or less	0.6	0.4	0.4	1.2	1.4	NMF
0.20 to 0.39	0.7	0.3	0.7	1.0	NMF[‡]	3.7
0.40 to 0.59	0.9	0.4	0.7	1.1	2.2	4.6
0.60 to 0.79	0.6	0.4	0.7	1.0	1.9	NMF
0.80 to 1.19	0.4	0.4	0.7	1.0	2.1	NMF
1.20 to 1.59	0.7	0.4	0.7	1.5	3.0	NMF
1.60 and over	0.4	0.4	0.6	1.9	NMF	NMF

Median rather than *mean* values are used in order to avoid distortions in the data that might occur if some extreme values were used in calculating mean data.

[*] As defined in Table 1–4.
[†] As defined in Table 1–4.
[‡] NMF indicates "not a meaningful figure" since the value would be based on three or fewer observations out of 1,448.

find the common stock of the average U.S. NFC in 1975 sold for only about 60 percent of book value (calculated at replacement cost).

In view of this depressed situation for the *average* company, the relatively high ratios shown in the final two columns of Table 1–6 for the companies that best satisfy the assumptions of Table 1–3 are particularly noteworthy and impressive.

At an admittedly broad level of generality, there appears to be a reasonably good fit between the rational economic model of security valuation presented in Table 1–3 and the actual "market defined" level of security prices observed at December 31, 1975. For our present purposes the evidence relating to this fit is sufficient since our primary objective is to present a rather detailed analysis of some individual firms later in the chapter. In particular, the objectives for the remaining parts of this chapter are:

1. The identification of specific firms that have historically occupied very attractive real-investment-opportunity profiles;
2. The presentation of evidence suggesting that a small but significant number of U.S. NFCs (the Hall of Fame firms) have in fact consistently managed to earn rates of return that exceed the cost of equity capital for these firms;
3. An estimation of the very substantial value created for shareholders (where this value creation is measured by the spread between market and book values) by the managements of the firms identified in (2) above; and
4. An examination of some of the salient characteristics of the firms noted in (2) and (3) above.

IDENTIFICATION OF FIRMS HISTORICALLY ENJOYING ATTRACTIVE INVESTMENT OPPORTUNITIES

In any given year a relatively small number of U.S. NFCs earn rates of return on common equity (ROEs) that are five or more percentage points above the median[30] ROE for all firms. This is not surprising, since on visual inspection the distribution of corporate ROEs appears to be roughly normal. Figure 1–1 presents the distribution of corporate ROEs for the 1,448 firms characterized previously. The data shown are for the

---

[30] I use *median* rather than *mean* values for this comparison since the mean value can be significantly influenced by a few firms with very high positive or negative values for this variable. For example, in 1968 one firm in the sample had a return on common equity equal to −1,103 percent. This single observation significantly distorts the mean ROE calculation of all 1,448 firms for 1968, but has no extraordinary effect on the median value.

FIGURE 1–1

Probability distribution of corporate profitability for 1448 U.S. non-financial corporations in the best year (1966), worst year (1971), and last year (1975) of the decade 1966–1975

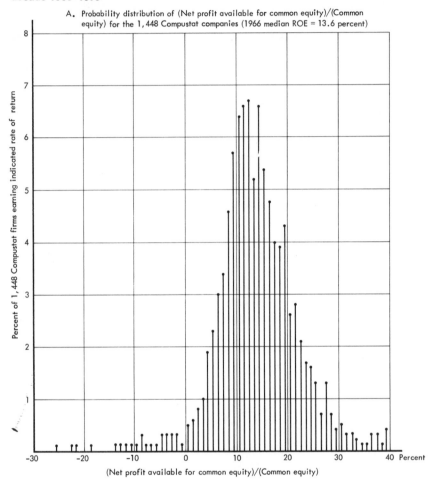

A. Probability distribution of (Net profit available for common equity)/(Common equity) for the 1,448 Compustat companies (1966 median ROE = 13.6 percent)

(Net profit available for common equity)/(Common equity)

best (1966), worst[31] (1971), and last year (1975) of the decade 1966–75.

One could predict with a fair degree of accuracy the number of firms that would earn, in any given year, an ROE exceeding the median value by five percentage points. This is neither terribly interesting nor remarkable. What is interesting is that many of the same firms, year after year, turn up with the superior ROE performance. The number of firms in our 1,448-firm sample that earned rates of return on common equity exceed-

---

[31] 1971 was the worst year of the decade not in terms of median ROE, but rather in terms of the number of firms with ROEs exceeding 15 percent, as shown in Table 1–7.

FIGURE 1–1 (continued)

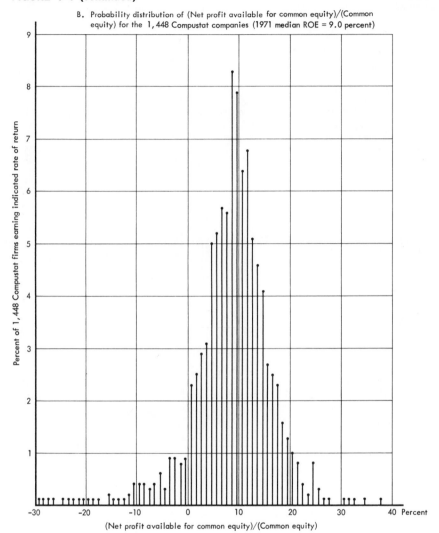

B. Probability distribution of (Net profit available for common equity)/(Common equity) for the 1,448 Compustat companies (1971 median ROE = 9.0 percent)

Percent of 1,448 Compustat firms earning indicated rate of return

(Net profit available for common equity)/(Common equity)

ing 15.0 percent in each of the ten years 1966–75 is shown in Table 1–7. The number of firms that earned rates of return on common equity in excess of 15 percent in *all ten years* is 72. If a company with an ROE of 15 percent in one year was no more likely to earn a 15 percent ROE in the following year than any other firm, then from the Table 1–7 data one would expect, statistically, 0.0008 firms out of 1,448 to have earned a 15 percent ROE for all ten years in succession. In fact, more than one third of the 214 firms that achieved an ROE in excess of 15 percent in the worst year of the decade (1971) earned such a return in *every* year of the

28

FIGURE 1–1 *(concluded)*

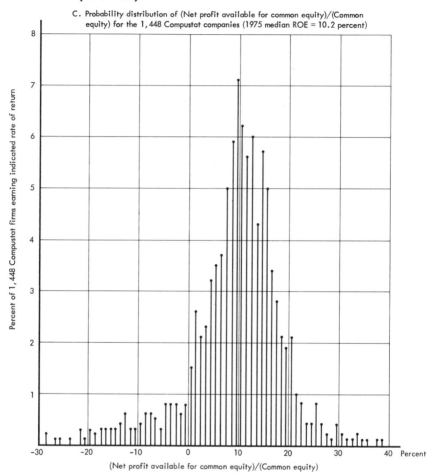

C. Probability distribution of (Net profit available for common equity)/(Common equity) for the 1,448 Compustat companies (1975 median ROE = 10.2 percent)

(Net profit available for common equity)/(Common equity)

decade. The persistence of high-return performance is remarkably strong. Of the 150 firms with five straight years of ROE performance exceeding 15 percent in the years 1966–70, almost half succeeded in keeping the string going during the next five years, as indicated in Table 1–8.[32]

---

[32] At first glance the data of Table 1–8 may appear to conflict with the conclusions of I.M.D. Little, A. C. Rayner, J. Lintner, and R. Glauber in their respective researches on the stability of growth in reported earnings per share (EPS) over successive time periods. In fact, the conclusions do not conflict for two reasons. First, success in exceeding an ROE benchmark of 15 percent over a significant time period does not necessarily lead to growth in EPS at all, let alone consistent growth. For example, a firm whose ROE declined from 30 percent to 15 percent over a five-year time period would probably find its EPS declining, but the firm would still pass the

TABLE 1-7
Number and fraction of sample NFCs earning ROEs in excess of
15% (1966-1975)

Year	Median ROE in year	Firms out of 1,448 earning ROEs in excess of 15%	
		(number)	(percentage)
1966	13.6%	599	41
1967	12.3	485	33
1968	11.7	392	27
1969	10.8	323	22
1970	8.9	227	16
1971	9.0	214	15
1972	9.9	240	17
1973	11.5	342	24
1974	11.5	439	30
1975	10.2	338	23

TABLE 1-8
Persistence of high-ROE performance among sample firms (1966-1975)

Number of years of ROE performance exceeding 15% (1966-1970)	Number of additional years of ROE performance exceeding 15% (1971-1975)	Number of firms with indicated ROE performance (1966-1975)
5	0	17
5	1	5
5	2	14
5	3	12
5	4	30
5	5	72
Total		150

The group of firms with ten successive years of ROE performance in excess of 15 percent is presented in Table 1-9. In this exhibit the data are arranged (a) by industry group and (b) in descending order of observed market-value/book-value ratio as of December 31, 1975. Listing these firms accomplishes the first of the four objectives outlined on page 25, and allows us to move on to determine which of these firms, if any, have actually achieved returns on equity in excess of their equity capital costs.

15 percent ROE test. Second, the authors cited above did not segment their data on the EPS growth-consistency of firms by ROE performance. As noted in Chapter 2 (page 86) rapid growth in EPS can be achieved in a number of ways, only one of which is sustainable over a significant time frame. Since a requirement for sustainable rapid growth in EPS is a high level of ROE performance, high-ROE companies could conceivably achieve somewhat greater predictability of growth in EPS across five-year time periods than that achieved by firms categorized more broadly.

TABLE 1-9

Profit after tax/common equity and market-value/book-value ratios for 72 U.S. NFCs with ten successive years of ROEs in excess of 15%

Line No.	Industry	Company	ROE 1966	1967	1968	1969	1970	1971	1972	1973	1974	1975	10-year average ROE	1975 Market-value/Book-value ratio
1	Drugs—Ethical	American Home Products	.241	.239	.243	.255	.253	.250	.257	.280	.281	.278	.262	5.83
2		Merck & Co.	.278	.259	.245	.241	.243	.246	.244	.258	.257	.241	.250	5.52
3		Schering-Plough	.200	.200	.211	.221	.209	.211	.231	.255	.248	.233	.231	4.76
4		Eli Lilly	.205	.192	.211	.211	.207	.187	.204	.213	.211	.189	.203	3.73
5		Smithkline Corp.	.287	.269	.249	.231	.227	.215	.206	.206	.204	.201	.223	2.78
6		Marion Labs	.501	.442	.409	.377	.334	.314	.308	.276	.253	.261	.294	2.32
7		Searle, G. D.	.258	.276	.271	.272	.267	.249	.242	.221	.213	.202	.232	1.96
8		Rorer-Amchem	.338	.316	.274	.226	.227	.220	.211	.217	.208	.202	.225	1.93
9		Robins, A. H.	.257	.249	.235	.220	.198	.211	.201	.193	.171	.150	.195	1.66
10	Drugs—Proprietary	Tampax	.369	.367	.354	.346	.368	.377	.364	.339	.311	.295	.340	3.88
11		Bristol-Myers Co.	.250	.199	.187	.195	.191	.172	.169	.185	.194	.200	.190	3.11
12		Sterling Drug	.224	.216	.206	.201	.197	.191	.183	.181	.172	.162	.187	2.18
13	Cosmetics	Avon Products	.371	.373	.353	.358	.361	.344	.330	.304	.237	.265	.314	3.86
14		Chesebrough-Ponds	.200	.208	.209	.213	.188	.184	.174	.172	.174	.169	.182	3.38
15		Revlon, Inc.	.160	.169	.154	.160	.155	.168	.160	.159	.161	.165	.161	2.83
16		Gillette Co.	.326	.303	.284	.264	.241	.210	.220	.222	.202	.169	.230	2.13
17	Tobacco	R. J. Reynolds	.174	.175	.163	.155	.170	.178	.169	.172	.182	.177	.172	1.51
18	Beverages—Soft drinks	Dr. Pepper	.243	.244	.248	.246	.258	.268	.260	.255	.227	.240	.248	4.34
19		Coca-Cola Co.	.221	.225	.222	.221	.224	.228	.228	.227	.192	.195	.215	4.01
20		PepsiCo Inc.	.198	.181	.176	.174	.169	.164	.163	.160	.157	.167	.167	2.65
21	—Bottler	PepCom Industries	.355	.336	.337	.323	.305	.256	.232	.220	.232	.353	.245	1.10
22	—Distillers	Heublein, Inc.	.741	.523	.429	.410	.320	.277	.171	.192	.192	.191	.221	3.07
23	Foods—Packaged	Kellogg Co.	.222	.214	.205	.201	.202	.207	.209	.205	.205	.257	.215	3.95
24	—Confectionery	Russell Stover Candies	.270	.259	.234	.194	.202	.206	.207	.201	.172	.207	.208	2.10
25	Soaps	Procter & Gamble	.157	.172	.164	.160	.166	.169	.176	.171	.163	.158	.166	3.46
26	Retail—Food chains	Dillon Cos.	.183	.167	.178	.155	.160	.176	.192	.193	.210	.220	.193	3.28
27		Lucky Stores, Inc.	.253	.299	.287	.258	.248	.238	.206	.194	.209	.215	.225	2.74
28		Winn-Dixie	.222	.202	.202	.200	.187	.196	.196	.190	.202	.190	.198	2.72
29		Weis Markets	.217	.211	.201	.184	.190	.184	.166	.158	.174	.176	.181	1.35
30	—Drug stores	Longs Drug Stores	.245	.241	.233	.227	.215	.225	.208	.199	.199	.201	.211	4.94
31		Eckerd (Jack)	.299	.323	.308	.362	.318	.163	.177	.194	.164	.158	.188	2.98
32	—Apparel	Loehmann's	.282	.317	.256	.245	.177	.212	.156	.154	.172	.198	.199	1.78
33		Rockower Bros.	.182	.201	.163	.214	.156	.177	.185	.207	.176	.187	.185	0.74
34	—Shoes	Melville Corp.	.269	.293	.275	.259	.239	.236	.217	.201	.160	.222	.222	2.23
35	—Mail order	New Process Co.	.315	.296	.330	.497	.512	.514	.292	.253	.201	.316	.334	3.86
36	—Disc. dept.	Caldor, Inc.	.171	.200	.216	.217	.208	.207	.176	.172	.151	.163	.180	1.21

Specialized services

#	Category	Company												
37	Freight forwarding	Emery Air Freight	.444	.415	.435	.379	.376	.328	.338	.336	.328	.289	.340	8.40
38	Eating places	McDonald's Corp.	.209	.225	.250	.264	.167	.192	.181	.199	.204	.210	.202	5.64
39	Insurance brokers	Marsh & McLennon	.252	.249	.259	.264	.278	.250	.233	.260	.269	.259	.257	5.30
40	Business management	Dun & Bradstreet	.225	.209	.197	.210	.209	.199	.204	.209	.197	.193	.203	3.50
41	Pest control	Rollins, Inc.	.245	.243	.230	.210	.231	.273	.223	.224	.211	.210	.225	3.06
42	Accounting	H&R Block	.507	.460	.483	.553	.420	.244	.292	.299	.294	.272	.312	2.48
43	Engineering	Stone & Webster	.178	.183	.184	.174	.243	.190	.186	.176	.242	.210	.200	1.41
44	Protective	Wackenhut	.170	.162	.192	.267	.249	.213	.196	.212	.192	.180	.202	1.30
45	Publishing—Broadcasting	Dow Jones & Co.	.322	.297	.313	.317	.241	.204	.252	.271	.231	.237	.261	3.69
46	—Books	Prentice-Hall, Inc.	.301	.302	.277	.270	.237	.223	.218	.226	.209	.192	.234	2.04
47	Trucking	Roadway Express	.193	.187	.163	.150	.157	.240	.246	.222	.230	.203	.209	4.76
48		Yellow Freight Systems	.229	.166	.215	.170	.170	.246	.245	.221	.241	.204	.218	4.19
49		Merchants, Inc.	.192	.166	.158	.163	.164	.189	.192	.194	.215	.160	.182	0.79
50	Office and Business machines	IBM	.158	.170	.191	.177	.171	.162	.169	.179	.182	.174	.174	2.94
51		Xerox	.280	.240	.224	.212	.210	.202	.199	.201	.189	.179	.201	2.12
52	Chemicals and	National Chemsearch	.295	.264	.226	.212	.205	.204	.211	.226	.233	.209	.221	4.43
53	preparations	Nalco Chemical	.201	.205	.205	.202	.160	.182	.188	.205	.196	.203	.194	3.82
54		Lubrizol	.190	.184	.207	.192	.201	.187	.185	.216	.248	.203	.206	3.47
55	Photographic	Eastman Kodak	.266	.214	.204	.197	.181	.173	.198	.210	.184	.165	.193	4.62
56	Auto Parts—Wholesale	Genuine Parts	.156	.163	.161	.154	.156	.173	.163	.167	.175	.184	.168	3.60
57	—Mfgr.	Purolator, Inc.	.262	.245	.221	.197	.189	.176	.176	.174	.171	.163	.186	1.72
58		Champion Spark Plug	.213	.211	.203	.193	.183	.190	.191	.200	.176	.159	.188	1.52
59	Electrical equipment	Emerson Electric	.183	.187	.180	.172	.168	.161	.160	.165	.171	.161	.168	3.17
60		Thomas & Betts Corp.	.256	.226	.207	.199	.163	.169	.198	.215	.205	.162	.195	3.13
61		Square D	.247	.210	.203	.215	.196	.207	.209	.188	.188	.173	.200	2.41

Energy related

#	Category	Company												
62	Oil—Crude producer	Louisiana Land & Exp.	.399	.392	.363	.340	.316	.318	.284	.275	.334	.255	.313	2.36
63	Petroleum refining	Quaker State Oil Refining	.181	.170	.181	.201	.209	.178	.170	.187	.201	.185	.187	1.89
64	Nat. gas transmission	Kaneb Services	.190	.185	.179	.183	.190	.193	.202	.206	.299	.305	.235	1.88
65		Panhandle Eastern Pipe Line	.215	.209	.193	.184	.181	.150	.166	.164	.160	.154	.172	0.92
66	Mining—Gold	Campbell Red Lake Mines	.334	.311	.343	.283	.187	.241	.340	.454	.509	.332	.362	4.58
67	Smelting and refining	Atlas Consol. Mining	.459	.365	.494	.590	.538	.432	.366	.577	.304	.191	.404	1.49

Miscellaneous

#	Category	Company												
68	Plumbing supplies	MASCO	.245	.209	.216	.195	.168	.174	.158	.183	.186	.192	.185	3.42
69	Business forms	Moore Corp.	.171	.168	.160	.165	.158	.152	.159	.169	.203	.175	.170	3.30
70	Wholesale foods	Malone & Hyde	.180	.174	.167	.172	.168	.171	.166	.162	.173	.185	.172	2.13
71	Machinery—Specialty	Dover Corp.	.218	.178	.165	.175	.175	.171	.165	.182	.195	.183	.180	1.51
72	Jewelry, yearbooks	Jostens Inc.	.196	.194	.192	.183	.175	.172	.184	.176	.171	.176	.179	1.42

IDENTIFYING FIRMS WHOSE ROEs EXCEED THEIR
EQUITY CAPITAL COSTS

Persistently high ROE performance is generally praised as evidence of superior management skill by business partisans, and damned as prima facie evidence of monopoly by advocates of expanded antitrust enforcement. In 1972, for example, the late Senator Philip A. Hart[33] filed a bill entitled "The Industrial Reorganization Act S.1167." Title I, Section 101.(b) of the bill stated:[34]

> There shall be a rebuttable presumption that monopoly power is possessed
> (1) by any corporation if the average rate of return on net worth after taxes is in excess of 15 percentum over a period of five consecutive years out of the most recent seven years preceding the filing of the complaint . . .

The bill went on to state that:

> A corporation shall not be required to divest monopoly power if it can show—
> (1) Such power is due solely to the ownership of valid patents, lawfully acquired and lawfully used, or
> (2) such a divestiture would result in a loss of substantial economies.
> The burden shall be upon the corporation to prove that monopoly power should not be divested pursuant to paragraphs (1) and (2) of the above subsection . . .

Clearly there are some dangers associated with arbitrarily selecting a single ROE number and (a) declaring that any firm that consistently surpasses that level of performance must be earning returns in excess of equity capital costs, or (b) concluding that earning a high ROE *alone* is evidence that a firm is extracting monopoly rents. Happily, the Hart bill never gained much support.

Some of the firms listed in Table 1–9, for example, subject shareholders to more than average levels of systematic *risk,* as will be explained later in this chapter. For other firms, particularly those in the drug and heavily-advertised consumer products fields, the book value of common equity (the denominator upon which the ROE is calculated) is systematically understated. This phenomenon results from a divergence between the economic logic associated with *capitalizing* and *amortizing* advertising

---

[33] Senator Hart was Chairman of the Subcommittee on Antitrust and Monopoly, a subcommittee of the Committee on the Judiciary.

[34] The text of this bill can be found in the *Congressional Record,* vol. 119, no. 38, March 12, 1973.

and research and development expenditures, and the immediate *expensing*[35] of these expenditures required by GAAP.

Finally, for those firms with heavy fixed asset commitments, or heavy commitments to inventory, the historical cost orientation of GAAP tends to overstate the *real* rate of return on common equity earned by the firm. Each of the potential problem areas noted above must be examined in turn in order to determine whether the ROE reported by a firm truly exceeds its capital costs.

CALCULATING THE COST OF EQUITY CAPITAL: *NOMINAL* VERSUS *REAL* COST

Modern portfolio theory[36] suggests that the cost of equity capital for a firm can be calculated according to the following equation.[37]

$$K_e = R_f + \beta(K_m - R_f),$$

where

K_e = the cost of equity capital for a specific firm;

R_f = the rate of return required by investors on a risk-free asset (the rate on short-term [90-day] U.S. Treasury bills is generally considered a good approximation of the risk-free rate);

K_m = the investor's required rate of return on investment in a stock of average market risk. This is the rate that would be required on a portfolio consisting of all stocks, weighted in accordance with their respective market values;

---

[35] Financial Accounting Standards Board, "Statement of Financial Accounting Standards No. 2—Accounting for Research and Development Costs," October 1974. While all firms were not required to immediately expense research and development expenditures in financial statements prior to the year beginning January 1, 1975, as a practical matter most firms did follow this practice prior to that date.

[36] The definition of risk in modern portfolio theory encompasses only that portion of *total* risk that is market related (i.e., systematic risk). All other risk (i.e., unsystematic risk) is ignored on the assumption that its impact is effectively cancelled out by the diversification in each individual shareholder's total equity portfolio. As Gordon Donaldson has pointed out in a paper entitled "The Management of Risk and Return in the Individual Business Firm" (Mimeo, May 1977), unsystematic risk (that risk peculiar to an industry or a firm) is precisely the type of risk for which a management group is often held most clearly accountable. Thus, it would not be at all surprising to find managers sometimes assessing risk differently (and quite justifiably so from their perspective) from the way prescribed by the shareholder-wealth maximization objective assumed in modern portfolio theory.

[37] A quite readable summary of modern portfolio theory (popularly called the Capital Asset Pricing Model) can be found in F. Modigliani and G. A. Pogue, "An Introduction to Risk and Return," *Financial Analysts Journal*, March–April 1974 and May–June 1974. A more rigorous discussion of the theory can be found in Michael C. Jensen, "Capital Markets: Theory and Evidence," *Bell Journal of Economics and Management Science*, Autumn 1972.

$\beta =$ the measure of market risk associated with the common stock of a particular firm. For a firm of average market risk, $\beta = 1.0$ by definition.

At December 31, 1975, the 90-day Treasury bill rate (which represents a close approximation of R_f, the risk-free rate) was 5.2 percent. Since the *real* (inflation-adjusted) rate of return on Treasury bills over the period 1929–74 was about 0.1 percent[38] we can make the somewhat heroic assumption[39] that investors at December 31, 1975, were probably anticipating a near-term future inflation rate of about 5.1 percent.[40] Since investors realized a *real* (inflation-adjusted) rate of return of 8.8 percent on common equities over the 1929–74 period,[41] using logic similar to that outlined above we can assume that the required nominal rate of return on a security of average market risk (K_m) was probably about 8.8 percent + 5.1 percent = 13.9 percent at December 31, 1975.

Using these values and the market risk factors (β's) appropriate for each firm,[42] it is possible to approximate the *nominal* cost of equity capital for each NFC at December 31, 1975. By removing the inflation factor, it is also possible to estimate a *real* cost of equity capital for each firm at that date.

The relevant calculation for each of the 72 U.S. NFCs reporting a nominal ROE in excess of 15 percent for each of the ten years 1966–75 is presented in Columns 2 and 3 of Table 1–10. The complete calculation for one firm, Avon Products, is carried out below.

Nominal cost of equity capital for Avon:

$$K_e = R_f + \beta(K_m - R_f)$$
$$= 5.2 + 1.25(13.9 - 5.2)$$
$$= 16.1\%.$$

Real cost of equity capital for Avon:

---

[38] R. G. Ibbotson and R. A. Sinquefeld, "Stocks, Bonds, Bills, and Inflation: Year-by-Year Historical Returns (1929–1974)" *Journal of Business,* January 1976.

[39] During the period 1929–74 the average rate of inflation (annual rate of change in the Consumer Price Index) was 2.1 percent. During the period 1966–74 the rate was 5.5 percent. The 5.1 percent rate was thus fairly close to the experience of the decade prior to 1975.

[40] This was equal to the 90-day Treasury bill rate of 5.2 percent as of December 31, 1975, less the historical (1929–74) real rate of return on Treasury bills, which was 0.1 percent.

[41] R. G. Ibbotson and R. A. Sinquefeld, "Stocks, Bonds, Bills, and Inflation."

[42] A number of commercial services supply market risk factors (β values) calculated on a regular basis. Among these are "Security Risk Evaluation," Merrill Lynch, Pierce, Fenner & Smith, Inc., and "Capital Market Equilibrium Statistics," Wilshire Associates, Incorporated.

$$K_e = R_f + \beta(K_m - R_f)$$
$$= 0.1 + 1.25(8.8 - 0.1)$$
$$= 11.0\%.$$

After the adjustment for market risk (but before any adjustment for capitalizing and then amortizing advertising and research and development expenditures, and before any adjustment for inflation), Column 8 of Table 1–10 suggests that 64 of the 72 high-return companies enjoyed ROEs in excess of their equity capital costs in 1976. Since the ROEs earned by most of these firms in 1976 approximated the average returns earned over the period 1966–75 (Column 4, Table 1–10), by implication most of these firms had earned nominal unadjusted rates of return in excess of their equity capital costs for over a decade.[43]

Once a firm's equity capital cost is defined, the next step is to define the acutal rate of return on equity capital achieved by the firm adjusted for:

a. aberrations caused by generally accepted accounting principles related to expenditures for advertising and research and development, and

b. aberrations caused by generally accepted accounting principles relating to the use of *historical cost* rather than *replacement cost* for the major nonmonetary asset items.

ADJUSTING THE GAAP-REPORTED *ROE* FOR ADVERTISING AND *R&D* EXPENDITURES

Advertising and research and development expenditures both generate economic benefits extending substantially beyond the point in time at which the expenditure occurs. Because these expenditures are written off immediately under GAAP, an economic asset (which might be labeled "capitalized advertising" or "capitalized research and development")

---

[43] In fact, every one of the eight firms whose nominal ROE in 1976 did not equal or exceed their nominal equity capital costs as of December 31, 1975 failed to meet this test because their ROE performance in 1976 was below their ten-year average ROE. Conversely, however, 3 of the 72 firms passed this particular test in 1976 that would not have passed it on the basis of their ten-year average ROEs.

The average annual inflation rate during the period 1966–74 was 5.5 percent. This was not markedly different from the 5.1 percent inflation rate that we assumed was incorporated into investor expectations in the mid-1970s. Thus, to the extent that (a) nominal ROEs achieved in the 1966–75 decade were similar to the nominal ROEs achieved in 1976 (as the comparison between Columns 4 and 5 of Table 1–10 would suggest), and (b) real costs of equity capital are relatively stable over time, it is reasonable to assume that real ROEs have, on average, exceeded real equity costs over the full decade 1966–75 for most of those firms that produced this result in 1976.

TABLE 1-10

Calculation of the size of the spread separating returns to equity from equity capital costs for the 37 high-ROE firms for which replacement cost data *are* available

Line No.	Firm	(1) Market risk factor (β)	(2) Estimated cost of common equity — Nominal	(3) Estimated cost of common equity — Real	(4) Profit/common equity (1966–1975 average)	(5) Profit/common equity (1976)	(6) 1976 Profit/common equity adjusted for: Advertising and R&D	(7) 1976 Profit/common equity adjusted for: Advertising and R&D and replacement cost	(8) Nominal returns earned in excess of capital costs — Unadjusted (5) − (2)	(9) Nominal returns earned in excess of capital costs — Adjusted for advertising and R&D (6) − (2)	(10) Real returns earned in excess of capital costs adjusted for advertising and R&D and replacement cost (7) − (3)
1	Marsh & McLennan	0.87	.128	.077	.257	.274	.274	.274	.146	.146	.197*
2	Louisiana Land & Exploration	1.02	.141	.090	.313	.243	.243	.241	.102	.102	.151*
3	Kellogg	0.83	.124	.073	.215	.267	.244	.185	.143	.120	.112*
4	Dow Jones	1.13	.150	.099	.261	.240	.234	.197	.090	.084	.098*
5	Dun & Bradstreet	1.02	.141	.090	.203	.204	.203	.184	.063	.062	.094*
6	Schering-Plough	1.02	.141	.090	.231	.222	.197	.176	.081	.056	.086*
7	Melville Corp.	1.35	.169	.118	.222	.249	.251	.200	.080	.082	.082*
8	American Home Products	1.03	.142	.091	.262	.286	.232	.172	.144	.090	.081*
9	Avon Products	1.25	.161	.110	.314	.286	.273	.189	.125	.112	.079*
10	Merck	0.97	.136	.085	.250	.234	.205	.156	.098	.069	.071*
11	IBM	0.96	.136	.085	.174	.188	.177	.152	.052	.041	.067*
12	Dover Corp.	1.17	.154	.103	.180	.198	.198	.163	.044	.044	.060*
13	Revlon	1.04	.142	.091	.161	.179	.176	.148	.037	.034	.057*
14	Eli Lilly	0.99	.138	.087	.203	.186	.168	.143	.048	.030	.056*
15	Lubrizol	0.96	.136	.085	.206	.195	.183	.140	.059	.047	.055*
16	Bristol-Myers	1.16	.153	.102	.190	.208	.176	.147	.055	.023	.045*
17	Smithkline	1.04	.142	.091	.223	.199	.160	.128	.057	.018	.037*
18	MASCO Corp.	1.61	.192	.141	.185	.215	.224	.172	.023	.032	.031*
19	Nalco Chemical	1.46	.179	.128	.194	.238	.222	.156	.059	.043	.028*
20	Coca-Cola	1.33	.168	.117	.215	.210	.197	.138	.042	.029	.021*
21	McDonald's	1.71	.201	.150	.202	.210	.216	.171	.009	.015	.021*
22	Reynolds, R. J.	0.86	.127	.076	.172	.166	.169	.094	.039	.042	.018*
23	Genuine Parts	1.48	.181	.130	.168	.183	.183	.145	.002	.002	.015*
24	Sterling Drug	0.95	.135	.084	.187	.147	.117	.098	.012	(.018)	.014
25	Chesebrough-Ponds	1.45	.178	.127	.182	.171	.162	.141	(.007)	(.016)	.014*
26	Square D	1.14	.151	.100	.200	.196	.187	.111	.045	.036	.011
27	Gillette	1.01	.140	.089	.230	.154	.134	.099	.014	(.006)	.010
28	Lucky Stores	1.16	.153	.102	.225	.189	.189	.111	.036	.036	.010
29	Xerox	1.18	.155	.104	.201	.165	.158	.113	.010	.003	.009
30	Robins, A. H.	1.42	.176	.125	.195	.156	.156	.132	(.020)	.003	.007
31	Champion Spark Plug.	0.93	.133	.082	.188	.142	.138	.087	.009	.005	.005
32	PepsiCo.	1.46	.179	.128	.167	.181	.182	.127	.002	.003	(.001)
33	Eastman Kodak	1.03	.142	.091	.193	.162	.151	.087	.020	.009	(.004)
34	G. D. Searle	1.17	.154	.103	.232	.141	.132	.092	(.013)	(.022)	(.011)
35	Purolator	1.47	.180	.129	.186	.128	.129	.089	(.052)	(.051)	(.040)
36	Quaker State Oil Refining	1.47	.180	.129	.187	.139	.136	.065	(.041)	(.044)	(.064)
37	Panhandle Eastern	1.02	.141	.090	.172	.146	.146	.005	.005	.005	(.085)

*See footnote 54 for the signification of this designation.

TABLE 1-10 (continued)

Calculation of the size of the spread separating returns to equity from equity capital costs for the 35 high-ROE firms for which replacement cost data are not available

Line No.	Firm	(1) Market risk factor (β)	(2) Nominal	(3) Real	(4) Profit/common equity (1966-1975 average)	(5) Profit/common equity (1976)	(6) Advertising and R&D	(7) Advertising and R&D replacement cost†	(8) Unadjusted (5) − (2)	(9) Adjusted for advertising and R&D (6) − (2)	(10) Real returns earned in excess of capital costs adjusted for advertising and R&D and replacement cost (7) − (3)†
			Estimated cost of common equity				1976 Profit/ common equity adjusted for:		Nominal returns earned in excess of capital costs		
38	PepCom Industries	1.27	.162	.111	.245	.328	.328	—	.166	.166	—
39	Emery Air Freight	1.22	.158	.107	.340	.305	.304	—	.147	.146	—
40	Campbell Red Lake Mines	0.66	.109	.058	.362	.219	.219	—	.110	.110	—
41	Dillon Cos.	0.87	.128	.077	.193	.235	.235	—	.107	.107	—
42	Tampax	1.24	.160	.109	.340	.278	.263	—	.118	.103	—
43	Dr. Pepper	1.53	.185	.134	.248	.313	.278	—	.128	.093	—
44	H&R Block	1.43	.176	.125	.312	.272	.255	—	.096	.079	—
45	Yellow Freight	1.20	.156	.105	.218	.230	.230	—	.074	.074	—
46	Kaneb Services	1.28	.163	.112	.235	.233	.233	—	.070	.070	—
47	New Process Co.	1.10	.148	.097	.334	.267	.214	—	.119	.066	—
48	Roadway Express	1.12	.149	.098	.209	.205	.205	—	.056	.056	—
49	Atlas Consolidated Mining	1.03	.142	.091	.404	.194	.194	—	.052	.052	—
50	Russell Stover Candies	1.24	.160	.109	.208	.212	.212	—	.052	.052	—
51	Longs Drug	1.07	.145	.094	.211	.196	.196	—	.051	.051	—
52	Winn-Dixie	0.99	.138	.087	.198	.187	.184	—	.049	.046	—
53	Rorer-Amchem	1.08	.146	.095	.225	.202	.190	—	.056	.044	—
54	Merchants	0.96	.136	.085	.182	.178	.178	—	.042	.042	—
55	Prentice-Hall	0.90	.130	.079	.234	.174	.167	—	.044	.037	—
56	Stone & Webster	1.42	.176	.125	.200	.213	.213	—	.037	.037	—
57	National Chemsearch	1.08	.146	.095	.221	.182	.182	—	.036	.036	—
58	Rollins	1.34	.169	.118	.225	.205	.203	—	.036	.034	—
59	Caldor	1.13	.150	.099	.180	.183	.182	—	.033	.032	—
60	Loehmann's	1.07	.145	.094	.199	.176	.176	—	.031	.031	—
61	Rockower Brothers	1.41	.176	.125	.185	.204	.205	—	.028	.029	—
62	Malone & Hyde	1.20	.156	.105	.172	.182	.182	—	.026	.026	—
63	Weis Markets	1.16	.153	.102	.181	.178	.178	—	.025	.025	—
64	Procter and Gamble	0.94	.134	.083	.166	.170	.153	—	.036	.019	—
65	Thomas & Betts	1.20	.156	.105	.195	.182	.174	—	.026	.018	—
66	Jostens	1.29	.164	.113	.179	.180	.180	—	.016	.016	—
67	Heublein	1.48	.181	.130	.221	.197	.194	—	.016	.013	—
68	Marion Laboratories	1.21	.157	.106	.294	.145	.168	—	(.012)	.011	—
69	Moore Corp.	0.94	.134	.083	.170	.142	.142†	—	.008	.008†	—
70	Emerson Electric	1.24	.157	.106	.168	.170	.164	—	.013	.007	—
71	Eckerd (Jack)	1.37	.171	.120	.188	.168	.167	—	(.003)	(.004)	—
72	Wackenhut	1.43	.176	.125	.202	.144	.144	—	(.032)	(.032)	—

† No data on advertising or R&D expenditures are publicly available.

disappears from the balance sheet. So do the offsetting entries for deferred taxes and net worth, which, by definition, would combine to equal the value of the capitalized asset. The effect of capitalizing and then amortizing advertising and research and development expenditures would be to increase net worth, and (so long as advertising and research and development expenditures were growing annually[44]) to increase reported profits. For most firms the percentage increase in net worth would be larger than the percentage increase in net profits, thus leading to a reduction in the firm's adjusted ROE (Table 1–10). The specific calculations that are appropriate for one firm, Avon Products, Inc., are presented in the appendix.

At the conceptual level the adjustments noted above are quite straightforward. Operationally, the adjustments are more difficult. The difficulty arises in defining a reasonable economic *life* for the advertising and research and development expenditures of a firm, and also specifying a reasonable amortization *schedule* for the advertising and research and development assets. Clearly these variables ought to differ for different firms, and indeed perhaps should even be different for different product types within a single firm.

Fortunately the likely range of error one could make by adopting uniform assumptions on economic life and amortization rates for advertising and R&D expenditures across firms are not critical in verifying the points I wish to establish.[45] For that reason I will simply follow, without lengthy discussion, some precedents established by others in the exploration of these issues. Thus, advertising expenditures will be assumed to have a six-year economic life. The assumed amortization rate for advertising assets will follow the double declining balance method. Readers wishing to examine more carefully the economic rationale for these particular choices should consult the first of the articles on the accounting for advertising expenditures, and the impact of accounting policy on reported profitability as noted in Footnote 46.

Arguments similar to those raised above can be applied to research and development expenditures. Given the normally long lead times be-

---

[44] If expenditures on advertising and research and development for a given firm were constant over time, the GAAP definition of expense and the economic definition of expense for advertising and research and development in any year would, of course, be equal.

[45] The magnitude of the ROE change that can be attributed to the capitalization and amortization of advertising and R&D expenditures (Column 5 versus Column 6 of Table 1–10) is usually rather small in relation to the spread between real ROEs and real equity capital costs for the firms appearing in Table 1–10.

[46] Leonard W. Weiss, "Advertising, Profits, and Corporate Taxes," *The Review of Economics and Statistics*, November 1969, pp. 421–30; or Harry Bloch, "Advertising and Profitability: A Reappraisal," *Journal of Political Economy*, March/April 1974, pp. 267–86; or Yoram Peles, "Amortization of Advertising Expenditures in the Financial Statements," *Journal of Accounting Research*, Spring 1970.

fore R&D expenditures produce the opportunity for revenue generation, and the length of the product life cycle generally associated with pro-prietary products (particularly in the drug industry) a *ten-year* life was applied to R&D expenditures. Straight line amortization at the rate of 10 percent per year was applied to the R&D asset. Readers wishing to examine more carefully the economic rationale for these particular choices should consult the first of the articles on the accounting for R&D expen-ditures, and the impact of accounting policy on reported profitability as noted in Footnote 47.

In the appendix, sample calculations for Avon Products, Inc., are carried out that convert GAAP-determined profit and book value data into the more economically meaningful figures resulting from capitalizing and then amortizing expenditures on advertising and R&D. "Adjusted ROE" calculations (taking into account the capitalization and amortization of advertising and R&D expenditures) are then presented in Column 6 of Table 1–10 for each of the 72 high-ROE firms first described in Table 1–9. Table 1–10 (Column 9) suggests that prior to any adjustment for inflation (but after adjustments for risk, and the capitalization and amortization of advertising and R&D expenditures), 63 of the 72 high-return companies enjoyed equity returns in 1976 that were in excess of their equity capital costs.

ADJUSTING *ROE* FOR THE EFFECT OF INFLATION: REPLACEMENT COST ACCOUNTING

One final adjustment can be made to reported ROEs to adjust, at least partially, for inflation.[48] During periods of rapid inflation, ROE calcula-tions based on GAAP can greatly overstate true profitability.[49] True profit-ability is necessarily based on *current,* not *historic,* cost levels. In an effort to capture a significant part of the impact of inflation on a firm's opera-tions and profitability, the U.S. Securities and Exchange Commission (as

---

[47] Rosalind Schulman in Joseph Cooper, ed., *The Economics of Drug Innovation* (Washington: American University, 1969), pp. 213–21; or Vernon A. Mund in Joseph Cooper, pp. 125–38; or Harold A. Clymer in Joseph Cooper, pp. 109–24.

[48] A further refinement of the ROE data might include an adjustment to interest expense to reflect current rates rather than the rates that a firm might enjoy on debt issued previously when rates were significantly different. As we will show momentarily (footnote 56) the firms noted in Lines 1–37 of Table 1–11 had a negligible amount of fixed-rate long-term debt at below-market rates on December 31, 1976. Such an ad-justment would thus simply further complicate our analysis without adding any significant benefit.

[49] Readers interested in pursuing this line of argument can explore it in greater detail in the following articles: S. Davidson and R. L. Weil, "Inflation Accounting: The SEC Proposal for Replacement Cost Disclosures," *Financial Analysts Journal,* March/April 1976; or Richard F. Vancil, "Inflation Accounting—The Great Contro-versy," *Harvard Business Review,* March–April 1976.

of December 25, 1976) required large[50] firms to report domestic inventories and net plant and equipment[51] at replacement as well as historic cost. The reporting of this information makes it possible (again in a rather crude[52] fashion) to adjust a firm's income statement and balance sheet to isolate a portion of the effect of inflation on profitability.

The calculation of the profit, book value, and ROE impact of utilizing replacement cost accounting is presented for Avon Products in the appendix. While the requisite replacement cost data are available for only the first 37 of the 72 firms listed in Table 1–10, it is interesting to note (from Column 10 of Table 1–10) that for 31 of these firms, real rates of return on adjusted equity exceed real equity costs.[53] This was true in 1976, and

---

[50] S.E.C. Accounting Series Release No. 190 (dated March 23, 1976, and effective December 25, 1976) "requires registrants who have inventories and gross property, plant and equipment which aggregate more than $100 million and which comprise more than 10 percent of total assets to disclose the estimated current replacement cost of inventories and productive capacity at the end of each fiscal year for which a balance sheet is required and the approximate amount of cost of sales and depreciation based on replacement cost."

[51] Cash and accounts receivable represent assets whose replacement cost is equal to historic cost. This is not generally true for inventories, or net plant and equipment, however. To the extent the SEC's requirements ignore land, foreign inventory, and foreign net plant and equipment, and other nonmonetary asset items, it does not capture the *full* economic impact of inflation accounting. In addition, replacement cost accounting generally ignores the impact of inflation on monetary assets and liabilities. In analyzing the potential profitability of *future* business operations, however, this latter omission is entirely reasonable.

[52] Replacement cost data as reported to the SEC do not, for example, reflect operating cost savings that would result from the replacement of existing assets with new assets utilizing current technology.

[53] For another three of these 37 firms, a poorer ROE performance in 1976 than that which characterized the prior decade caused them to fail to achieve a *real* ROE that exceeded their *real* equity capital cost as of December 31, 1976. Conversely, one firm passed this particular test in 1976 that would not have passed it on the basis of its ROE average for the prior decade.

When equity capital costs are compared with actual return-on-equity performance data, the ROE performance data should be calculated using *beginning-of-year* common equity values unless new equity is issued during the year. In situations where a significant amount of new equity is issued by a firm during the year, the average of beginning-of-year and end-of-year common equity values might be the most appropriate figure to use in the ROE calculation. At the time this book was written, replacement cost data (which are utilized in the calculation of adjusted book values in Table 1–11) were not available for points in time prior to December, 1976. Profit data were not yet available for 1977. All of the *adjusted* ROE data of Table 1–10 thus had to be based upon end-of-year common equity rather than beginning-of-year or average common equity. In order to maintain consistency throughout the text, all ROE data (whether adjusted or unadjusted) have been calculated using end-of-year common equity. The use of end-of-year common equity produces a modest downward bias in the reported spreads between rates of return on equity, as reported in this book, and the cost of common equity. For the firms listed in Lines 1–37 of Table 1–10, for example, 1976 unadjusted ROEs would have been, on average, 2.8 percentage points and 1.4 percentage points higher, respectively, if beginning-of-year or average common equity values had been utilized. For firms with lower levels of profitability and average dividend payout ratios, the downward bias brought about by utilizing end-of-year common equity would, in general, be smaller.

in most cases was probably equally true for the prior decade as well for reasons noted in the second paragraph of Footnote 43.

It can be fairly safely stated that most of the firms that show a positive figure in Column 10 of Table 1–10 do, in fact, earn rates of return on equity that exceed their equity capital costs.[54] These are bona fide Hall of Fame firms. One further caveat, however, should be offered at this point. Our list of firms that have consistently earned rates of return in excess of equity capital costs was drawn from a sample of 72 firms that had achieved ROEs in excess of 15 percent in *every year* of the decade 1966–75. This sample in no sense purports to be exhaustive with regard to firms that qualify as having consistently earned ROEs in excess of equity capital costs. Indeed, if a firm's cost of equity capital were relatively low (as a result of limited systematic risk), it might consistently achieve ROEs in excess of equity capital costs and not appear in the 72-firm sample. Similarly, there is no magic in defining "consistently" as ten years out of ten with ROEs in excess of 15 percent. Numerous companies might have earned ROEs in excess of their equity capital costs in *many,* but not *all,* of the years 1966–75. Such firms would not necessarily appear on the 72-firm list. In short, the 72-firm list in Table 1–10 simply picks up the most likely candidates.

Having identified a list (admittedly not exhaustive) of firms that have consistently earned ROEs in excess of equity capital cost, we have achieved the second objective outlined on page 25. This allows us to move on to the third objective, which is to estimate the very substantial value created for shareholders by the managements of those firms whose returns on equity exceed their equity capital costs.

VALUE CREATION: MARKET VALUE VERSUS ADJUSTED BOOK VALUE FOR HIGH-*ROE* FIRMS

As noted in Table 1–10, the data needed to adjust GAAP-determined book values for the effects of advertising, R&D, and inflation are available

---

[54] Errors in calculating the value of Column 10, Table 1–10, can arise from a number of sources, several of which have already been noted. For this reason, small positive values in this column (in the range of 0.01 or 0.02) should not be taken as compelling evidence that a particular firm is actually achieving a real ROE that exceeds its equity capital cost. For example, the β utilized in calculating a firm's cost of equity capital in Table 1–10 is determined via regression techniques. The value so determined is simply an estimate of the *true* β of the firm's common stock. If uncertainties surrounding the true value of β were the only uncertainty associated with defining the size of the spread indicated in Column 10, Table 1–10, then we could say (with a minimum of 90 percent confidence in each case) that the 24 firms with starred data is Column 10 of Table 1–10 were actually earning rates of return on equity that exceeded their equity capital costs. The use of standard error data relating to the β calculation (combined with the use of the t-distribution) permits us to determine, statistically, this confidence interval.

for only 37 of the 72 previously described high-ROE firms.[55] The market value of the common equity securities of these 37 firms exceeds the adjusted book value of their equity by some $57.6 billion at December 31, 1976 (Column 7, Table 1–11).[56] This created value, as the model developed earlier in the chapter suggests, arises from investor perceptions (often buttressed by a favorable historical record) regarding the volume, duration, and degree of extraordinary profitability anticipated from the firm's *existing* investments and *future* investment opportunities.

A substantial part of the message conveyed by Chapter 1 is captured in Column 7 of Table 1–11. The message is simply this. *Managers who are successful in either shaping or simply taking advantage of the competitive environment so as to earn returns in excess of their capital costs create enormous wealth for their shareholders.* The game is clearly worth the candle. How some of the firms in Table 1–11 have played the game is the subject of Chapters 3 to 9.

We have now examined, empirically, the degree of wealth creation achieved by firms listed in Table 1–10 that have succeeded in producing returns on equity that exceed their equity capital costs. This fulfills the third objective noted on page 25. The fourth objective noted on page 25 remains. We shall now examine, briefly, some of the important characteristics of the 72 high-ROE firms.[57]

SALIENT CHARACTERISTICS OF HIGH-*ROE* FIRMS—ENTRY BARRIERS

Firms that consistently earn rates of return on equity that exceed their equity capital costs can invariably attribute their success to the existence of some entry barrier(s) in the competitive environment. This is true as

---

[55] Replacement cost data are available only for domestic U.S. firms whose fiscal years end after December 24, 1976, and whose gross assets plus inventories exceed $100 million. Thirteen of 35 high-ROE firms for which replacement cost data are not available had their 1976 fiscal year end prior to December 25, 1976.

[56] One could argue that if the long-term debt of these firms were valued at *market* rather than *book* values, the spread between the market value of the equity of these firms and the adjusted book value of the equity of these firms would be reduced. In fact, the impact would be insignificant. At December 31, 1976, the firms listed in Lines 1–37 of Table 1–11 had a book value total of $5.5 billion of long-term debt outstanding. Of this total, $0.4 billion was floating-rate debt, $1.3 billion was not identified as to rate, and $3.8 billion was fixed-rate debt. Of the fixed-rate, non-convertible debt, less than $0.5 billion carried an interest rate of less than 7.5 percent. These facts make it quite clear that adjusting the long-term debt of these firms to *market* rather than *book* values would have no significant impact on the calculation of the adjusted book value of the equity securities of these firms.

[57] While some of the characteristics are causally related to the ability of these firms to earn ROEs in excess of their capital costs, others are not. Some characteristics simply result from the fact that these firms achieve high ROEs, and have no causal link to that success.

a general proposition, extending beyond just those high-ROE firms listed in Table 1–10. If competitive entry barriers did not exist, the action of competition would simply drive equity returns down to the level of equity costs. Entry barriers exist in a number of forms that have been well catalogued and described, primarily by specialists in the field of industrial organization economics.[58]

There are four broad catagories of entry barriers.[59] *Unique products*[60] (often called differentiated products) can be created and protected from competition by patents, trademarks, and persuasive advertising. Because of their real or perceived uniqueness, such products face limited competition and can sometimes be priced at levels that produce returns in excess of capital costs.

Scale economies in the production, marketing, or maintenance of products sometimes exist that allow the most efficiently organized competitor(s) to enjoy costs that are below those of less efficiently positioned competitors. To the extent that the benefits of these cost advantages are captured for shareholders, the efficient producer can achieve returns in excess of capital costs, while still pricing his product no higher than that of the less efficient competitor.

Absolute cost advantages often occur in the extractive industries, where some competitors control scarce resources that can be developed and marketed at costs that are far below that enjoyed by less fortunately positioned competitors. The firms that control the scarce low-cost resource can often earn returns that substantially exceed their capital costs, while pricing their product at competitive levels. Finally, the *capital requirements* associated with participation in a market can be so high in some businesses that most potential competitors are, as a practical matter, precluded from either entering or effectively exploiting the market. This fact allows the financially well positioned firms already participating in the market to price their products so as to produce returns in excess of capital costs.

Once a catalog of entry barriers has been described, one could go through the list of firms presented in Table 1–10 in an effort to pinpoint

---

[58] See, for example, Joe S. Bain, *Barriers to New Competition* (Cambridge, Mass.: Harvard University Press, 1956); or John M. Vernon, *Market Structure and Industrial Performance—A Review of Statistical Findings* (Boston: Allyn and Bacon, Inc., 1972); or F. M. Scherer, *Industrial Market Structure and Economic Performance* (Chicago: Rand McNally & Co., 1970).

[59] The catalog of identifiable entry barriers and the understanding of the relationships between these barriers and enhanced profitability have been enriched substantially since Bain's seminal research, which described these four categories. For a sample of some new directions in research in the field of industrial organization see, for example, Michael E. Porter, *Interbrand Choice, Strategy, and Bilateral Market Power* (Cambridge, Mass.: Harvard University Press, 1976).

[60] The use of the word product here is meant to refer to services as well as products in the usual sense.

TABLE 1-11

Calculation of the values created for shareholders by firms that earn returns on equity that exceed their equity capital costs (data for 37 firms for which replacement cost data are available)

Line	Firm	(1) Market value of firm's common equity @ 12/31/76 ($ millions)	(2) Book value — Unadjusted ($ millions)	(3) Book value — Adjusted for advertising and R&D ($ millions)	(4) Book value — Adjusted for advertising and R&D and replacement cost ($ millions)	(5) = (1) − (2) Value created — Unadjusted ($ millions)	(6) = (1) − (3) Value created — Adjusted for advertising and R&D ($ millions)	(7) = (1) − (4) Value created — Adjusted for advertising and R&D and replacement cost ($ millions)	(8) MV/BV ratio — Unadjusted	(9) MV/BV ratio — Adjusted for advertising and R&D	(10) MV/BV ratio — Adjusted for advertising and R&D and replacement cost
1	Marsh & McLennan	777	170	170	170	606	606	606	4.6	4.6	4.6
2	Louisiana Land & Exploration	1,078	398	398	400	681	681	678	2.7	2.7	2.7
3	Kellogg	2,106	487	566	694	1,618	1,539	1,411	4.3	3.7	3.0
4	Dow Jones	535	126	130	152	409	405	383	4.2	4.1	3.5
5	Dun & Bradstreet	807	234	240	259	573	566	547	3.5	3.4	3.1
6	Schering-Plough	2,420	707	804	919	1,713	1,616	1,501	3.4	3.0	2.6
7	Melville Corp.	661	244	255	279	417	406	382	2.7	2.6	2.4
8	American Home Products	5,019	968	1,267	1,592	4,050	3,751	3,427	5.2	4.0	3.2
9	Avon Products	2,845	589	638	841	2,256	2,207	2,004	4.8	4.5	3.4
10	Merck	5,145	1,090	1,429	1,751	4,055	3,716	3,394	4.7	3.6	2.9
11	IBM	42,063	12,749	14,639	17,029	29,313	27,423	25,033	3.2	2.9	2.5
12	Dover Corp.	338	158	158	187	180	180	150	2.1	2.1	1.8
13	Revlon	1,338	456	545	613	882	792	725	2.9	2.5	2.2
14	Eli Lilly	3,292	1,079	1,332	1,516	2,214	1,960	1,776	3.1	2.5	2.2
15	Lubrizol	737	262	295	376	475	441	360	2.8	2.5	2.0
16	Bristol-Myers	2,155	740	1,022	1,151	1,415	1,133	1,004	2.9	2.1	1.9
17	Smithkline	1,190	361	549	627	829	641	563	3.3	2.2	1.9
18	MASCO Corp.	672	219	235	274	454	437	399	3.1	2.9	2.5
19	Nalco Chemical	682	183	206	273	498	476	409	3.7	3.3	2.5
20	Coca-Cola	4,734	1,357	1,514	1,901	3,378	3,220	2,833	3.5	3.1	2.5
21	McDonald's	2,163	525	566	682	1,637	1,597	1,481	4.1	3.8	3.2
22	Reynolds, R. J.	3,137	2,068	2,198	3,609	1,069	939	(472)	1.5	1.4	0.9
23	Genuine Parts	657	207	207	229	450	450	428	3.2	3.2	2.9
24	Sterling Drug	995	564	779	868	430	216	127	1.8	1.3	1.2
25	Chesebrough-Ponds	805	317	374	426	488	431	379	2.5	2.2	1.9
26	Square D	664	226	246	397	439	418	268	2.9	2.7	1.7
27	Gillette	839	505	672	789	334	167	50	1.7	1.2	1.1
28	Lucky Stores	576	243	243	309	333	333	266	2.4	2.4	1.9
29	Xerox	4,653	2,179	2,611	3,278	2,474	2,043	1,375	2.1	1.8	1.4
30	Robins, A. H.	314	201	244	276	113	69	37	1.6	1.3	1.1
31	Champion Spark Plug.	490	318	345	435	172	145	55	1.5	1.4	1.1
32	PepsiCo.	1,953	753	870	1,052	1,200	1,083	901	2.6	2.2	1.9
33	Eastman Kodak	13,896	4,026	4,806	7,782	9,870	9,090	6,114	3.5	2.9	1.8
34	G. D. Searle	687	436	621	706	251	66	(19)	1.6	1.1	1.0
35	Purolator	131	96	98	122	36	33	9	1.4	.13	1.1
36	Quaker State Oil Refining	348	185	192	300	163	155	48	1.9	1.8	1.2
37	Panhandle Eastern	802	587	587	1,782	219	219	(980)	1.4	1.4	0.5
37(a)	Total	111,704	36,011	42,052	54,047	75,694	69,650	57,652			

TABLE 1-11 (continued)
(data for 35 firms for which replacement cost data are not available)

Line	Firm	(1) Market value of firm's common equity @ 12/31/76 ($ millions)	(2) Unadjusted ($ millions)	(3) Adjusted for advertising and R&D ($ millions)	(4) Adjusted for advertising and R&D and replacement cost ($ millions)	(5) Unadjusted ($ millions)	(6) Adjusted for advertising and R&D ($ millions)	(7) Adjusted for advertising and R&D and replacement cost ($ millions)	(8) Unadjusted	(9) Adjusted for advertising and R&D	(10) Adjusted for advertising and R&D and replacement cost
			Book value of firm's common equity			Value created			Market-value/book-value ratio		
38	PepCom Industries	18	14	14	—	4	4	—	1.3	1.3	—
39	Emery Air Freight	294	52	54	—	242	240	—	5.7	5.5	—
40	Campbell Red Lake Mines	198	35	35	—	163	163	—	5.7	5.7	—
41	Dillon Cos.	261	96	96	—	165	165	—	2.7	2.7	—
42	Tampax	412	118	125	—	293	286	—	3.5	3.3	—
43	Dr. Pepper	272	50	62	—	223	211	—	5.5	4.4	—
44	H&R Block	257	73	79	—	185	178	—	3.5	3.3	—
45	Yellow Freight	611	147	147	—	463	463	—	4.2	4.2	—
46	Kaneb Services	106	53	53	—	53	53	—	2.0	2.0	—
47	New Process Co.	102	39	39	—	63	63	—	2.6	2.6	—
48	Roadway Express	920	209	209	—	711	711	—	4.4	4.4	—
49	Atlas Consolidated Mining	235	132	133	—	102	102	—	1.8	1.8	—
50	Russell Stover Candies	105	54	54	—	51	51	—	1.9	1.9	—
51	Longs Drugs	358	87	92	—	271	266	—	4.1	3.9	—
52	Winn-Dixie	973	336	363	—	637	610	—	2.9	2.7	—
53	Rorer-Amchem	288	144	170	—	144	118	—	2.0	1.7	—
54	Merchants	34	39	39	—	(6)	(6)	—	.9	.9	—
55	Prentice Hall	232	110	130	—	122	102	—	2.1	1.8	—
56	Stone & Webster	252	148	148	—	104	104	—	1.7	1.7	—
57	National Chemsearch	268	90	90	—	178	178	—	3.0	3.0	—
58	Rollins	325	109	116	—	216	209	—	3.0	2.8	—
59	Caldor	72	46	52	—	24	20	—	1.5	1.4	—
60	Loehmann's	23	14	14	—	9	9	—	1.6	1.6	—
61	Rockower Bros.	29	28	29	—	1	0	—	1.0	1.0	—
62	Malone & Hyde	169	77	77	—	92	92	—	2.2	2.2	—
63	Weis Markets	154	101	101	—	53	53	—	1.5	1.5	—
64	Procter & Gamble	7,729	2,357	2,971	—	5,372	4,758	—	3.3	2.6	—
65	Thomas & Betts	310	93	105	—	216	205	—	3.3	3.0	—
66	Jostens	93	53	53	—	40	40	—	1.7	1.7	—
67	Heublein	883	371	473	—	512	410	—	2.4	1.9	—
68	Marion Laboratories	125	58	70	—	67	55	—	2.2	1.8	—
69	Moore Corp.	1,009	424	424	—	585	585	—	2.4	2.4	—
70	Emerson Electric	1,972	689	753	—	1,283	1,219	—	2.9	2.6	—
71	Eckerd (Jack)	546	186	195	—	360	352	—	2.9	2.8	—
72	Wackenhut	15	16	16	—	0	0	—	1.0	1.0	—
73	Subtotal	19,650	6,650	7,580	—	13,000	12,070	9,900*	—	—	—
74	Total	131,354	42,661	49,632	—	88,694	81,720	67,552	—	—	—

*Assumes the same ratio relationship between Columns 7 and 5 in Line 73 as that indicated in Line 37(a).

the specific entry barrier(s) that permit each firm to earn premium rates of return. To accomplish this task with rigor could easily be the work of a lifetime. Instead, in Chapters 3 to 9 we shall look, in some depth, at a few of the firms listed in Table 1–10 (as well as some others) in an effort to understand how the managers of some firms have acted to create value for their equity shareholders through the effective utilization of entry barriers.[61]

SALIENT CHARACTERISTICS OF MANY HIGH-*ROE* FIRMS—FOCUSED PRODUCT LINES

Most of the firms listed in Table 1–10 are highly focused in their business activities. Indeed, a high fraction of their sales is in a single line of business, according to the way these firms define their lines of business in 10K reports to the SEC.[62] Table 1–12 summarizes this information. It indicates that 61 percent of these high-ROE firms have more than 70 percent of their total sales in a single line of business.

In addition to being highly focused, many of the high-ROE firms in Table 1–10 have achieved the largest *national* market share in the industries in which they compete. Indeed, the 72 high-ROE firms of Table 1–10 enjoy the dominant national market position in at least 22 lines of

TABLE 1–12
Degree of focus in the lines of business of 72 high-ROE firms—1976

Fraction of firm's sales in its principal line of business	Firms with this fraction of total sales in their principal line of business	
	(number)	*(percentage)*
0.91–1.00	30	41
0.81–0.90	4	6
0.71–0.80	10	14
0.61–0.70	7	10
0.51–0.60	8	11
0.41–0.50	7	10
0.31–0.40	4	6
0.21–0.30	1	1
0.11–0.20	1	1
0–0.10	0	0
	72	100%

[61] The firms selected for analysis in greater depth in Chapters 3–9 in no sense represent a random sample of the 72 firms. The firms were selected instead for the clarity with which value-creation, value-transfer, and value-destruction phenomena could be highlighted.

[62] Since firms do not report their line-of-business data to the SEC according to SIC categories, this measure of diversification in their business activities is quite imprecise. It does at least give an indication, however, of the degree to which many of these firms have rather sharply focused their area of business operations.

business.[63] To the extent opportunities for achieving scale economies at the national level exist in the businesses represented, the firms shown in Table 1–10 are certainly advantageously positioned to reap these scale economies.

SALIENT CHARACTERISTICS OF MANY HIGH-*ROE* FIRMS—REDUNDANT CASH

The *very* rich, I am told, are cursed by an inability to spend wealth faster than it accumulates. Their wealth simply grows and grows. So it is with corporations. Annually a surprisingly large number of U.S. NFCs report levels of cash and marketable securities that are more than sufficient to (*a*) meet normal transactions requirements and (*b*) repay all of their outstanding short- and long-term borrowings. In 1975, for example, 151 firms in the sample of 1,448 firms enjoyed this luxury (Line 10, Table 1–13). Some 60 of these firms had basked in such splendor for at least a decade (Line 11, Table 1–13). In effect, these firms enjoy the equivalent of a debt-free capital structure and a large pool of redundant cash.[64] Indeed, it would be accurate to characterize these firms as having *negative* leverage, or what economists would call a net-creditor position.

Who are the firms that enjoy the benefits of a capital structure that is free from financial risk? Are they only firms facing great operating risk whose managers seek to reduce total corporate risk by adopting an all-equity or even negatively leveraged capital structure? The answer appears to be no! The firms most likely to have redundant cash are firms with very high ROEs whose equity capital retentions outpace the investment requirements of their product-markets. As shown in Line 1 of Table 1–14, 38.3 percent of the 72 firms with ROEs exceeding 15 percent for the years 1966–75 also had redundant cash in *every* year of this decade. A significant fraction of those high-return firms simply do not face a supply of attractive investment opportunities in their existing markets that is commensurate with their ability to generate equity capital through earn-

---

[63] It should be noted that "markets" are defined here so broadly as to limit the economic significance of the information. As will be shown in Chapter 4, for example, competition in the retail grocery trade has economic relevance primarily at the *city* level, not the *national* level. Thus, while the Dillon Companies, Lucky Stores, Winn-Dixie, and Weis Markets (Lines 26–29, Table 1–9) might all be dominant in many of the local areas in which they operate, none of these firms ranks higher than fifth in terms of its share of national retail grocery trade.

[64] Redundant cash, as defined here, equals all cash and marketable securities less an amount equal to the sum of (1) borrowed money, and (2) 6 percent of all non-cash assets. The 6 percent figure noted above is assumed to be the amount of cash and marketable securities needed to meet normal operating needs. FTC data for the 1974–75 period show firms in the category "all manufacturing" holding cash and marketable securities equal to about 6 percent of noncash assets.

TABLE 1-13

A. Number of firms out of Compustat 1,448 stockpiling redundant cash in each of the years 1966–1975

Line	Year	Number	Percentage
1	1966	270	18.7
2	1967	237	16.4
3	1968	229	15.9
4	1969	179	12.4
5	1970	162	11.2
6	1971	169	11.7
7	1972	164	11.3
8	1973	151	10.4
9	1974	123	8.5
10	1975	151	10.4

B. Number of years in the ten-year period 1966–1975 during which redundant cash was stockpiled by each of the 151 Compustat firms holding redundant cash as of December 31, 1975

Line	Number of years in the period 1966-1975 during which redundant cash was held	Number	Percentage
11	10	60	39.7
12	9	13	8.6
13	8	11	7.3
14	7	11	7.3
15	6	9	6.0
16	5	11	7.3
17	4	6	4.0
18	3	1	0.6
19	2	11	7.3
20	1	18	11.9
21		151	100.0%

ings retentions. Why these firms do not return this redundant cash to their shareholders in the form of higher dividends or share repurchases (or use it to acquire other businesses) is an open research question that might well be answered differently for each firm. It is interesting to note, however, that the existence of redundant cash (and, by definition,[65] redundant equity capital) substantially reduces a firm's reported ROE. For example, absent its $3.7 *billion* pool of redundant cash (and equity capital) at December 31, 1975, IBM's ROE would have risen from 17.4 percent to 23.7 percent (Lines 1, 2, Table 1–15). If IBM had chosen to both (*a*) eliminate its redundant cash and (*b*) leverage itself to the same point as its *least* leveraged competitor in 1975, the firm's ROE would have

---

[65] Redundant cash and redundant equity capital are equal, by definition, since redundant cash is calculated on the assumption that all debt is repaid before cash can be deemed "redundant."

TABLE 1-14

Historical data indicating the propensity of firms with very high rates of return on common equity to stockpile redundant cash over extended time periods

Return on common equity	1,448 Compustat firms		151 Compustat firms with redundant cash at 12/31/75		60 Compustat firms with ten successive years of redundant cash at 12/31/75	
	Number	Percentage	Number	Percentage	Number	Percentage
1. Exceeding 15% in each of the years 1966–75	72	(5.0)	23	15.2	23	(38.3)
2. Exceeding 15% in at least 5 out of 7 of the years 1969–75 (but not including the firms in (1) above)	80	(5.5)	29	19.2	12	(20.0)
3. Less than 6% in at least 6 of the years 1966–75	178	(12.3)	12	8.0	1	(1.7)
4. Other than that characterized by (1) to (3) above	1,118	(77.2)	87	57.6	24	(40.0)
	1,448	100.0	151	100.0	60	100.0

Note: All cash and marketable securities over an amount equal to the sum of (1) borrowed money, (2) customer deposits, and (3) 6 percent of all noncash assets is considered to be redundant cash.

TABLE 1-15

Calculation of the effect of a change in financial structure (via the removal of redundant cash and/or utilizing debt capital) on the reported profit/common equity ratios of the IBM Corp. and Avon Products, Inc. (1966–1975)

Line	Profit/common equity ratio	1966	1967	1968	1969	1970	1971	1972	1973	1974	1975
	IBM Corp.										
1	As reported to shareholders	0.158	0.170	0.191	0.177	0.171	0.162	0.169	0.179	0.182	0.174
2	Adjusted to remove redundant* cash. . .	0.158	0.170	0.229	0.188	0.173	0.172	0.193	0.217	0.231	0.237
3	Adjusted to remove redundant cash and to achieve the debt/equity ratio of the least leveraged competitor[†] in the industry.	—	—	—	—	—	—	—	—	—	0.324
	Avon Products, Inc.										
4	As reported to shareholders	0.371	0.373	0.353	0.358	0.361	0.344	0.330	0.304	0.237	0.265
5	Adjusted to remove redundant* cash. . .	0.546	0.542	0.511	0.413	0.422	0.453	0.470	0.395	0.291	0.454

* All cash and marketable securities less an amount equal to the sum of: (1) borrowed money, (2) 6 percent of all noncash assets is considered to be redundant cash. In removing this redundant cash (via dividends or share repurchases) for the calculation in Line 2, this redundant cash is assumed to have yielded 4 percent after taxes. The derivation of Line 5 can be found in Table 3A–1.

[†] At December 31, 1975, IBM's principal competitors had borrowed-money/net-worth ratios as follows: Burroughs 0.47, Control Data 0.76, Sperry Rand 0.82, and NCR 0.99. In the Line 3 calculation, IBM is assumed to have borrowed $2,495 million at an after-tax cost of 5 percent, and to have paid out this amount via dividends or share repurchases, thereby achieving a debt/equity ratio of 0.47.

risen to about 32.4 percent (Line 3, Table 1–15).[66] IBM's unleveraged capital structure and its enormous pool of redundant capital have clearly reduced the obviousness of IBM's enormous profitability.

The profitability of Avon Products, when cast in a framework similar to that suggested in the IBM example above, is even more staggering (Lines 4–5, Table 1–15). No other firm in a similar size class comes even close to the level of profitability of this truly remarkable firm.

SALIENT CHARACTERISTICS OF MANY HIGH-*ROE* FIRMS—OVERVALUATION

One final note should be added to complete Chapter 1. That note relates to the great degree of optimism shown by investors in valuing high-ROE firms. The circled values in Columns 5–7 of Table 1–16 depict an interesting phenomenon. The market-value/adjusted-book-value ratios of 16 of the 37 inflation-adjusted high-ROE firms fall *above* the ratios that would be expected for these firms based upon a *30-year* extrapolation of their historical performance measured along the three critical value-creating dimensions originally outlined in Table 1–3. This overvaluation is demonstrated as follows.[67] Column 6 of Table 1–16 contains the calculated market-value/adjusted book-value ratio for each firm assuming that its *real* ROE at December 31, 1975, was exactly equal to its *real* cost of equity capital, and that its *real* equity returns and costs would remain equal in the future. Under these circumstances the market-value/adjusted-book-value ratio for the firm should obviously be 1.0, as is shown in Column 6 of Table 1–16. Now let's change these assumptions, however, and assume that *real* equity returns for the 30 years following December 31, 1975, would exceed *real* equity costs by the amount indicated in Column 3 of Table 1–16. Then assume further that each firm would, for the next 30 years, expand its equity base at the rate achieved during the prior decade as indicated in Column 4 of Table 1–16. Given this set of investor expectations, the calculated (and economically rational) market-value/adjusted-book-value ratio for each firm would be as indicated in Column 7 of Table 1–16.

Clearly, as of December 31, 1975, a large number of high-ROE firms faced some quite impressive (and, in at least a few cases, essentially

---

[66] It should be noted that the elimination of redundant cash and/or leveraging a firm's capital structure would, of course, increase the firm's β and its cost of capital. This effect is examined in the appendix to Chapter 3.

[67] "Overvaluation" here refers to the notion (Table 1–3) that the economic value of a firm's equity securities is a function of the firm's real investment opportunity profile and the discounted value of the cash flows streaming from these investment opportunities.

TABLE 1-16

Actual market-value/book-value ratio data versus the *range* of market-value/book-value ratio data projected (based on an extrapolation of historical performance) for 37 high-ROE firms for which replacement cost data are available

Line	Firm	(1) 1975 Redundant cash/ Common equity	(2) Estimated real cost of equity capital (K_e)†	(3) Real returns on equity earned above real equity† cost	(4) 10-Year average annual reinvestment rate‡	(5) Market value/ adjusted book value §	(6) (7) Projected market-value/ adjusted-book-value ratio range‖	
1	Marsh & McLennan	.35	.077	.197	0.50	4.6	1.0 to	14.4
2	Louisiana Land & Exploration	—	.090	.151	0.42	2.7	1.0 to	5.8
3	Kellogg	.06	.073	.112	0.43	3.0	1.0 to	4.4
4	Dow Jones	.31#	.099	.098	0.40	3.5	1.0 to	3.1
5	Dun & Bradstreet	.14	.090	.094	0.53	3.1	1.0 to	3.9
6	Schering-Plough	.19	.090	.086	0.83	2.6	1.0 to	6.4
7	Melville Corp.	.21	.118	.082	0.71	2.4	1.0 to	4.0
8	American Home Products	.26	.091	.081	0.38	3.2	1.0 to	2.6*
9	Avon Products	.44	.110	.079	0.40	3.4	1.0 to	2.4*
10	Merck	—	.085	.071	0.52	2.9	1.0 to	2.9
11	IBM	.32	.085	.067	0.72	2.5	1.0 to	3.6
12	Dover Corp.	—	.103	.060	0.76	1.8	1.0 to	3.2
13	Revlon	—	.091	.057	0.82	2.2	1.0 to	3.4
14	Eli Lilly	.05	.087	.056	0.69	2.2	1.0 to	2.8
15	Lubrizol	.12	.085	.055	0.68	2.0	1.0 to	2.7
16	Bristol-Myers	—	.102	.045	0.72	1.9	1.0 to	2.3
17	Smithkline	—	.091	.037	0.39	1.9	1.0 to	1.6
18	MASCO Corp.	—	.141	.031	1.24	2.5	1.0 to	3.3

	(1)				(Range)		
19	Nalco Chemical	.06	.128	.028	0.63	2.5	to	1.5 **
20	Coca-Cola	.22	.117	.021	0.56	2.5	to	1.4 **
21	McDonald's	—	.150	.021	1.26	3.2	to	2.4
22	Reynolds, R. J.	—	.076	.018	0.55	0.9	to	1.4
23	Genuine Parts	.04	.130	.015	0.85	2.9	to	1.4 **
24	Sterling Drug	—	.084	.014	0.59	1.2	to	1.3
25	Chesebrough-Ponds	—	.127	.014	0.88	1.9	to	1.4 **
26	Square D	—	.100	.011	0.39	1.7	to	1.2 *
27	Gillette	—	.089	.010	0.50	1.1	to	1.2
28	Lucky Stores	—	.102	.009	0.77	1.9	to	1.2 *
29	Xerox	—	.104	.009	0.81	1.4	to	1.2
30	Robins, A. H.	.13	.125	.007	0.76	1.1	to	1.1
31	Champion Spark Plug	—	.082	.005	0.60	1.2	to	1.1 *
32	PepsiCo	—	.128	(.001)	0.73	1.9	to	1.0
33	Eastman Kodak	.10	.091	(.004)	0.57	1.8	to	0.9
34	G. D. Searle	—	.103	(.011)	0.79	1.0	to	0.8
35	Purolator	—	.129	(.040)	0.67	1.1	to	0.5 **
36	Quaker State Oil Refining	—	.129	(.064)	0.73	1.2	to	0.3 **
37	Panhandle Eastern	—	.090	(.085)	0.62	0.5	to	0.1

* See Footnote 71.

** See Footnote 71.

† Data drawn from Table 1-10. It should be noted that the data in Columns (2) through (7) do not reflect the removal of the redundant cash noted in Column (1). The Column (1) data are presented solely to indicate the extent of redundant capital in individual high-ROE firms.

‡ Reinvestment rate is defined as the average annual increase in the firm's common equity divided by its average annual profit after taxes.

§ Data drawn from Table 1-11.

‖ The *left* side of this range assumes that the firm's *real* ROE changes immediately to the level of its *real* cost of equity capital and remains there in the future. The *right* side of this range assumes that the firm's real ROE remains at variance from its real cost of equity capital as indicated in Column (3) for the next 30 years, and that the firm's reinvestment rate remains at the level indicated in Column (4) for the next 30 years.

A deduction for unfulfilled subscription liabilities would reduce this redundant cash significantly.

unachievable[68]) investor expectations. A number of factors may be contributing to this phenomenon. These include:

1. The depressing effect of redundant cash[69] upon reported returns on equity as noted in the cases of IBM and Avon Products (Table 1–15). The relative importance of redundant cash (in relation to reported net worth) is indicated for each firm in Column 1 of Table 1–16;

2. The anticipation that the spread separating real returns from equity capital costs will, for some of these firms, improve in the future over what they had been in 1976;[70]

3. The anticipation that reinvestment opportunities in relation to net profits beyond 1976 will accelerate above the levels experienced during the decade 1966–75; and

4. The possibility that market valuations for some of these high-ROE firms have simply become detached, at least temporarily, from economic reality.[71]

This last point is a particularly important one. It suggests that significant imperfections[72] in the U.S. equity markets may well exist in the valuation of individual securities such as those listed in Table 1–16. These

---

[68] An example of essentially unachievable implied investor expectations is described in the Avon Products, Inc., example in Chapter 3.

[69] The impact of this phenomenon would be to *decrease* the projected market-value/adjusted-book-value ratio. Partially offsetting this effect, however, is the fact that reinvestment rates (Column 4 of Table 1–16) are *overstated* somewhat in comparison to what they would have been absent the accumulation of redundant cash. An overstated reinvestment rate for a high-return firm tends to overstate the projected market-value/adjusted-book-value ratio.

[70] Twelve of the sixteen firms whose adjusted-market-value/book-value ratios fell above the projected upper boundary value in Columns 6 and 7 of Table 1–16, for example, earned a lower nominal ROE in 1976 than their average nominal ROE in the prior decade (Column 5 versus Column 4, Table 1–10). If the average nominal ROE achieved by these firms during the prior decade were substituted for the nominal ROE achieved in 1976, the adjusted-market-value/book-value ratio for six of these firms would then fall below the projected upper boundary value in Columns 6 and 7 of Table 1–16.

[71] As noted in Footnote 54, errors in estimating the β for each firm can introduce significant error in the calculation of a firm's cost of equity capital, and thus in the value appearing in Column 7, Table 1–16. If uncertainty surrounding the *true* value of β were the only uncertainty in determining the Column 7 value, then we could say (with a minimum of 90 percent confidence in each case) that the firms with starred data in Column 7, Table 1–16 were "overvalued." For the six firms with double stars, we could make this statement with a minimum of 95 percent confidence in each case.

[72] In a 1963 article on share valuation, Burton Malkiel reached the equivalent conclusion. Malkiel's valuation model was similar in concept to the model presented in Chapter 1, but the Malkiel model focused on the rationality of a firm's price/earnings ratio based on a maximum *five*-year extrapolation of growth performance. See Burton G. Malkiel, "Equity Yields, Growth, and the Structure of Share Prices," *The American Economic Review,* December 1963.

are securities that are traded broadly and deeply by seemingly sophisticated investors. The possibility that such market imperfections may exist presents significant opportunities for *value transfers*, a subject that will be explored in greater detail in Chapters 2, 3, 7, and 9.

APPENDIX

CAPITALIZING AND AMORTIZING ADVERTISING EXPENDITURES

The accounting requirement that advertising and research and development expenditures be immediately expensed can lead to an understatement of a firm's total profits, while at the same time producing an overstatement of a firm's overall profitability (ROE). Avon Products, for example, increased its media advertising expenditures very significantly in 1976 (Lines 8–13, Column 1, Table 1A–1). If the economic benefits of Avon's advertising outlays were assumed to decay over six years at the rates indicated in Lines 1–6, Column 1, Table 1A–1, then in 1976 the firm experienced an economic amortization of its advertising assets equal to $20.1 million (Line 14, Column 3, Table 1A–1). This $20.1 million figure represents the *economic* cost of advertising for the firm in 1976. The GAAP *accounting* cost of advertising for the firm in 1976 was, however, $29.3 million.

Given our assumptions, Avon's 1976 pretax profit, according to the *economic* definition of profit, should have been $9.2 million higher than the firm's pretax profit calculated according to the GAAP definition of profit. The firm's after-tax profit (applying Avon's 1976 tax rate of 50.4 percent per Line 3, Table 1A–3) should have been $9.2 × (1.0 − 0.504) = $4.6 million higher according to the *economic* definition of profit.

This profit increase is only part of the story, however. Had Avon capitalized its media advertising expenditures each year, the unamortized balance of the firm's advertising asset at December 31, 1976, would have been $36.2 million (Line 14, Column 2, Table 1A–1). This figure is determined by multiplying the numbers in Lines 1–6, Column 2, by the numbers in Lines 8–13, Column 1, and summing the results (Lines 8–13, Column 2) to arrive at the $36.2 million total. Were this advertising asset to appear on Avon's balance sheet, there would obviously have to be some offsetting liabilities. Since reported pretax profits would have been increased by $36.2 million over the period 1971–76 as a result of capitalizing advertising expenditures, after-tax profits would also have been increased. If we again apply Avon's 1976 tax rate of 50.4 percent, Avon's retained earnings at December 31, 1976, would have risen by $36.2 (1.0 − 0.504), or $18.0 million. Avon's tax liability would have risen by the bal-

TABLE 1A-1

Adjustments to Avon Products' costs and assets at December 31, 1976 (caused by capitalizing advertising expenditures and amortizing these expenditures over six years using the double declining balance method of amortization)

Line	Year	(1) Amortization rate for advertising expenditures (6-year DDB)	(2) Outstanding balance of advertising expenditures made in year 1 that remains unamortized at the end of each year	(3) Amortization of advertising asset in year 1976 from advertising program in year ($ millions)
1	1	0.333	0.667	9.8
2	2	0.222	0.445	3.7
3	3	0.148	0.297	1.9
4	4	0.099	0.198	1.5
5	5	0.066	0.132	1.1
6	6	0.132	0	2.1
7	Total	1.000		20.1

	Year	Actual advertising expenditures in year ($ millions)	Unamortized advertising asset at 12/31/76 remaining from advertising expenditures in year ($ millions)
8	1976	29.3	19.5
9	1975	16.8	7.5
10	1974	12.7	3.8
11	1973	15.6	3.1
12	1972	17.1	2.3
13	1971	16.2	0.0
14	Total		36.2
15	Actual advertising expenditures in 1976.	29.3	
16	Calculated advertising expense in 1976.	20.1	
17	Cost improvement impact in 1976 .	9.2	

Note: Accountants will recognize that this amortization schedule does not follow the double declining balance method during the last half of the six-year period. The impact of this difference is negligible. The method used here is that proposed in Weiss, L. W., "Advertising, Profits, and Corporate Taxes," *Review of Economics and Statistics*, November 1969.

TABLE 1A-2

Adjustments to Avon Products' costs and assets at December 31, 1976 (caused by capitalizing R&D expenditures and amortizing these expenditures over ten years using the straight-line method of amortization)

Line	Year	(1) Amortization rate for R&D expenditures (10-year SLD)	(2) Outstanding balance of R&D expenditures made in year 1 that remains unamortized at the end of each year
1	1	0.100	0.90
2	2	0.100	0.80
3	3	0.100	0.70
4	4	0.100	0.60
5	5	0.100	0.50
6	6	0.100	0.40
7	7	0.100	0.30
8	8	0.100	0.20
9	9	0.100	0.10
10	10	0.100	0
11		1.000	

Line	Year	Actual R&D expenditure in year ($ millions)	(2) Unamortized R&D asset at 12/31/76 remaining from R&D expenditure in year ($ millions)	(3) Amortization of R&D asset in year 1976 from R&D program in year ($ millions)
12	1976	13.5	12.2	1.4
13	1975	12.8	10.2	1.3
14	1974	14.6	10.2	1.5
15	1973	18.3	11.0	1.8
16	1972	14.4	7.2	1.4
17	1971	11.7	4.7	1.2
18	1970	9.6	2.9	1.0
19	1969	8.5e	1.7	0.9
20	1968	7.3e	0.7	0.7
21	1967	6.3e	0	0.6
22	Total		60.8	11.8
23	Actual R&D expenditure in 1976.	13.5		
24	Calculated R&D expense in 1976.	11.8		
25	Cost improvement impact in 1976	1.7		

ance of $36.2 — $18.0, or $18.2 million. Since these taxes would be reported only to shareholders, and not actually paid to the Internal Revenue Service[73] for the years 1971–76, this $18.2 million figure would appear as a liability entitled "deferred taxes."

The bookkeeping adjustments needed to capitalize and then amortize Avon's advertising expenditures have the net result of boosting Avon's 1976 profits by $4.6 million and increasing the firm's net worth at December 31, 1976, by $18.0 million. When these adjustments are made to profits and net worth as calculated according to GAAP, Avon's 1976 ROE declines from 28.6 percent to 28.5 percent as shown in Table 1A–3 (Lines 14–15, 18–19, and 24–25). While this decline is not particularly noteworthy in the Avon Products example, the effect can be quite substantial for a firm with high (in relation to net worth) and rapidly growing advertising expenditures. Firms marketing branded consumer products often fall into this category. In the case of Dr. Pepper, for example, this adjustment would reduce the firm's 1976 reported ROE from 31.3 percent to 27.8 percent.

CAPITALIZING AND AMORTIZING R&D EXPENDITURES

Research and development expenditures are quite analogous to advertising expenditures. The economic benefits of R&D expenditures almost certainly appear more slowly however, and the benefits may last somewhat longer. This is reflected in Lines 1–10, Column 1, of Table 1A–2. Here we assume that the economic benefits of R&D expenditures extend over ten years and that the R&D asset is amortized according to a straight-line pattern. Given Avon's past pattern of R&D expenditures, this set of assumptions produces:

a. a cost reduction for 1976 equal to $1.7 million when an *economic* definition of R&D cost is used in place of the *GAAP* definition (Line 25, Column 1, Table 1A–2)

b. a capitalized R&D asset at December 31, 1976, equal to $60.8 million when an *economic* definition of R&D cost is used in place of the *GAAP* definition (Line 22, Column 2, Table 1A–2).

When these cost and asset items are tax-effected and work their way into Avon's financial statements, the firm's ROE in 1976 declines from 28.5 percent to 27.3 percent as shown in Table 1A–3 (Lines 15–16, 19–20, and 25–26).

Again (as was the case in the advertising example) the impact of capitalizing and then amortizing R&D expenditures is not particularly profound in the Avon situation. The impact is far greater for firms with

---

[73] It is assumed that Avon would continue to expense advertising expenditures for tax purposes as permitted by IRS regulation.

TABLE 1A-3
Calculation of the adjustments to Avon Products' profit/common-equity ratio (caused by
(1) capitalizing and amortizing advertising, (2) capitalizing and amortizing R&D,
(3) replacement cost accounting for inventory and plant and equipment)

Line		1976 ($ million)
1	Profit before taxes	339.4
2	Income taxes	171.0
3	Income tax rate	0.504
4	Profit after taxes	168.4
5	Preferred dividends	0.0
6	Profit after taxes available for common stock	168.4
7	Change in costs—Advertising adjustment (Line 17, Column 1, Table 1A-1)	(9.2)
8	Change in costs—R&D adjustment (Line 25, Column 1, Table 1A-2)	(1.7)
9	Change in costs—Replacement cost of goods sold (from Avon's 10K Report to the SEC dated 12/31/76)	21.6
10	Change in costs—Replacement cost depreciation* (from Avon's 10K Report to the SEC dated 12/31/76)	8.2
11	Tax-effected change in profits after tax from:—Advertising	4.6
12	Tax-effected change in profits after tax from:—R&D	0.8
13	Tax-effected change in profits after tax from:—Replacement cost of goods sold and replacement cost depreciation[†]	(14.8)
14	Profit after taxes available for common stock (historical reporting)	168.4
15	PAT to common—Adjusted for advertising (Line 14 + Line 11)	173.0
16	PAT to common—Adjusted for advertising, R&D (Line 15 + Line 12)	173.8
17	PAT to common—Adjusted for advertising, R&D, replacement cost of goods and depreciation (Line 16 + Line 13)	159.0
18	Common equity (historical reporting)	589.4
19	Common equity (adjusted for advertising: equal to line 18 + (1 − tax rate) (Line 14, Column 2, Table 1A-1)	607.4
20	Common equity (adjusted for advertising, R&D: equal to Line 19 + (1 − tax rate) (Line 22, Column 2, Table 1A-2)	637.6
21	Increase in net plant (replacement cost)	172.8
22	Increase in inventory (replacement cost)	30.7
23	Common equity (adjusted for advertising, R&D, net plant and inventory: Equal to Line 20 + Line 21 + Line 22)	841.1
24	Profit after tax/common equity (historical reporting)	0.286
25	Profit after tax/common equity (adjusted for advertising)	0.285
26	Profit after tax/common equity (adjusted for advertising, R&D)	0.273
27	Profit after tax/common equity (adjusted for advertising, R&D, net plant and inventory)	0.189

*Depreciation other than that included in cost of goods sold.
†Under standard accounting conventions, no tax benefits would be associated with the increased level of costs resulting from the application of replacement cost accounting to existing assets since such benefits would not, in fact, be received from the IRS. On new investments, however, tax benefits would be realized. Since new investment is often more critical to the valuation of the equity of high-ROE firms than old investments (Table 1-3), for our purposes it is reasonable to impute a tax impact into the calculation.

large (in relation to net worth) and rapidly growing R&D expenditures. Pharmaceutical firms generally fall into this category. In the case of Merck & Co., for example, this adjustment would reduce the firm's 1976 ROE from 22.6 percent to 20.5 percent.

ROE VERSUS TRUE (DCF) RETURNS

It is possible to make adjustments such as those indicated above to GAAP profitability calculations in order to bring them more closely into line with an economic notion of profitability. Nevertheless, some problems inherent in the measurement system still remain. An ROE calculation, no matter how carefully adjusted, does not *necessarily* equal the true yield (measured on a DFC basis) produced by the cash flows properly allocable to a firm's equity capital. Solomon has demonstrated this phenomenon with a series of relatively simple examples.[74] Stauffer has developed the issues in considerably more analytic detail.[75] In comparing GAAP-calculated ROEs with his own true discounted-cash-flow (DCF) rates of return, Stauffer notes that ". . . the magnitude of these discrepancies is small for most industries other than pharmaceuticals, oil producing companies, and a few other 'discovery intensive' industries."[76] In the pharmaceutical industry (the industry with the widest discrepancies) Stauffer finds a divergence between GAAP and true discounted cash flow returns to the firm's equity investment as indicated in the table below.[77]

	GAAP ROE	True DCF ROE	Difference (percentage points)
Firm A	17.5%	15.0%	2.5
Firm B	20.1%	16.4%	3.7
Firm C	9.8%	12.1%	(2.3)
Firm D	29.4%	21.2%	8.2
Firm E	20.4%	16.3%	4.1
Firm F	13.3%	13.1%	0.2

In Table 1–10 we are comparing a true discounted-cash-flow concept (the cost of equity capital in Column 2) against an accounting measure of returns on a firm's equity capital (Columns 4, 5, 6, and 7). Happily in

---

[74] Ezra Solomon, "Return on Investment: The Relation of Book Yield to True Yield," in *Research in Accounting Measurement,* American Accounting Association, 1966.

[75] Thomas R. Stauffer, "The Measurement of Corporate Rates of Return: A Generalized Formulation," *Bell Journal of Economics and Management Science,* Autumn 1971; and Thomas R. Stauffer, "Profitability Measures in the Pharmaceutical Industry," in Robert B. Helms, *Drug Development and Marketing,* The American Enterprise Institute for Public Policy Research, 1975.

[76] Ibid., pp. 112–13.

[77] Ibid., p. 110.

most of our Table 1–10 examples the spread between equity capital costs (both unadjusted and adjusted) is sufficiently large so that the measurement error is not critical.

ADJUSTING FOR INFLATION—*REAL* VERSUS *NOMINAL* EQUITY COSTS AND *ROE's*

Column 6 of Table 1–10 adjusts historically reported ROEs to reflect the effects of capitalizing and then amortizing advertising and research and development expenditures. One final adjustment remains. That is to incorporate into the data the impact of inflation. Numerous articles have appeared in recent years that describe the adjustments that must be made to a firm's income statement and balance sheet in order to account correctly for the impact of inflation. Three broad approaches have been described. These are (1) current-replacement-value accounting (CRVA), (2) general-price-level accounting (GPLA), and (3) specific-and-general-price-level accounting (SPLA).[78]

The critical issue in choosing a specific method for capturing the impact of inflation relates to the use to which the adjusted data will be put. Our concern here is largely with the value-creation potential of a firm's *future* investment opportunities. Thus we need to look forward to estimate future profitability. Accordingly, in our definition of net profits we will ignore holding gains or losses (realized and unrealized) from both tangible[79] and net monetary assets. Our definition of profit is quite close to that described by Davidson as "sustainable income."[80] There is one difference between Davidson's definition of "sustainable income" and our own definition of inflation-adjusted income as outlined in Table 1A–3. On *new* investment we would gain the tax benefits associated with the higher level of costs usually reflected in current-replacement-value accounting. For the investments already in place, however, we would not receive any tax benefits from the utilization of CRVA, as Davidson's definition of "sustainable income" properly reflects. Given the future orientation of our data need, Table 1A–3 reflects a definition of profit that incorporates in the calculations tax benefits from CRVA.

As with advertising and R&D expenditures, we also need to examine the impact of inflation accounting (of the CRVA variety described above)

---

[78] Richard F. Vancil, "Inflation Accounting," p. 59.

[79] In this context "tangible" refers to inventory and property, plant and equipment.

[80] Sidney Davidson and Roman L. Weil, "Inflation Accounting," p. 59. According to Davidson (pages 58–60 of the article noted), "changes in this number over time probably measure the growth capability of the firm better than the growth in any other income figure. This is the income number that financial analysts probably should pay most attention to in assessing growth prospects for the company, hence in assessing potential for appreciation of the firm's shares in stock markets."

on the reported profitability of Avon Products. As shown in Line 9, Table 1A–3, the December 31, 1976, replacement cost of products sold by Avon in 1976 was $21.6 million higher than that reported under GAAP accounting. Depreciation based on CRVA was $8.2 million higher than that reported under GAAP accounting (Line 10, Table 1A–3). The value of net plant was increased by $172.8 million through the use of CRVA (Line 21, Table 1A–3) and inventories were revalued upward by $30.7 million through the use of CRVA (Line 22, Table 1A–3).

As Avon looks forward to future investments, the net effect of CRVA on the firm is to reduce the *real* (inflation-adjusted) ROE to 18.9 percent (Line 27, Table 1A–3). When this figure is compared to Avon's 11.0 percent *real* cost of equity capital, it is clear that Avon enjoys about a 7.9 percentage point spread between its equity cost and the returns on equity (projected forward) of its past investments (Line 9, Column 10, Table 1–10).

PART
TWO

Processes by which
shareholder values are
created, transferred, and
destroyed

2

The levers that managers can utilize to enhance shareholder values

Chapter 1 was concerned primarily with identifying and measuring the value enhancement for shareholders produced by a select group of U.S. NFCs that consistently achieved rates of return that exceeded their capital costs. Little was said in Chapter 1 about how these firms came to enjoy their enviable status. Even less was said about any role that may have been played by the management of each firm in achieving the individual success stories reflected in Table 1–9.

Chapter 2 will shift our focus from a demonstration of both the existence and the significant dollar amount of created value in American industry, to an examination of the general *processes* through which managers can act to create, transfer, and destroy shareholder value. As noted in the Introduction, a checklist of value-enhancing opportunities that might be appropriate for each and every firm will not emerge from Chapter 2. Only broadly defined areas of opportunity will be explored. Indeed, the goal of Chapter 2 is *to focus attention on those broad areas of opportunity that need to be examined in a systematic fashion if managers are to exploit fully the value-enhancing potential of the decision choices they face on a regular basis.* The chapter suggests that a systematic exploration of value-enhancing opportunities should represent an integral part of the general management process. Managers who attempt less miss a significant part of the management challenge.

VALUE CREATION

The economic value of any investment is a function of the future cash flows anticipated from that investment, and the cost of the capital required to finance the investment. From the general equation for calculating the value of a stream of future cash flows, it is clear that managers can work to increase the value of a specific real-asset investment by influencing either (1) the cash flows or (2) the discount rate that is appropriate for the given investment risk.

$$\text{NPV} = \sum_{i=0}^{n} \frac{(\text{Revenues} - \text{Costs})_i}{(1 + k_0)^i},$$

where

NPV = net present value, and
k_0 = the cost of capital.

As the numerator in the above equation suggests, there are three ways to increase the cash flows produced by a business with a given asset base.

1(a) Cash flow from an investment can be increased, for example, if the product involved can be consistently *priced higher* than would have been possible without the existence of some entry barrier.

The barrier here could be, for example, the existence of patents or some form of successful product differentiation. The barrier might also result from the simple exercise of market power such as that enjoyed by a monopolist. In Chapter 4 we will explore examples of firms that may have gained a portion of their superior returns because of an ability to price their products somewhat higher than competitors.

1(b) Cash flow from an investment can also be increased by achieving *lower costs* than that experienced by competitors, again perhaps as a result of the existence of some barrier that prevents all competitors from achieving equal costs.

The barrier in this instance could be, for example, scale economies achievable by only the largest firms in a market, or the ownership of captive sources of low-cost raw materials. In Chapters 3, 4, and 6 we will explore examples of firms that have achieved superior returns in part because of the lower costs that they incur in the production, distribution, and service of their products.

1(c) Cash flow from an investment can also be increased if a firm can reduce the capital intensity of its business below that of its competitors.

A retailer with a competitive cost advantage could, for example, lower the prices it charges. This would presumably produce an increase in sales measured against assets employed, thus reducing the capital intensity of the firm's operations. We will observe in Chapters 3 and 9 that differences in the level of capital intensity achieved by different competitors in a business (where capital intensity is defined as revenue/assets) can substantially change the cash flows produced from a given asset base.

As we move our focus from the numerator to the denominator of the valuation formula noted above, our attention shifts from cash flows to capital costs. Reducing capital costs represents another broad area of opportunity for increasing the value of any investment. To the extent that the capital costs associated with an investment can be reduced, the value of that investment increases. The discount rate (capital cost) that is appropriate for a specific investment is a function of three factors. These are (a) the cost of debt financing, (b) the cost of equity financing, and (c) the specific composition of a firm's capital structure.[1] Mathematically this relationship can be represented as follows:

$$k_0 = w_d k_d + w_e k_e,$$

where

k_0 = the weighted cost of capital,
k_d = the cost of debt (after tax),
k_e = the cost of equity (after tax),
w_d = the debt proportion in the capital structure,
w_e = the equity proportion in the capital structure.

Value creation via the reduction of capital costs occurs to the extent that a firm can:

2(a)   design a *debt* security that appeals to a special niche in the capital markets and thereby attract funds at a cost lower than the free-market rate for equivalent risk investments;

2(b)   design an *equity* security that appeals to a special niche in the capital markets and thereby attract funds at a cost lower than the free-market rate for equivalent risk investments; or

2(c)   design a *capital structure* that weights the utilization of debt and equity so as to achieve a lower capital cost overall than that enjoyed by competitors.

Finally, value can be created by lowering capital cost if:

2(d)   A firm reduces its *business risk* vis-a-vis competition.

Chapter 5 deals with the design of debt securities that appeal to special market niches as noted in 2(a). Chapters 7 and 9 address, in a similar fashion, the design of equity securities that appeal to special market

---

[1] This capital cost derivation holds where the specific project in question is in the same risk class as the firm overall. When this is not the case, adjustment for risk must be made. See, for example, Mark E. Rubenstein, "A Mean-Variance Synthesis of Corporate Financial Theory," *Journal of Finance*, March 1972.

niches as noted in 2(b).[2] The design of a capital structure that produces lower capital costs, as outlined in 2(c) above, is a complex problem both in theory and in practice. For that reason, a short digression on this topic might be quite useful.

Value creation—The capital structure decision

The influence of a firm's capital structure on its capital costs has long been a subject of great interest to both business practitioners and financial theorists. The mainstream views of these two groups were often at variance in the past. More recently, however, practice and theory have converged to a considerable degree.[3] While there is still little agreement as to how to determine, in practice, a firm's optimal capital structure, there continues to be generalized support for the view that the capital structure decision does have an effect on share values, and that the optimum capital structure (that is, the capital structure with the lowest cost) for most firms includes debt capital.

To illustrate this view, Table 2–1 outlines, hypothetically, how changes in a firm's capital structure (that is, its debt/total-capital ratio) would influence the total market value of that firm's securities. Reduced to its simplest form, the exhibit suggests that a stream of earnings before interest and taxes (designated EBIT in Line 9) can be sold to investors in a variety of packages, each representing a different capital structure deci-

---

[2] As will be clear later, particularly in Chapters 7 and 9, the design of an equity security to give it appeal to a special niche in the capital markets can often be described more accurately as *value transfer* rather than *value creation*.

[3] The early evolution in the theory of optimal capital structure can be traced in the following articles:

1. Franco Modigliani and Merton H. Miller, "The Cost of Capital, Corporation Finance, and the Theory of Investment," *American Economic Review*, June 1958, vol. 48, pp. 261–97.
2. Franco Modigliani and Merton H. Miller, "Corporate Income Taxes and the Cost of Capital: A Correction," *American Economic Review*, June 1963, vol. 53, pp. 433–43.
3. Donald E. Farrar and Lee L. Selwyn, "Taxes, Corporate Financial Policy and Return to Investors," *National Tax Journal*, December 1967, pp. 444–54.
4. Joseph E. Stiglitz, "Taxation, Corporate Financial Policy, and the Cost of Capital," *Journal of Public Economics*, January 1973, pp. 1–34.

The most recent advances in the theory of the capital structure decision include:

5. Stewart C. Myers, "Determinants of Corporate Borrowing," *Journal of Financial Economics*, November 1977, pp. 147–76.
6. Michael C. Jensen and William H. Meckling, "Theory of the Firm: Managerial Behavior, Agency Costs and Ownership Structure," *Journal of Financial Economics*, October 1976.
7. John Lintner, "Bankruptcy Risk, Market Segmentation and Optimal Capital Structure," in *Risk and Return in Finance*, I. Friend and J. Bicksler, eds. (Cambridge, Mass.: Ballinger Publishing Company, 1977).

TABLE 2–1

Hypothetical example of how changes in a firm's capital structure can influence (1) the total market value of its securities (and especially the value of a share of common stock) and (2) its competitive strength within an industry

Line		Debt in capital structure					Derivation of data presented
		0%	10%	20%	30%	40%	
1	Interest rate required on debt (%) . . .	8.0	8.2	8.6	9.4	11.0	Assumed
2	After-tax cost of debt capital (%) . . .	4.0	4.1	4.3	4.7	5.5	Note 2
3	After-tax cost of equity capital (%) . .	12.0	12.4	13.0	14.2	16.6	Assumed
4	After-tax cost of total capital (%) . . .	12.0	11.6	11.3	11.4	12.2	Notes 3, 4
5	Book value of debt ($)	0	500	1,000	1,500	2,000	Assumed
6	Book value of equity ($)	5,000	4,500	4,000	3,500	3,000	Assumed
7	Book value of total capital ($)	5,000	5,000	5,000	5,000	5,000	(Line 5)+(Line 6)
8	EBIT return actually achieved on total capital (%)	24.0	24.0	24.0	24.0	24.0	Assumed
9	EBIT[1] ($)	1,200	1,200	1,200	1,200	1,200	(Line 8)X(Line 7)
10	Interest expense ($)	0	41	86	141	220	(Line 5)X(Line 1)
11	Profit before taxes ($)	1,200	1,159	1,114	1,059	980	(Line 9)−(Line 10)
12	Taxes ($)	600	580	557	530	490	(Line 11)X0.50
13	Profit after taxes ($)	600	579	557	529	490	(Line 11)−(Line 12)
14	Market value of debt ($)	0	500	1,000	1,500	2,000	
15	Market value of equity ($)	5,000	4,673	4,285	3,729	2,952	(Line 13)÷(Line 3)
16	Market value of EBIT stream ($) . . .	5,000	5,173	5,285	5,229	4,952	(Line 14)+(Line 15)
17	Number of shares outstanding	50	45	40	35	30	50−[(Line 14)÷(100)]
18	Book value per share ($)	100	100	100	100	100	(Line 6)÷(Line 17)
19	Market value per share ($)	100	104	107	106	98	(Line 15)÷(Line 17)

Calculation of the EBIT necessary to meet the return required on invested capital

		Firm					
		(A)	(B)	(C)	(D)	(E)	
20	EBIT return required on capital (%). .	24.0	23.2	22.5	22.7	24.5	(Line 4)X(2) and Note 4
21	EBIT required ($)	1,200	1,157	1,126	1,135	1,216	(Line 7)X(Line 20) X.01
22	Interest ($)	0	41	86	141	220	
23	Profit before taxes ($)	1,200	1,116	1,040	994	996	
24	Taxes ($)	600	558	520	497	498	
25	Profit after taxes ($)	600	558	520	497	498	Comparable
26	Market value of debt ($)	0	500	1,000	1,500	2,000	to method
27	Market value of equity ($)	5,000	4,500	4,000	3,500	3,000	used above.
28	Market value of EBIT stream ($) . . .	5,000	5,000	5,000	5,000	5,000	
29	Number of shares outstanding	50	45	40	35	30	
30	Book value per share ($)	100	100	100	100	100	
31	Market value per share ($)	100	100	100	100	100	

Excess pretax profit available for (a) windfall gain in equity prices for shareholder, (b) product price reduction to consumers, (c) market share battle with competitors, or (d) organizational slack.

32		$ 0	43	74	65	(16)	(Line 9)−(Line 21)

Note 1: The calculations assume that the EBIT figures in Lines 9 and 21 represent perpetuities, and that all profits are paid to shareholders in the form of dividends.

Note 2: Assuming a 50 percent tax rate, the after-tax cost of debt capital is equal to 50 percent of Line 1.

Note 3: Return required on total capital is calculated by multiplying the percentage debt in the firm's capital structure by the return required on that debt, and adding to this amount the percentage equity in the firm's capital structure multiplied by the return required on that equity.

Note 4: The data in Line 4 are rounded for convenience in presentation. The data in Lines 20 and 32 are derived, however, from unrounded Line 4 data.

General note: From a theoretical standpoint all of the calculations in this exhibit should be based on the use of *market-value* weights for debt and equity in the firm's capital structure, not *book-value* weights as are utilized above. Using market-value weights in the examples cited above would significantly complicate an otherwise easy-to-follow set of calculations, without significantly affecting the final results for most firms. For this reason, book-value weights have been used above.

sion.[4] More important, each packaging alternative can result in a different total market value for the total stream of earnings available (Line 16).

Assume, for example, that investors demand the increasing pattern of returns (which produce the capital costs outlined in Lines 2 and 3 of Table 2–1) in exchange for taking on the added risk associated with the higher debt levels indicated. If we further assume that the firm initially has no debt in its capital structure, and that our objective in making a debt/total-capital ratio choice is to maximize the market value of a share of common stock, then from the example of Table 2–1 it is clear that the unleveraged firm should issue $1,000 in debt in order to retire ten shares of its own common stock. This would move its capital structure to the optimum position at 20 percent debt. At this position, the firm's after-tax cost of capital is minimized (Line 4, Table 2–1), the total value of the firm's EBIT stream is maximized (Line 16, Table 2–1), and the value of a single share of the firm's common stock is maximized (Line 19, Table 2–1). Absent the indicated rise in the price of a share of common stock (Line 19, Table 2–1), the transition to a capital structure that included 20 percent debt would cause the firm's shareholders to earn a return higher than that required to compensate them adequately for the risk they incurred. As suggested by the valuation model in Chapter 1, under these circumstances the total value of each share of common stock would rise. The rise would continue until the return measured against the market value of a share of stock was reduced to the required rate, giving the shareholders in the Table 2–1 example a windfall gain of $7 per share from simply altering the firm's capital structure from one including no debt to one including 20 percent debt.[5]

The Table 2–1 example squarely raises the issue of how the selection of a specific capital structure can enhance a firm's competitive position. As shown in Line 21 of Table 2–1, firms with increasingly efficient capital structures can deliver the required rate of return to their capital providers at lower earnings levels than is possible for less efficiently financed competitors. Firm C, for example, needs an EBIT stream of only $1,126 to satisfy its security holders' return requirements. Firm A, because of its less efficient capital structure, needs an EBIT stream of $1,200 to satisfy its security holders' return requirements. The $74 cost advantage enjoyed by Firm C over Firm A is noted in Line 32 of Table 2–1. It is important to recognize that this cost advantage is no different from a cost advan-

---

[4] In this example the investment claims sold to investors are limited, somewhat artificially, to straight debt and common equity.

[5] It is assumed in this exhibit that the transition from 0 percent debt to 20 percent debt is made in one jump in which ten shares of common stock are repurchased using $1,000 of debt capital carrying an interest rate of 8.6 percent. If the transition were made in stages, with an interim step at a 10 percent debt ratio, a slightly different final result would emerge.

tage produced from any other nonproprietary source. Its competitive effect can be just as telling as a cost advantage based, for example, on superior manufacturing efficiency. It is equally important to recognize, however, that efficiencies in capital structure are quite easily replicated by competitors. There is no entry barrier to the use of this particular technique. Indeed, in a perfectly competitive situation, all firms in the Table 2–1 example would be forced to adopt the capital structure of Firm C.

As was the case in each of the previously noted areas of potential value creation, our discussion of capital structure has not yet benefited from an examination of field examples. These examples will be presented in Chapters 5 and 8.

Value creation—The reduction of business risk

The short digression into the issue of capital structure has left untouched the one final area of potential value creation that is possible via the reduction of capital costs. That area relates to the reduction of business risk, which was noted earlier as Item $2(d)$ on page 67.

As shown in the equation below, the cost of equity capital related to a specific investment is a function of three factors. These are the *risk-free* (that is, Treasury bill) rate, the degree of *business risk* inherent in the investment, and the degree of *financing risk* inherent in the choice of the capital structure supporting the investment.[6]

$$k_e = (\text{Risk-free rate}) + (\text{Business risk}) + (\text{Financing risk}),$$

where

k_e = the cost of equity capital.

There is little a firm can do to influence the risk-free rate. In addition, its financing risk is largely defined by the capital structure decision. The one remaining avenue for reducing the equity cost component in a firm's total cost of capital is to achieve a reduction in the firm's business risk.

How might the business risk of a specific project, or a firm, be reduced? A specific example involving a natural gas producer might occur as follows. The natural gas producer agrees with an intrastate pipeline to commit its output under a take-or-pay contract at a price that floats with the market. The pipeline is happy to make this agreement since it now

---

[6] The appendix to Chapter 3 includes a calculation showing how the portion of a firm's equity capital cost resulting from its *financing risk* may be determined. Given knowledge of a firm's equity capital cost, the risk-free rate, and the portion of a firm's equity capital cost attributable to its financing risk, it is simply a matter of subtraction to determine the portion of a firm's equity capital cost that is attributable to its *business risk*. It should be repeated here that in our determination of a firm's equity capital cost we are adopting the assumptions of the capital-asset-pricing model described in Chapter 1. According to this model, only systematic or market-related risk has an effect on the cost of equity capital for a specific firm.

has a stable source of gas. The natural gas producer should be happy too, since it now has a guaranteed outlet at no concession in price. This reduction in business risk for the gas producer should produce a corresponding reduction in the firm's equity capital cost.[7]

In this particular example it is assumed that all of the valuation benefits created on the natural gas producer's side of the transaction remain with the natural gas producer. In reality the allocation of these benefits would be the subject of negotiation between the natural gas producer and the pipeline company.

While the natural gas example is fairly straightforward, more detailed designs for the reduction of business risk in actual field situations are explored in Chapters 5 and 6.

Realizing the benefits of a competitive advantage

Whenever a firm is successful in gaining a competitive advantage, the firm faces a choice as to how the fruits of that advantage will be allocated. The options available to the firm can be grouped into four broad categories, which can be characterized as follows:

Option 1—Shareholder wealth model
Option 2—Consumer wealth model
Option 3—Marketing competition model
Option 4—Organizational slack model.

The option or combination of options that the firm elects to pursue in enjoying its competitive advantage will have a substantial impact on all of the players with a stake in the firm's operations. This can be shown in the following way. Assume that Firms $A-E$ as listed in the bottom half of Table 2–1 have achieved pretax profits in excess of the market-required rates to the extent noted in Line 32. This could result from *any* of the sources of value creation labeled $1(a)$ through $2(d)$, not just from a competitive advantage based on a more efficient capital structure.

Table 2–2 can be combined with the data of Line 32, Table 2–1, to show what a firm with a competitive advantage arising from any[8] source can do to other less fortunately situated competitors when product-markets are not completely efficient.

---

[7] In the context of the capital-asset-pricing model introduced in Chapter 1, this implicitly assumes that the systematic (that is, market-related) risk of the gas producer's common stock is reduced as a result of the take-or-pay contract.

[8] Table 2–2 demonstrates the alternative uses for a competitive advantage that is produced as a result of the lowering of a firm's capital costs (Items $2(a)$ through $2(d)$ of page 67. A slightly modified version of Table 2–2 would be required to show the alternative uses for a competitive advantage based on increased cash flows from a given investment base (Items $1(a)$ through $1(c)$ of page 66).

TABLE 2-2
**Hypothetical price, operating cost, and EBIT comparisons relating to the options available
for realizing the benefits of a competitive advantage**

			Firm			
	A	B	C	D	E	
Option 1—Shareholder wealth model						
Units sold	3	3	3	3	3	
Unit price	1,000	1,000	1,000	1,000	1,000	
Sales.	3,000	3,000	3,000	3,000	3,000	
Operating costs	1,800	1,800	1,800	1,800	1,800	
EBIT	1,200	1,200	1,200	1,200	1,200	
EBIT required	1,200	1,157	1,126	1,135	1,216	Benefits of excess
Excess pretax profits	0	43	74	65	(16)	profits flow to shareholders.
Option 2—Consumer wealth model						Potential excess profits absorbed by product price reductions.
Units sold.	3	3	3	3	3	
Unit price.	1,000	986	975	978	1,005	
Sales.	3,000	2,957	2,926	2,935	3,016	
Operating costs	1,800	1,800	1,800	1,800	1,800	
EBIT	1,200	1,157	1,126	1,135	1,216	
EBIT required	1,200	1,157	1,126	1,135	1,216	
Excess pretax profits	0	0	0	0	0	
Option 3—Marketing competition model						
Units sold	3	3	3	3	3	
Unit price	1,000	1,000	1,000	1,000	1,000	Potential excess profits absorbed by marketing or product cost increases.
Sales.	3,000	3,000	3,000	3,000	3,000	
Operating costs . . .	1,800	1,843	1,874	1,865	1,784	
EBIT	1,200	1,157	1,126	1,135	1,216	
EBIT required	1,200	1,157	1,126	1,135	1,216	
Excess pretax profits	0	0	0	0	0	
Option 4—Organizational slack model						
Units sold.	3	3	3	3	3	
Unit price.	1,000	1,000	1,000	1,000	1,000	Potential excess profits absorbed by redundancies or above-market compensation.
Sales.	3,000	3,000	3,000	3,000	3,000	
Operating costs . . .	1,800	1,843	1,874	1,865	1,784	
EBIT	1,200	1,157	1,126	1,135	1,216	
EBIT required	1,200	1,157	1,126	1,135	1,216	
Excess pretax profits	0	0	0	0	0	

Option 1—The shareholder wealth model

In Option 1 of Table 2–2 we assume that the five identical firms (noted in Lines 20–31 of Table 2–1) sell three units of product each year at prices and with operating costs that are assumed to be equal for all firms. As shown in Line 19 of Table 2–1, under these conditions the shareholders of Firms B–D receive windfall gains as a result of their competitive advantage. The shareholders of Firm A achieve no increment in value, and the shareholders of Firm E sustain a decline in their share price in order to maintain the rate of return to a new shareholder at the level that is consistent with the degree of risk assumed. In this example, which has been labeled the "Shareholder Wealth Model," the firms that have achieved a competitive advantage decide to capitalize on this advantage not by cutting price or increasing expenditures (perhaps to enhance product quality or strengthen the marketing effort) but rather by passing all of the benefits immediately to their shareholders in the form of increased profits.

The overall impact of Option 1 behavior would be to (1) leave the consumer no better off as a result of the competitive advantages achieved by Firms B–D; and (2) pass all of the benefits of the increased efficiency on to the efficient firms' shareholders. Option 1 type behavior would have a completely neutral long-run competitive impact. Market shares for those firms enjoying a competitive advantage would not change. Investors in these firms would simply enjoy a higher stock price than the shareholders of less ably managed firms. The Option 1 behavior choice would, of course, be impossible if both product markets and the securities markets were perfectly competitive. Under conditions of perfect competition in product as well as financial markets, all five of the firms in this example would be driven to the same product-price, product-cost, and capital-cost position, and product prices would fall to the level set by Firm C in Option 2.

Option 2—The consumer wealth model

As an alternative to reaping the harvest of its competitive advantage in the form of immediate gains for shareholders, Firm C might have chosen to cut its product price to a level that exactly met the return requirements of those investors who furnished its $5,000 original capitalization. Thus, according to Line 32 of Table 2–1, the product price for this most efficient of the five firms is assumed to fall to $2,926/3 = $975.33 per unit. This represents a total price cut of $74/3 or $24.67 per unit. Other producers of this product (assuming they are unable to replicate Firm C's competitive advantage) have two choices. They might either price above the low-price leader in an effort to preserve investor returns (but thereby almost certainly begin an inexorable downward spiral) or they could price in line with the low-price leader in an effort to preserve market share (but thereby produce inadequate returns and reduced stock prices).

The overall impact of Option 2 behavior would be to (1) benefit consumers via reduced prices, and (2) leave the efficient firms' shareholders with no windfall gain in market value from the more efficient operation.[9]

---

[9] If investors expected that firms enjoying a competitive advantage (and adopting the price-reduction option) would thereby generate and participate in future in-

Option 2 behavior would have maximum long-run competitive impact. Unless Firm C's competitors responded with price reductions, they would probably face a very bleak future.

Option 3—The marketing model

A third option is open to the firm with a competitive advantage. That option is to spend more money on advertising, promotion, and/or product quality. As in Option 2 the most efficient producer has $74/3 or $24.67 per unit in extra profits to work with in an effort to build his market share. Other producers, not so advantageously positioned, again face choices similar to those explored in Option 2. They might either refuse to match the expenditure increases of the more efficient producers in an effort to preserve investors' returns (but thereby almost certainly lose some market share), or they might meet these expenditure increases in an effort to preserve their market shares (but thus produce inadequate returns and reduced stock prices).

The overall impact of Option 3 behavior would be to (1) potentially benefit the consumer (to the extent these expenditure increases generated added product value), and (2) leave the efficient firms' shareholders with no immediate windfall gains in market value from the more efficient operation.[10]

Option 3 behavior could have a significant competitive impact, but it would be considerably less inflammatory than Option 2 behavior. Unless Firm C's competitors matched Firm C's aggressive marketing programs, these competitors would probably begin to lose market share.

Option 4—The organizational slack model

One final option is open to the firm with a competitive advantage. This option is to introduce or increase organizational slack by spending money on redundant physical capacity and redundant manpower, or by paying wages, salaries, and perquisites that exceed competitively defined market rates.[11]

---

vestments with returns in excess of capital costs, then the shareholders of such firms would gain a benefit from their firm's competitive advantage in spite of the price-reduction strategy.

[10] As was the case in Option 2, if investors expected that firms enjoying a competitive advantage (and adopting an Option 3 strategy) would thereby generate and participate in future investments with returns in excess of capital costs, then the shareholders of such firms would gain a benefit from their firm's competitive advantage in spite of the Option 3 strategy).

[11] The concept of organizational slack is developed in considerable detail in R. M. Cyert and J. G. March, *A Behavioral Theory of the Firm* (Englewood Cliffs, N.J.: Prentice-Hall, Inc., 1963), chaps. 3 and 9. Some evidence relating to the magnitude and economic significance of organizational slack (or "X inefficiency") is presented

The overall impact of Option 4 behavior would be to (1) offer no benefit to the consumer, (2) offer potential, substantial financial benefits to the employees and management of the otherwise more profitable producers, and (3) leave the otherwise more profitable firm's shareholders with no immediate windfall gains in market value. As was the case with Option 1 behavior, Option 4 behavior would have a neutral long-run competitive impact. Market shares for those firms enjoying a competitive advantage would not change. Indeed, their greater efficiency would be largely *invisible* to consumers, competitors, and shareholders, since it would be offset by inefficiencies elsewhere. As we will discuss in Chapter 10, Option 4 behavior has some potentially significant consequences in terms of social welfare.

The material presented above on the distribution of the benefits resulting from a firm's competitive advantage represents a quite simplified version of reality.[12] Firms rarely embrace but a single option over time, for example. Indeed, firms may sometimes pursue strategies that simultaneously utilize portions of *all four* of the options presented above. Alternatively, firms may cut prices (Option 2) only long enough to gain a dominant share of the market, and then revert to Option 1 in order to maximize shareholder wealth. In spite of the simplified nature of the examples cited above, it is, nonetheless, useful to work through some hypothetical situations to see specifically how the realization of the benefits of a firm's competitive advantage can influence a firm's product prices, costs, equity values, and growth opportunities.

Such analysis also points up the importance of carefully examining the trade-offs involved in managing the distribution of the benefits produced as a result of the successful achievement of a competitive advantage.

VALUE TRANSFER

The previous portion of this chapter focused on areas in which managers can *create* value for their shareholders. We dealt, one by one, with the variables shown on the right-hand side of the valuation equation presented on page 66. Our objective has been to find ways to coax the

---

in Harvey Leibenstein, *Beyond Economic Man: A New Foundation for Microeconomics* (Cambridge, Mass.: Harvard University Press, 1976). A discussion of some limits to managerial discretion in both the development and allocation of organizational slack can be found in David W. Mullins, Jr., "Product Market Inefficiency, Capital Market Inefficiency, and a Managerial Theory of the Firm," unpublished paper, 1978.

[12] It is clear that managers can adopt strategies outlined as Options 2 through 4 even in the absence of current "excess" profits. Trading off current profits in anticipation of larger future profits (even in situations where present profits are inadequate) is not at all unusual. We shall see one example of such a tradeoff in Chapter 8.

numerator of this term *up* while attempting to persuade the capital markets to pare the denominator *down*. There is an entirely separate path, however, by which managers can improve the wealth position of all or some subset of their existing shareholder group. This second path involves management actions that concentrate on the left-hand side of the valuation equation outlined on page 66. In the next portion of this chapter we will focus on how a manager can capitalize on differences between the calculated *economic value* of a firm's securities (that is, the net present value), and the empirically observed *market value* of those same securities. The process here is one of finding or creating potential imperfections in the securities markets, and thus generating opportunities for value transfer.

In recent years a considerable amount of empirical research has been undertaken to assess the efficiency of the U.S. capital markets. In a completely efficient market, value transfers of the variety noted above would be impossible, since securities would always be correctly priced in relation to the riskiness of their expected returns. The sufficient conditions for complete market efficiency include:

a. the absence of transaction costs,
b. the prompt and costless dissemination of all relevant information to all investors, and
c. complete agreement by all participants on the implications of current information for both the current price and the distributions of future prices for each security.[13]

While conditions sufficient to assure complete market efficiency are only imperfectly approximated in practice, some significant intermediate degrees of market efficiency have been identified. These types of market efficiency are known in the literature as (1) the weak form, (2) the semi-strong form, and (3) the strong form of the efficient-markets hypothesis. The weak form holds that past security prices are without value in predicting future security prices, since the current price reflects all of the information contained in historical prices. Charts, trading rules, and so on can thus have no predictive value in estimating future share prices. The empirical evidence in favor of the weak form of the efficient-markets hypothesis is quite persuasive.[14]

The semi-strong form of the efficient-markets hypothesis holds that all publicly available information about a stock is immediately reflected in its price. Once earnings, dividends, stock splits, and the like for an individual firm have been publicly announced, it is not possible to earn a

[13] John Lintner, "Inflation and Security Returns," *Journal of Finance,* May 1975, p. 265.

[14] See, for example, Paul H. Cootner, *The Random Character of Stock Market Prices* (Cambridge, Mass.: The MIT Press, 1964).

superior risk-adjusted return from trading in the firm's stock. The empirical evidence accumulated to date appears to support the semi-strong form of the efficient-markets hypothesis,[15] although there is some evidence suggesting that support for the semi-strong form must be qualified.[16]

The strong form of the efficient-markets hypothesis holds that all information that is known to *anyone* (including, for example, insiders and/or professional analysts who attempt to create private information from a superior interpretation of publicly available data) is properly reflected in security prices. The empirical evdence that supports the strong form of the efficient-markets hypothesis is significant,[17] but not compelling. Indeed, studies by Jaffe,[18] Scholes,[19] and Neiderhoffer[20] suggest (not surprisingly) that both insiders and securities market-makers with access to more complete information about the company or the market for its securities do earn superior rates of return.

The managers that we will observe making decisions with value transfer potential in Chapters 2–9 are all insiders. Since they have access to information about the future prospects of their firms that is not available to outsiders, it might not be terribly surprising to find these managers making decisions concerning the sale or exchange of newly issued equity securities of their firms in ways that tend to benefit all or some subset of their shareholder group. Indeed it is a fundamental proposition of this book that all or some subset of the existing shareholders sometimes benefit if managers can transfer wealth:

3(a)   at the expense of shareholders of *other* firms; or

---

[15] See, for example, (1) Philip Brown and Victor Niederhoffer, "The Predictive Content of Quarterly Earnings," *Journal of Business,* October 1968, pp. 488–97; and (2) Eugene F. Fama, Lawrence Fisher, Michael C. Jensen, and Richard Roll, "The Adjustment of Stock Prices to New Information," *International Economic Review,* February 1969, pp. 1–21.

[16] See, for example, Victor Niederhoffer, "The Predictive Content of First Quarter Earnings Reports," *Journal of Business,* January 1970, pp. 60–62.

[17] See, for example, (1) Michael C. Jensen, "The Performance of Mutual Funds in the Period 1945–1964," *Journal of Finance,* May 1968, pp. 389–416; (2) Eugene F. Fama, "Efficient Capital Markets: A Review of Theory and Empirical Work," *Journal of Finance,* May 1970, pp. 383–423; and (3) Eugene F. Fama and J. D. MacBeth, "Tests of the Multiperiod Two-Parameter Model," *Journal of Financial Economics,* May 1974.

[18] Jeffrey F. Jaffe, "Special Information and Insider Trading," *Journal of Business,* July 1974, pp. 410–28.

[19] Myron S. Scholes, "The Market for Securities: Substitution Versus Price Pressure and the Effects of Information on Share Prices," *Journal of Business,* April 1972, pp. 179–211.

[20] Victor Niederhoffer and M. F. M. Osborne, "Market Making and Reversal on the Stock Exchange," *Journal of the American Statistical Association,* December 1966, pp. 897–916.

3(b)   at the expense of *new* investors purchasing *newly issued* shares of the firm in question;[21] or

3(c)   at the expense of a *subset* of the existing shareholder group. This subset is induced to sell their equity interest back to the firm for cash or securities[22] that do not participate meaningfully in the fruits of the firm's future success.[23]

Value transfers via acquisition

An example of the first situation noted above follows. Firm X acquires Firm Y. Firm Y's shares are assumed to be rationally valued in the market. Specifically the economic value of Firm Y's shares (as measured in terms of the valuation model of Chapter 1) is roughly equal to the market value of these shares. Firm X pays a modest premium over the market price for Firm Y's shares, and the acquisition is completed via an exchange of stock. The market value of Firm X's stock substantially exceeds its economic value (as measured in terms of the valuation model of Chapter 1). To the extent that market values and economic values tend to converge in the long run (as is argued in Chapter 1), in this example Firm X's shareholders will be the beneficiaries of a value transfer accomplished at the expense of Firm Y's shareholders. The conglomerate acquisition phenomenon of the 1960s was, in part, an example of value transfers of this variety on a fairly grand scale.[24] We will examine clinical examples of value transfers, also of this variety, in Chapter 7.

---

[21] It should be noted that item 2(b) described on p. 67 and item 3(b) described above are usually equivalent.

[22] Securities as used in this sense would include such instruments as debt or nonconvertible preferred stock.

[23] A fourth method for accomplishing value transfers involves a firm's own *debt* holders. If the loan covenants of a firm's outstanding debt securities permitted the firm to issue significant amounts of equal- or senior-ranked debt and use the proceeds to repurchase its own common stock, then the common shareholders of the firm could benefit from a stock-repurchase program at the expense of the holders of its outstanding debt. The outstanding debt holders would suffer an increased risk of default with no compensating payment. The market value of the outstanding debt would fall, and the value of the stock would rise. This form of value transfer is not separately categorized above since in practice it appears to have quite limited aggregate value-transfer potential. A discussion of additional examples of value transfers from bondholders to shareholders can be found in the following:

1.   Eugene F. Fama and Merton H. Miller, *The Theory of Finance* (Hinsdale, Ill.: Dryden Press, 1972), pp. 178–81; and
2.   Charles W. Haley and Lawrence P. Schall, *The Theory of Financial Decisions* (New York: McGraw-Hill, 1973), pp. 218–20.

[24] A highly readable exposition of the value-transfer aspects of the conglomerate acquisition phenomenon of the 1960s can be found in Marvin M. May, "The Earnings Per Share Trap: The Chain Letter Revisited," *Financial Analysts Journal*, May–June 1968.

In a study utilizing FTC merger data covering the period 1948–62, Gershon

Value transfers via new stock issues

There is a second broad category of value-transfer opportunities. In this second category a firm can also take advantage of imperfections in the securities markets when its stock price seems to be optimistically detached from economic reality as explained in Chapter 1. In this instance, however, instead of engaging in an acquisition program, the firm sells its own common stock for *cash* at a price that substantially exceeds a rational valuation for these securities. We will see examples of this form of value transfer in Chapters 7 and 9. In Chapter 9 we will also see that when a firm enjoys an overvalued equity security, the capital structure decision ought[25] to be resolved in precisely the fashion that is frequently observed in practice (that is, the firm meets its external financing requirements largely through the sale of equity, and utilizes very little debt). This observable fact is not easily explained if one makes the assumption that the securities markets are always efficient.

Value transfers via share repurchases

The third and final major source of value-transfer opportunity relates to corporate share repurchases. Sometimes the management group of a firm views the future investment potential of the firm quite differently from the way other investors view these prospects. This divergence may arise because the managers of the firm have an information advantage[26] that gives them a more complete understanding of the firm's potential. It may also arise from hubris or extreme optimism on the part of management, or extreme pessimism on the part of investors. If the divergence is suffi-

---

Mandelker concluded that the stockholders of *acquired* firms, on average, enjoyed abnormally *high* securities market returns as a result of mergers. The example utilized above assumes a quite different result, such as that which occurred during the conglomerate fad of the mid-to-late 1960s. The inevitable collapse in the share prices of acquisitive conglomerates left the owners of many firms acquired for stock (assuming they retained their shares) with abnormally *low* securities-market returns. More recently the trend in premiums paid to acquire firms via cash-tender offers suggests a return to the pattern found by Mandelker, in which abnormally *high* securities-market returns are earned by shareholders of acquired firms. (See Gershon Mandelker, "Risk and Return: the Case of Merging Firms," *Journal of Financial Economics,* December 1974, pp. 303–35.)

[25] Wealth transfer can, of course, occur in a less ethically questionable fashion. For example, a particular business unit could simply be worth less in the hands of one owner than in the hands of some other owner. GE's marginally viable computer business in 1970 was almost certainly worth more as part of an enlarged Honeywell computer operation than it was as a part of the General Electric Company. While the sale of GE's business to Honeywell might be described in part as a wealth transfer, as we shall see in Chapter 6 the transaction clearly created value via improved scale economies.

[26] See, for example, Jeffrey E. Jaffe, "Special Information and Insider Trading," *Journal of Business,* July 1974, pp. 410–28.

ciently large, management's share ownership is large,[27] and the firm has access to the required financing, a major share-repurchase program might be undertaken. Regardless of the source of management's more optimistic assessment of the firm's future prospects, if management's view turns out to be accurate, wealth is transferred from nonbelievers to believers in the firm's potential.[28]

Annual share repurchases of U.S. NFCs are relatively modest, amounting to less than $3.0 billion per year.[29] That portion of share-repurchase programs that are undertaken with wealth transfer as the principal objective must certainly be far smaller than $3.0 billion per year.[30] We will not devote a chapter to the exploration of this phenomenon, but it is worth noting by way of example that Teledyne Inc., over the five-year period 1972–76, repurchased almost two thirds of its originally outstanding shares. The data in Table 2–3 suggest that the wealth transferred from one subset of shareholders to another subset of shareholders in this example has been quite significant. Over 24 million Teledyne shares were reacquired between December 31, 1971, and December 31, 1976, at an average price slightly above $20, versus a share price of $69½ on December 31, 1976.

Those shareholders retaining their Teledyne shares over the period extending from December 31, 1971, through December 31, 1976, enjoyed an annual compounded rate of return on their investment equal to 26.3 percent. An investment in the S&P 500 stocks held over the same period would have produced an annual compounded rate of return on investment equal to 4.5 percent. Adjusting Teledyne's stock price performance

---

[27] While a significant management stake in the equity ownership of a firm is certainly not a prerequisite for a major share-repurchase program, casual empirical observation leads me to conclude that the two are usually closely related.

[28] In a study of 42 tender-offer share repurchases completed between 1953 and 1969, Kenneth R. Marks found that on average, and after adjusting for risk, the common stocks of the firms repurchasing their shares did not exceed the return from the market during the period immediately following the conclusion of the tender offer. This study did not attempt to segment the data according to the degree of management ownership. In addition, performance of the firm's stock versus the market was observed for only one year following the tender offer. See Kenneth R. Marks, "The Stock Price Performance of Firms Repurchasing Their Own Shares," *The Bulletin, New York University Graduate School of Business Administration,* 1976–1.

[29] Between 1970 and 1976, for example, the average annual rate of equity security retirements (including financial as well as nonfinancial corporations) was $2.6 billion. This figure includes calls of preferred stock, and repurchases of both common stock and preferred stock by public tender, open-market purchases, and cash payments in connection with liquidations, reorganizations, and mergers. Source: U.S. Securities and Exchange Commission, "Statistical Bulletin," April 1977.

[30] Share-repurchase plans are often used to offset the dilution caused by the exercise of options issued under stock option plans, and for other corporate purposes of a similar nature. When repurchases are relatively small in scale, their principal objective is unlikey to be wealth transfer.

TABLE 2-3
Profitability, stock price, and common stock repurchase history of Teledyne, Inc., 1971-1976

	(1) Profit/Common-equity ratio	(2) Debt/equity* ratio	(3) Market-value/Book-value ratio	(4) End-of-period share price ($/share)†	(5) Tender-offer price ($/share)	(6) Means of payment for tendered shares	(7) Shares reacquired (000's)	(8) Shares reissued (000's)	(9) Shares outstanding (000's)	(10) Shares owned by chairman‡ (000's)	(11) Percentage of outstanding shares owned by chairman||
1971											
4th quarter §	—			19-3/8							
Year	0.089	0.44	1.0	—					30,616	643	2.1
1972											
1st quarter				26							
2d quarter				22-7/8							
3d quarter				18							
4th quarter				20-3/8	20	Cash	8,962				
Year	0.116	0.85	1.0	—			8,962	1,318	22,973	636	2.8
1973											
1st quarter				17-1/8							
2d quarter				13-1/2							
3d quarter				14-3/4							
4th quarter				15-1/8							
Year	0.124	1.20	0.6	—			588	795	23,210	655	2.8
1974											
1st quarter				12-3/4	14	Cash	1,679				
2d quarter				12-1/2	20	Debenture	3,963				
3d quarter				10							
4th quarter				10-1/4							
Year	0.058	1.67	0.4	—			5,642	833	18,401	663	3.6
1975											
1st quarter				11-1/2	16	Debenture	1,885				
2d quarter				21-5/8							
3d quarter				19-3/4	18	Cash	3,830				
4th quarter				22-1/8							
Year	0.215	1.09	0.7	—			5,715	926	13,612	679	5.0
1976											
1st quarter				50-3/4	40	Cash	2,500				
2d quarter				68							
3d quarter				78							
4th quarter				69-1/2							
Year	0.279	0.38	1.7	—			3,162	968	11,418	700	6.1

*The equity figure in this calculation is based on market, not book values.
†Teledyne paid a 3 percent stock dividend in each of the years noted above. The share price is not adjusted for this split.
‡Shares owned by the chairman are as of December 31 of the years 1971-73. After 1973 the data are as of January 31 of the following year.
§Teledyne's fiscal year ended in October through 1973. Starting with the first quarter of 1974, the company's fiscal year was changed to match the calendar year.
||Primarily because of five separate 3 percent stock dividends between December 31, 1971, and early 1977, the Teledyne chairman's stock holdings have increased significantly during this period.

for the higher risk faced by the Teledyne investor (as reflected in changes in the stock's β that can be attributed to the changing capital structure of the firm) would not alter the conclusion that Teledyne's investors have achieved superior risk-adjusted rates of return in the latter part of the period covered by Teledyne's share repurchases.[31]

Value transfers—General considerations

As a general rule, *securities* markets are thought to be a good deal more efficient than *real product* markets. For this reason, it is unlikely that the broad area of value transfer offers anything like the total dollar potential (at the aggregate level) for enhancing shareholder values that is presented to managers attempting to create rather than simply transfer value. In spite of this fact, market valuation "errors" produce value-transfer opportunities that are hardly trivial in magnitude. A case in point is Avon Products. When the market's judgment of Avon's value (up to 1972) is compared to this firm's historical (and likely future) performance along the important value-creation dimensions outlined in Chapter 1, it is clear that the securities markets were valuing this company's common stock quite irrationally for an extended period of time, a factor we shall explore in greater detail in Chapter 3. This irrationality did not even begin to be corrected until 1973–74 (Table 2–4). By this date Avon's security prices returned to levels that (although still exceeding a reasonable upper boundary according to Table 1–16) could be explained more readily using a rational economic model. The valuation error here was multi-billion dollar in scale as indicated by Column 5 of Table 2–4. While Avon's management did not capitalize on this valuation error in recent times via corporate equity sales or mergers, managers of firms with security prices similarly bloated (but on a somewhat less grand scale in terms of total market value) did take advantage of this ephemeral blessing.[32] We shall see examples of this in Chapters 7 and 9.

---

[31] The single-year rates of return enjoyed by Teledyne's shareholders versus the single-year rate of return enjoyed by investors in the S&P 500 were as follows:

Year	Rate of return to Teledyne's investors (%)	Rate of return to S&P 500 investors (%)
1972	3.0	18.7
1973	(37.7)	(14.5)
1974	(26.6)	(26.0)
1975	122.4	36.9
1976	223.4	23.6

A method for calculating the change in a stock's β value that is attributable to a change in capital structure will be presented in the appendix to Chapter 3. Teledyne's β-adjusted returns are not calculated above since Teledyne's market performance so clearly exceeded that which could be explained in terms of the firm's β value.

[32] Avon did, in fact, attempt a minor acquisition for stock in 1975. The stock market reaction was so negative, however, that the merger aborted.

TABLE 2-4

One example of a dramatically large securities market valuation error of relatively long duration in the common stock of Avon Products, Inc.

	(1)	(2)	(3)	(4)	(5)	(6)
		Growth in Common equity/ Profit after tax	Market value/ Book value	Market value/ Adjusted book value	Total market value of common stock outstanding ($ billions)	Total book value of common stock outstanding ($ billions)
	ROE					
1966	0.371	—	15.6	—	2.3	0.15
1967	0.373	0.39	23.3	—	4.1	0.18
1968	0.353	0.38	18.1	—	3.7	0.20
1969	0.358	0.40	21.0	—	4.9	0.24
1970	0.361	0.39	18.6	—	5.1	0.27
1971	0.344	0.39	18.3	—	5.8	0.32
1972	0.330	0.50	20.9	—	7.9	0.38
1973	0.304	0.50	8.3	—	3.7	0.44
1974	0.237	0.22	3.5	—	1.7	0.47
1975	0.265	0.38	3.9	—	2.0	0.52
1976	0.286	0.39	4.9	3.4	2.8	0.59
Average	0.321	0.39	—	—	—	—

Source: Compustat data for Columns 1–3, 5–6; Table 1–11 for Column 4.

One important characteristic of value-transfer opportunities deserves special mention. Market valuation errors sometimes arrive on a manager's doorstep quite by accident.[33] When the fancy of investors turns to a particular industry, their enthusiasm (as reflected in the spread investors sometimes create between *market* value and the upper boundary of a rationally computed *economic* value) can be quite breathtaking. Reality will, of course, ultimately intrude upon this process. Indeed, one could argue that the management challenge in the area of value transfers, given these circumstances, is one of simply having the presence of mind to act before the spotlight passes on!

Some managers have to create their own opportunities in the area of value transfers. Fate is rarely kind enough to deliver overvaluation errors without assistance. For many years, one way for a firm to provide investors with the encouragement necessary to open up a spread between market and economic value was to generate rapid growth in earnings per share. High-ROE firms such as those noted in Chapter 1 often generate rapid growth in earnings per share over long time periods. When such firms retain a significant fraction of their earnings, and enjoy attractive reinvestment opportunities that are commensurate with their earnings retentions, then rapid growth in earnings per share is practically assured. For example, a firm that earns a 20 percent ROE and maintains a 50 percent dividend payout ratio will see its earnings per share grow by 10 percent per year so long as its ROE and number of shares outstanding remain constant. The growth in earnings per share simply equals the ROE multiplied by the earnings retention ratio.

A high ROE can often justify a high market-value/adjusted-book-value ratio for a firm's common stock as indicated in Chapter 1. In addition, as indicated above, high-ROE firms often produce rapid growth in earnings per share. It is the next step in a chain of (il)logic that has made many an investor poorer, if not wiser. That step of illogic is to assume that rapid growth in earnings per share, in and of itself, justifies a high market-value /adjusted-book-value ratio. Indeed, as noted in Table 1–3, for a firm to be rationally valued in excess of its adjusted book value, it must (now and in the future) enjoy investment opportunities that promise rates of return that exceed capital costs.

The existence of high-return investment opportunities makes it possible for managers to produce higher-than-average growth in earnings per share, with consistency, over a relatively long time span. But higher-than-average earnings-per-share growth can also be produced, over a shorter time span, by:

---

[33] Obviously, not all valuation errors arise by accident. In the late 1960s, for example, active touting of stocks by managers eager to boost the price of their shares was not exactly unknown.

1. an earnings turnaround in which, for example, a firm's ROE grows from a depressed 2 percent to a more normal 10 percent over a five-year period;
2. the absence of any cash dividend or gradual (say over five years) reduction in a firm's dividend payout ratio;
3. a gradual (say over five years) but significant upward shift in a firm's debt/equity ratio;
4. the systematic sale of high market-value but low cost-basis assets, such as those assets that might have been acquired in acquisitions accounted for as a pooling-of-interests;
5. the chain-letter acquisitions of low price/earnings ratio firms (or assets) by higher price/earnings ratio firms.[34]

Earnings-per-share growth generated from any of the five sources listed above is not sustainable over the long run, although in the past the securities markets have sometimes overvalued the securities of firms producing rapid earnings-per-share growth from one or more of these sources.[35]

VALUE DESTRUCTION

There is one final area in which managers can influence shareholder values. That is in the area of *value destruction*. Occasionally managements of firms determine that they and/or their shareholders would best be served by a strategy that wreaks havoc with the firm's competitors, perhaps even driving some of the competitors to or near bankruptcy. Such a strategy could cripple certain competitors, thereby destroying at least a portion of the value of those firms' securities. At a minimum such firms would face reduced access to the capital markets, thereby restraining their growth. A more severe result would be the elimination of these competitors from the marketplace entirely. Either result would facilitate the expansion of the aggressive firm, perhaps thereby enhancing the value of its securities (once the battle had subsided) above the level believed to be obtainable absent any battle.

Product price cutting is one management action that can create quite spectacular results in the area of value destruction. Although other com-

---

[34] See Marvin M. May, "The Earnings per Share Trap," and Harry H. Lynch, *Financial Performance of Conglomerates* (Cambridge, Mass.: Division of Research, Graduate School of Business Administration, Harvard University, 1971).

[35] While I have not attempted to categorize the bases and duration of strings of EPS growth (or the valuation impact of such growth) for the 1,448 firms representing the sample of U.S. NFCs in Chapter 1, this project would make an interesting research topic.

petitive actions can produce similar results, such results generally take longer to achieve by other methods. Since price cutting that is designed to destroy competition is probably illegal,[36] care must be taken to assure that any damage done to competition as a result of price cutting is an *incidental result* of a broader strategy rather than the *principal objective* of that strategy.[37]

It is much easier to identify the impact of price cutting on competition in an industry than it is to characterize the intent that led to the decision to cut price. This difficulty has not, however, impeded the U.S. Department of Justice's efforts to describe as predatory IBM's price reductions in the peripheral equipment market in the early 1970s. Indeed, in an economic analysis presented to a U.S. District Court in late 1974, the Justice Department argued as follows at several different points in a brief on the economics of the industry.

> IBM's effort to destroy the viability of peripherals companies represented an integrated strategy comprised of pricing policy changes and fighting machines.[38]

✻ ✻ ✻ ✻ ✻

> The second link in IBM's peripherals strategy was the . . . [new lease] . . . plans, which had a pronounced effect on PCMs.[39] The plans offered 8 percent and 16 percent discounts for IBM peripherals on 1- and 2-year leases, respectively. In addition, however, the plans also eliminated addi-

---

[36] Section 3 of the Robinson-Patman Act states: "It shall be unlawful for any person engaged in commerce, in the course of such commerce, to be a party to, or assist in, any transaction . . . to sell, or contract to sell goods at unreasonably low prices for the purpose of destroying competition or eliminating a competitor."

Section 2 of the Sherman Act states: "Every person who shall monopolize, or attempt to monopolize, or conspire with any other person or persons, to monopolize any part of the trade or commerce among the several States, or with foreign nations, shall be deemed guilty of a misdemeanor. . . ."

Section 5 of the Federal Trade Commission Act states: "Unfair methods of competition in commerce, and unfair or deceptive acts or practices in commerce, are hereby declared unlawful."

[37] The economic and legal aspects of predatory pricing are reviewed at length in a series of articles and replies by Phillip Areeda, Donald F. Turner, and F. M. Scherer that appeared in the February 1975 and March 1976 issues of the *Harvard Law Review*. A review of some litigated predatory pricing cases that ended in convictions can be found in Roland H. Koller, II, "The Myth of Predatory Pricing: an Empirical Study," *Antitrust Law and Economics Review*, Summer 1971.

[38] *United States of America* v. *International Business Machines Corporation*, 69 CV 200, U.S. District Court, Southern District of New York, "An Economic Analysis of the Market for General Purpose Digital Computer Systems," December 10, 1974, p. 77.

[39] PCM's or "plug compatible manufacturers" produce equipment that is interchangeable with similar equipment manufactured by IBM.

tional use charges for those machines on which they had not already been eliminated. This meant actual rental reductions of 30–40 percent.[40]

✿✿✿✿✿

The effect on PCM's was devastating. IBM documents show that in the first seven months after the fixed term plan was announced, PCM tape and disk drive installations fell 62 percent and 48 percent, respectively.[41]

✿✿✿✿✿

More importantly, the plan provided a warning to the investment community as to the real risks faced by PCM'ers.[42]

✿✿✿✿✿

Once the PCM firms began to establish themselves as profitable, ongoing enterprises, IBM brought to bear its pricing and fighting machine weapons. And suddenly the market was filled with the "dying company" . . . just as IBM staff members had predicted in the briefing that preceded the decision to go ahead with the [new lease plan].[43]

The Justice Department alleged that IBM's actions in the situation noted above represented a bold and highly successful example of value destruction. IBM has a considerably different view. IBM argued as follows in a private antitrust suit alleging similar abuses in more limited product areas:

IBM's prices for its disc products at issue—both before and after the price reductions—were always significantly profitable (greater than 20% of revenue).[44]

✿✿✿✿✿

Beginning in 1968 and 1969, [other companies] copied IBM's disc products and began marketing their copies to IBM's customers at prices significantly below IBM's prices.[45]

✿✿✿✿✿

IBM was rapidly losing business to such discounted copies (in 1968 IBM's share of disc products manufactured in the U.S. was 89%; one year later (1969)it had dropped to 68%; the next year (1970) it dropped to

---

[40] *U.S.* v. *IBM*, p. 79.

[41] Ibid., p. 79.

[42] Ibid., p. 80.

[43] Ibid., p. 84.

[44] *California Computer Products, Inc.* v. *International Business Machines Corp.;* 77–1563; U.S. Court of Appeals, Ninth Circuit, "Brief of Appellee International Business Machines Corporation," September 26, 1977, p. 3.

[45] Ibid., p. 2.

51%). IBM either had to improve the price/performance of its disc products or go out of the disc business.[46]

* * * * *

IBM's market share of disc products manufactured in the United States has continued to decline; from 51% in 1970, to 30% in 1971 and to 25% in 1975.[47]

* * * * *

Price reductions anticipated to return a reasonable profit have consistently been held by the courts to be lawful means of competition and not evidence of willful acquisition or maintenance of monopoly power.[48]

* * * * *

An agreement among competitors limiting profitable price competition so that suppliers can exact higher prices from consumers would be per se unlawful and a criminal violation of Section 1 of the Sherman Act. A court order accomplishing the same result would be unthinkable.[49]

IBM won a directed verdict of acquittal in the District Court which tried the private antitrust action referred to above. That judgment is being appealed, however. The Jusice Department's suit continues with IBM only beginning its defense as of mid-1978.

How the Justice Department's case will end is obviously unclear, but both sides will have ample time to test the legal foundations of their positions. A final resolution of the Justice Department's case (and its likely appeals) is not expected until at least 1981, some 12 years after the case was first filed.[50]

In part because of legal pitfalls, examples of competitive behavior whose primary objective is value destruction appear infrequently, particularly in the price-cutting area. Nevertheless, in Chapters 8 and 9 we will examine some examples of competitive actions that may have had value-destruction consequences, presumably as incidental results of broader corporate objectives.

SUMMARY

Chapter 2 focuses on those broad areas of opportunity that managers ought to address in their efforts to enhance shareholder values. The goal of the chapter is to challenge managers to pick their way through the elements of the valuation formula, consciously and systematically pok-

---

[46] Ibid., p. 3.

[47] Ibid., p. 4.

[48] Ibid., pp. 4–5.

[49] Ibid., p. 12.

[50] J. Thomas Franklin, "An Overwhelming Antitrust Case Against IBM," *Computers and People*, February 1977, p. 18.

$$\text{NVP} = \sum_{i=0}^{n} \frac{(\text{Revenues} - \text{Costs})_i}{(1 + k_0)^i},$$

ing at specific elements here and there, in an effort either (a) to increase the left hand side of the equation, or (b) to identify and perhaps capitalize on the perceived valuation errors of others.[51]

As indicated in the chapter, the array of weapons that can be used to create, transfer, or destroy shareholder values is surprisingly broad. The management challenge, obviously, is to identify and then exploit one or two areas of opportunity that promise to produce significant value enhancement for a firm's shareholders at a particular point in time. With that thought in mind, we will now move from a concern about general processes for enhancing shareholder values to the realities of actual management action. Chapters 3 through 9 will carefully explore how a number of firms have handled this important management challenge.

---

[51] As we will observe in Chapter 10, efforts aimed at creating, transferring, and destroying shareholder value have ethical as well as economic and legal consequences that need to be carefully considered by managers.

PART THREE

Examples of firms creating, transferring, and destroying shareholder values

A. VALUE CREATION
    3. Avon Products, Inc.
    4. The Grocery Retailing Industry
    5. Freeport Minerals Company
    6. General Electric Company

B. VALUE TRANSFER
    7. The Computer Leasing Industry

C. VALUE DESTRUCTION
    8. The Great Atlantic & Pacific
        Tea Company, Inc.

D. VALUE CREATION, TRANSFER, AND
    DESTRUCTION
    9. The Levitz Furniture Corporation

VALUE
CREATION

Avon Products, Inc.

In Chapter 1, Avon Products, Inc., was noted as one of the most profitable large firms in the United States. The firm was a spectacular success story in the area of *value creation*. In Chapter 2, Avon was again cited, this time for having achieved a market value for its common equity in the late 1960s and early 1970s that appeared consistently to exceed, by billions of dollars, the rationally defined economic value of the firm's common equity. The Avon example was cited as evidence demonstrating that inefficiency in the valuation mechanisms of the capital markets could exist on a fairly grand scale over substantial time periods in securities that were broadly traded by seemingly sophisticated professional investors.[1] This chapter will examine in considerably more detail the issues relating to Avon that were first raised in Chapters 1 and 2. The chapter focuses first on the source of Avon's extraordinary profitability.

Avon Products, Inc., was the largest cosmetics company in the United States. In 1976 the firm marketed its 600 products directly to the consumer on a house-to-house basis through 335,000 independent domestic and 560,000 international representatives. As shown in Table 3–1, house-to-house selling was one of the most important channels for the distribution of cosmetics products.

Avon's dominance of the house-to-house distribution channel was impressive. Avon's sales reached $1.4 billion in 1976. One of Avon's largest

---

[1] On December 31, 1976, the trust departments of 67 banks held 24.4 percent of the total number of Avon shares outstanding. On the same date 54 mutual funds held 7.0 percent of the total number of Avon shares outstanding. The source of these data is "Spectrum 3" and "Spectrum 1," Computer Directions Advisors, Inc., December, 1976.

TABLE 3-1

Share of cosmetics, toiletries, and fragrances sold in the U.S. through various channels of distribution, 1950-1975

Year	Chain and independent drug stores	Department and specialty stores	Food stores	Variety stores	House to house	Other
1950	.... 37%	27%	6%	11%	14%	5%
1955	 29	22	18	7	20	3
1960	 26	18	24	9	21	3
1965	 27	15	23	9	20	5
1970	 26	13	23	7	23	8
1975	 25	12	24	7	24	8

Source: *Avon Products, Inc.—A New Look* (Boston: Harvard Business School, 1977), p. 25. Original data sources listed in the above document included the Cosmetic, Toiletry, and Fragrance Association and *Drug Topics*.

competitors in the house-to-house sales of cosmetics, Mary Kay Cosmetics, Inc., achieved sales of $46 million in 1976.[2] The sales gap separating Avon from other house-to-house cosmetics firms was extremely wide.

Avon's dominance of the cosmetics business overall was far less dramatic than its dominance of the house-to-house distribution channel for cosmetics sales. Avon estimated that it enjoyed a 15 percent share of the U.S. cosmetics and toiletries market. Avon's sales of $1.4 billion in 1976 were only about 50 percent greater than the $950 million in sales reported by Revlon,[3] the second largest cosmetics firm in the United States and the largest cosmetics company selling through retail establishments.

While Revlon was somewhat close to Avon in terms of sales volume, Revlon was not close to Avon in terms of profitability. Neither were any of the other large cosmetics and toiletries firms such as Gillette, Chesebrough-Pond's, Faberge, or Alberto Culver. As Table 3–2 indicates, while Revlon earned a very attractive ROE during the decade 1967–76 (indeed Revlon qualified for the Table 1–9 list of Hall of Fame firms that earned consistently high ROEs), its ROE each year was always 10 to 20 percentage points *lower* than that earned by Avon.

Avon versus Revlon profitability

In attempting to identify why Avon's ROE performance is so exceptional, we can use Avon's nearest competitor (Revlon, Inc.) as a benchmark. The profitability of any firm can be easily broken down into three broad components. These are the *capital intensity* of the firm's opera-

---

[2] Mary Kay Cosmetics, Inc. products were sold primarily via the "party plan" method of in-home selling.

[3] Revlon, Inc., 10K Report to the SEC.

TABLE 3-2
Return on equity for Avon Products, Inc., and Revlon, Inc., 1967-1976

	Profit-after-taxes/net-worth ratio	
Year	Avon	Revlon
1967	0.374	0.159
1968	0.353	0.207
1969	0.359	0.163
1970	0.361	0.156
1971	0.344	0.168
1972	0.330	0.160
1973	0.304	0.159
1974	0.237	0.161
1975	0.265	0.165
1976	0.286	0.179

tions, its *profit margins,* and its utilization of *leverage.* An equation that accomplishes this segmentation of important profitability factors (a slightly modified version of the well-known du Pont formula) is shown below.

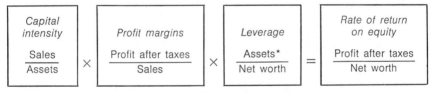

* Since assets are, by definition, equal to total liabilities plus net worth, the ratio "assets/net worth" is equivalent to [total liabilities plus net worth]/net worth. This latter ratio is nothing more than a measure of the intensity of a firm's utilization of non-equity financing.

The financial performances of Avon Products and Revlon for the past decade are cast in the format noted above in Table 3–3. Table 3–3 shows quite clearly where Avon's performance surpasses that of Revlon. Over the decade 1967–76 Avon was able to achieve an average of $1.68 in sales for every $1.00 of assets employed (Line 1, Table 3–3). Revlon was able to achieve an average of only $1.07 in sales for every dollar of assets employed (Line 2, Table 3–3). In terms of profits-to-sales ratios, a similar differential is apparent between the two firms. Avon enjoyed average after-tax profits in relation to sales of 12.0 percent (Line 3, Table 3–3). Revlon had to settle for a lower ratio, equal to 8.1 percent, over the decade (Line 4, Table 3–3). Only in the area of leverage utilization did Revlon's ratio exceed that of Avon. Revlon had an average of $1.90 of assets for every $1.00 of equity, but Avon had only $1.59 of assets for each $1.00 of equity (Lines 6 and 5, Table 3–3).

TABLE 3-3

Comparative capital intensity, profit margin, leverage, and profitability ratio data for Avon Products, Inc. versus Revlon, Inc., 1967-1976

Line	1967	1968	1969	1970	1971	1972	1973	1974	1975	1976	1967-76 Average
Sales/Assets ratio											
1 Avon	1.73	1.68	1.80	1.72	1.72	1.68	1.62	1.68	1.59	1.55	1.68
2 Revlon	1.36	1.13	1.08	1.06	0.98	0.95	0.99	1.03	1.00	1.09	1.07
Profit-after-taxes/Sales ratio											
3 Avon	0.138	0.128	0.128	0.130	0.125	0.124	0.118	0.089	0.107	0.117	0.120
4 Revlon	0.076	0.076	0.080	0.075	0.087	0.085	0.085	0.082	0.083	0.085	0.081
Assets/Net-worth ratio											
5 Avon	1.57	1.64	1.55	1.61	1.60	1.58	1.59	1.59	1.56	1.57	1.59
6 Revlon	1.62	1.85	1.89	1.98	1.97	1.96	1.88	1.90	1.98	1.92	1.90
Profit-after-taxes/Net-worth ratio											
7 Avon	0.374	0.353	0.359	0.361	0.344	0.330	0.304	0.237	0.265	0.286	0.321
8 Revlon	0.159	0.207	0.163	0.156	0.168	0.160	0.159	0.161	0.165	0.179	0.168

Sources: Annual reports.

Table 3–3 indicates broadly why Avon's financial performance exceeded that of Revlon. Important details are missing from the analysis to this point, however, and we need to probe further in order to fill in these details.

Avon's capital intensity advantage

Avon was able to achieve a higher level of sales from a dollar of assets than Revlon for two reasons. First, and by far most significant, Avon has a much shorter receivables collection period than Revlon as indicated by the accounts-receivable/sales ratios for these firms (Lines 1 and 2, Table 3–4). Avon's terms of trade require its independent representatives to pay for their merchandise within about ten days after it is received.[4] Revlon's terms to its retail and/or wholesale accounts run as long as 90 days for some health products.[5] Since the Avon representative is not required to carry any inventory (and receives cash in payment for merchandise delivered to customers), these credit terms are not at all onerous. The shortened inventory-receivable-cash cycle associated with direct selling accrues directly to Avon in the form of greatly reduced capital requirements for the financing of accounts receivable. Revlon enjoys no such benefit in its sales to retail and/or wholesale establishments.

The second major reason that Avon was able to achieve more sales per dollar of assets relates to inventory turnover. Avon was able to turn its inventories, on average, 50 percent faster than Revlon as indicated in Lines 3 and 4 of Table 3–4. Avon's direct selling method is again a key factor in the superiority of this performance measure. Avon's representatives sold the company's products in a series of "campaigns" each lasting two to three weeks. In each campaign a limited selection (usually 50 to 75) of the 600 items in the Avon product line were featured and heavily promoted. Since the bulk of the sales in each campaign were *featured* items, Avon's marketing approach effectively shrank the product

---

[4] Avon ran sales campaigns on a two-week cycle domestically and on a three-week cycle outside the United States. Avon's representatives were required to enclose payment for products ordered in the immediately *prior* campaign with their orders from the *latest* campaign. Avon's representatives generally received their merchandise within five days after their order was sent to the company. Orders mailed in by representatives on Monday were generally in the representatives' hands by Friday.

[5] The terms of trade in the cosmetics industry vary along a number of dimensions such as type of product (that is, cosmetic versus toiletry), retailer volume, and historic relationship between the manufacturer and the retailer. Payment terms are an item of negotiation as are other items such as (a) cooperative advertising allowances, (b) allowances for in-store beauty advisors, and (c) other forms of in-store promotion.

TABLE 3-4
Comparative *capital intensity* ratio data for Avon Products, Inc. versus Revlon, Inc. 1967–1976

Line	1967	1968	1969	1970	1971	1972	1973	1974	1975	1976	1967–76 Average
Accounts-receivable/Sales ratio											
1 Avon	.074	.068	.067	.065	.064	.068	.072	.071	.073	.075	.070
2 Revlon	.194	.196	.264	.286	.325	.290	.277	.246	.208	.181	.245
Inventory/Sales ratio											
3 Avon	.120	.124	.149	.151	.126	.125	.156	.175	.125	.123	.137
4 Revlon	.162	.158	.214	.257	.241	.243	.232	.276	.216	.189	.219
Net-fixed-assets/Sales ratio											
5 Avon	.181	.184	.206	.196	.224	.190	.182	.170	.170	.158	.186
6 Revlon	.137	.123	.148	.174	.178	.175	.155	.143	.129	.145	.151

Sources: Annual reports.

line at any point in time, thereby improving the inventory turns.[6] Avon's campaigns, coupled with promotional push from the independent representatives, gave Avon considerable flexibility in terms of "forcing" demand. This strength enabled Avon to deal rapidly with slower moving items, thereby increasing Avon's inventory turnover.

Accounts receivable, inventory, and net fixed assets accounted for 80 percent or more of the noncash[7] assets of both Avon and Revlon. The net fixed asset category represents the principal area of capital utilization not yet addressed. As shown in Lines 5 and 6 of Table 3–4, Avon required a slightly higher level of net fixed assets to support a dollar of sales volume than Revlon, but this difference was quite modest. In summary, then, Avon's capital intensity was far lower than Revlon's, primarily because of differences in the credit terms and inventory-turnover rates achieved by each firm. The advantage in Avon's favor could, in each instance, be attributed to Avon's direct-sales marketing approach.

Avon's profit-margin advantage

A second broad area in which Avon outperformed Revlon (as well as the other major cosmetics and toiletries firms) was in profit margins. Avon's average gross margin generally ran slightly ahead of Revlon's average gross margin, although the differences over a ten-year period averaged less than one percentage point (Lines 1 and 2, Table 3–5). The real differences in financial performance did not show up in *gross* margins. Instead, they showed up in *pretax* profit margins. This is where the differences are most dramatic between a direct-marketing organization such as Avon and a retail-establishment marketer such as Revlon. Almost the entire difference in pretax profit margins separating Avon from Revlon (Lines 3 and 4, Table 3–5) can be attributed to the differences in the advertising/sales ratios of these two firms (Lines 7 and 8, Table 3–5).

Simply stated, Revlon was forced to spend an average of 10.1¢ of each sales dollar in order to pull the firm's products through their retail channels. Avon spent an average of only 1.6¢ of each sales dollar on advertising, since the firm's independent representatives personally performed the advertising function in the course of their house-to-house selling.

A partitioning of the average pretax-profit margin differential separat-

---

[6] Avon managed its inventory position in featured products by testing each "campaign" in a number of representative market areas four weeks ahead of the date the campaign was to be introduced nationally. Deliveries from suppliers could be either speeded up or slowed down based on the sales response in these sample market areas.

[7] Cash and marketable securities represented a significant fraction of total assets for both Avon and Revlon. Later in the chapter we will explore the effect that the removal of redundant cash would have upon the key financial-performance ratios of Avon and Revlon.

TABLE 3-5
Comparative profit margin ratio data for Avon Products, Inc. versus Revlon, Inc., 1967–1976

Line	1967	1968	1969	1970	1971	1972	1973	1974	1975	1976	1967–76 Average
Gross-profit/Sales ratio											
1 Avon	.656	.657	.655	.650	.659	.659	.654	.617	.648	.651	.651
2 Revlon	.599	.620	.644	.639	.651	.658	.657	.656	.646	.650	.642
Pretax-profit/Sales ratio											
3 Avon	.265	.266	.259	.260	.253	.253	.233	.189	.217	.237	.243
4 Revlon	.151	.153	.150	.131	.144	.144	.155	.149	.157	.161	.150
After-tax-profit/Sales ratio											
5 Avon	.138	.128	.128	.130	.125	.124	.118	.089	.107	.117	.120
6 Revlon	.076	.076	.080	.075	.087	.085	.085	.082	.083	.085	.081
Advertising/Sales ratio											
7 Avon	—	—	—	—	.019	.017	.014	.010	.013	.020	.016
8 Revlon	—	—	—	—	.118	.095	.102	.107	.091	.091	.101

Sources: Annual reports and 10K reports to the SEC.

ing Avon from Revlon over the decade 1967–76 produces the following results:

Pretax-profit/Sales ratio for Avon	0.243
Pretax-profit/Sales ratio for Revlon	0.150
Pretax-profit/Sales ratio difference	(0.093)
Gross-margin/Sales ratio difference	0.009
Advertising/Sales ratio difference	0.085
Other SGA/Sales ratio difference	(0.001)
Pretax-profit/Sales ratio difference	(0.093)

As noted earlier, Avon's direct marketing approach gave this firm a superior position in terms of its *capital intensity*. As shown in Table 3–5, the direct-marketing approach also gave the firm a superior position in terms of its *profit margin*.

Avon's leverage position

The one important area influencing profitability where Avon fell below Revlon was in the utilization of leverage. As shown in Lines 5 and 6 of Table 3–3, Avon had an average of $1.59 of assets for each $1.00 of net worth over the decade 1967–76. Over this same time period Revlon had an average of $1.90 of assets for each $1.00 of net worth. At first glance one might conclude that Revlon must have utilized borrowed money more aggressively than Avon in order to achieve its higher leverage ratio. In fact, the explanation is a bit more complex. As indicated in Table 3–6,

TABLE 3–6
Cash and marketable securities versus borrowed money for Avon Products, Inc. and Revlon, Inc. at December 31, 1976 ($ millions)

	Avon	Revlon
Cash and marketable securities. . . .	$362.3	$268.5
Borrowed money	30.8	235.7

Avon in 1976 held several hundred million dollars of redundant capital in the form of cash and marketable securities. Revlon, on the other hand, held cash and marketable securities in an amount roughly equal to its interest-bearing debt.

If these firms were to utilize their redundant cash and marketable securities first to repay borrowings and then to reduce net worth (either by paying dividends to shareholders or by repurchasing shares), then the profitability analysis for Avon and Revlon would appear as indicated in Table 3–7.

TABLE 3-7
Profitability analysis of Avon Products, Inc. versus Revlon, Inc. for 1976 (after adjustments to remove redundant cash and marketable securities from each firm)

	$\dfrac{Sales}{Assets}$	X	$\dfrac{Profit\ after\ taxes}{Sales}$	X	$\dfrac{Assets}{Net\ worth}$	=	$\dfrac{Profit\ after\ taxes}{Net\ worth}$
Avon	2.26	X	0.113	X	2.13	=	0.547
Revlon	1.49	X	0.087	X	1.41	=	0.172

[handwritten annotation in left margin: "avon here is made 3x more profitable"]

The true profitability of Avon's product-market position emerges only when the firm's redundant cash and marketable securities are removed. When this is accomplished, it is clear that in 1976 Avon produced a return in excess of 50 percent on the equity invested in its product-market operations.[8] Obviously the firm earned a very modest return on the equity invested in cash and marketable securities.

The source of Avon's superior profitability

At this point the bases of Avon's remarkable profitability have been isolated by contrasting the economics of Avon's direct sales against the economics of Revlon's distribution through retail establishments. Three factors accounted for almost all of the difference in observed profitability between Avon Products, Inc., and Revlon, Inc. The factors favoring Avon were (a) a shorter accounts-receivable collection period, (b) a more rapid inventory turnover, and (c) a reduced need for media advertising. Avon's 900,000 independent sales representatives form the basis of Avon's competitive advantage in the sale of the firm's products. These independent representatives are the entry barrier that allows Avon to achieve the enormous level of profitability indicated in Tables 3-3 and 3-7.

Value creation for Avon's shareholders

Now that the nature of Avon's entry barrier and the economic bases for the firm's high level of profitability have been established, we can directly examine the question of *value creation*. Specifically, how much value has been created for Avon's shareholders as a result of Avon's remarkable profitability?

---

[8] One other quite interesting observation emerges from the Table 3-7 analysis. Avon's large volume of spontaneously generated liabilities (that is, its income tax and retail sales-tax liabilities) combined with its limited asset requirements (due to a short accounts-receivable collection period and a rapid inventory turnover) made Avon a more highly leveraged firm than Revlon, absent the effects of redundant cash and capital-structure decisions.

Chapter 1 showed that Avon's ROE for 1976 (when adjusted for the replacement cost of inventory and fixed assets, and for the capitalization and amortization of advertising and research and development expenditures) amounted to 18.9 percent (Line 27, Table 1A–3). Avon's *real* cost of equity capital amounted to 11.0 percent (Line 9, Column 3, Table 1–10). Avon thus achieved a *real* ROE in 1976 that was 7.9 percentage points in excess of the firm's *real* cost of equity capital (Line 9, Column 10, Table 1–10).

Based on Avon's historical pattern of annual growth in net worth (equal to 40 percent of annual net profits), the upper limit on the rationally determined economic value of Avon's common stock (measured in relation to adjusted book value) should have been about 2.4 (Line 9, Column 7, Table 1–16). In fact, at December 31, 1976, the actual market-value/adjusted-book-value ratio of Avon's common stock was 3.4 (Line 9, Column 5, Table 1–16). What could account for this presumably irrational overvaluation? The data of Table 3–7 come quickly to mind. Could it be that Avon's profitability was understated as a result of not explicitly dealing with the issue of the firm's redundant cash and marketable securities? If so, perhaps the rationally defined market-value/adjusted-book-value ratio for Avon's common stock has also been understated.

Valuation impact of removing redundant capital

This possible explanation for the observed overvaluation turns out to be invalid. Avon's *real* ROE in 1976 after the elimination of the firm's redundant cash and marketable securities was 0.279. The derivation of this figure is described in the appendix to this chapter. The firm's *real* cost of equity capital (after adjustment for the elimination of the firm's redundant cash and marketable securities) was 0.117. This figure is also derived in the appendix. Eliminating Avon's redundant capital increases the spread between the firm's real rate of return and its real cost of equity capital from the previously reported 0.079 (Line 9, Column 10, Table 1–10) to 0.162.[9] Eliminating Avon's redundant cash and marketable securities has a second result, however. It highlights the very *modest* rate at which Avon has been able to make new investments in high-return product-market opportunities.[10] Indeed, absent investments in the form of redundant cash and marketable securities, Avon's net worth would have grown annually by an amount equal to only 18.1 percent of the

---

[9] This equals the real ROE of 0.279 minus the real cost of equity capital of 0.117.

[10] The accumulation of redundant cash and marketable securities causes a firm's net worth to grow more rapidly than would be the case if the redundant cash and marketable securities were utilized to pay dividends or repurchase the firm's common stock.

firm's annual profits over the period 1966–76 (Line 13, Column 7, Table 3A–1). Over the period 1971–76, Avon's net worth would have grown annually by an amount equal to only 8.4 percent of annual profits (Line 14, Column 7, Table 3A–1).

If these adjusted data relating to real ROE, real cost of equity capital, and rate of reinvestment are assumed in the valuation formula utilized in constructing Table 1–16, the upper range of the rational economic-value/ adjusted-book-value ratio for Avon's common stock turns out to be 3.1 for the higher reinvestment-rate assumption (18.1 percent of annual profits) and 2.6 for the lower reinvestment-rate assumption (8.4 percent of annual profits).

Making these adjustments does not, however, help to close the gap between the observed market-value/adjusted-book-value ratio for Avon's common stock and the upper boundary of the rationally determined economic-value/adjusted-book-value ratio for Avon's common stock. If Avon's redundant capital were removed, the firm's market value and book value would both decline. If Avon's market value and book value both declined by equal amounts (as they should in theory), this would increase the observed market-value/adjusted-book-value ratio of Avon's common stock at December 31, 1976, to 4.7 (Line 3, Column 3, Table 3–8). In short, adjustments designed to remove Avon's redundant capital do not change one essential fact:

> *Avon's market price at December 31, 1976, substantially exceeded the rationally defined upper boundary value that was calculated by extrapolating Avon's historical profitability and growth performance 30 years into the future.*

Partitioning the value created for Avon's shareholders—1976

The value created for Avon's shareholders can be estimated by simply subtracting the adjusted book value of the firm's equity from its market value. This is done in Table 3–8. It is a simple task to partition this created value into one portion that can be attributed to the capitalization of present and future returns that are in excess of capital costs, and a second portion that is due simply to investor expectations that are unlikely to be realized. The $2.0 billion of shareholder wealth created by Avon at December 31, 1976 (Line 2, Column 5, Table 3–8), can be partitioned as follows. A *maximum* upper range of $1.2 billion can be attributed to the capitalization of present and future returns that are in excess of capital costs (Line 2, Column 6, Table 3–8) while *at least* $800 million should be attributed to investor expectations that are unsupported by an extrapolation of Avon's past financial performance (Line 2, Column 7, Table 3–8). Interestingly, this allocation is not significantly influenced by the

TABLE 3-8
Market value versus book value ratio data (variously defined) for Avon Products, Inc. common stock at December 31, 1976

	(1)	(2)	(3) = (1)/(2)	(4)	(5) = (1)–(2)	(6) = (4)X(2)–(2)	(7) = (1)–(2)–(6)
	Market value of common equity ($ millions)	Book value of common equity ($ millions)	Market-value/ Book-value ratio	Upper boundary of economically rational Market-value/ Book-value ratio	Value created ($ millions)	Economically rational portion of value created ($ millions)	Overvaluation portion of value created ($ millions)
Historical data	2,845	589	4.8	n.a.*	2,256	n.a.	n.a.
Historical data adjusted for replacement cost. . .	2,845	841	3.4	2.4	2,004	1,177	827
Historical data adjusted for replacement cost and the removal of redundant capital	2,552	548	4.7	3.1	2,004	1,151	853

*n.a. = not applicable.

removal of Avon's redundant capital, as the figures in Line 3 of Table 3–8 suggest. In this example, the valuation impact of the *reduced ROE* associated with holding redundant cash is fully offset by the *higher apparent rate of reinvestment* resulting when the firm accumulates cash and marketable securities.

Partitioning the value created for Avon's shareholders—1972

The apparent "overvaluation" of Avon's stock in 1976 cannot be attributed to complications in the use of the valuation model caused by Avon's accumulation of redundant cash. Investors have simply overvalued this security. This finding (which is based on data for one point in time, i.e., December 31, 1976) can be significantly extended if the analysis is moved back several years to a time when Avon's market value was equal to over 20 *times* its adjusted book value.

As shown in Table 2–4, from 1967 through 1972 Avon enjoyed a market-value/book-value ratio that averaged over 20. In 1972, Avon's market-value/book-value ratio was 20.9. Table 3–9 presents data equivalent to that found in Lines 1 and 2 of Table 3–8, except that the data are now for 1972 rather than for 1976. Line 2 of Table 3–9 suggests that Avon's over-valuation in 1972 probably exceeded $3.5 *billion*. While Avon has clearly created enormous wealth for its shareholders as a result of its remarkable profitability, Avon's share price has for many years included an impressive premium above that explained by the application of a rational valuation model to Avon's *historic* profitability and growth performance. More importantly, Avon's stock price in 1972 included a premium above that explained by the application of a rational valuation model to Avon's likely *future* profitability and growth performance. In order to economically justify the market-value/book-value ratio that Avon's common stock enjoyed at December 31, 1972, investors would have to assume that Avon's sales would rise from $1 billion in 1972 to *$55 billion* in 2002. This is a 55-fold increase. The calculation assumes 30 years of continued profitability and equity capital costs at the levels achieved in 1972. By comparison, a 5 percent compounded rate of growth in, for example, GNP (or the total market for cosmetics and toiletries) would produce a 4.3-fold expansion over this same 30-year time period. A 55-fold expansion (viewed in the context of Avon's existing 15 percent market share of the U.S. domestic cosmetics and toiletries market) simply cannot be achieved by Avon.

In short, Avon has had the best of both worlds. Shareholder value has been created as a result of the extraordinary profitability made possible by Avon's principal competitive weapon. That weapon was the firm's 900,000 independent sales representatives. Shareholder value has *also* been

TABLE 3-9
Market value versus book value ratio data (variously defined) for Avon Products, Inc. common stock at December 31, 1972

	(1)	(2)	(3) = (1)/(2)	(4)	(5) = (1)−(2)	(6) = (4)×(2)−(2)	(7) = (1)−(2)−(6)
	Market value of common equity ($ millions)	Book value of common equity ($ millions)	Market-value/ Book-value ratio	Upper boundary of economically rational Market-value/ Book-value ratio*	Value created ($ millions)	Economically rational portion of value created ($ millions)	Overvaluation portion of value created ($ millions)
Historical data	7,900	379	20.9	n.a.†	7,521	n.a.	n.a.
Historical data adjusted for replacement cost . .	7,900	470	16.8	9.2	7,430	3,854	3,576

*This calculation assumes a real ROE of 25.0 percent, a real cost of equity capital equal to 6.9 percent, and an annual growth of net worth equal to 40.1 percent of annual profits. It should be noted that Avon's real cost of equity capital was quite low in 1972 as a result of Avon's low beta of 0.78. For many years prior to Avon's profit decline in 1974, the firm enjoyed a beta coefficient that was significantly below 1.0.
†n.a. = not applicable.

created as a result of investor expectations that in recent years have consistently been out of line with reality.

Overvaluation—A value-transfer opportunity

While the issue of *value transfers* is reserved for Chapter 7, the enormous dollar significance of Avon's overvaluation almost demands a brief digression into this area. As noted in Chapter 2, valuation errors often present *value-transfer* opportunities. Since Avon's shares appeared to be so greatly overvalued in the late 1960s and early 1970s, one might wonder (1) whether this overvaluation was perceived by Avon's management, and (2) if it was perceived, whether any serious effort was undertaken to utilize the overvaluation to benefit Avon's existing shareholder group. At best one can only infer the answers to such questions from management actions.

Column 2 of Table 3–10 suggests that Avon's growth in earnings per share began to slow noticeably in 1973. Given Avon's extremely high market valuation, and the concomitant high expectations of investors, this was a serious problem. As Avon's business softened in mid-1973, a number of Avon's officers divested substantial fractions of their personal holdings of Avon common shares. Ten officers sold between 20 percent and 92 percent of their direct and indirect holdings of Avon shares during the months of July and August, 1973.[11] Avon reported an unusually low rate of earnings-per-share growth in the third quarter of 1973 (Column 2, Table 3–10). Avon's stock price fell sharply in response to the company's profit problem (Column 3, Table 3–10). The price slide began in late September 1973.

In the four-year period spanning March 1974 through March 1978, Avon's stock price was never *above* $55 per share. During the first eight months of 1973, Avon's share price was never *below* $109. The ten Avon officers who sold shares valued at $3.6 million during July and August, 1973, completed their sales at an average price of $110 per share. This figure was equal to roughly twice the price of Avon's shares a few months later when knowledge of Avon's profit problems was widespread.[12]

As noted earlier, Avon's common stock was dramatically overvalued in the late 1960s and early 1970s. Avon issued no new shares of common stock during this period other than the nominal number of shares issued

---

[11] On average these ten officers divested 54 percent of their direct and indirect holdings of Avon stock, as reported in the U.S. Securities and Exchange Commission publication, "Official Summary of Securities Transactions and Holdings."

[12] Two shareholders brought derivative class-action lawsuits against certain Avon officers and directors in late 1973. Their complaint alleged that during 1973 certain Avon officers and directors sold shares of capital stock of Avon on the basis of inside information regarding adverse developments in connection with the financial affairs of Avon, and that they profited from such sales.

TABLE 3-10
Quarterly market price and profit performance of Avon Products, Inc., 1971–1976

Quarter	(1) Earnings per share in quarter ($)	(2) EPS growth over same quarter of prior year (%)	(3) Market value per share ($)	(4) Book value per share* ($)	(5) Market-value/ Book-value ratio	(6) Dow Jones Industrial Average
1971						
1st	0.26	18	96-3/4	4.74	20.4	904
2d	0.36	13	110-3/8	4.81	22.9	891
3d	0.39	11	98-1/2	4.91	20.1	887
4th	0.88	6	100-3/8	5.50	18.3	809
1972						
1st	0.29	12	115	5.47	21.0	941
2d	0.46	28	114-1/4	5.61	20.4	929
3d	0.46	18	124-1/2	5.75	21.7	953
4th	0.95	8	136-3/4	6.55	20.9	1,021
1973						
1st	0.35	21	134	6.55	20.5	959
2d	0.50	9	123-1/2	6.80	18.2	892
3d	0.48	4	100	6.93	14.4	947
4th	1.01	6	63-3/4	7.71	8.3	857
1974						
1st	0.29	(17)	53-5/8	7.62	7.0	847
2d	0.38	(24)	47-1/2	7.62	6.2	802
3d	0.40	(17)	19-1/4	7.64	2.5	608
4th	0.86	(15)	28-3/4	8.13	3.5	616
1975						
1st	0.29	0	37-1/4	8.10	4.6	768
2d	0.47	24	47-1/2	8.23	5.8	879
3d	0.52	30	36	8.40	4.3	794
4th	1.12	30	34-7/8	9.04	3.9	852
1976						
1st	0.40	38	42-5/8	9.04	4.7	999
2d	0.59	26	47-1/4	9.18	5.1	1,003
3d	0.63	21	47-7/8	9.36	5.1	990
4th	1.28	14	49-1/2	10.15	4.9	1,005

*4th quarter data are actual; data for the first three quarters of each year are estimated.

through the exercise of stock options. During this period Avon's enormous overvaluation was never utilized to the advantage of Avon's shareholder group via the value-transfer techniques outlined in Chapter 2. The valuation spotlight dimmed considerably at Avon before the firm's management acted (at least at the *corporate* level) to capitalize on this valuation error.

It was not until late in 1975 (when Avon's share price was well under $50 per share) that Avon's management announced a plan to acquire another firm for Avon stock. On December 5, 1975, Avon announced that it had entered into a preliminary agreement to acquire the common stock of Monarch Capital Corp. (a life insurance firm) for about $120 million in market value of a new Avon convertible preferred stock. The proposed transaction represented Avon's first significant diversification via acquisition. Immediately following the announcement of Avon's plans, the market value of Avon's common shares declined by $300 million. One week later both firms announced the termination of merger discussions, stating that "the unexpected reaction of the stock market to the announcement of the agreement in principle has made further discussions unfeasible."[13] The announcement of the cancellation of the proposed merger did not precipitate any equivalent perceptible *rise* in the value of Avon's shares.

One might speculate that Avon's diversification attempt was perceived by investors as official acknowledgment that Avon's opportunities for internal growth in its traditional high-return product-market areas were declining. This was simply another way of saying that management, via the attempted diversification, may have signaled to investors a belief that Avon's stock was overvalued. The Monarch acquisition might have been beneficial in the long run for Avon's existing shareholder group. It probably would have fit the *value-transfer* criteria described in Chapter 2. Avon's dramatic break with its nonacquisition tradition, however, may have conveyed a clear message to investors. Given these circumstances, the act of attempting to capitalize on a value transfer opportunity might have been precisely the event that precipitated the disappearance of that value-transfer opportunity.

In any case it is clear that Avon's management was far more effective in *creating* value for its shareholders than in *transferring* value for its shareholders.

APPENDIX

Chapter 1 described a model that could be utilized to calculate the rational economic value of a firm's common stock. The model required as input:

---

[13] *The Wall Street Journal,* December 12, 1975.

1. The size of the percentage-point spread projected to be earned on common equity over the cost of the firm's common equity;
2. The volume of future capital-investment opportunities promising average rates of return equal to the level indicated in (1) above; and
3. The number of years during which the exceptional returns noted in (1) and (2) would continue to be available before these returns were forced to the level of the firm's cost of common equity by, for example, competitive pressures.

Avon had historically increased its net worth annually by an amount equal to 40 percent of the firm's net profits (Line 9, Column 4, Table 1–16). On average, the firm's investments produced an ROE of 32.1 percent (Line 7, Column 11, Table 3–3). Dealing with average figures is quite hazardous in the Avon example, however, since Avon was not able to increase its investment in the firm's product-market areas at a rate equal to 40 percent of average annual profit. A significant fraction of Avon's earnings retentions were invested instead in money-market instruments that produced very modest rates of return on equity.

When a nonfinancial corporation holds significant amounts of redundant capital (as evidenced by a portfolio of cash and marketable securities that greatly exceeds any outstanding borrowings), this redundant capital tends to *depress* the firm's apparent ROE and *overstate* the firm's apparent ability to invest capital in attractive projects as evidenced by the annual growth of its net worth in relation to reported profits.

One way to counteract the problem noted above in analyzing the product-market profitability of a firm is to reconstruct the firm's ROE. One can assume that cash and marketable securities in excess of amounts needed for normal operations are first used to repay all borrowed money and next used either to repurchase shares of the firm's common stock, or simply to pay dividends to shareholders. Naturally, when redundant capital is removed, the profits of the firm must be altered to reflect any interest expense saved, and any interest income forgone as a result of the elimination of both borrowed money and the excess marketable securities portfolio.

When the adjustment process described above is performed for Avon, the key financial-performance measures for the firm improve dramatically over the ratios presented in Table 3–3. In particular, Avon's average ROE during the period 1967–76 increases from 32.1 percent (Line 7, Column 11, Table 3–3) to 45.0 percent (Line 12, Column 11, Table 3A–1).

Table 3A–1 isolates the average profitability of Avon's product-market investments from the profitability of the firm's money-market investments. The ROE data of Table 3A–1 still have one major shortcoming, however. They are *nominal* ROE data. These data need to be adjusted further to produce *real* ROE data for use in the valuation model. This

TABLE 3A-1

Selected financial data needed to adjust Avon Products, Inc.'s ROE to reflect the removal of redundant capital, 1966–1976

Line	Year	(1) Cash and marketable securities ($ millions)	(2) Debt outstanding plus operating cash needs ($ millions)	(3) Redundant capital ($ millions)	(4) Net worth ($ millions)	(5) = (4)–(3) Net worth minus redundant capital ($ millions)	(6) Profit after taxes adjusted for debt paydown and redundant capital elimination ($ millions)	(7)	(8) Sales/ Assets ratio	(9) Profit/ Sales ratio	(10) Assets/ Equity ratio	(11) Profit/ Sales ratio
1	1966	81.4	31.5	49.9	149.3	99.6	54.3	—	2.09	0.133	1.96	0.546
2	1967	88.3	32.2	56.1	175.1	119.0	64.4	—	2.19	0.136	1.83	0.542
3	1968	112.0	47.6	64.4	201.9	137.5	70.3	—	2.10	0.126	1.94	0.511
4	1969	89.4	56.0	33.4	235.2	201.8	83.3	—	1.90	0.127	1.72	0.413
5	1970	110.8	68.3	42.5	274.3	231.8	97.9	—	1.91	0.129	1.72	0.422
6	1971	146.9	71.0	75.9	317.1	241.2	109.1	—	2.03	0.125	1.78	0.453
7	1972	183.5	68.0	115.5	379.1	263.6	123.8	—	2.08	0.123	1.83	0.470
8	1973	198.5	88.6	109.9	447.1	337.2	133.1	—	1.92	0.116	1.78	0.395
9	1974	180.6	87.3	93.3	471.6	378.3	110.2	—	1.93	0.087	1.73	0.291
10	1975	290.2	64.1	226.1	524.3	298.2	135.3	—	2.20	0.104	1.97	0.454
11	1976	362.3	69.8	292.5	589.4	296.9	162.4	—	2.26	0.113	2.13	0.547
12	1967–1976 Average	—	—	—	—	—	—	—	2.05	0.119	1.84	0.450
13	1966–1976 Average increase in adjusted-net-worth/average-annual-profits						0.181					
14	1971–1976 Average increase in adjusted-net-worth/average-annual-profits						0.084					

can be done for the year 1976 by simply adding the net worth adjustments found in Lines 18–23 of Table 1A–3 to the net worth data of Line 11, Column 5, Table 3A–1. The profit adjustments of Lines 14–17 of Table 1A–3 must similarly be subtracted from the profit data of Line 11, Column 6, Table 3A–1. This produces a *real* ROE for Avon in 1976 (absent redundant capital) equal to 0.279.

Determining Avon's *real* ROE after adjustment for redundant capital yields one of the three pieces of information required to determine an upper boundary for the rational economic value of a share of Avon's common stock in relation to the firm's adjusted book value. The next step is to determine Avon's *real* cost of equity capital assuming the firm were to disgorge its redundant capital.

A paydown of debt by utilizing some of Avon's cash and marketable securities, coupled with the removal of Avon's redundant capital (via dividends or share repurchases), would, of course, change Avon's financial risk.[14] Since a change in Avon's financial risk would change the β of Avon's common stock, Avon's cost of equity capital would obviously change as a result of any change in the firm's capital structure. The relationship between the β of an unleveraged firm and the β of that same firm with a leveraged capital structure is:[15]

$$\beta^L = \beta^U \left[1 + \frac{D}{E}(1 - T) \right],$$

where

β^L = the beta of a leveraged firm with a debt ratio equal to D/E,
β^U = the beta of the same firm assuming no debt,
D/E = the debt-to-equity ratio of the firm,
T = the corporate tax rate.

The equation above is equivalent to:

$$\beta^U = \frac{\beta^L}{\left[1 + \left(\frac{D}{E} \right) \left(1 - T \right) \right]}$$

Were Avon to disgorge its "negative leverage" (that is, the amount of cash and marketable securities in excess of its debt plus normal operating

---

[14] A reduction in Avon's cash and marketable securities might also increase Avon's *business* risk since cash and marketable securities usually have low market covariability.

[15] Mark E. Rubinstein, "A Mean-Variance Synthesis of Corporate Financial Theory," *Journal of Finance,* vol. 28, March 1973.

This equation implicitly assumes that the market value of a firm's common stock is increased by the discounted value of the tax savings associated with tax deductibility of interest payments on debt.

cash requirements), the firm's debt-to-equity ratio would *increase* from $\dfrac{-292.5}{2552}$ to zero.[16] The β of Avon's common stock would *increase* (as shown by the calculation below) from 1.25 to 1.33:

$$\beta^U = \frac{\beta^L}{1 + \left(\dfrac{D}{E}\right)\left(1 - T\right)}$$

$$= \frac{1.25}{1 + \left(\dfrac{-292.5}{2552}\right)\left(0.50\right)}$$

$$= 1.33.$$

With a β of 1.33, Avon's *real* cost of equity capital in 1976 would, according to the calculation below, rise to 11.7 percent:

$$K_e = R_f + \beta(K_m - R_f)$$
$$= 0.001 + 1.33\,(0.088 - 0.001)$$
$$= 0.117.$$

Once Avon's *real* ROE and its *real* cost of equity capital have been determined (assuming the elimination of the firm's redundant capital), one fact remains. Before an upper boundary for the rational economic value of a share of Avon's common stock (in relation to the firm's adjusted book value) can be determined, an estimate is needed of the volume of future capital investment opportunities (offering real average ROEs of 27.9 percent) that Avon can expect in the future.

Over the period 1966–76 and over the period 1971–76, Avon annually expanded its net worth (adjusted for the removal of redundant cash and marketable securities) by an amount equal to 18.1 percent and 8.4 percent of adjusted annual profits, respectively (Lines 13 and 14, Column 7, Table 3A–1). If the real ROE, capital cost, and reinvestment performance of Avon in 1976 could be continued for 30 years in the future, the rational economic value of an Avon share would range from 2.6 to 3.1 times the adjusted book value (with redundant capital eliminated) of the firm's common stock at December 31, 1976.

---

[16] The figure $-292.5 relates to the amount of Avon's redundant capital that is held in the form of cash and marketable securities (Line 11, Column 3, Table 3A–1). The figure of $2,552 million relates to the market value of Avon's common stock at December 31, 1976 (Line 9, Column 1, Table 1–11) less the $292.5 million of redundant capital. Note that debt and equity in the calculation of Avon's capital structure are taken at their *market* values rather than their *book* values.

$$4 \quad | \quad \begin{array}{l} \text{VALUE} \\ \text{CREATION} \end{array}$$

The grocery retailing industry

Chapter 1 identified four Hall of Fame grocery retailers. The firms were Lucky Stores, Winn-Dixie, the Dillon Companies, and Weis Markets (Table 1–9, Lines 26–29). These firms had consistently enjoyed rates of return on equity that exceeded 15 percent over the ten year period 1966–75. Their rates of return on equity also exceeded their cost of equity. Unlike the high-ROE drug and consumer products firms noted in Table 1–9, the four grocery firms noted above had no important proprietary products. Further, none of the four firms enjoyed *national* dominance of the grocery retailing industry. Indeed, they ranked 5, 6, 16 and 31, respectively, in terms of national grocery sales in 1976.[1]

Since the most profitable grocery retailers lack the distinguishing characteristics that are often associated with high-ROE firms, it might be useful to try to identify the factor or factors that *do* contribute to high rates of return in grocery retailing. This would provide some insight into the one or more ways in which successful grocery retailers have *created value* for their shareholders. The identification of the key profitability variables in grocery retailing requires some understanding of both the evolution and the market structure of this industry.

Grocery retailing in the post–World War II era has been marked by three distinct trends. *First*, the industry has consolidated into fewer and larger corporate entities. Chain stores, retailer-owned cooperatives, and wholesaler-sponsored voluntary groups have all significantly increased

---

[1] *Progressive Grocer*, April 1977, pp. 126, 130.

TABLE 4-1
Distribution of grocery store sales 1945–1975

Type of retailer	Percentage of grocery store sales			
	1945	1955	1965	1975
Chain	35	36	42	50
Cooperative and voluntary groups*	30	39	49	44
Unaffiliated independents	35	25	9	6
Total	100	100	100	100

*In an effort to protect their markets, some wholesalers became partially integrated with their retail customers. Many independent retailers joined this trend because it promised the advantages of large-scale buying and merchandising. Arrangements between wholesalers and independents have assumed two basic forms: the retailer-owned cooperative food wholesaler and the wholesaler-sponsored voluntary retail group. Groups of independents so affiliated with a particular wholesaler commonly are referred to as voluntary or cooperative groups or chains.
Source: *Progressive Grocer*, April 1976, p. 76.

their national market shares at the expense of unaffiliated independents. Unaffiliated independents saw their market share decline from 35 percent to 6 percent (Table 4–1).

Within the chain-store category, The Great Atlantic & Pacific Tea Company (A&P) showed a dramatic loss of market share at the national level after 1954 (Line 1, Table 4–2).[2] Other chains in the top 20 made consistent and substantial gains in their market shares (Lines 2–6, Table 4–2).[3]

Second, the average size of retail grocery outlets has grown substantially during the post–World War II period. The average selling space in newly constructed supermarkets more than doubled between 1953 and 1976 as shown in Table 4–3.

The transformation of the distribution channels in grocery retailing

---

[2] In Chapter 8 we will explore the efforts of A&P's management to reverse this trend with the WEO price reduction program, which was put in place nationally at A&P in early 1972.

[3] A&P was, until 1973, the largest U.S. grocery retailer. In 1973, A&P was overtaken by Safeway Stores, Inc.

As unaffiliated independents have disappeared, the share of market achieved by chain stores has begun to level out. Buzzell et al. note the following factors as contributing to this result:

"First, independents through affiliation with cooperative or voluntary wholesalers have gained the staff services and, in many instances, even the financial muscle formerly available only to the chains. Secondly, independents are not as frequently unionized as the chains. This situation may result in somewhat lower wage rates. Such differences are important, particularly in the operation of the consumer-desired and labor-intensive service departments. In addition, the lack of union restrictions for independents may result in greater flexibility in hours of operation."

(Robert D. Buzzell et al., "The Consumer and the Supermarket—1980," a study sponsored by Family Circle and the National Association of Food Chains, 1976, p. 24.)

TABLE 4-2
National market share of the 20 largest U.S. grocery chains, 1948-1975

Line	Rank of chains	1948	1954	1958	1963	1967	1972	1975
1	A&P.	10.7%	11.3%	11.1%	9.4%	8.3%	6.6%	4.9%
2	Other chains in top four . .	9.4	9.6	10.6	10.6	10.7	11.5	13.0
3	5th to 8th largest chains . .	3.6	4.5	5.8	6.6	6.7	7.1	7.6
4	9th to 20th largest chains. .	3.2	4.5	6.6	7.4	8.7	11.9	11.5
5	Top 20 largest chains	26.9%	29.9%	34.1%	34.0%	34.4%	37.1%	37.0%
6	Top 20 largest chains, excluding A&P	16.2%	18.6%	23.0%	24.6%	26.1%	30.5%	32.1%

Source: Joint Economic Committee, Congress of the United States, *The Profit and Price Performance of Leading Food Chains, 1970-1974*, p. 11.

TABLE 4-3
Median size of selling area in newly constructed supermarkets, 1953-1976

Year	Median area (sq. ft.)
1953	9,400
1958	13,100
1963	13,000
1967	14,000
1972	17,600
1976	20,400

Source: Super Market Institute, Inc., "Facts About New Supermarkets Opened in [1953, 1958, 1963, 1967, 1972, 1976]."

toward large-volume outlets has been quite pronounced. In 1948, only 12 percent of national grocery store sales were made in stores selling more than $1 million per year. By 1972, 72 percent of all national grocery sales occurred in stores with annual sales volumes of $1 million or above (Table 4-4).

Third and finally, as the grocery retailing industry was consolidating at the *national* level, it was also consolidating at the *city-market* level. The most rapid increase in city-market concentration appears to have taken place in the early post–World War II period. Unfortunately, consistent data covering the period from 1945 to 1975 are not available. In selected individual city markets for which fragmentary data are available, however, the increase in concentration in grocery retailing between 1948 and 1954 is noteworthy. It amounted to almost seven percentage points in only six years (Table 4-5).

More complete and consistent data covering the period 1954 to 1972 show a continuation of the increase in concentration of local markets (Table 4-6), but the increase is certainly less dramatic than that shown

TABLE 4-4

Number of grocery stores in operation and percentage of total U.S. retail grocery sales
made in stores ranked by size (1948, 1958, 1967, 1972)

Size	Number of stores	Percentage of industry sales
1948		
Store sales of:		
$5,000,000 and above	24*	1*
$1,000,000 to $4,999,000	1,887*	11*
$300,000 to $999,000	11,557	26
less than $300,000	312,733	62
Total	326,201	100
1958		
Store sales of:		
$5,000,000 and above	96	2
$1,000,000 to $4,999,000	10,236	44
$300,000 to $999,000	17,461	23
less than $300,000	215,003	31
Total	242,796	100
1967		
Store sales of:		
$5,000,000 and above	455	5
$1,000,000 to $4,999,000	18,540	56
$300,000 to $999,000	21,480	20
less than $300,000	168,015	19
Total	208,490	100
1972·		
Store sales of:		
$5,000,000 and above	1,687	13
$1,000,000 to $4,999,000	23,307	59
$300,000 to $999,000	22,206	14
less than $300,000	131,179	14
Total	178,379	100

*Estimated.

Note: The index of food prices measured in constant 1948 dollars is as follows: 1948 = 1.00, 1958 = 1.15, 1967 = 1.23, 1972 = 1.48. To a modest extent the upward shift in volume per store simply reflects inflation.

Source: U.S. Department of Commerce, Bureau of the Census, Census of Retail Trade, 1948, 1958, 1967, 1972.

in the earlier period. It took *18 years* to increase the average four-firm concentration level by seven percentage points between 1954 and 1972.

Scale economies at the store and city-market levels

The increasing *size* of retailing outlets and the increasing *concentration* of city-markets in grocery retailing was the inevitable outgrowth of the appearance of scale economies at both the individual-store and city-market levels. Once automobile use became widespread in the United States, larger grocery stores became more cost-efficient. The trend toward increased efficiency in the marketplace is apparent from the following statistic. About 150,000 selling units disappeared between 1948 and 1972 (Table 4–4) as larger stores replaced smaller, less efficient outlets.

TABLE 4–5
Market share of leading grocery chains in selected metropolitan areas, 1948 and 1954

	Percentage of food store sales	
Metropolitan area	1948	1954
Altoona, Pa., top two chains	29.8	41.4
Atlanta, Ga., top four chains	43.7	43.1
Denver, Colo., top two chains	21.1	26.8
Indianapolis, Ind., top three chains	30.8	37.5
Manchester, N. H., top two chains	37.4	40.1
Peoria, Ill., top three chains	24.2	31.6
Phoenix, Ariz., top two chains	20.9	33.1
Roanoke, Va., top two chains	21.7	32.0
Spokane, Wash., top two chains	22.4	26.0
Stockton, Calif., top three chains	12.5	10.9
Utica-Rome, N. Y., top four chains	18.2	34.6
Average (unweighted)	25.7	32.5

Source: U.S. Federal Trade Commission, *Economic Report on the Structure and Competitive Behavior of Food Retailing*, January 1966, p. 7.

Expense data for some of the earliest supermarkets opened in the late 1930s demonstrate rather dramatically the influence of scale economies at the *individual store* level. As shown in Table 4–7, operating expenses in relation to sales for the largest supermarkets in one A&P division in 1938 were about seven percentage points below the average level of operating expenses for all of A&P's stores, the bulk of which were not supermarkets and therefore achieved far lower weekly sales volumes.[4]

TABLE 4–6
Average four-firm concentration in food retailing for 194 SMSAs, 1954–1972

Year	Four-firm concentration level
1954	45.1%
1958	49.2
1963	50.0
1967	50.7
1972	52.1

Note: Standard Metropolitan Statistical Areas (SMSAs) generally contain one central city of 50,000 or more inhabitants, plus the surrounding metropolitan area. SMSAs are usually, but not always, geographically coextensive with the county surrounding the SMSA's core city. Approximately 70 percent of all retail sales take place in SMSAs.
Source: Joint Economic Committee, Congress of the United States, *The Profit and Price Performance of Leading Food Chains, 1970–1974*, p. 16.

[4] In 1938 only 6.1 percent of A&P's total sales were made in stores large enough to be described as supermarkets, although practically any large self-service store was called a supermarket in the 1930s. As indicated in Table 4–7, even stores with only $4,100 in weekly sales were designated as supermarkets by A&P in 1938. The generally accepted definition of a supermarket in 1977 is a departmentalized food store with sales of at least $1 million per year.

TABLE 4–7

Analysis of A&P's expense rates (all stores, 1937, and Central Western supermarkets, 1938; in percentage of sales)

Item	All A&P stores, 1937	All A&P supermarkets, Central Western Division, 1938, average sales per store per week ($ thousands)				
		$4.1	$6.1	$8.4	$12.4	$17.5
Clerks' salaries	3.76%	3.52%	3.41%	3.55%	3.53%	3.44%
General branch.	2.70	2.13	1.72	1.53	1.57	1.84
Advertising	0.60	1.04	0.80	0.85	0.70	0.80
Handling and delivery . .	2.51	1.16	1.16	1.01	0.98	0.96
Rent and write-off. . . .	1.39	2.44	1.78	1.55	1.23	1.10
Managers' salaries	4.75	2.53	1.75	1.32	1.10	0.74
Total*	15.71%	12.82%	10.62%	9.81%	9.11%	8.88%

*Does not include an allocated charge for supervision and administration.

Source: Adelman, M.A., *A&P: A Study in Price-Cost Behavior in Public Policy* (Cambridge, Mass.: Harvard University Press, 1959), p. 60.

Scale economies are equally apparent at the level of *city-markets*. These scale economies come in areas such as advertising and warehousing. Newspapers are the primary vehicle for grocery store advertising. Since newspaper advertising generally has to be purchased in units that are geographically equivalent to an entire city, the grocery retailer with a large market share in a city advertises more efficiently than the grocery retailer with a smaller market share. As a result, in cities where a grocery retailer controlled a large market share, the chain could achieve the desired market coverage necessary to remain competitive with the expenditure of a smaller fraction of its revenues on advertising. The relevant data for one grocery retailer are shown in Table 4–8.

TABLE 4–8

Advertising expenses as a percentage of sales versus average market share for various branches of The National Tea Company, 1958

Branch	Advertising/Sales Ratio		Average market share
Indianapolis	1.20%		24.9%
Denver	0.82	6-city average = 0.99%	20.0
Chicago.	0.95		16.6
Sioux City	1.06		14.8
Minneapolis	1.21		13.3
New Orleans.	0.75		11.5
St. Louis	1.39		10.2
Kalamazoo.	1.13	6-city average = 1.37%	8.3
Davenport	1.52		7.2
Milwaukee	1.30		7.0
Memphis	1.44		5.1
Detroit	1.45		5.1
All branches	1.14%		

Source: U.S. Federal Trade Commission, *Economic Report on the Structure and Competitive Behavior of Food Retailing*, January 1966, p. 96.

The average expenditure on advertising between the six divisions with the highest market shares and the six divisions with the lowest market shares in the example above differed by 0.38 percentage point.[5] The significance of the spread is apparent only when one recognizes that pretax profit margins on sales in grocery retailing usually range between 1 percent and 2 percent. Scale economies in advertising *alone* can thus have a very substantial impact on a grocery retailer's ROE.

Profitability versus local-market share

Cost efficiencies such as those in advertising at the city-market level translate directly into added contribution margins.[6] Indeed, as shown in Table 4–9, for one large national grocery retailer that was closely studied in the late 1950s, the relationship between the profit contribution of stores in specific city-markets and the chain's share of market in those same city-markets was startling. In referring to these data, the FTC's chief economist stated, "I have never seen a closer relationship between the market dominance of a firm in an individual market, or group of markets, and its profitability. . . ."[7]

Alternative expansion strategies

The response of chain grocery retailers to the changing economics of their business was quite predictable. In the early post–World War II era, chains began aggressively to build their market positions. Expansion pro-

---

[5] If advertising allowances were netted out, this spread would drop from 0.38 percentage point to 0.28 percentage point. If both advertising allowances and trading-stamp expenses were netted out, the spread would rise to 0.45 percentage point.

[6] The contribution margin data of Table 4–9 do not include warehouse and corporate overhead expenses, which generally averaged around 2 percent per year.

[7] U.S. Federal Trade Commission, In the Matter of National Tea Company, Docket 7453, Findings as to the Facts, Conclusions and Order, March 4, 1966, p. 57.

The relative importance of scale economies versus market power in the linkage between grocery-chain profitability and local-market share has been the subject of long and heated debate. A recent study (noted as the data source for Table 4–2) suggested that "monopoly overcharges" (that is, revenues earned from price levels above those likely to prevail in fully competitive markets, which price levels were made possible by a high concentration in local markets) may have equaled $662 million for the four largest firms in each SMSA during the year 1974. The evidence presented in support of this conclusion was not compelling. Rebuttal arguments can be found in the "Statement of Dr. Ray A. Goldberg before the Joint Economic Committee," Congress of the United States, March 30, 1977. For our present purpose it is not critical to determine whether the profit enhancement linked to high local-market share stems from scale economies or market power. For the moment we need only focus on the fact that local market share is an important profit variable. We will consider some of the social-welfare implications of the market power issue later, in Chapter 10.

TABLE 4-9

Profit contribution versus city-market share for the National Tea Company's
operations in 399 cities, 1958

City-market share (percent)	Profit contribution as percentage of sales	Number of cities in data base
35.0 and over	6.5	29
25.0 to 34.9%	5.5	44
20.0 to 24.9%	5.7	47
15.0 to 19.9%	4.0	55
10.0 to 14.9%	3.7	83
5.0 to 9.9%	1.6	93
4.9 and under	(2.3)	48
		399

Source: U.S. Federal Trade Commission, In the Matter of National Tea
Company, Docket 7453, Findings as to the Facts, Conclusions and Order,
March 4, 1966, p. 54.

gressed both internally and through acquisitions. Some chains, such as
the National Tea Company, had *national* ambitions. They embarked on
expansion strategies (including numerous acquisitions) that quickly pro-
pelled them into toehold positions in a large number of widely dispersed
city-markets across the country. National Tea's president articulated his
goals during the 1950s quite clearly:

> While National Tea Company now operates in only 18 states, we are
> looking forward to the 48. . . .
>
> . . . Our future is pin-pointed on the map—it is just a question of how far
> and how fast we can move—always, of course, living within our means
> for best operating results.
>
> . . . This is my aim [   ]. We plan to cover the United States like a
> book.[8]

Having achieved a truly national market position, National Tea would
then be able to turn its attention to building up its toehold positions in
individual city-markets.

National Tea's strategy represented a rapid dash for national coverage. Winn-Dixie, another fast-growing chain, adopted a quite different
strategy. Using both acquisitions and internal growth, Winn-Dixie drove
for *deep* market penetration in a limited geographic region. The acquisition histories of National Tea and Winn-Dixie, as well as some other
active acquirers during the period 1948–63, are presented in Table 4–10.

Government intervention into retail grocery mergers

The intensity of the merger activity in grocery retailing and the rapid
concentration of individual city-markets ultimately attracted the interest

---

[8] U.S. Federal Trade Commission, In the Matter of National Tea Company,
Docket 7453, Findings as to the Facts, Conclusions and Order, March 4, 1966,
pp. 10–11.

TABLE 4–10
Sales growth and acquisition acitivity of selected retail grocery chains, 1948–1963

Line		Sales ($ millions)		Number of grocery firms acquired 1948-1963	Sales volume of grocery firms acquired ($ millions) 1948-1963	Sales volume acquired as a percentage of total sales growth 1948-1963
		1948	1963			
1	National Tea.	$270	$1,057	36	$584	74%
2	Kroger	825	2,102	12	312	24
3	Winn-Dixie.	79	831	19	254	34
4	Allied Supermarkets .	20	397	10	168	46
5	First National Stores .	354	723	3	167	45
6	Grand Union.	116	667	22	162	29

Sources: U.S. Federal Trade Commission, *Economic Report on the Structure and Competitive Behavior of Food Retailing*, January 1966, p. 165; and Moody's Industrial Manual, 1964.

of the U.S. Federal Trade Commission in the late 1950s. In March 1959, the FTC filed a complaint against National Tea charging that certain of the firm's acquisitions violated antitrust laws. For about two years, the threat posed by this suit reduced the enthusiasm of the ten largest grocery retailers for additional acquisitions (Column 3, Table 4–11). Once these firms regained their resolve, the pace of acquisition activity among the ten largest grocery retailers began to pick up. Perhaps in response to this trend, in January 1962 the FTC filed *another* suit, this time against Grand Union (Line 6, Table 4–10).

In 1963, FTC hearing examiners recommended that the Commission drop the actions against National Tea and Grand Union for lack of evidence. In each case the Commission overruled the recommendation of its hearing examiner and proceeded with the complaint.

In June 1965, Grand Union settled the FTC complaint by entering into a consent decree that, among other things, prohibited further grocery store acquisitions for ten years. In early 1966, the FTC found that several of National Tea's acquisitions had violated Section 7 of the Clayton Act. The firm was prohibited from making any further food store acquisitions for a period of ten years without FTC approval.

By the mid-1960s, the FTC had clearly reduced the acquisition activity of the *larger chains*, although the pace of *total* grocery store acquisitions continued unabated. After 1965, the ten largest grocery chains (which had previously led the merger parade) were no longer able to participate meaningfully (Columns 3 and 4, Table 4–11).

Those firms, such as National Tea, that had opted to gain toehold positions in numerous (but geographically scattered) city-markets found themselves in economically untenable positions. They were precluded from acquiring their way into viable city-market positions. Instead, they had to fight their way up via internal growth.

TABLE 4-11

Acquisition activity of the ten largest grocery retailing firms (versus that of all manufacturing and mining firms and all food retailers), 1949-1974

Year	(1) Total assets of acquired manufacturing and mining firms ($ millions)	(2) Annual sales of food retailers acquired by all firms ($ millions)	(3) Annual sales of food retailers acquired by ten leading food chains ($ millions)	(4) = (3) ÷ (2) Sales of food retailers acquired by ten leading food chains as percentage of total sales of all acquired food retailers
1949	89	66	47	71
1950	186	4	1	25
1951	202	28	19	68
1952	374	71	53	75
1953	779	88	61	69
1954	1,445	76	31	41
1955	2,169	559	267	48
1956	1,882	450	141	31
1957	1,202	319	170	53
1958	1,070	517	261	50
1959	1,432	319	24	8
1960	1,535	307	36	12
1961	2,003	518	292	56
1962	2,251	306	157	51
1963	2,536	568	416	73
1964	2,303	312	153	49
1965	3,254	558	35	6
1966	3,329	539	73	14
1967	8,259	1,350	0	0
1968	12,580	1,155	199	17
1969	11,043	498	13	3
1970	5,904	688	22	3
1971	2,460	435	28	6
1972	1,886	1,236	3	0
1973	3,149	206	11	5
1974	4,471	1,591	14	1

Sources: Joint Economic Committee, Congress of the United States, *The Profit and Price Performance of Leading Food Chains, 1970-1974*, p. 20; U.S. Federal Trade Commission, *Statistical Report on Mergers and Acquisitions*, November 1976, p. 93.

The more attractively positioned chains, such as Winn-Dixie, had already achieved deep individual city-market penetration by 1966. Winn-Dixie could thus enter into a consent decree in 1966, secure in the knowledge that its competitive position was economically sound.[9] Indeed, the fruits of Winn-Dixie's superior strategy have been visible for decades, as the ROE data presented below suggest.

			ROE			Average local-market share*	
Firm	1955	1960	1965	1970	1975	1958	1972
Winn-Dixie	22.8%	23.0%	22.1%	18.7%	19.0%	17.2%	16.2%
National Tea . . .	13.5%	10.5%	8.9%	6.1%	(7.1)%	8.6%	8.9%

*Data for 1958 are the weighted average share of food-store sales in those counties where each firm operated. The source of the 1958 data is: U.S. Federal Trade Commission, In the Matter of National Tea Company, Docket 7453, Findings as to the Facts, Conclusions, and Order, March 4, 1966, p. 5. Market share data for 1972 include only those sales for each chain in 153 SMSA's. The 1972 data are unweighted. For these reasons, comparisons should be made only across the *firms* within a specific year, and not across the *years* for a specific firm. The source of the 1972 data is: Joint Economic Committee, Congress of the United States, *The Profit and Price Performance of Leading Food Chains, 1970–1974,* March 1977, p. 38.

In terms of value creation for its shareholders, Winn-Dixie's strategy has been extraordinarily successful. By way of contrast, the ambition to be a national force in grocery retailing caused National Tea to stretch itself thinly in too many markets simultaneously. This was a strategic error that we will see repeated in the 1970s by another retailer, the Levitz Furniture Corporation (Chapter 9).

The links among city-market share, profitability, and value creation

The importance of city-market share to profitability in grocery retailing has endured for decades.[10] It continues to be critical in the 1970s, and

---

[9] Winn-Dixie entered into a consent decree with the FTC on September 14, 1966. The agreement prohibited Winn-Dixie from acquiring any retail grocery stores in the United States for a period of ten years without the prior approval of the FTC.

[10] It should be noted that grocery-chain executives in their public comments generally resist the notion that profitability is linked to local-market share. For example, Mr. W. S. Mitchell, president of Safeway Stores, Inc., was asked the following question while testifying before the Joint Economic Committee of the U.S. Congress on December 17, 1974: "Is there a direct relationship between the market position of food chains and their profitability?" Mr. Mitchell's response was:

This is a difficult question to answer because we don't know of any reliable measure of "market position" and therefore have nothing to measure "profitability" against. (Most of the published measures of so-called "market shares" seem to be based either on some consumer popularity survey or on some arbitrary allocation related to number of store outlets.) . . .

nothing on the horizon suggests that this factor will lose importance in the future. A recent study (based on financial data from 68 operating divisions of 11 grocery chains during the period 1970–74) linked profit margins to (*a*) market share and (*b*) market concentration within local markets. The relationship is depicted in Figure 4–1.

Figure 4–1 reflects a significant refinement in the statistical arguments that link profitability to local-market share. The relationship between profitability and local-market share is so strong, however, that it emerges fairly clearly even when market-by-market data are aggregated and become total *firm*-performance data. For example, data are publicly available that make it possible to define, crudely,[11] an average city-market

FIGURE 4–1

Estimated profit/sales ratio for various levels of local market share and local market concentration ratios based on data for 1970, 1971. and 1974

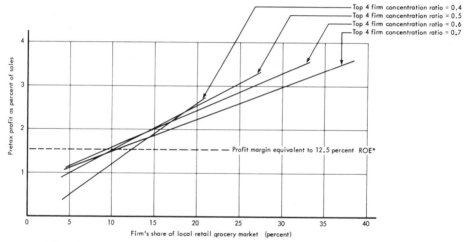

* Based on 1975 data relating to the operating results and financial structure of the supermarket industry, a pretax profit margin of 1.55 percent would produce a 12.5 percent after-tax return on net worth. The data source for this information is Supermarket Institute, *1975 Annual Financial Review*, 1976, pp. 7–9.

Source: Joint Economic Committee, Congress of the United States, *The Profit and Price Performance of Leading Food Chains, 1970–1974*, March 1977, p. 56.

. . . Within any given area, we may very well have stores ranging the whole spectrum in sales and profits. That is, two stores in the same city may have entirely different operating results even though both are on the same price structure and have similar facilities. We think this situation could well reflect differences in local management abilities, customer make-up, location accessibility, and numerous other factors.

11 The definition is called "crude" for several reasons. First, the data include only 153 SMSAs for the year 1972. Thus, not all of the cities in which each of these chains operate are represented. Second, the data are unweighted. Thus, in computing the average market share for a specific firm, each of the 153 SMSAs in which the firm operates counts equally, regardless of the total sales significance of that market to the firm.

TABLE 4–12
Profitability versus average city-market share for selected retail grocery chains—1975

Line		(1) Sales ($ millions)	(2) Average city-market share	(3) Nominal returns earned in excess of equity capital costs	(4) Market-value/Book-value ratio	(5) Market value minus book value ($ millions)
1	Dillon Companies.	969	0.183	0.093	3.3	184
2	Safeway Stores	7,917	0.172	0.056	1.5	378
3	Winn-Dixie Stores.	2,962	0.162	0.053	2.7	503
4	Giant Foods.	832	0.149	(0.014)	0.6	(28)
5	Weis Markets.	369	0.137	0.024	1.4	31
6	Lucky Stores	3,109	0.129	0.063	2.7	387
7	Stop & Shop.	1,360	0.112	0.003	0.7	(27)
8	A&P	6,538	0.099	(0.110)	0.6	(184)
9	Kroger	4,803	0.090	(0.072)	0.6	(180)
10	National Tea.	1,472	0.089	(0.231)	0.5	(44)
11	Jewel	2,818	0.086	(0.064)	0.8	(69)
12	Grand Union.	1,611	0.072	(0.051)	0.6	(72)
13	Supermarkets General	1,550	0.071	(0.060)	0.6	(32)
14	Fisher Foods.	1,380	0.068	(0.001)	0.9	(9)
15	Albertson's.	1,271	0.066	0.040	1.8	73
16	Allied Supermarkets	1,049	0.063	(0.277)	0.4	(23)

Sources: Column 1 — *Progressive Grocer*, April 1977, p. 130.
Column 2 — Joint Economic Committee, Congress of the United States, *The Profit and Price Performance of Leading Food Chains, 1970–1974*, p. 38. Data for the Dillon Companies and Weis Markets are for the year 1975 and were derived from *Distribution Study of Grocery Store Sales in 264 Cities*, Fairchild Publications, Inc., 1977.
Column 3 — Derived from 1975 data according to the procedure followed in Column 8, Table 1–10.
Columns 4 and 5 — Compustat data for December 31, 1975.

share for 16 large grocery chains (Column 2, Table 4–12). Seven of these 16 chains produced average ROEs over the ten-year period 1966–75 that exceeded their estimated costs of equity capital in 1975. Nine of the chains did not meet this test (Column 3, Table 4–12). With one exception in each category, those firms with average city-market shares *above* ten percent consistently earned rates of return that exceeded their 1975 equity capital costs, while those firms with lower average city-market shares consistently earned rates of return *at or below* their 1975 equity capital costs.

The superior performance of the high-ROE firms is clearly reflected in the market-value/book-value relationships of their common stocks. Those firms included in Table 4–12 with average local-market shares exceeding 10 percent enjoyed market values more than $1 billion higher than their underlying book values at December 31, 1975 (Column 5, Lines 1–7, Table 4–12).

Many factors are obviously important in the overall profitability of retail grocery chains. Price, quality, store size, convenience, service, degree of unionization of the work force,[12] and management are all important variables that immediately come to mind. Nonetheless, one variable that consistently emerges as preeminent in the profit equation of grocery retailing is local-market share. Firms that have perceived the importance of this variable and achieved high local-market shares have been generally successful in *creating value* for their shareholders (Columns 4–5, Table 4–12). Firms that have ignored the importance of this variable, or have been unable to achieve high local-market shares have, in general, met with less success in value creation.

---

[12] Some indication of the influence of the degree of unionization in a grocery retailer's workforce on costs is noted in recent testimony before a Congressional committee. "One reliable industry source estimates that 55 percent of the 20 percent gross margin cost is labor cost and the nonunion differential in the form of restrictions, benefits and pensions would amount to 1 percent on sales difference between [union and nonunion] operations." (Statement of Dr. Ray A. Goldberg before the Joint Economic Committee, Congress of the United States, March 30, 1977.)

all economies of scale are local

↳ can get economies of scale simply by being dense.

Key: Newspaper advertising is impt.

Because truckloads everyday you don't need big shipmts or storage space.

VALUE
CREATION

Freeport Minerals Company

After five years of relatively low profitability, in 1964 the U.S. sulphur industry entered a period of tightening supplies and rising prices. Freeport Minerals Company,[1] the largest U.S. sulphur producer, enjoyed sharply increased profitability as this trend progressed through 1968 (Column 6, Table 5–1). During this period a number of firms, including Freeport, made substantial investments aimed at increasing their sulphur production in response to rising demand. In addition to its expansion in the sulphur industry, Freeport also embarked on a major diversification program to reduce the company's dependence on sulphur, a product that accounted for nearly 90 percent of the company's sales in the mid-1960s.

During the mid-1960s, Freeport was financially well positioned for significant diversification. The company was in a highly liquid financial position (Column 1, Table 5–1) and had essentially no debt in its capital structure (Column 2, Table 5–1). The price of its stock was also rising sharply through 1967 (Column 8, Table 5–1). While Freeport was anxious to capitalize on its strong financial position, the firm hoped to diversify through internal means rather than through acquisitions. Unfortunately, for a number of years the firm had been unable to find attractive investment opportunities that were large enough to absorb even a fraction of its available financial resources. In 1967, however, Freeport faced an opportunity to invest a significant amount of capital in developing a copper mine in Indonesia.

---

[1] In 1971 the Freeport Sulphur Company changed its name to the Freeport Minerals Company. The latter name will be used throughout this chapter.

TABLE 5-1
Financial position, profitability, and market valuation data of Freeport Minerals Co., 1956–1969

	(1) Cash and marketable securities ($ millions)	(2) Borrowed money ($ millions)	(3) Other liabilities ($ millions)	(4) Net worth ($ millions)	(5) Total liabilities and net worth ($ millions)	(6) Profit after tax/Net worth (%)	(7) Dividend payout ratio (%)	(8) Market value of equity ($ millions)	(9) Market value/Book value of equity
1954	9	0	15	51	66	19.9	60	170	3.3
1955	19	0	17	65	82	19.2	53	228	3.5
1956	19	0	17	71	88	18.9	56	236	3.3
1957	7	0	18	76	94	17.0	58	176	2.3
1958	70*	0	15	149*	164	8.8	57	248	1.7
1959	67	0	13	154	167	9.4	63	199	1.3
1960	64	0	63	141†	204	9.4†	68	235	1.7
1961	58	0	66	145	211	8.9	71	210	1.4
1962	59	0	33	149	182	8.6	71	172	1.2
1963	51	0	18	157	175	8.2	71	266	1.7
1964	54	0	61	166	227	9.2	60	341	2.1
1965	51	0	30	179	209	12.1	57	478	2.7
1966	63	8	35	196	239	16.4	51	593	3.0
1967	47	7	60	208	275	15.5	60	1,122	5.4
1968	43	7	56	227	290	17.8	54	683	2.0
1969	51	6	57	231	294	12.3	87	320	1.4

*In 1958, Freeport's cash and net worth grew dramatically as a result of the cash sale of the company's oil and gas interests for nearly $100 million.
†In 1960, Freeport wrote off its investment in subsidiaries located in Cuba. Profit data exclude the effect of this extraordinary charge.
Sources: Freeport Minerals Co. Annual Reports; *Bank and Quotation Record.*

Investigating the Indonesian copper mining opportunity

Two events combined to create this investment opportunity. First, in 1960 Freeport had confirmed[2] the existence of a major body of copper ore at an extremely inaccessible location in the Ertsberg, a mountain in Indonesia. At that time, however, the political climate in Indonesia was not attractive to foreign investment, as a pro-Communist government was in power. By early 1967, a change in the political climate in Indonesia prompted further investigation of the copper ore body. Second, the price of copper in world markets had risen by the mid-1960s (Table 5–2) to the point where mines that could not be developed economically at previous price levels were becoming economically more attractive.

Given these changes, Freeport moved to investigate fully the Ertsberg opportunity. The period between late 1967 and July 1968 was devoted to drilling and to analyzing the extent of the deposit. By July 1968, Freeport had determined that the Ertsberg contained 33 million tons of ore with an average copper content of 2.5 percent[3] and significant traces of gold and silver.

TABLE 5–2
Refined copper prices
(London Metal Exchange,
1955–1969)

Year	Price (¢/lb)
1955	43.9
1956	41.1
1957	27.4
1958	24.8
1959	29.8
1960	30.8
1961	28.7
1962	29.3
1963	29.3
1964	44.0
1965	58.6
1966	69.1
1967	51.2
1968	56.0
1969	66.3

---

[2] The ore body was actually discovered by a young petroleum geologist on a mountain-climbing expedition in 1936. The geologist's findings were published in Holland in 1939, but created no interest until the managing director of the East Borneo Co. received an exploration permit from the Indonesian government in 1959. At that point Freeport was contacted for financial and technical assistance in carrying out the exploration.

[3] The copper content of ores from U.S. mines usually ranged from 0.4 percent to 1.2 percent. In some African mines the copper content averaged as high as 3.0 percent.

At this point, the Bechtel Corporation (an engineering and construction firm) was asked to determine the cost and feasibility of establishing a mine site at an elevation of 9,200 feet in an uninhabited area separated from water transportation facilities by 39 miles of rain forest and 24 miles of precipitous mountain terrain. In December 1969, Bechtel reported that the proposed mining venture could be operational by the end of 1972, with a total development cost of $120 million.[4] At the mining rate projected, the ore body was expected to last for 13 years. The Ertsberg deposit was sufficiently rich in copper that production costs were expected to be among the lowest in the world.

The economics of the proposed venture

In evaluating the profitability of the proposed Indonesian mine, Freeport's management assumed that refined copper prices would probably not fall below an average of 40¢ per pound and would probably substantially exceed this figure. Indeed, over the prior 15 years, refined copper prices had averaged 42.9¢ per pound, and in the prior five years had not fallen below 50¢ per pound (Table 5–2). World copper consumption had continued to expand rapidly in the mid-1960s (Line 8, Table 5–3) in spite of significant price increases that were necessary to bring forth more production of ore from marginal mines. This situation caused reduced inventories of refined copper, increased use of copper scrap in the production of refined copper, and increased interest in new sources of copper ore.

At an assumed price of 40¢ per pound for refined copper, the Ertsberg investment promised to produce the cash flows shown in Table 5–4. When these cash flows were discounted at 15 percent and 20 percent (rates believed to be roughly consistent with the level of risk[5] in the proj-

---

[4] This estimate included construction costs escalated for anticipated inflation, an allowance for contingencies, interest and insurance during construction, organizational and pre-operating costs, and $4.5 million of working capital.

[5] The economics of the Ertsberg investment opportunity were examined throughout the 1968–69 time period. The beta coefficients of the common stocks of the four largest (but relatively undiversified) U.S. copper producers averaged 0.98 during this period. The interest rate on three-month Treasury bills averaged 5.9 percent over this period. According to the logic followed in Chapter 1, these data imply a nominal cost of equity capital equal to 14.4 percent for the average firm involved in domestic copper mining in the late 1960s. This is calculated as follows: $K_e \doteq R_f + \beta$ $(K_m - R_f)$ when $R_f = 5.9$; $\beta = 0.98$; and K_m equals the real rate of return demanded by investors on equity capital (8.8 percent) plus the anticipated rate of inflation (5.8 percent) embedded in the T-bill rate. While calculating an estimated cost of equity capital for the average firm involved in copper mining might be helpful in establishing a benchmark for the Ertsberg project, differences in the operating risk and financing risk at Ertsberg versus the average copper mining firm makes such comparisons a bit hazardous. For that reason, 15 percent to 20 percent was chosen by the author as an acceptable range for the estimated cost of equity capital committed to the Ertsberg project.

TABLE 5-3
World copper consumption and production by smelter location and origin of ore (000 tons)

Line		1963	1964	1965	1966	1967	1968	1969
	World copper consumption							
1	USA	1,580	1,683	1,855	2,240	1,595*	1,707*	1,914
2	Japan	339	504	471	532	679	766	888
3	West Germany	535	628	610	541	548	681	728
4	United Kingdom	615	698	717	653	567	594	603
5	All other free world	1,408	1,565	1,593	1,639	1,481	1,594	1,749
6	Total free world	4,477	5,078	5,246	5,605	4,870	5,342	5,882
7	Soviet sphere	850	955	955	1,010	1,070	1,122	1,211
8	Total world	5,327	6,033	6,241	6,615	5,940*	6,464*	7,093
	World copper production by smelter location							
9	USA	1,393	1,418	1,521	1,580	930*	1,352*	1,678
10	Zambia	637	704	767	656	698	732	775
11	Chile	615	647	615	667	695	687	713
12	Japan	325	377	403	446	518	605	694
13	West Germany	334	371	394	414	422	477	441
14	Canada	361	398	422	410	478	499	431
15	Zaire	298	305	318	349	352	359	401
16	All other free world	710	712	730	846	851	928	947
17	Total free world	4,673	4,932	5,170	5,368	4,944	5,639	6,080
18	Soviet sphere	752	858	903	968	1,050	1,108	1,185
19	Total world	5,425	5,790	6,073	6,336	5,994	6,747	7,265
	World copper production by origin of ore							
20	USA	1,208	1,251	1,356	1,408	950*	1,203*	1,535
21	Zambia	648	710	767	687†	731	755	793
22	Chile	662	685	645†	701	728	726	758
23	Canada	462	487	510	508	603	633	573†
24	Zaire	298	305	318	349	353	358	399
25	All other free world	967	961	969	1,098	1,084	1,168	1,242
26	Total free world	4,245	4,399	4,565	4,751	4,449	4,843	5,300
27	Soviet sphere	723	818	867	927	1,009	1,077	1,160
28	Total world	4,968	5,217	5,432	5,678	5,458	5,920	6,460

Note: Some countries with copper mines exported the ore to be smelted and refined elsewhere.
*Between July 15, 1967, and March 30, 1968, the U.S. copper producers were on strike. Copper mining, smelting, and consumption was cut significantly during this period.
†Production was interrupted in Chile in 1965, in Zambia in 1966, and in Canada in 1969.
Source: *Yearbook of the American Bureau of Metal Statistics, 1970.*

TABLE 5-4
The Ertsberg investment opportunity: Calculated cash flows ($ millions, assuming future world copper prices equal 40¢ per pound)

Line		1969	1970	1971	1972	1973	1974	1975	1976	1977	1978	1979	1980	1981	1982	1983	1984	1985	Total
	Sales																		
1	Copper*	—	—	—	—	52.0	52.0	52.0	52.0	52.0	52.0	52.0	52.0	52.0	52.0	52.0	52.0	52.0	676.0
2	Gold†	—	—	—	—	2.4	2.4	2.4	2.4	2.4	2.4	2.4	2.4	2.4	2.4	2.4	2.4	2.4	31.2
3	Silver‡	—	—	—	—	1.2	1.2	1.2	1.2	1.2	1.2	1.2	1.2	1.2	1.2	1.2	1.2	1.2	15.6
4	Total sales	—	—	—	—	55.6	55.6	55.6	55.6	55.6	55.6	55.6	55.6	55.6	55.6	55.6	55.6	55.6	722.8
5	Mining and milling costs §	—	—	—	—	6.2	6.2	6.2	7.5	7.5	7.5	7.5	7.5	8.8	8.8	8.8	8.8	8.8	100.1
6	Smelting, refining, freight, and misc.	—	—	—	—	14.3	14.3	14.3	14.3	14.3	14.3	14.3	14.3	14.3	14.3	14.3	14.3	14.3	185.9
7	Operating profits	—	—	—	—	35.1	35.1	35.1	33.8	33.8	33.8	33.8	33.8	32.5	32.5	32.5	32.5	32.5	436.8
8	Depreciation and amortization	—	—	—	—	8.9	8.9	8.9	8.9	8.9	8.9	8.9	8.9	8.9	8.9	8.9	8.9	8.7	115.5
9	Earnings before interest and taxes	—	—	—	—	26.2	26.2	26.2	24.9	24.9	24.9	24.9	24.9	23.6	23.6	23.6	23.6	23.8	321.3
10	Taxes @ 40% ||	—	—	—	—	10.5	10.5	10.5	10.0	10.0	10.0	10.0	10.0	9.4	9.4	9.4	9.4	9.5	128.6
11	Profit after tax	—	—	—	—	15.7	15.7	15.7	14.9	14.9	14.9	14.9	14.9	14.2	14.2	14.2	14.2	14.3	192.7
12	Depreciation and amortization	—	—	—	—	8.9	8.9	8.9	8.9	8.9	8.9	8.9	8.9	8.9	8.9	8.9	8.9	8.7	115.5
13	Cash flow from operations	—	—	—	—	24.6	24.6	24.6	23.8	23.8	23.8	23.8	23.8	23.1	23.1	23.1	23.1	23.0	308.2
14	Return of working capital #	—	—	—	—	0	0	0	0	0	0	0	0	0	0	0	0	4.5	4.5
15	Total cash return	—	—	—	—	24.6	24.6	24.6	23.8	23.8	23.8	23.8	23.8	23.1	23.1	23.1	23.1	27.5	312.7
16	Total cash investment	7.5	18.9	42.5	51.1	—	—	—	—	—	—	—	—	—	—	—	—	—	120.0

Net present value of cash flows (Lines 15 and 16)
| 17 | Discounted at 15% . . . . ($1.1) million |
| 18 | Discounted at 20% . . . . ($19.0) million |

*130 million lb. copper @ 40¢
†68,000 oz. gold @ $35
‡0.75 million oz. silver @ $1.65
§During the first three years of mining operations, costs were expected to be relatively low as a significant portion of the copper ore at Ertsberg was covered with very little overburden (non-ore-bearing material). Conventional open-pit mining at slightly higher cost would be undertaken in the middle years of the mine's life. More expensive underground mining would not be necessary until the latter years of mine operation.
|| For simplicity a 40 percent tax rate has been assumed. Indonesia granted tax concessions that made the Indonesian tax rate substantially lower than 40 percent. Additional taxes, reduced to some extent by statutory depletion allowance, would be incurred by Freeport Minerals Co. in the United States however.
#Of the $120 million in capital originally budgeted for the project, $4.5 million was for working capital.
Sources: Wall Street institutional research reports; Freeport Minerals Co. 10K Report to the SEC, 1969.

TABLE 5-5
The Ertsberg investment opportunity: Sensitivity analysis

Copper price (¢/lb)	Total investment ($ millions)	Net present value ($ millions) of cash flows at discount rate of 15%	20%
40	180	(35.9)	(51.6)
40	120	(1.1)	(19.0)
60	180	20.9	(10.9)
60	120	50.9	17.7

ect), the net present value of the project was determined to be −$1.1 million and −$19.0 million, respectively (Lines 17 and 18, Table 5–4). Single-point estimates of investment returns, while useful, were also quite limited. Indeed, given the hostility of the physical terrain at Ertsberg and the volatility of past copper prices, a sensitivity analysis regarding project returns was essential. The sensitivity of the investment returns to (a) changed copper price assumptions and (b) changed mine development cost assumptions is shown in Table 5–5.

As suggested by the net-present-value data, the economics of the Ertsberg project showed promise only if copper prices were assumed to average more than 40¢ per pound over the life of the project. In addition, the project carried with it some unusual risks. Not the least of these risks was the possibility of future expropriation, a problem that Freeport had experienced first-hand in the recent past.

After operating in various segments of the mining industry in Cuba for 30 years, Freeport had all of its Cuban-based assets expropriated by the Castro government in 1960. The expropriated investments included an almost-completed nickel-cobalt mining project at Moa Bay. Freeport had an equity investment of $19 million in the project, six steel and automobile companies had loaned the project $25.3 million, and nine U.S. banks had loaned the project $61.5 million. All of the project loans had been made without recourse to the Freeport parent company credit. Freeport had to write off its $19 million equity investment as a result of the expropriation, and the lenders wrote off their $86.8 million in loans as well.[6]

Negotiating a financing plan

The 1960 experience in Cuba made Freeport wary of large mining ventures in less developed and politically unstable areas of the world. This

---

[6] Freeport was able to write off (for tax purposes) *all* of the Cuban assets that were expropriated, not just its *equity interest* in these assets. As a result, Freeport was in the rather unique and enviable position of having turned a devastating event (the expropriation) into a significant economic benefit.

consideration alone would have *eliminated* any possibility that Freeport might have undertaken the Ertsberg project solely on Freeport's own credit. Fortunately for Freeport, by 1969 the governments of numerous industrialized nations had designed programs of credit guarantees to stimulate the export of products of domestic companies or to assure long-term sources of raw materials supply to domestic companies. Indeed, it was only a matter of days prior to the date that Freeport started looking for lenders to finance the Ertsberg project that the U.S. government signaled its interest in guaranteeing development loans to projects in Indonesia, apparently in an effort to support that country's new pro-Western government.

Government guarantee programs made it possible for the Freeport Minerals Co. to insulate itself from much of the risk (both operating and political) inherent in the proposed Indonesian venture. This solved only a part of Freeport's problem with the Ertsberg investment, however. Another problem related to the basic economics of the project. At an assumed 40¢ per pound copper price the project simply did not make economic sense unless Freeport's financing included some capital-cost subsidy.

By late 1969, Freeport had tentatively negotiated an extremely complex financing package for the Ertsberg project that solved both the problems of Freeport's risk-exposure, and the problem of the project's marginal economics at a copper price of 40¢ per pound.

Specifically, Freeport Minerals Co. formed a new Delaware corporate subsidiary, Freeport Indonesia, Inc. (FI), to undertake the mining venture. To induce FI to contract to sell two thirds of the mine output to a consortium of Japanese smelters,[7] the consortium agreed to lend FI $20 million in subordinated debt at an interest rate equal to 8.4 percent. This rate was equivalent to the actual cost incurred by the consortium in borrowing the funds made available to FI. The loan would be repayable at the rate of $3.3 million per year between 1975 and 1980 (Column 4, Table 5–6). The Export-Import Bank of Japan guaranteed the repayment of this loan.

A comparable lending arrangement was worked out with a German buyer. In exchange for a contract in which FI agreed to sell one third of the Ertsberg copper output to a German smelter, this buyer induced a German bank to lend FI $22 million of senior debt at 7 percent interest. This loan was repayable between 1974 and 1982 in escalating installments

---

[7] The ore mined at Ertsberg was expected to contain 2.5 percent copper. Prior to shipment, this ore would be upgraded to 30 percent contained copper. At this stage the copper concentrate would be sold to both the Japanese and German buyers, based on the value of contained copper, at prices essentially equivalent to those quoted on the London Metal Exchange for refined copper less prevailing world prices for smelting, refining, and transportation.

TABLE 5-6

The Ertsberg investment project: Proposed capital takedown plan and contractual loan principal repayment schedule ($ millions)

	(1)	(2)	(3)	(4)	(5)	(6)
	Senior debt			Junior debt	Equity	
	Insurance companies	U.S. banks	German bank	(Japanese ore buyers)	(Freeport Minerals Co.)	Total
Capital takedown						
1969	—	—	—	—	7.5	7.5
1970	6.7	3.1	2.4	6.3	0.4	18.9
1971	17.1	7.6	8.2	5.6	4.0	42.5
1972	16.2	7.3	11.4	8.1	8.1	51.1
Total . .	40.0	18.0	22.0	20.0	20.0	120.0
Loan principal repayment						
1974	—	7.2	0.7	—	—	7.9
1975	0.9	6.4	1.4	3.3	—	12.0
1976	2.2	4.4	2.1	3.3	—	12.0
1977	7.1	—	2.1	3.3	—	12.5
1978	6.3	—	2.8	3.4	—	12.5
1979	5.9	—	3.2	3.4	—	12.5
1980	5.9	—	3.3	3.3	—	12.5
1981	5.9	—	3.2	—	—	9.1
1982	5.8	—	3.2	—	—	9.0
Total . .	40.0	18.0	22.0	20.0	—	100.0

Source: Freeport Minerals Co., 10K Report to the SEC, 1969.

(Column 3, Table 5-6). The loan to FI was guaranteed by the Federal Republic of Germany.

Why the Japanese and German governments were prepared to offer such attractive terms to Freeport should be clear from Table 5-3. Japan and Germany were both large consumers of refined copper, and large smelters and refiners of copper concentrate (Lines 2, 3, 12, and 13 of Table 5-3). Neither country had any significant domestic source of copper ore, however. Since all of the large copper-exporting countries generally chose to concentrate and smelt their ore and export refined copper rather than copper concentrate (Lines 10, 11, 14, 15, and 21-24 of Table 5-3), Japanese and German smelters were somewhat frantic in the late 1960s to secure sources of copper concentrate in order to enable them to keep their smelters and refineries operating.

Of the $120 million needed to complete the Ertsberg project, $42 million was tentatively negotiated overseas; the remaining $78 million was arranged in three separate domestic transactions. A group of U.S. banks agreed to advance FI $18 million, repayable between 1974 and 1976 (Column 2, Table 5-6) at an interest rate ½ percent over the prime lending rate. Repayment of this senior bank debt was guaranteed by an agency of the U.S. government, the Export-Import Bank. The guarantee was possible because FI agreed to purchase $18 million of U.S. manufactured equipment for use in the project.

A group of U.S. insurance companies agreed to lend FI $40 million, repayable between 1975 and 1982 (Column 1, Table 5–6), at 9¼ percent interest.[8] Repayment of this senior debt was guaranteed by the Overseas Private Investment Corp.,[9] an agency of the U.S. government. The guarantee was possible because FI agreed to purchase $40 million of U.S. manufactured equipment for use in the project.[10]

Finally, FI was to be capitalized with $20 million of equity capital invested by Freeport Minerals Company. The Overseas Private Investment Corporation guaranteed Freeport Minerals' investment in FI against loss due to war, expropriation, and currency inconvertibility.

To protect Freeport Minerals, the Indonesian venture would be carried out by Freeport Indonesia, the new subsidiary. Freeport Minerals would not guarantee nor be responsible for FI's debt obligations.

Further to protect Freeport, the capital to be supplied by each party to the proposed $120 million financing would automatically increase in the event of a cost overrun by up to 20 percent on a pro-rata basis. Thus, the project could cost as much as $144 million before Freeport would have to worry about additional financing. The automatic financing of cost overruns of up to 20 percent of the project's anticipated cost was a novel and highly important part of the proposed financing. This feature greatly limited Freeport's potential exposure to cost overruns, and it also assured the availability of low-cost loans to the project in case cost overruns were experienced. Since Freeport Minerals offered the lenders no project-completion guarantee, the firm was also protected from an involuntary commitment of funds to finance overruns beyond 20 percent of the project's original anticipated costs.

The proposed financing package for the complex Ertsberg project is presented in simplified form[11] in Figure 5–1.

The value-creation process at Ertsberg

The outstanding business architect acts to create value for shareholders by operating in the areas of opportunity outlined in Chapter 2. The Ertsberg investment represents a very clear example of how value can be *designed* into a business investment. The enhancement in value

[8] The cost of the guarantee, 1¾ percent per year, raised the effective interest rate on this loan to 11 percent.

[9] At the time this guarantee was originally issued the guaranteeing agency was the Agency for International Development (AID). In 1971 AID's guarantee activity was taken over by the Overseas Private Investment Corporation (OPIC).

[10] This $40 million of U.S. purchases was in addition to the $18 million of U.S. purchases associated with the proposed bank borrowing.

[11] In fact, while Freeport Minerals provided essentially all of the equity capital invested in FI, Freeport Minerals actually owned only 87 percent of the equity in FI. For purposes of simplicity, all of the data in this chapter are presented as though Freeport Minerals owned 100 percent of the equity of FI at the outset of this investment.

FIGURE 5–1
Ertsberg copper mine investment project: Pictorial description of the loan guarantors, capital providers, and ore buyers involved

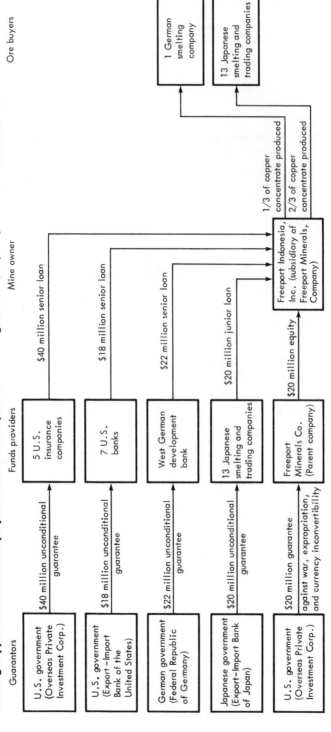

TABLE 5-7

The Ertsberg investment opportunity: Analysis of net present value
($ million)

Line		Discount rate*	
		15%	20%
1	Net present value of the cash flows associated with the *total* investment (Lines 17 and 18 of Table 5-4) . . . . .($ 1.1)		($19.0)
2	Net present value of the cash flows associated with the *equity investment* (Lines 14 and 15 of Table 5-8) $24.6		$12.1
3	Value created through the specific design of the transaction (Line 2—Line 1)† $25.7		$31.1

*The use of 15 percent to 20 percent as the relevant range of discount rates for the Ertsberg project is explained in Footnote 5.

†This calculation implicitly assumes that Freeport Minerals' equity investment in Freeport Indonesia would be exposed to a similar degree of risk under either the *all-equity* or the *high-leverage* alternatives for financing the Ertsberg project. The supporting logic for this assumption is presented in pp. 143-45. A more detailed discussion of risk adjustments associated with foreign capital investments can be found in Alan C. Shapiro, "Capital Budgeting for the Multinational Corporation," *Financial Management*, Spring, 1978.

built into the Ertsberg investment amounted to between $25 and $30 million as indicated in Table 5-7.

What is the source of this value creation? The economics of the Ertsberg project to Freeport Minerals were enhanced by:

a. the nonrecourse nature of the loans to FI;
b. government guarantees on loans to FI;
c. extremely high initial debt leverage in FI;
d. automatic financing of cost overruns up to 20 percent of the project's originally anticipated cost;
e. the absence of a project-completion guarantee from Freeport Minerals;
f. customer-supplied financing;
g. the involvement of several government guarantors, each of which was important to Indonesia's future development; and
h. life-of-mine contracts at LME prices.[12]

Table 5-8 (Lines 14–15) shows the economic effect of some of the above factors.

The conceptual basis of Freeport's investment analysis shifts in Table

---

[12] The contract prices actually were determined by reference to the price at which the principal copper producers in Chile and Zambia sold refined wirebars to major Western European fabricators in quantities under contracts for periods of one year or more. In fact, the producers in Chile and Zambia quoted, as their price, the official London Metal Exchange (LME) price for prompt delivery of electrolytic copper wirebars.

TABLE 5-8

Calculation of the cash flows (dividends) to Freeport Minerals Co. from Freeport Indonesia, Inc. assuming future world copper prices equal 40¢ per pound ($ millions)

Line		1969	1970	1971	1972	1973	1974	1975	1976	1977	1978	1979	1980	1981	1982	1983	1984	1985	Total
1	Earnings before interest and taxes*	—	—	—	—	26.2	26.2	26.2	24.9	24.9	24.9	24.9	24.9	23.6	23.6	23.6	23.6	23.8	321.3
2	Interest	—	—	—	—	8.9	8.9	8.3	7.4	6.1	4.6	3.0	1.4	0	0	0	0	0	48.6
3	Pretax profits	—	—	—	—	17.3	17.3	17.9	17.5	18.8	20.3	21.9	23.5	23.6	23.6	23.6	23.6	23.8	272.7
4	Taxes @ 40%	—	—	—	—	6.9	6.9	7.2	7.0	7.5	8.1	8.8	9.4	9.4	9.4	9.4	9.4	9.5	108.9
5	Profit after taxes	—	—	—	—	10.4	10.4	10.7	10.5	11.3	12.2	13.1	14.1	14.2	14.2	14.2	14.2	14.3	163.8
6	Depreciation and amortization	—	—	—	—	8.9	8.9	8.9	8.9	8.9	8.9	8.9	8.9	8.9	8.9	8.9	8.9	8.7	115.5
7	Cash flows from operations	—	—	—	—	19.3	19.3	19.6	19.4	20.2	21.1	22.0	23.0	23.1	23.1	23.1	23.1	23.0	279.3
8	Working capital changes†	—	—	—	—	19.3	(9.4)	(3.1)	(1.3)	0	0	0	(5.5)	0	0	0	0	4.5	4.5
9	Cash flow for debt repayments and dividends	—	—	—	—	0	28.7	22.7	20.7	20.2	21.1	22.0	28.5	23.1	23.1	23.1	23.1	27.5	283.8
10	Required debt repayment	—	—	—	—	0	7.9	12.0	12.0	12.5	12.5	12.5	12.5	0	0	0	0	0	81.9
11	Debt prepayment	—	—	—	—	0	0	0	3.0	3.9	4.3	4.8	2.1						18.1
12	Dividends‡	—	—	—	—	0	20.8	10.7	5.7	3.8	4.3	4.7	13.9	23.1	23.1	23.1	23.1	27.5	183.8
13	Cash investment (equity only)	7.5	0.4	4.0	8.1	—	—	—	—	—	—	—	—	—	—	—	—	—	—

Net present value of cash flows to equity (Lines 12 and 13)

14	Discounted at 15%	$24.6 million
15	Discounted at 20%	$12.1 million

*Data taken from Line 9, Table 5-4.

†$4.5 million of the $120 million capital investment in Freeport Indonesia, Inc., was to be used as working capital. Since under the various loan covenants dividends could not be paid unless net working capital was at least $10 million, $5.5 million of cash flow was retained and committed to net working capital as of December 31, 1974. Since the loans were entirely repaid by December 31, 1980, these covenants became inoperative and the $5.5 million of working capital not needed to support normal operations could be paid out in dividends.

‡Under various loan covenants no dividends could be paid until December 31, 1974. In addition, as outlined in footnote 15, under certain circumstances debt prepayments had to be made in conjunction with dividend payments.

Sources: Wall Street institutional research reports; Freeport Minerals Company 10K report to the SEC, 1969.

5–8. The focus is no longer on *total cash returns* and *total project invest-ment* as it was in Table 5–4 (Lines 15 and 16). The analysis focuses in-stead upon the *dividends* and *return of capital* that Freeport would ulti-mately realize from its investment, and Freeport's *capital at risk* (its equity investment) in the project (Lines 12 and 13 of Table 5–8). In effect, by its financing choice Freeport converted its ownership of oper-ating assets into a simple common-stock investment, thereby accepting only those liabilities consistent with common-stock ownership.

Freeport's actions to enhance the value of the Ertsberg project can be linked quite easily to the valuation formula presented in Chapter 2. As we think about dealing with each of the elements of this valuation form-ula, we might focus first on the numerator of the right-hand side of this equation.

$$\text{NPV} = \sum_{i=0}^{n} \frac{(\text{Revenues} - \text{Costs})_i}{(1 + k_0)^i}$$

Freeport locked in its customers with life-of-mine contracts at LME market prices. If Freeport produced the concentrate, Freeport's customers were required to accept it. Freeport would not be forced to reduce or suspend mining operations because of the lack of a market, or be forced to shade prices in order to flush out a buyer. For this reason Freeport's cash flow might sometimes be higher than that of an equivalently situated producer who lacked life-of-mine contracts at LME market prices. Free-port gave up little in entering these contracts,[13] but gained some modest value-creation benefits through the design of its customer contracts.

As we shift our attention from the *numerator* to the *denominator* of the valuation formula, the major value-creating design features of the Ertsberg project become apparent. The overall capital costs of a project are a function of leverage, the cost of debt capital, and the cost of equity capital as indicated in Chapter 2 and shown below.

$$k_0 = w_d k_d + w_e k_e,$$

where

k_0 = the weighted cost of capital,
k_d = the cost of debt (after tax),
k_e = the cost of equity (after tax),

---

[13] Freeport Indonesia may have given away one item of value in accepting these contracts that it could have retained in the absence of the contracts. FI represented to its customers (but did not guarantee) reasonably level production of copper ore at Ertsberg. As a practical matter, FI's life-of-mine contracts may have limited FI's operating flexibility in terms of the firm's ability to reduce the scale of its operations significantly (or temporarily cease operations entirely) during periods of unusually low copper prices.

w_d = the debt proportion in the capital structure,

w_e = the equity proportion in the capital structure.

In financing the Ertsberg project, Freeport was able to achieve $\frac{100}{120} =$ 83 percent initial debt financing. Absent government or Freeport Minerals Company guarantees, it is practically certain that the project, standing alone, could *not* have attracted any debt financing. The combined *project* and *sovereign* risks were simply too great. Government guarantees permitted the project to gain access to an extraordinarily large fraction of debt financing (at a very low cost, as we shall explore in a moment) thus greatly limiting Freeport's total capital exposure in the project. Since Freeport's equity investment was guaranteed against war, expropriation, and currency inconvertibility, Freeport retained only the operating, and not the sovereign, risk on its equity investment.

While government guarantees allowed Freeport Indonesia to leverage itself to an extraordinarily high degree, these government guarantees also created for Freeport an enormous capital-cost subsidy,[14] the magnitude[15] of which is indicated in Line 18 of Table 5–9. Instead of producing an after-tax cost that would be commensurate with a 15 percent to 20 percent overall capital cost for the entire project, the debt carried a rate that was more consistent with government borrowing (plus a modest insurance premium). The capital-cost subsidy on 83 percent of the total initial capital investment provided all[16] of the value creation indicated in Line 3, Table 5–7.

---

[14] FI was compelled (by the terms of the U.S. Export-Import Bank and OPIC loan guarantees) to purchase U.S. manufactured equipment costing $58 million for use at Ertsberg. FI may have had to pay a price premium over foreign manufactured equipment because of this requirement. If so, the capital-cost subsidy from the U.S. government guarantees may have been reduced somewhat.

[15] A complex set of dividend covenants required by the OPIC loan guarantor caused FI to have to *prepay* some of its debt if FI paid dividends that cumulatively exceeded an amount equivalent to a 15 percent rate of return on its original equity investment compounded over the period ending December 31, 1975. Once dividends totaling the allowed amount had been paid, FI had to prepay pro-rata (or FM had to substitute itself as guarantor for) $1 of FI's senior debt for each $1 of dividends paid by FI. The operation of these covenants is reflected in Lines 11 and 12 of Table 5–8. While the mandatory debt repayment schedule (Column 6, Table 5–6) was of primary importance in the value-creation area, these dividend covenants were also quite important. To the extent the lenders to FI received debt *pre*payments, the net present value of the project to Freeport Minerals was reduced. Indeed, the negotiations surrounding debt *pre*payments and dividend covenants may have been one of the few spots in the transaction where Freeport Minerals may not have extracted every drop of value-creation potential in the project.

[16] The other factors affecting the total value created are more difficult to quantify since they relate largely to changes in the level of risk to which Freeport's equity capital was exposed. In the example above, it is assumed that (*a*) the stabilization in cash flows produced by the customer contracts, (*b*) the probable willingness of customers to assist FI if the project got into financial difficulty, and (*c*) the reduced likelihood of (and compensation for) expropriation would *exactly offset* any added

TABLE 5-9

Freeport Indonesia, Inc.: Balance sheet, capital structure, and cost of capital

Line		1969	1970	1971	1972	1973	1974	1975	1976	1977	1978	1979	1980	1981	1982	1983	1984	1985
	Balance sheet																	
1	Net working capital	—	—	—	4.5	23.8	14.4	11.3	10.0	10.0	10.0	10.0	4.5	4.5	4.5	4.5	4.5	0
2	Plant and equipment	—	—	—	115.5	106.6	97.7	88.8	79.9	71.0	62.1	53.2	44.3	35.4	26.5	17.6	8.7	0
3	Total capital	—	—	—	120.0	130.4	112.1	100.1	89.9	81.0	72.1	63.2	48.8	39.9	31.0	22.1	13.2	0
4	Debt (11% interest rate)	—	6.7	23.8	40.0	40.0	40.0	39.1	34.9	25.2	16.1	7.2	0	—	—	—	—	—
5	Debt (7% interest rate)	—	5.5	21.3	40.0	40.0	32.1	24.3	16.8	13.4	9.1	4.1	0	—	—	—	—	—
6	Debt (8.4% interest rate)	—	6.3	11.9	20.0	20.0	20.0	16.7	13.4	10.1	6.7	3.3	0	—	—	—	—	—
7	Equity	7.5	7.9	11.9	20.0	30.4	20.0	20.0	24.8	32.3	40.2	48.6	48.8	39.9	31.0	22.1	13.2	0
8	Total capital	7.5	26.4	68.9	120.0	130.4	112.1	100.1	89.9	81.0	72.1	63.2	48.8	39.9	31.0	22.1	13.2	0
	Fractional weight in total capital structure†																	
9	Debt (11% interest rate)	—	0.254	0.345	0.333	0.307	0.356	0.390	0.388	0.311	0.223	0.114	—	—	—	—	—	—
10	Debt (7% interest rate)	—	0.208	0.309	0.333	0.307	0.286	0.243	0.187	0.165	0.126	0.065	—	—	—	—	—	—
11	Debt (8.4% interest rate)	—	0.239	0.173	0.166	0.153	0.178	0.167	0.149	0.125	0.093	0.052	—	—	—	—	—	—
12	Equity	1.000	0.299	0.173	0.167	0.233	0.178	0.200	0.276	0.399	0.558	0.769	1.000	1.000	1.000	1.000	1.000	—
13	Total capital	1.000	1.000	1.000	1.000	1.000	1.000	1.000	1.000	1.000	1.000	1.000	1.000	1.000	1.000	1.000	1.000	—
	Calculation of weighted average cost of capital†																	
14	Debt (6.6% after-tax cost)*	—	0.017	0.023	0.022	0.020	0.023	0.026	0.026	0.021	0.015	0.008	—	—	—	—	—	—
15	Debt (4.2% after-tax cost)*	—	0.009	0.013	0.014	0.013	0.012	0.010	0.008	0.007	0.005	0.003	—	—	—	—	—	—
16	Debt (5.0% after-tax cost)*	—	0.012	0.009	0.008	0.008	0.009	0.008	0.007	0.006	0.005	0.003	—	—	—	—	—	—
17	Equity (20% after-tax cost)	0.200	0.060	0.035	0.033	0.047	0.036	0.040	0.055	0.079	0.112	0.154	0.200	0.200	0.200	0.200	0.200	—
18	Total capital cost	0.200	0.098	0.080	0.077	0.088	0.080	0.084	0.096	0.113	0.137	0.168	0.200	0.200	0.200	0.200	0.200	—

* Assumes a 40 percent income tax rate.
† Utilizes book-value weights.
Sources: Tables 5–6 and 5–8.

Additional value may have been created for Freeport Minerals' share-holders since the cost of FI's equity capital was probably reduced by the design of the Ertsberg project. The equity risk (and thus the equity cost) is a function of three components: the risk-free interest rate, the business risk (operating and sovereign[17]), and the financing risk. As a result of the governmental guarantee of Freeport's equity against war, expropriation, and currency inconvertibility, the downside risk of ex-propriation was eliminated. Perhaps equally important, however, the risk of losing the upside potential of the investment through expropria-tion was also greatly reduced by the presence of loan guarantors who were both sovereign entities and important partners in the future eco-nomic development of Indonesia.

Both the timing of the Indonesian project and the physical location of the project were also important in reducing the expropriation risk. Since Freeport first confirmed the attractiveness of the Ertsberg ore body in 1960, the company had been carefully laying the groundwork for the possibility of an Indonesian investment. When the political climate was favorable and government loan guarantees became available, Freeport was first in line. Ertsberg thus became a showcase project for several of the parties to the transaction. From the standpoint of the Indonesian government, Ertsberg was the bell cow. It was designed to attract addi-tional investments into the country from other firms. Ertsberg's physical location in the remote province of Irian Jaya was also significant in reduc-ing the risk of expropriation. The project was unlikely to become highly politicized since it was essentially invisible to the bulk of the Indonesian population.

Finally, the financing risk associated with FI's high leverage was prob-ably reduced somewhat by the fact that some of the lenders to FI were also the project's customers. In the event of financial difficulty at Erts-berg, these lenders might be a good deal more accommodating than un-related lenders, since they could conceivably suffer significant operating problems themselves if the Ertsberg project failed for lack of adequate financing.

In short, excellent timing, design creativity, and a bit of good luck all

---

risk to equity capital produced by leveraging FI. In the text that follows, it is argued that these benefits may do even more in terms of value creation than simply offsetting the added financing risk.

[17] Advocates of modern portfolio theory generally part company with business practitioners on the issue of whether nonsystematic risk (that is, risk that affects a *single firm* without affecting the *market* as a whole) has any importance in deter-mining a firm's cost of equity capital. Modern portfolio theory rests on the assump-tion that nonsystematic risks (such as the risk of government expropriation) can be diversified out of an investor's portfolio, and therefore have no influence on the cost of a firm's equity capital. As Donaldson points out (Footnote 36, Chapter 1), business practitioners often make their investment decisions (and financial design decisions) in the belief that nonsystematic risk does indeed have an effect on the cost of equity capital.

helped to make the Ertsberg project economically viable. While the specifics of the Ertsberg project may have limited transferability outside of the mining industry, the basic principles involved are quite broadly based. Pipelines, oil tankers, aircraft, railroad rolling stock, shopping centers, and other commercial real estate properties have all been financed by utilizing one or more of the value-enhancing features present in the Ertsberg example. The important factor is that the outstanding financial architect, by examining the areas of value-creation opportunity present in a project (or a whole business) can sometimes accomplish a truly significant value transformation. In the Ertsberg example, the Indonesian nation received tax payments, added employment, and a "showcase" project designed to attract additional foreign investment; German and Japanese ore buyers received an assured source of copper ore (thereby protecting a large domestic smelter investment); and Freeport's shareholders enjoyed the opportunity to make an investment that, absent the $25 to $30 million of net-present-value benefits created through capital-cost subsidies, might not have been economically justifiable.

The aftermath—Freeport Indonesia, 1973–1977

Reality often diverges sharply from forecasts. The Ertsberg project is no exception. Before the project was complete, the plant and equipment expenditures at Ertsberg had outrun the original budget by almost 50 percent (Line 13, Table 5–10). Freeport Minerals and all of the project lenders increased their commitments by 20 percent. This brought Freeport Minerals' investment in FI up to $24 million. The balance of the financing need was funded out of the project's own cash flow in 1973 and 1974, thereby making it impossible to pay the dividend anticipated in 1974 (Line 9, Table 5–10).

Both capital and operating costs in the 1973–77 period escalated far beyond the expectations of 1969. On the other hand, in the 1973–74 period, copper prices in both current and constant dollars (Lines 2 and 3, Table 5–10) far exceeded the 40¢ forecast of 1969. Indeed, in 1974 the Ertsberg project earned four times the level of pretax profit anticipated at a 40¢ per pound copper price (Line 4, Table 5–10). By mid–1975, however, copper prices had fallen substantially from their previous highs. In addition, Freeport had concluded that the underground mining operations scheduled to commence in 1981 (Table 5–4, Note §) would be uneconomic at the copper prices prevailing in 1975. For this reason, depreciation charges were *doubled* in mid-1975 in order to fully depreciate Freeport's fixed assets as the remaining economically extractable ore was recovered through open-pit mining. Because of a substantial cash buildup and a shortening in the anticipated life of the mine, Freeport also began to *prepay* its lenders more rapidly than originally anticipated (Line 16, Table 5–10).

TABLE 5-10

Freeport Indonesia, Inc.: Actual versus forecast financial performance (1973–1976)

Line		1973 Forecast	1973 Actual	1974 Forecast	1974 Actual	1975 Forecast	1975 Actual	1976 Forecast	1976 Actual	1977 Forecast	1977 Actual
	Production and market data										
1	Copper shipments (millions of lbs)	130.0	77.3	130.0	142.4	130.0	136.9	130.0	151.2	130.0	124.0
2	Copper price (¢/lb)	40	81	40	93	40	56	40	64	40	59
3	Copper price (constant 1969 ¢/lb)		67		69		38		41		36
	Income statement data ($ millions)										
4	Profit before taxes and special depreciation charge*	17.3	23.5	17.3	69.3	17.9	13.6	17.5	20.7	18.8	2.2
5	Special depreciation charge*	0.0	0.0	0.0	0.0	0.0	6.1	0.0	18.5	0.0	15.6
6	Profit before taxes	17.3	23.5	17.3	69.3	17.9	7.5	17.5	2.2	18.8	(13.4)
7	Taxes	6.9	7.3	6.9	24.9	7.2	.6	7.0	(2.1)	7.5	(4.9)
8	Profit after tax	10.4	16.2	10.4	44.4	10.7	6.9	10.5	4.3	11.3	(8.5)
9	Dividends	0	0	20.8	0	10.7	10.1	5.7	4.8	3.8	0
10	Proceeds from sale of 8.5% of stock in FI	0	0	0	0	0	0	0	8.3	0	0
	Balance sheet data ($ millions)										
11	Marketable securities	13.8	6.9	4.4	47.4	1.3	19.1	0.0	9.9	0.0	6.5
12	Other net working capital	10.0	5.6	10.0	14.4	10.0	15.5	10.0	16.7	10.0	3.6
13	Plant and equipment	106.6	152.8	97.7	157.5	88.8	149.6	79.9	120.6	71.0	98.0
14	Total assets	130.4	165.3	112.1	219.3	100.1	184.2	89.9	147.2	81.0	108.1
15	Reserve for taxes	0.0	7.4	0.0	28.5	0.0	21.9	0.0	11.8	0.0	4.9
16	Debt	100.0	117.7	92.1	106.2	80.1	86.7	65.1	60.3	48.7	36.6
17	Equity	30.4	40.2	20.0	84.6	20.0	75.6	24.8	75.1	32.3	66.6
18	Total liabilities	130.4	165.3	112.1	219.3	100.1	184.2	89.9	147.2	81.0	108.1

*As noted on p. 146. In mid-1975 Freeport Indonesia doubled the rate of depreciation on ore mined at Ertsberg in order to depreciate fully all fixed assets at the time when reserves reachable by surface mining techniques were exhausted.

Sources: Forecast data are drawn from Tables 5–8 and 5–9; actual data are drawn from Freeport Minerals Co. Annual Reports and 10K Reports to the SEC.

In 1976, Freeport encountered encouraging indications of additional underground copper mineralization a short distance from the existing operation. This promised to extend the life of its mining investment. In the interests of conservatism, however, depreciation charges were maintained at double the original rate.

Also in 1976, the Indonesian government asked to acquire an investment in FI, and was sold 8.5 percent of the stock in FI for $8.3 million.[18] The net result of these capital transactions can be seen in Lines 9 and 10 of Table 5–10.[19]

Finally, for a number of months in 1977 copper prices fell to levels that in *real* terms had not been experienced since the 1930s. Freeport Indonesia suffered an after-tax loss of over $8 million in 1977 (Line 8, Table 5–10).

At year-end 1977 it was too early to tell whether the Ertsberg investment would ultimately prove to be an economic success for Freeport Minerals' shareholders. Indeed, by year-end 1977, Freeport had not even recovered its original cash investment in Freeport Indonesia, let alone any return on that investment. Were copper prices to remain indefinitely at the depressed levels of 1977, the Ertsberg would almost certainly not be an economic success. The success of the project and the value created by its financial design are quite separate issues, however. The purpose of this chapter was to demonstrate that systematic thinking about methods for enhancing the value of an investment project can have a significant payoff for shareholders. As shown in Table 5–7, the architectural skill brought to bear on the Ertsberg project enhanced its value by some $25 million to $30 million. In hindsight, this benefit may turn out to be inadequate to overcome the negative effect of present copper prices. Nonetheless this accomplishment stands as a reality quite independent of the Ertsberg's ultimate economic success.

---

[18] This implicitly placed a valuation of $97.5 million on 100 percent of the equity in FI, versus an original cash investment in FI which was equal to $24 million.

[19] As noted in footnote 11, Freeport Minerals actually owned only 87 percent of the equity in Freeport Indonesia prior to this stock sale transaction. The dividends and stock sale proceeds actually realized by Freeport Minerals in the first five years of FI's operation were thus:

	100% ownership ($ million)	Freeport Minerals' 87% share ($ million)
1975 Dividend	10.1	8.8
1976 Dividend	4.8	3.9
1976 Stock sale	8.3	6.8
1977 Dividend	0	0
Total	23.2	19.5
Original investment	24.0	24.0

VALUE
CREATION

General Electric Company

On May 20, 1970, the General Electric Company announced a plan to sell the major portion of its computer business to Honeywell, Inc.[1] The sale arrangement brought to a close an unsuccessful 14-year effort aimed at establishing GE in a major position in the main frame computer market.[2]

This chapter will explore why GE left the main frame computer business in 1970, and examine in detail the design of the firm's exit strategy. It will show how GE's management team *created value* out of a hopelessly uneconomic market position, a task that two other firms, RCA and Xerox, were unable to replicate in *their* later, rather inglorious exits from the main frame computer business. Our examination of GE's performance in the computer industry will begin with a brief review of the main frame computer industry in 1970. The chapter will show how GE was positioned in this industry in 1970, and what options the firm enjoyed with regard to future investments in the computer business. Finally the chapter will compare the success of GE's exit from the computer business to that of similar divestiture efforts by RCA and Xerox.

The main frame computer industry—1970

In 1970 the main frame computer manufacturing industry represented one of the most highly concentrated and one of the most profitable large

---

[1] GE retained the time-sharing and process-control segments of its computer business. In 1974, in a separate transaction, GE sold its process-control business to Honeywell.

[2] "Main frame" refers to the central processing units of a computer where numerical calculations are actually performed. This is distinct from input and output devices (peripheral equipment) such as card readers and tape drives.

industries in the United States. The IBM Corporation, as noted in Chapter 1, was the prime beneficiary of the success of this industry. IBM accounted for almost 70 percent of the industry's total shipments,[3] and practically all of the industry's profits. No other competitor in the industry in early 1970 had achieved a market share even one tenth the size of IBM's, as indicated in Table 6–1. This somewhat unusual disparity in market shares led IBM's competitors to be referred to in the trade, somewhat derisively, as the "Seven Dwarfs."[4]

The main frame computer industry in 1970 was made up of firms with widely varying degrees of commitment to computer manufacturing, as suggested in Table 6–1. IBM, as a highly focused firm, received almost all of its revenue from computer operations. Xerox, RCA, and GE, on the other hand, achieved less than ten percent of their annual revenue from computers.

As suggested by Table 6–2, the main frame computer manufacturing business had been extremely unprofitable for many years for most of the firms that attempted to compete across the board with IBM.[5] The poor performance achieved by these firms could be attributed to a number of factors. One of the more important such factors was scale diseconomies.[6] Scale diseconomies vis-à-vis IBM were particularly apparent in expenditures for research and development, an issue that will be explored later in the chapter.

---

[3] The issue of market definition and IBM's share of relevant markets, submarkets, and sub-submarkets in the electronic data processing (EDP) industry is the subject of considerable dispute. The share of market figure noted above is one that is commonly (although perhaps erroneously) used in the industry. It should be noted that IBM's market share varies dramatically according to one's definition of the "market," as indicated below:

	IBM Market Share	
Market Definition	1957	1972
Plaintiff's definition (9 companies)	83%	63%
Companies identified by Plaintiff as having manufactured general purpose digital computer systems	72%	49%
Top 100 EDP Companies deposed in Census	56%	37%
All EDP Companies deposed in Census	55%	32%

Source: *U.S.* v. *IBM*, 69 CV 200, Pretrial Brief for Defendant International Business Machines Corporation, January 15, 1975, p. 229.

[4] Xerox's share of the main frame computer industry was so small (Table 6–1) that it was not even included among the Seven Dwarfs.

[5] It should be noted that the extent of these losses was not made public by either GE or RCA prior to the sale of their computer operations. Indeed, GE's senior management wished to avoid the disclosure of these losses "if at all possible" (*U.S.* v. *IBM*, Plaintiff Exhibit 371A, p. 79).

Sperry Rand, Honeywell, GE, and RCA were considered to be broad-line manufacturers. Burroughs and NCR were somewhat specialized, while Xerox and Control Data were highly specialized.

[6] Other factors often cited were poor management, the alleged exercise of market power by IBM, and the existence of other entry barriers that prevented these firms from reaching a more efficient scale of operations.

TABLE 6-1

Corporate capital, revenue, market shares, and relative commitment to the computer industry of various competitors in the computer market in 1969

	Sales value of computers shipped ($ millions)	Market share in terms of sales value of computer shipments (percent)	Total corporate capital* ($ millions)	Total corporate revenue ($ millions)	Sales value of computers shipped as percentage of total revenues	Percentage of total earnings from computers
IBM	4,950	69.0	5,906	7,197	83	85
Sperry Rand	400	5.6	977	1,710	36	30
Honeywell	340	4.7	956	1,281	27	20
Burroughs	305	4.3	907	759	36	10
General Electric . .	290	4.0	3,554	8,448	3	loss
Control Data . . .	255	3.6	984	1,084	53	35†
RCA	230	3.2	1,875	3,222	7	loss
National Cash Register	195	2.7	1,104	1,255	16	loss
Xerox	75	1.1	1,099	1,483	8	8†
Others	130	1.8	—	—	—	—
Industry total, 1969. . . .	7,170	100.0				

*Includes short-term loans, long-term debt, and shareholders' equity.

†In 1970, these companies were reportedly sustaining a loss in their computer operations.

Sources: International Data Publishing Co., annual reports, and author's estimates.

TABLE 6-2
Profitability of computer operations of selected broad-line computer manufacturers

| Year | Profit after taxes— computer operations ($ millions) | |
	General Electric	RCA
1969	4.7*	(10.8)
1968	(11.4)	(13.6)
1967	(42.6)	(15.3)
1966	(55.8)	(12.9)
1965	(39.7)	(4.6)
1964	(14.3)	(1.3)
1963	(12.1)	(4.3)
1962	(10.8)	(10.6)
1961	(8.2)	n.a.[†]
1960	(4.0)	n.a.
1959	(3.4)	n.a.
1958	(3.4)	n.a.
1957	(3.3)	n.a.

*While GE's computer division's losses had turned into very modest profits by 1969, this improvement was somewhat deceptive since in 1970 the firm was poised for a costly new effort aimed at developing a fourth generation of computer equipment. If this development effort had been undertaken by GE, it would have quickly plunged GE's computer operations back into a loss position.

[†]n.a. = not available.

Sources: Honeywell, Inc. Proxy Statement, August 21, 1970, p. 9; *U.S.* v. *IBM*, Plaintiff Exhibit 380, p. 1; RCA Corporation Annual Report, 1971, p. 35.

Since scale diseconomies were such a very important element in the profitability equation for the broad-line manufacturers, practically all of them set as a corporate target the achievement of at *least* a 10 percent market share during the 1970s.[7] For example, RCA's president, Robert Sarnoff, stated publicly that "RCA is prepared to commit whatever resources are necessary to achieve the number two position in the industry . . ."[8]; and "[We plan to achieve] a 10 percent market share by the mid-nineteen seventies."[9] Similarly, GE's chairman, Fred Borch, felt

---

[7] Arguments about the size of scale economies in the data processing industry can be found in far greater abundance than hard economic evidence on the size of these economies. Gerald W. Brock has gathered some of the more persuasive data regarding the importance of scale economies in manufacturing, marketing, maintenance, and software development in his book entitled *The U.S. Computer Industry, A Study of Market Power* (Cambridge, Mass.: Ballinger Publishing Co., 1975), pp. 27–41.

[8] *Business Week*, September 19, 1970, p. 83.

[9] *The New York Times*, October 15, 1970.

that "GE needed 15 percent of the world market to keep from being at the mercy of sturdy competitors."[10]

The most cursory review of the computer manufacturing industry in 1970 reveals two seemingly irreconcilable facts. First, the broad line Dwarfs all planned to expand significantly their market shares. Second, it appeared that IBM's own plans left little room for the Dwarfs to achieve their aspirations. This was the reality of the computer industry in 1970.

GE's computer division in 1970

For GE the goal of reaching a 10 percent to 15 percent market share at some future date was not new. Indeed, in the early 1960s the goal of GE's computer division was to achieve a 10 percent share by 1970.[11] Toward that end, in April of 1964 GE purchased a 50 percent interest in a French manufacturer of medium-size computers with a sales volume exceeding that of GE's U.S. computer operations. In August of 1964, GE acquired a controlling interest in an Italian manufacturer of small computers with sales equal to about one third of the U.S. operation.[12]

> With Milan [Italy] building small computers, Paris [France] medium-sized ones, and Phoenix [GE's U.S. computer headquarters] the big machines—so the broad plan went—GE would mount a frontal assault on Fortress IBM and, by 1970, capture 10 percent of the exploding computer market.[13]

Sometime during the mid-1960s, after the company began realizing huge losses through its equity interest in the French affiliate, and after IBM had demonstrated tremendous market success with its third-generation System/360 line of computers, GE essentially abandoned its hope of achieving a 10 percent market share by 1970. The timing had been missed, and another opportunity would not be present until the technology for a new generation of computer equipment was in place. That moment of opportunity did not return until 1969. In 1969, prior to the introduction of a fourth generation of computer equipment, GE had a new opportunity to join a battle from which it had pulled back in 1966. In April 1969, the top management of GE's computer division formulated a battle plan that was designed to:

---

[10] *Fortune,* October, 1970, p. 156.

[11] *Forbes,* April 1, 1967, p. 22.

[12] GE presumably made its acquisitions overseas rather than domestically in order to avoid antitrust problems.

[13] *Fortune,* June 1, 1967, p. 92.

obtain 10 percent of the value of total new systems shipped in 1975 in the [rental price] range between $500 and $80,000 per month.[14]

In order to achieve this goal, six new computer models were to be introduced, with deliveries scheduled to commence in the third quarter of 1972. GE's computer planners estimated that to achieve their 10 percent market share goal, one third of GE's computer shipments would have to displace IBM systems, and that to displace these IBM systems GE would have to offer equipment with a "20–40 percent price/performance advantage over IBM's competitive offerings."[15]

If the objective of GE's computer division plans were *fully met*, the revenues, pretax profits, and cash-flow profile resulting from the program to develop, build, and market the machines would be as shown in Table 6–3.[16] The cumulative capital needs for the proposed investment peaked at $685 million in 1974, and cumulative pretax losses reached a maximum

TABLE 6-3

Fifteen-year profile of revenue, pretax profit and cash flow relating to GE's proposed investment in a new broad line of computers—April 15, 1969

	Annual data ($ millions)			Cumulative life cycle data ($ millions)		
	Revenue	Profit before taxes	Cash flow	Revenue	Profit before taxes	Cash flow
1969	0	(47)	(24)	0	(47)	(24)
1970	0	(89)	(45)	0	(136)	(69)
1971	50	(143)	(103)	50	(279)	(172)
1972	200	(159)	(182)	250	(438)	(354)
1973	470	(122)	(204)	720	(560)	(558)
1974	770	22	(127)	1,490	(538)	(685)
1975	1,000	203	53	2,490	(335)	(632)
1976	1,090	329	231	3,580	(6)	(401)
1977	1,080	413	317	4,660	407	(84)
1978	960	421	341	5,620	828	257
1979	800	401	284	6,420	1,229	541
1980	650	373	248	7,070	1,602	789
1981	480	312	180	7,550	1,914	969
1982	320	240	100	7,870	2,154	1,069
1983	210	122	80	8,080	2,276	1,149
1984	120	60	40	8,200	2,336	1,189

DCF internal rate of return = 17.4%

Source: *U.S.* v. *IBM*, Plaintiff Exhibit 322, pp. 8, 11, 13.

---

[14] This price range represented 91 percent of the total market based on the sales value of installed equipment. (*U.S.* v. *IBM*, Plaintiff Exhibit 353, p. 48.)

[15] Ibid., p. 53.

[16] The financial implications of what was described as the "base-case" strategy are presented in Table 6–3. GE also considered seven other alternatives to the "base-case" strategy, all of which were less ambitious in terms of revenue generation.

of $560 million in 1973. The investment promised a 17 percent discounted-cash-flow rate of return on investment over the full life cycle of the product generation.

On the other hand, if GE achieved more limited market success for its new line of computers, the consequences of this shortfall would come in the form of reductions in the anticipated positive cash inflows in years 1975–84. A marketing failure would not reduce the early cash *outflows* from the investment nearly as much as it would reduce the later cash *inflows*. This was true since development expenditures of $265 million would be incurred, and marketing and manufacturing expenditures exceeding $100 million would be incurred before GE shipped its first new computer system!

GE's corporate office in 1970

As GE's computer division was preparing its battle plan for the 1970s, GE's corporate headquarters was undertaking a review of its commitments in high growth–major loss markets. A "Ventures Task Force" consisting of GE's chief financial officer, its chief strategic planning officer, and its general counsel was established by GE's Chairman, Fred Borch, in October 1969. The task force's mandate was to review GE's potential in computers, nuclear power, and jet engines, areas in which the firm had made major new investment commitments in the recent past. The computer business was the first item on the task force's agenda. The need for this review was stated quite simply by a member of the Ventures Task Force.

> For the first time in our generation, at least, we face the necessity for an allocation of corporate resources which are not adequate to meet all of our readily identifiable needs—during a period when the Company is under special pressure to demonstrate its ability to grow earnings.[17]

The "special pressure" noted above stemmed from GE's rather uninspired profit performance in the years between 1963 and 1969 (Lines 3 and 10 of Table 6–4). In 1963, when Fred Borch took over as chairman of GE, sales, profits, and capital expenditures had been relatively flat for six years (Lines 1, 3 and 6 of Table 6–4). In an effort to get the company's growth on a trend line substantially steeper than the GNP, Borch began looking for markets with strong growth and profit potential. These markets had to be large enough to justify a substantial commitment of managerial resources, that is, ones in which GE could hope to achieve $1 billion in sales. Three businesses were finally selected that

---

[17] *U.S.* v. *IBM,* Plaintiff Exhibit 371A, p. 75.

TABLE 6-4
General Electric Corporation financial data 1957–1969

Line		1969	1968	1967	1966	1965	1964	1963	1962	1961	1960	1959	1958	1957
1	Sales ($ millions)	8,448	8,382	7,741	7,177	6,214	5,319	5,177	4,986	4,667	4,383	4,466	4,236	4,489
2	Increase in sales (%)	0.8	8.3	7.8	15.5	16.8	2.7	3.8	6.8	6.5	(1.9)	5.0	(5.6)	7.1
3	After-tax profit ($ millions)	278	357	361	339	355	220*	272*	257*	238	219	278	238	251
4	Dividends ($ millions)	235	235	234	235	217	198	183	178	176	176	174	174	173
5	Depreciation ($ millions)	351	300	280	234	188	170	149	146	132	125	124	128	123
6	Plant and equipment expenditures ($ millions)	531	515	562	485	333	238	149	173	180	166	97	109	157
7	Plant and equipment expenditures/depreciation	1.5	1.7	2.0	2.1	1.8	1.4	1.0	1.2	1.4	1.3	0.8	0.9	1.3
8	Long-term debt ($ millions)	673	749	723	476	364	192	203	222	229	245	274	300	300
9	Net worth ($ millions)	2,540	2,493	2,342	2,212	2,107	1,944	1,889	1,764	1,655	1,569	1,494	1,350	1,275
10	After-tax profit/equity (%)	11.0	14.8	15.9	15.7	17.5	11.5	14.9	15.0	14.8	14.3	18.6	17.6	19.7

* After write-off of $24, $12, and $149 millions in 1962, 1963, and 1964 respectively, arising out of utility claims relating to a price-fixing antitrust suit brought against electrical equipment suppliers by the U.S. Department of Justice.

Sources: GE Annual Reports; *Moody's Industrial Manual*, 1970.

met the necessary criteria. They were nuclear power, computers, and commercial jet engines. All three were seen as "futures" businesses, that is, ones that would require a significant trading off of *current* for *future* earnings.

One especially attractive feature of the three businesses chosen for emphasis at GE in the mid-1960s related to the fact that their earnings drag and peak cash requirements were expected to follow quite predictably one behind the other. According to GE's plan, as the nuclear power business became self-sustaining in terms of profit and cash flow in the late 1960s, corporate resources could be shifted into computers. As GE built to a 10 percent to 15 percent share of the computer business and the division began to pay its own way in the early 1970s, the firm's cash flow could be funneled into building the large jet engines required for the wide-bodied jets and supersonic transports of the mid- to late-1970s. Unfortunately, the duration and scale of the losses incurred in the nuclear power business and the computer business had sent the whole plan somewhat awry by 1970.

GE's strategy in developing its nuclear power business had been based upon quoting fixed-price turnkey contracts to utility companies. The initial financial outcome of this market development strategy can be seen in Line 1 of Table 6–5. The enormous losses incurred in 1968 and 1969 arose mainly from two sources, misestimates of the *amount* of labor needed to construct complete plants and misestimates of the *cost* of that labor. One industry analyst calculated that labor man-hour overruns cost GE about $200 million in U.S. plant sites and $50 million on foreign plant sites. Higher-than-expected rates of inflation in labor costs probably cost GE an additional $200 million.[18] The absolute size of the nuclear power losses were quite beyond anything GE's management had anticipated.

In the computer area, the short-term profit situation beyond 1969 looked as bad as, if not worse than, it did in nuclear power (Line 9 versus Line 1, Table 6–5). In late 1969 the internal profit forecasts for the computer division (assuming the new product development program received corporate approval) looked as shown in Table 6–6.

The profit and loss implications of simultaneously maintaining a commitment to nuclear power, computers, and commercial jet aircraft engines as shown in Table 6–5 were simply unacceptable to GE's top management. They were not prepared to accept continuing losses averaging $200 million per year beyond 1969, as they had been forced to accept in 1968 and 1969 (Line 16, Table 6–5). The cash-flow implications of continued participation in all of these businesses were equally unacceptable. Indeed, as GE's chief financial officer noted,

---

[18] GE appears to have priced the contracts on the assumption of annual inflation rates of 4 percent to 5 percent across the board for all items. Construction labor costs, however, rose by as much as 20 percent per year in some areas.

TABLE 6-5

Estimated profit contribution data for major product categories of the General Electric Corporation: 1968–1972 (Estimates as of early 1970; $ millions)

Line		Pretax profit				
		Completed years		Forecast years		
		1968	1969	1970	1971	1972
1	Nuclear turnkey	(150)	(150)	(50)	(20)	0
2	Other nuclear	(30)	(25)	(35)	(5)	(25)
3	Turbine generators	114	82	110	200	224
4	Transmission and distribution	70	62	63	88	90
5	Total utility business	4	(31)	88	263	289
6	Commercial jet engines division	(30)	(50)	(60)	(135)	(75)
7	Other heavy capital goods	85	65	50	60	70
8	Total heavy capital goods	55	15	(10)	(75)	(5)
9	Computer division	(30)	(1)	(50)	(78)	(88)
10	Other light industrials	225	161	134	190	220
11	Total light industrials	195	160	84	112	132
12	Consumer products	255	215	95	280	300
13	Aerospace and defense	65	50	30	30	25
14	Non-operating earnings*	71	84	85	90	90
15	Total	645	493	369	700	836
16	Pretax profit from nuclear, computer, and jet engine businesses	(240)	(226)	(195)	(238)	(188)
17	Pretax profit from other operations	885	719	573	938	1,024
18	Total pretax profit	645	493	369	700	836

*Primarily GE Credit Corporation.
Sources: Author's projections based on data from *U.S.* v. *IBM*, Plaintiff Exhibit 362, p. 11; and Wall Street institutional reports.

TABLE 6-6
GE computer division net-profit-after-tax forecast, 1970–1975 ($ millions)

	1970	1971	1972	1973	1974	1975	Total
Existing product line	5	8	26	37	50	47	173
Proposed new product line	(29)	(43)	(59)	(58)	(51)	(18)	(258)
Next proposed product line . . .	(1)	(4)	(11)	(19)	(26)	(32)	(93)
Contingency	0	0	0	(20)	(20)	(10)	(50)
Total	(25)	(39)	(44)	(60)	(47)	(13)	(228)

Note: These profit forecasts for the new product line are not consistent with those presented in Table 6–3. The two forecasts were based on somewhat different assumptions at different points in time, and Table 6–3 is a *pretax profit* forecast while the forecast noted above is an *after-tax* forecast.
Source: *U.S.* v. *IBM*, Plaintiff Exhibit 362, p. 11.

our debt to capital ratio had been climbing. And we just said [ ] there is a breaking point where we will lose our triple A rating as a corporation if we continue to pile on debt and if we try to do all of these things that we have got on our plate right now.[19]

Once the financial implications noted above were recognized at the GE corporate level, GE's computer division was doomed. The computer division in particular was selected for elimination for the following reasons. *First,* owing to the nature of its contractual relationships, GE was locked into the nuclear business for eight to ten years; in the commercial jet engine business, the firm was locked in for four to six years.[20] GE thus had little flexibility in terms of getting out of these two businesses. In the words of a senior GE officer, "disengagement is not an available option in these businesses."[21] Disengagement, was, however, an available option for the computer business. *Second,* unlike computers, in the nuclear power and commercial jet engine businesses GE could operate in a competitive posture more to the firm's taste. In the nuclear field, for example, GE held a 30 percent to 35 percent share of the market.[22] In the commercial jet engine field, GE expected to command a 20 percent to 25 percent share of market.[23]

> . . . in both cases, unlike computers—GE would appear to have in hand or in prospect more of the ingredients of a conventional GE successful business posture (in terms of market share; contributed value; cost leadership; technical resources; sales organization; maintenance and service operations).[24]

---

[19] *U.S.* v. *IBM,* Testimony by Reginald H. Jones, Trial Transcript, pp. 8831–32.
[20] Ibid., Trial Transcript, p. 8759.
[21] *U.S.* v. *IBM,* Plaintiff Exhibit 371A, p. 76.
[22] *U.S.* v. *IBM,* Testimony by Reginald H. Jones, Trial Transcript, p. 8761.
[23] Ibid., p. 8762.
[24] *U.S.* v. *IBM,* Plaintiff Exhibit 371A, p. 76.

Finally, and perhaps most importantly, after an intensive study of the computer business in late 1969 and early 1970, the Ventures Task Force reported to GE's chairman that:

> It is our conclusion that the [proposed plan for achieving a 10 percent share of market in computers] is, in part, based on questionable assumptions, that it entails very high risks, and that it is doubtful that it could be kept to time and cost schedules. Even if General Electric Co. were in a position to undertake such an ambitious program, and we don't believe it is, we would not recommend that it invest the requested sums in such a hazardous project.[25]

The reasons for GE's failure in computers

It is useful to reflect upon GE's failure to achieve an acceptable position in the computer business. Three successive chief executives of GE have cited essentially the same factors. Ralph Cordiner stated (as recalled by his successor once removed) that General Electric's mistake "was that it failed to realize the opportunity and therefore made an inadequate allocation of resources, both human and physical, to the business."[26] Fred Borch stated that the mistakes were,

> . . . I think, first, in having the business, which was a very small one, of course, to begin with, at too low a level in the company to attract the level of managerial competence and technical competence that should have been brought into play in the business. That, I think, would be the most serious mistake. Had that been handled correctly to begin with, the resources would have been made available that were needed. But the real picture of what was needed to compete very aggressively and very successfully in the business never came up high enough in the organization to make a good business decision on it.
>
> That would be, I would say, the most significant mistake that we made.[27]

Reginald Jones stated that:

> . . . by the time that we caught up with the size of the opportunity it was truly a lost opportunity and it would have required inordinate investments to catch up and achieve a position of significance.[28]

While GE lagged far behind IBM in terms of market participation in the mid-1950s, the firm at that time had the financial strength vis-a-vis IBM to permit it to force its way to a much larger share of the market.

---

25 Ibid., p. 10.

26 *U.S.* v. *IBM,* Testimony of Reginald H. Jones, Trial Transcript, p. 8869.

27 *U.S.* v. *IBM,* Deposition of Fred J. Borch, June 20, 1974, p. 20.

28*U.S.* v. *IBM,* Testimony of Reginald H. Jones, Trial Transcript, pp. 8869–70.

This particular competitive advantage disappeared rapidly, however. In the six years between 1955 and 1961, IBM's after-tax profit and operating cash flow grew from about one third of the level achieved by GE to near parity (Table 6–7). By the early 1960s GE had lost the opportunity to build a dominant position in computers on the basis of financial strength. Having lost this potentially important benefit by 1961, GE had to accept one of three possible "nondominance" strategies for dealing with its computer operations. The firm could either (a) leave the business; (b) maintain its market position and accept the role of a marginal producer in a rapidly growing business with little or no return on an ever-increasing investment base; or (c) build its market position—not to the level of dominance, but to a level where an acceptable[29] return could be earned on a much larger investment base than that anticipated in (b).

In the early 1960s GE clearly opted for alternative (c). Unfortunately, the losses incurred by GE's overseas acquisitions were so large during the mid-1960s that by 1969 the company found itself in a status (b) competitive posture after having sustained a pattern and level of losses associated with building a status (c) market position.

When IBM announced its fourth generation of computers in 1970, GE's market position and map of possible alternative competitive choices looked almost exactly as they had ten years earlier, in 1960. This time, however, GE confronted a desire to achieve alternative (c) from a much weaker financial position vis-à-vis IBM than the firm had enjoyed in 1960. Indeed, in 1969 GE's after-tax profit and operating cash flow were less than one third of IBM's (Table 6–7) and the computer industry had grown so large that "success" in achieving a 10 percent share of the market implied that for six years GE would have to commit essentially *all* of what might be called the corporation's *discretionary* cash flow into that one small corner of the firm's operations known as the computer division! This rather startling fact can be explained as follows. GE's annual profit after taxes between 1967 and 1969 averaged about $350 million (Line 3, Table 6–4). During this period dividends averaged about $235 million per year (Line 4, Table 6–4). GE thus generated only about $115 million of cash flow that was available to support the growth of both old and new businesses. This assumes, of course, that cash flow arising from depreciation in existing businesses had to be reinvested in them in order to maintain their earning power. This $115 million of *discretionary* cash flow can be matched against the $685 million in cash flow over six years that GE estimated would be required

---

[29] "Acceptable" is defined here to mean a rate of return on capital equal to the cost of that capital.

TABLE 6-7

Profits and cash flow data for major computer manufacturers, 1955–1969 ($ millions)

	Profit after taxes								Operating cash flow							
	1955	1957	1959	1961	1963	1965	1967	1969	1955	1957	1959	1961	1963	1965	1967	1969
Broad line computer manufacturers																
IBM	(73)	111	(176)	253	363	477	652	(934)	(139)	230	(351)	456	573	1000	1515	(1942)
GE	(209)	251	(278)	238	272	355	361	(278)	(306)	368	(400)	360	398	543	641	(629)
RCA	48	39	40	36	66	101	148	151	66	53	64	70	113	163	299	333
Sperry Rand	46	28	37	24	27	32	64	81	—	53	72	70	87	110	149	182
Honeywell	19	21	29	25	35	38	42	63	26	29	40	40	60	75	102	145
Somewhat specialized computer manufacturers																
Burroughs	12	10	11	11	9	18	35	55	17	18	19	25	26	48	78	119
NCR	18	23	22	30	22	29	35	44	26	32	38	49	58	75	114	146
Highly specialized computer manufacturers																
Xerox	1	1	2	5	23	62	100	161	3	4	5	15	50	132	218	391
Control Data	—	—	—	1	3	8	8	52	—	—	0	2	12	22	40	100

Sources: Annual reports; *Moody's Industrial Manual*, 1970; Value Line Investment Survey.

to achieve a 10 percent share of the computer market (Table 6–3). To achieve economic viability in computers in the 1970s, GE would have to put practically all of its discretionary cash flow into this business.[30] If the gamble were successful GE would then have become a distant number two in the computer industry, with a market share equal to one sixth that of the leading firm!

In short, IBM in the computer business had employed and benefitted from precisely the type of competitive strategy that GE pursued in almost all of its other business areas. That was to be the dominant firm and the cost leader. IBM had so far outdistanced its nearest competitors, and its markets had grown to enormous size so rapidly, that the simple passage of time was now helping to raise the entry barriers faced by a broad-line computer manufacturer to insurmountable heights. In hindsight it is clear that GE bungled the scale and timing of its entry into the computer business in the early 1950s, and given IBM's skill, this error effectively doomed GE's broad-line strategy.

Table 6–8 presents an interesting basis for comparing the financial competences of various firms to mount an aggressive strategy aimed at capturing computer market share. The sharp alteration in relative strength over time (as measured by earnings and cash flows in Table 6–7) between GE and IBM has already been noted. The competitive importance of other factors such as a firm's *debt policy*, its *dividend-payout policy*, and its *market value/book value* ratio should also be noted. It should be clear from the market value/book value ratio data of Table 6–8, that (at least in relation to historical ROE performance) most of the firms engaged in the computer business in 1969 enjoyed stock prices that substantially exceeded a rational economic valuation as described in Chapter 1. To the extent this was true, these firms could raise the equity capital needed to support rapid growth in computers at a very low cost.[31] Unfortunately, the highly diversified firms with a broad line of computer products (such as GE, Sperry Rand, and RCA) were at a significant comparative disadvantage in raising equity capital "on the cheap." They did not enjoy market value/book value ratios for their common stocks that were quite as bloated as some of their less diversified competition.

In the area of debt policy, most firms in the computer business, with the notable exception of IBM, had very high debt-to-equity ratios. This made them a good deal more vulnerable to product obsolescence than

---

[30] This overstates the magnitude of the problem somewhat, since GE's existing computer product line in 1970 could have been the source of some cash flow to fund the new line. In addition, if GE were to maintain its long-term debt ratio at about 40 percent of equity, $115 million of retained earnings per year would have generated $46 million of borrowing power, which could then be added to GE's discretionary cash flow.

[31] The notion that a bloated stock price lowers a firm's equity capital cost will be explored in detail in Chapter 9.

TABLE 6-8
Selected financial statistics for major computer manufacturers, 1955–1969

	Debt/equity ratio (%)								Dividend payout ratio (%)	
	1955	1957	1959	1961	1963	1965	1967	1969	1967	1969
Broad-line computer manufacturers										
IBM	104	60	50	36	27	16	20	13	37	44
GE	9	25	19	15	11	23	44	42	66	84
RCA	97	87	76	52	48	43	79	83	38	43
Sperry Rand	94	68	85	95	101	75	57	50	16	21
Honeywell	19	32	25	30	37	51	76	94	39	29
Somewhat specialized computer manufacturers										
Burroughs	36	98	107	98	104	95	87	118	24	19
NCR	49	61	28	41	51	43	91	92	30	29
Highly specialized computer manufacturers										
Xerox	38	24	32	91	67	82	58	44	27	28
Control Data	—	—	6	56	88	78	164	49	0	0

	Return on equity (%)								Market-value/book-value ratio	
	1955	1957	1959	1961	1963	1965	1967	1969	1967	1969
Broad-line computer manufacturers										
IBM	20.6	15.1	17.4	18.5	18.9	18.6	17.0	17.7	9.2	7.9
GE	19.5	19.7	18.6	14.8	14.9	17.5	15.9	11.0	3.7	2.9
RCA	18.7	13.5	12.5	7.9	12.4	16.9	17.4	14.9	4.1	2.1
Sperry Rand	18.8	8.2	10.6	7.1	6.9	7.7	10.7	11.3	3.7	1.8
Honeywell	16.2	12.1	13.9	9.5	10.9	10.1	9.7	10.2	4.4	4.4
Somewhat specialized computer manufacturers										
Burroughs	13.2	9.6	8.9	8.2	5.6	10.7	14.2	13.2	6.2	6.5
NCR	13.2	12.2	11.1	12.3	7.5	9.0	7.3	7.1	3.0	3.0
Highly specialized computer manufacturers										
Xerox	14.6	13.6	17.9	38.8	43.7	39.9	26.4	22.5	16.4	10.8
Control Data	—	—	15.3	8.6	10.5	8.9	9.3	7.2	12.1	2.6*

*Control Data's market value/book value ratio fell from 12.1 at December 31, 1967, to 2.6 at December 31, 1969, primarily because of the firm's 1968 minnow-whale acquisition of the rather unglamorous Commercial Credit Corporation.

Sources: Annual Reports; *Moody's Industrial Manual*, 1970; Value Line Investment Survey.

their more powerful rival, IBM—a firm that had historically moved toward less and less reliance upon debt in its capital structure. Thus, at the close of 1969, when many computer companies were extended to the point of having the highest debt ratios in their history, IBM had essentially no debt, a cash position of almost $1.5 billion, and a whole line of fourth-generation computer products ready for introduction in 1970.

Finally, the relatively high dividend payout ratios of firms such as GE and RCA made their capital raising more difficult, since they had a smaller fraction of their earnings available for retentions, and a smaller *discretionary* cash flow.

In effect, this type of analysis suggests that while no firm looked particularly well situated financially to take on IBM with a broad-line product strategy, firms like GE and RCA by 1970 may have been foolhardy even to broach a challenge. A distinguishing feature of GE's management was that they recognized this fact. Other managements in the industry did not.

GE's exit from the computer business

A key management challenge for GE in 1970 was to plan a graceful and financially advantageous exit from the main frame computer manufacturing business. GE's formal effort to disengage from the main frame computer business commenced on February 2, 1970, following a presentation by the Ventures Task Force to GE's chairman. The task force's prognosis for a successful sales effort was not particularly comforting at that time.[32]

> It's not that we have great enthusiasm for or optimism over a sale oriented strategy, but rather that we have *so little choice remaining* . . . [italics mine].[33]

In light of its concern, the Ventures Task Force proposed the following course of action.

> We are very much aware of the need to prevent a climate of a fire sale developing in the course of test-marketing a sale strategy. Our preliminary approach should be designed to get the maximum sense of our competitors' attitudes, while at the same time avoiding the appearance of initiating any discussions oriented to the sale approach: in short, we need a plan which conceals our objectives but provides the opportunity for explorations.

---

[32] Part of the caution reflected by the Ventures Task Force could undoubtedly be attributed to the fact that if their recommendation to sell the computer division were accepted (as it was), the members of this task force would undoubtedly be given the job of actually selling it (as they were)!

[33] *U.S. v. IBM,* Plaintiff Exhibit 371A, p. 80.

In our discussions with third parties it would be important to indicate that GE still has [   ] three options (sale, joint venture, purchase) very much before it for ultimate decision. Our emphasis would be on our study of the structure of the computer industry and the extreme hazards faced by any one dwarf for the long term when confronted by the continuing dominance of IBM.[34]

＊＊＊＊＊

We of course do not know what prospects we have of successfully completing a sale-oriented strategy. Our inventory of physical assets and our going-concern value in this business—except perhaps for our European investments—offer only limited leverage: what we do have is our potential as a competitor. Any dwarf would rest easier if that potential were to be under his control; and would be deeply concerned if it were to go to another dwarf.[35]

＊＊＊＊＊

The preferred course in our opinion would be to conduct at least one tentative reading of the possible interest of a competitor in acquiring some or all of our equipment business.[36]

The proposed exploration of interests with potential buyers of GE's main frame computer business took place between February and April of 1970. In April, the Ventures Task Force reported as follows to GE's Board of Directors:

The choice as to where to begin was simple. Control Data Corp. [CDC] had approached GE on its own initiative a full year ago. Early this year they again showed interest in acquiring our [computer] equipment business. Accordingly, we decided to begin our exploration with CDC. We have had two sessions with CDC. It is evident that:

- They share our view of the industry trends and necessity for restructuring.
- Apparently they would like to acquire GE's [computer] equipment business but it is clear to both of us that they are not currently in a position to finance such an acquisition. We have serious reservations about the future of CDC and any sale to them would require us to hold a substantial amount of their paper while they embarked on a strategy that involved a rather poor match of product lines.
- From our point of view, no further exploratory discussions are contemplated.

---

[34] Ibid., p. 81.
[35] Ibid., p. 84.
[36] Ibid., p. 86.

Xerox appeared a logical second candidate on the basis of their out-standing capability to finance an acquisition plus their interest in the [computer] business as evidenced by the acquisition of [Scientific Data Systems].

Following an initial contact with Xerox we were requested to submit to them a memorandum we have developed covering our views on the structure of this industry. Since we have not heard further from Xerox, we have concluded that they have little or no interest.

Honeywell ranked high in our studies of optimum fit . . . and we have discussed the structure of the industry with them in some depth. We find that, while they have minor differences of opinion on emphasis and timing, they are in essential agreement with our views. Our dis-cussions then centered on the feasibility, in a very broad sense, of com-bining resources. The main advantages that would result from such a combination are a larger revenue base; a higher market share; a stronger and broader-based marketing and service organization; and improved financial results through elimination of redundant costs, initially most significantly in the area of product development programs.[37]

＊＊＊＊＊

New product line plans of Honeywell are comparable to product and market strategies under consideration in GE. It appears that both com-panies are just starting their [new product] design efforts and that they are largely similar. This is advantageous because it appears that neither company has progressed beyond the point at which major re-investment would be required to reorient product development programs.

We exchanged sufficient financial data with Honeywell to enable us to prepare an order-of-magnitude estimate of the operating results for the combined computer equipment business of the two companies.

We assumed for purposes of these estimates that Honeywell's account-ing practices, which are more liberal than GE's, would be used by the joint venture. The principal changes having a favorable effect in 1970 are in the treatment of engineering and manufacturing period costs and in the amortization period for equipment leased to customers ($17 million). . . .

We estimated that reductions in engineering costs totaling $34 million could be realized through management action, $12 million in current product lines and $22 million on advanced products.[38]

＊＊＊＊＊

There would also be additional savings, probably only achievable over several years, in combining management, supporting and overhead func-

[37] *U.S.* v. *IBM*, Plaintiff Exhibit 331A, pp. 36, 37.
[38] Ibid., pp. 39, 40.

tions of the businesses such as finance, [public] relations, marketing, headquarters, manufacturing, pooled purchasing, duplicate field facilities, etc.[39]

* * * * *

Also I want to underscore the extreme urgency of progressing the Honeywell negotiations as rapidly as possible. Because of the growing number of persons privy to our deliberations and the possibility that our partner will try to force our hand by leaking or threatening publicity, we are increasingly vulnerable to a serious loss of customer and employee loyalty at the very time when this loyalty is our single most valuable asset. Moreover, we face a continuing erosion of all our basic values in this business due to declining competitive sufficiency of our product offerings and rising vulnerability of our [installed base of leased computers]. Hence, we must press ahead through this perilous period with all possible dispatch.[40]

Discussions with Honeywell commenced in March of 1970. In May the terms of a sale agreement were publicly announced. In the intervening ten weeks, negotiations had produced agreement as to *what* GE was selling, *how much* Honeywell would pay for what GE was selling, and *what form* the payment by Honeywell would take.

As suggested in Table 6–9, what GE was selling was a *market share large enough to produce significant scale economies for Honeywell*. GE's business was operating essentially at breakeven in 1970 (Column 3, Table 6–9). When GE's operations were combined with Honeywell's, however, the resulting efficiencies, according to GE's calculations, would nearly double the earnings before taxes of Honeywell's computer operations from $39 million (Column 4, Table 6–9) to $76 million (Column 7, Table 6–9).

GE's book investment in its computer division amounted to about $180 million. For this investment Honeywell agreed to pay:

1. 1.5 million shares of Honeywell stock, with a market value of $154 million immediately prior to the sale announcement;
2. $110 million of 9⅛ percent subordinated notes due 1975 and 1977 that were interest-free for the first year, and payable (or *prepayable*) in cash or in Honeywell common stock, at the option of Honeywell;
3. 18.5 percent of the common stock of the combined enterprise (to be called HIS) consisting of GE's and Honeywell's computer operations. GE's equity interest in the new entity was to be the subject of a cross-option agreement. Either GE or Honeywell could force GE's 18.5 percent interest to be exchanged for Honeywell common stock

---

[39] Ibid., p. 40.
[40] Ibid., pp. 41, 42.

TABLE 6-9

Enhancement of profitability resulting from the scale economies achieved by combining the GE and Honeywell computer divisions ($ millions; estimated internally by GE's management—April 1970)

Line		(1) GE Computer Division before accounting adjustments	(2) Accounting adjustments to GE*	(3) GE Computer Division after accounting adjustments	(4) Honeywell Computer Division	(5) GE/Honeywell combined before merger savings	(6) Projected merger savings	(7) GE/Honeywell combined after projected merger savings
1	Revenue	475	–	475	457	932	–	932
	Costs							
2	Manufacturing	201	(10)	191	164	355	–	355
3	Marketing	109	–	109	122	231	–	231
4	Engineering	74	(7)	67	47	114	(34)	80
5	Field engineering	64	–	64	61	125	–	125
6	G&A and other	21	–	21	24	45	–	45
7	Total	469	(17)	452	418	870	(34)	836
8	Interest expense	20	–	20	–	20†	–	20
9	Income before taxes and minority interest	(14)	(17)	(3)	(39)	42	(34)	(76)

Note: The "revenue" data of this table do not agree with the data relating to the "sale value of computers shipped" for GE which are shown in Table 6–1. This is not an inconsistency, since the two measures are quite different. Similarly, the income data in Column 1 of Table 6–9 do not match the profit data of Table 6–2. Differences in the method of allocating corporate expenses (including interest) account for this variation.

* These adjustments were required to place GE's more conservative accounting on a basis comparable with that of Honeywell.

† Does not include $10 million of added interest originally estimated by GE.

Source: *U.S. v. IBM*, Plaintiff Exhibit 331A, p. 54A.

after January 1, 1975. The exchange would give GE a block of stock in Honeywell with a value equal to GE's interest in the average annual profit of HIS (during the two calendar years preceding the exercise of the option) multiplied by the average price/earnings ratio of Honeywell's common stock (during the year preceding the exercise of the option). The transaction can be diagrammed as in Figure 6–1.

FIGURE 6–1

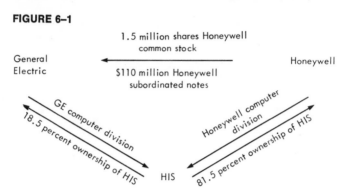

The package of Honeywell securities involved in this transaction looks like an incredible hodgepodge. In fact, the package was a tour de force of financial architecture. It was intricately designed to satisfy the following requirements:

1. Honeywell was sufficiently constrained financially that not a dime of cash could be involved in the transaction, either immediately or in the near future.
2. GE was bargaining to recover at least the book value of its investment of $180 million in the sale transaction.
3. The sale transaction had to minimize the dilution of Honeywell's earnings caused by the payment of several hundred million dollars for GE's computer division. Given the modest earnings of GE's computer division (Table 6–2), this was no small task.
4. Honeywell had to wind up owning more than 80 percent of the equity in the combined computer venture in order to permit the filing of a consolidated tax return.

How did the package of securities exchanged satisfy the objectives of each of the parties? *First,* the deal included no cash or near-cash. Indeed, the Honeywell subordinated debt (the nearest thing to cash in the package) was prepayable in Honeywell common stock. It was in fact prepaid with Honeywell common stock as soon as interest on the debt began to accrue following the one-year moratorium. This subordinated debt was effectively Honeywell common stock from the outset of the deal. Its debenture feature (without interest for the first year) simply made it possible to defer the earnings dilution that would have resulted from the immediate issuance of additional Honeywell stock until the scale economy savings promised by the merger were in fact realized. *Second,* GE received securities with a market value (at the time of the exchange) substantially in excess of the book value of its investment. GE contributed 43 percent of the net assets of HIS[41] and received 18.5 percent of its stock. In exchange for the implicit 43 − 18.5 = 24.5 percentage point reduction in its ownership interest in HIS, GE received Honeywell stock and debentures valued as indicated below. The "discounted" valuation figure reduces the "market" or "face" value figure to reflect the limited marketability of GE's interest in Honeywell.[42]

	Market* or face value (in millions)	"Economic" or discounted value (in millions)
1.5 Million shares of Honeywell common	$154	$108
$110 Million Honeywell subordinated debt	110	77
	$264	$185

*This value was calculated as of the date of the public announcement of the transaction in May 1970.

The equity in HIS was implicitly valued by the parties, according to the calculation above, at about $185 million ÷ 24.5, or $7.6 million per 1 percent of ownership interest. This translates into a value of $140 million for GE's 18.5 percent residual interest in HIS. GE thus received Honeywell securities with a total *economic* value of $185 million + $140 million, or $325 million. This amount was $145 million above the $180 million *book* value of GE's investment in its computer division.[43]

---

41 *U.S.* v. *IBM*, Plaintiff Exhibit 331A, p. 55.

42 The discount assumed here is 30 percent. It reflects GE's agreement not to sell its interest in a fashion that would tend to depress Honeywell's stock price, and the fact that GE's shares in Honeywell were all held in a voting trust, and could not be voted by GE.

43 GE did not value the securities received from Honeywell for shareholder reporting purposes until October 1, 1970, the date the transaction was completed. Between the date the terms of the transaction were first announced (May 20, 1970) and the date it closed (October 1, 1970), the price of a share of Honeywell's common stock declined by 14 percent from a price of $103 to a price of $89⅛. This decline, plus GE's extraordinary conservatism in valuing the securities received from Honeywell, reduced GE's *immediate* reported profit on the transaction to less than $2 million, after recognition of incurred and anticipated costs and expenses in connection with the discontinuance of the computer business. By valuing the Honeywell

Third, the only dilution to Honeywell's earnings came from the 1.5 million Honeywell shares issued in the transaction. The subordinated debenture produced no earnings dilution, as noted above, until offsetting scale economies had been realized. More importantly, the cross-option agreement was designed to swap out GE's minority interest in HIS's earnings at a value linked directly to the price/earnings ratio of Honeywell's common stock. This method of computing the purchase price under the cross-option agreement was "intended to result in no material dilution of Honeywell's earnings per share as a result of the exercise of the cross-option."[44] The mechanics of a hypothetical calculation showing this result are presented in Table 6–10. The actual *outcome* of the exercise of the cross-option agreement is presented in the Appendix to this chapter.

Fourth, and finally, since GE retained only 18.5 percent of the equity ownership of HIS, Honeywell was able to gain the tax benefits of consolidation with HIS.[45]

TABLE 6-10

Hypothetical example of the calculation of Honeywell's earnings per share before and after the exercise of the cross-option agreement relating to GE's 18.5% interest in HIS

	Before swap	After swap
Profit after tax—HIS ($ millions)	100	100
Profit after tax—Other Honeywell operations (($ millions)	200	200
Profit after tax before minority interest ($ millions)	300	300
GE's minority interest in HIS ($ millions)	18.5	0
Total Honeywell profit after tax ($ millions)	281.5	300
Total Honeywell shares outstanding (millions).	28.15	30
Honeywell earnings per share ($)	(10.00)	(10.00)

Note: Recalculating Honeywell's EPS to reflect the effect of this swap involves the following:
1. Assume Honeywell's common stock sells for 10 times earnings, or $100 per share.
2. GE's $18.5 million interest in HIS's profits would entitle GE to receive $18.5 X 10 = $185 million worth of Honeywell common stock.
3. At $100 per share, this $185 million value would entitle GE to receive 1.85 million Honeywell shares.

---

securities received in this transaction extremely conservatively, GE tucked away a large pool of potential capital gains to be realized as these Honeywell securities were sold in future years.

By December 31, 1976, GE had received about $190 million in cash from the sale of Honeywell shares. In addition, GE held about $100 million in market value of Honeywell stock (or securities that could ultimately be converted into Honeywell stock). Between October 1, 1970, and December 31, 1976, the value of a share of Honeywell stock had declined from $89⅛ to $48¼.

[44] Honeywell, Inc., Proxy Statement of August 21, 1970, p. 1.

[45] In addition to the domestic benefits of a tax consolidation, Honeywell also obtained foreign tax-loss carryforwards exceeding $100 million. These were concentrated largely in France, and could be used only to offset income earned in the computer business in France.

Summary of GE's exit

GE's sale of its computer division to Honeywell in 1970 was a master-piece of strategic analysis, timing, and financial engineering. GE was the first of the Dwarfs to realize that it could not make an economic success out of a broad-line computer manufacturing strategy. It was, accordingly, the first to get out of this business. GE timed its exit well, in that immediate product-development savings could be realized by a buyer in 1970, since a number of the Dwarfs were just beginning to develop their next-generation products. Being the first of the Dwarfs to leave the business, GE also enjoyed a larger pool of potential buyers for its business. This was true since any one Dwarf probably would be unable to digest, in a managerial sense, more than a single computer acquisition over a time period spanning several years. Finally, GE was able to persuade Honeywell to pay an enormous sum of money for a division that had essentially no value to GE as an ongoing entity.[46] In fact, the division probably had *negative* value to GE in terms of what it would have cost to close it down.

GE created a very significant improvement in the value of its share-holders' position in the computer industry by improving Honeywell's economies of scale, and by persuading Honeywell to pay handsomely for that improvement. While GE failed miserably *in* the main frame computer business, it succeeded brilliantly in getting *out* of it. The value GE's management created for shareholders in its exit was quite substantial, the more so when compared with the exit performances of RCA and Xerox.

The withdrawal of RCA and Xerox

The contrast between GE's skillful exit from the computer business and the later withdrawals of RCA and Xerox is worth some note. When RCA finally exited from the computer business in 1971, the company sustained a $210 million after-tax loss.[47] In 1971 there was, realistically, only one buyer for RCA's business. Mohawk Data Sciences made a proposal to acquire the bulk of RCA's computer business, but Mohawk's

---

[46] The international computer operations of GE did have value in 1970. Indeed, GE's share of the earnings of the Bull Companies amounted to $7.8 million in 1969. GE's domestic computer operations probably had significant negative value, however, on a going-concern basis.

[47] In 1971 RCA established reserves of $490 million related to the discontinuation of its computer business. The establishment of this reserve created a $250 million after-tax loss in 1971. By 1973 it was clear that RCA's losses on the discontinuation would be less than originally anticipated. After the elimination of tax benefits, $40 million was returned to earned surplus in 1973, thereby reducing RCA's after-tax loss to $210 million.

weak financial position eliminated them as a serious contender.[48] Honeywell was preoccupied with its earlier GE acquisition. Only Sperry Rand was left. The deal was cut on terms essentially dictated by Sperry Rand.[49] Sperry Rand bought the bulk of RCA's rental base, but only a small portion of its other computer-related assets, at a price ($116 million) that reportedly allowed Sperry Rand to earn $200 million on the RCA equipment base between 1972 and 1975.[50] While RCA's management created significant value as a result of its exit from the computer business, much of the value created went to *Sperry Rand's* shareholders.

Xerox's entry into and exit from the computer industry were even more remarkable. Xerox made its entry into the computer business just shortly before GE began planning its exit. In early 1969, Xerox paid $910 million in stock for Scientific Data Systems, Inc. (SDS), a fast-growing scientific computer manufacturer with a net worth of $78 million. In 1968 SDS had achieved a 16.5 percent ROE based on its average equity outstanding during the year. Over the 1965–68 period, SDS had expanded its equity base at a rate equal to 2.8 times annual earnings. The price Xerox paid was about twelve times SDS's book value. From the analysis presented in Chapter 1, this valuation logically would have carried with it some quite fancy expectations on the part of Xerox's management as to the *size* and *profitability* of future investment opportunities in computers. As shown in Table 6–11, at the time of the SDS acquisition Xerox expected to expand SDS's pretax profits from $20 million in 1968 to $77 million by 1973.

Indeed, two years after the SDS acquisition, Xerox's chief financial officer was quoted as follows:

> Our policy has really been to find the company that we think is good for us, [ ] and then you damn well pay what you have to to get it. If we really want a company we don't want to get into a lot of haggling. If you're right about a company, the actual price you pay is not very important five years or so down the pike.[51]

---

[48] *U.S.* v. *IBM*, Plaintiff Exhibit 402, p. 3, 4.

[49] RCA sold its lease base (plus other assets with a book value of $23 million) for consideration that ultimately totaled $127 million ($116 million in net-present-value terms). RCA received $70.5 million in cash at the closing. Additional payments were earned as a result of the performance of the lease base. RCA's staff originally argued that the lease base alone should not be sold for less than $133 million, since this was the net present value of the cash flows anticipated from a run-off of the lease base under RCA's management. This $133 million figure did not include the $23 million book value of other assets included in the sale transaction. (*U.S.* v. *IBM*, Plaintiff Exhibit 405A, p. 19.)

[50] *Datamation*, April 1976, p. 100.

[51] Chris Welles, "Xerox: Whatever Happened to Act II," *Corporate Financing*, July/August 1971, p. 26.

TABLE 6-11

Xerox Data Systems—Computer operations (trend of long-range plan projections of sales and pretax profits versus actual results; $ millions)

Line		(1)	(2)	(3)	(4)	(5)	(6)	(7)	(8) Actual revenue achieved
		1969	1970	1971	1972	1973	1974	1975	
	Preacquisition period								
1	1966	*	*	*	*	*	*	*	55
2	1967	*	*	*	*	*	*	*	72
3	1968	*	*	*	*	*	*	*	101
	Postacquisition period								
4	1969	*	*	*	*	*	*	*	*
5	1970	*	*	*	*	*	*	*	*
6	1971	*	*	*	*	*	*	*	*
7	1972	288	*	*	70	*	*	*	70
8	1973	365	*	*	89	73	*	*	65
9	1974	*	*	*	108	83	67	*	66
10	1975	*	*	*	112	104	76	72	*
11	1976	*	600	*	109	111	93	94	*

Line		1969	1970	1971	1972	1973	1974	1975	Actual pretax profit achieved
		Pretax profit estimate in long-range plan of							
	Preacquisition period								
12	1966	*	*	*	*	*	*	*	8
13	1967	*	*	*	*	*	*	*	13
14	1968	*	*	*	*	*	*	*	20
	Postacquisition period								
15	1969	*	*	*	*	*	*	*	22
16	1970	*	*	*	*	*	*	*	(36)
17	1971	*	*	*	*	*	*	*	(44)
18	1972	61	*	*	(29)	*	*	*	(47)
19	1973	77	*	*	(25)	(23)	*	*	(45)
20	1974	*	*	*	(5)	(27)	(25)	*	(42)
21	1975	*	*	*	3	(22)	(22)	(44)	*
22	1976	*	100	*	13	(14)	(18)	(32)	*

* Indicates data not available.

Sources:
1. Scientific Data Systems, Inc., 1968 Annual Report to shareholders.
2. *U.S.* v. *IBM*, Deposition of C. Peter McColough, Deposition Exhibit 5305-002, March 12, 1976, p. 7.
3. Xerox Corporation, 1975 Annual Report to shareholders, pp. 26-27.

Xerox's hopes for its newly acquired computer division were quickly dashed as SDS's pretax profits fell from over $20 million in 1969 to a loss of more than $30 million in 1970 (Column 8, Table 6–11). SDS's pretax losses remained in the $40 million range after 1970. While Xerox's long-range forecasts for the division between 1972 and 1975 always projected an improving posture (Columns 4, 5, 6, and 7 of Table 6–11), the actual operating results of the division were extremely unfavorable (Column 8, Table 6–11) both in relation to revenues and in absolute magnitude.

TABLE 6-12

Calculation of the estimated economic loss (excluding the opportunity cost of money) associated with the participation of General Electric, RCA, and Xerox in the main frame computer manufacturing business ($ millions)

	GE	RCA	Xerox
Excess of purchase price paid over the book value of acquisitions	35	0	832
Net losses sustained from operations	171*	124	109
Net losses sustained in the disposition of operations	(145)†	210	84
Total estimated economic loss	61	334	1,025

*This figure equals $204 million of reported operating losses less $35 million of excess purchase price paid over the book value of acquisitions. The $35 million figure was written off by GE as a charge to operations at the time GE acquired the securities in question.

†The $145 million *profit* figure from the disposition of GE's computer operation is equal to the $325 million discounted value of Honeywell securities received (per page 171) less the $180 million book value of GE's investment in its computer division. As noted in footnote 43, because of a sharp decline in the value of Honeywell's common stock, GE's ultimate cash realization from its Honeywell securities may be closer to $300 million than $325 million.

Sources:

GE Data—*U.S.* v. *IBM*, Plaintiff Exhibit 380, p. 1; Honeywell, Inc., Proxy Statement of August 21, 1970, p. 9; *Forbes*, April 1, 1967, p. 21.

RCA Data—RCA Annual Report, 1971, pp. 34-35; *U.S.* v. *IBM*, 69 CV 200, Plaintiff Exhibit 350A, p. 2.

Xerox Data—Xerox 10K Report to the SEC, 1975, pp. 10-11, and Notes to Consolidated Financial Statements, pp. 2-3; *The Wall Street Journal*, July 22, 1975; *U.S.* v. *IBM*, Deposition of C. Peter McColough, Exhibit 5305, pp. 16-17, March 12, 1976.

Six years after the SDS acquisition, Xerox withdrew from the computer business, leaving its common shareholders with an economic loss of $1 billion as indicated in Table 6-12. Table 6-12 demonstrates with considerable force the benefit of systematic thinking in the area of *value creation*. GE shareholders benefitted very significantly from the skill of GE's management team in planning and executing a strategy for enhancing the value of its market position in the computer industry. This enhancement in value came largely from the scale economies noted in Table 6-9. To the extent GE persuaded Honeywell to pay a price for its computer assets that may have exceeded the economic value of these assets, the GE divestiture also serves as a bridge to our next broad area of investigation—the area of value transfers.

APPENDIX

Table 6–10 presents a hypothetical example of how the cross-option agreement relating to GE's 18.5 percent equity interest in HIS was intended to operate. Unfortunately, the mechanics of the formula did not produce the intended result. In the last half of 1974, Honeywell's earnings per share fell to less than 60 percent of the level of the prior year. This earnings collapse occurred at about the same time that broad-based stock market price averages were falling to the lowest levels experienced in two decades. With pressure coming from *both* an earnings decline and the general erosion in market prices, Honeywell's stock price fell from about $80 per share in January 1974 to a little over $20 per share in November 1974.

This stock price decline was doubly disastrous for Honeywell. In the cross-option agreement made with GE in 1970, GE had the right to put[52] its 18.5 percent ownership interest in HIS to Honeywell after December 31, 1974. The price to be paid in Honeywell stock equalled 18.5 percent of HIS's after-tax profits (averaged over the prior two years) multiplied by Honeywell's average price/earnings ratio (averaged over the prior year). As noted earlier in this chapter, this formulation was designed to achieve an exchange of interests that would produce no dilution in earnings per share for Honeywell's shareholders. Under normal circumstances, Honeywell's earnings and price/earnings ratio would have been reasonably stable, and the valuation formula would produce the anticipated result. A very rapid slide in Honeywell's stock price, however, had a dramatic and unanticipated effect on the cross-option valuation formula.

HIS's profits are not publicly reported by Honeywell in a form that can be directly utilized in the cross-option pricing formula. Some estimates of HIS's after-tax profits can be made from the data that Honeywell does report, however. If we utilize the assumed profitability data for HIS that are shown in Table 6A–1, it is possible to calculate that GE should have been entitled to receive about 1.1 million shares of Honeywell common stock if the firm had chosen to exercise its option at January 1, 1975. This figure is based on the assumption that GE should have received an *equity interest* in Honeywell equal to its *profit interest* in Honeywell as calculated in Line 9, Table 6A–1. The operation of the formula utilized in the cross-option agreement, however, would have given 3.5 million shares[53] to GE had GE exercised its option as of January 1, 1975 (Line 10, Table 6A–1).

---

[52] This "put" permitted GE to force Honeywell to acquire GE's interest in HIS upon terms agreed to in Honeywell's 1970 acquisition of GE's computer division.

[53] As was the case in Line 9, Table 6A–1, this calculation is based upon the HIS profitability data presented in Line 1, Table 6A–1.

TABLE 6A-1
Calculation of the number of Honeywell shares issuable under the original terms of the GE-Honeywell cross-option agreement relating to GE's 18.5% ownership interest in HIS

Line		(1) 1974 ($ millions)	(2) %	(3) 1973 ($ millions)	(4) %	(5) Combined—1973-74 ($ millions)	(6) %
1	Profit after tax—HIS	12	15	40	39	52	29
2	Profit after tax—Other	68	85	62	61	130	71
3	Profit after tax—Total	80	100	102	100	182	100
4	Honeywell common shares outstanding at 12/31/74				19.5 million		
5	GE's minority interest in HIS's earnings				0.185		
6	GE's minority interest in Honeywell's *total* earnings,* 1973-74 (Equal to Line 5 X Line 1, Column 6)				0.0536		
7	Honeywell's average price/earnings ratio in 1974 per cross-option formula calculation				14.14		
8	Honeywell's stock price/share at 12/31/74 per cross-option formula calculation				$19.20		

9 Calculation of the number of Honeywell shares issuable to GE as of 1/1/75 if the cross-option agreement had been based upon equity ownership pro rata with profit interest

$$\frac{\text{Honeywell shares issuable for GE's interest in HIS}}{\text{Total Honeywell shares outstanding after issuance of shares to GE}} = 0.0536$$

$$\frac{x}{19.5+x} = 0.0536$$

x = 1.1 million Honeywell shares

10 Calculation of the number of Honeywell shares issuable to GE as of 1/1/75 based on the *actual* terms of the cross-option agreement

$$x = \frac{(\text{Profit of HIS averaged over two years}) \times (\text{GE's minority interest in HIS}) \times (\text{Honeywell's average P/E ratio})}{\text{Honeywell's share price}}$$

$$x = \frac{(\$52) \times (0.5) \times (0.185) \times (14.14)}{\$19.20}$$

x = 3.5 million Honeywell shares

*This calculation of total earnings includes GE's minority interest.

Obviously the architects of the cross-option agreement never anticipated a set of circumstances that might lead to the issuance of new shares equal to 18 percent of Honeywell's capitalization at December 31, 1974, in order to eliminate a minority interest with a claim on 5.4 percent of the firm's total earnings. Fortunately for Honeywell, GE had no desire to test the enforceability of its contract. Instead, in November 1974, GE settled to receive a fixed number of Honeywell shares that ranged from 1.5 million to 2.2 million based on the date chosen by either GE or Honeywell to exercise the option. In early 1977 Honeywell exercised its option and GE received the maximum number of Honeywell shares.

VALUE
TRANSFER

The computer leasing industry

This chapter deals with the second major category of opportunity in the area of value transformation. It examines how the managements of a number of firms, all lessors of main frame computer systems, *transferred* value by taking advantage of major imperfections in the market valuations of their equity securities. Managers can sometimes transfer wealth for the benefit of all (or some subset) of their existing shareholders:

1. at the expense of shareholders of *other* firms; or
2. at the expense of investors purchasing *newly issued* shares of the firm in question; or
3. at the expense of a *subset* of the existing shareholder group.

We will explore how the managements of numerous firms participating in the computer leasing business transferred value across different shareholder groups utilizing the methods noted in (1) and (2) above. This value transfer occurred in the midst of a $1 billion swing in the market value of computer leasing common equities that took place during the period 1966–70.

Background on computer leasing

Most users of general purpose computers in the late 1960s leased rather than owned their computer equipment. Widespread leasing had long been a custom in the data processing industry. Prior to 1956 this phenomenon could be explained by IBM's unwillingness to offer its data processing equipment for sale. As a result of a consent decree signed in 1956, IBM was required to "offer for sale all equipment which it offers for lease and must establish a sales price for such equipment which will have a commercially reasonable relationship to its lease charges for the same equipment."[1] While this consent decree made the outright purchase of IBM data processing equipment possible, most users of IBM equipment continued to favor the one-year lease contract.[2] A short-term lease freed the user from any risk of technological obsolescence and made "trading-up" a simple matter if the user's data processing needs outgrew the capacity of the machine in question.

The popularity of the one-year lease contract, over time, produced a strong competitive advantage for IBM. As noted in Chapter 6, growth in the computer industry entailed huge capital requirements. For example, a typical computer selling for $1,000,000 might have a manufacturing cost of about $400,000. All other corporate operating expenses (such as engineering, selling, and administrative overhead) might add another $300,000 to the machine's cost, leaving a pretax profit of $300,000 for the manufacturer if the machine were sold outright.[3] The same computer installed under a manufacturer's standard lease contract would produce annual revenues of about $238,000, but the expenses associated with earning this revenue would amount to $460,000 during the first year, as shown in Table 7–1.

If the computer's basic manufacturing cost of $400,000 were depreciated over four years using the sum-of-the-years' digits method, the first year depreciation expense would be $160,000. The "other" costs (such as marketing, engineering, etc.) of $300,000 were immediately charged off as an expense. This led to a first-year loss of $222,000 on the leased

TABLE 7–1
First-year financial statement relating to the lease of a hypothetical computer with a sales price equal to $1,000,000

Revenue		$238,000
Depreciation	$160,000	
Other costs	300,000	
Total costs		460,000
Pretax profit (loss)		(222,000)
Income tax (credit)		(111,000)
After tax profit (loss)		(111,000)
Add: Depreciation		160,000
Cash inflow from lease		49,000
Cash outflow to manufacturer		400,000
Net cash outflow in first year		$351,000

[1] *United States* v. *International Business Machines Corporation,* 1956 Trade Cas. 71, 117 (S.D.N.Y. 1956).

[2] After the first year, IBM's standard lease became cancellable upon 90 days' notice.

[3] Barton M. Biggs, "Numbers Game," *Barron's,* July 24, 1967, p. 3; Digital Equipment Corp. Annual Report, 1967.

machine. If corporate income from other sources were available to offset the loss on this lease transaction, tax savings would eliminate half of this loss, or $111,000. Adding depreciation, a noncash expense, to the after-tax loss gives $49,000 as the first-year operating cash inflow from the leased computer. Since the manufacturer was assumed to have incurred an initial cash outflow of $400,000 to produce the machine, the lease transaction during the first year would cause a net cash drain of $351,000.

From this analysis it is easy to see why a large volume of computer shipments placed on lease could be, from a cash-flow standpoint, very damaging to a manufacturer. Since IBM enjoyed a cash flow twice as large as its nearest rival in 1965 (Table 6–7), this firm benefitted substantially from the demonstrated preference of users for short-term leases. For precisely the reasons indicated above, cash shortages in the mid to late 1960s forced manufacturers such as Honeywell to encourage outright sales or long-term leases (three to five years) against which they could immediately borrow almost the total discounted value of the future contractual lease payments. The need to limit the volume of shipments placed on one-year leases put a computer manufacturer such as Honeywell at a competitive disadvantage since many lessees favored one-year contracts in order to avoid obsolescence risk and the need to show a large future lease obligation in a footnote to their balance sheets.

Theoretically IBM assumed the risk of massive annual equipment returns since the company was protected only by one-year leases. In practice, however, a lessee rarely returned a piece of equipment in less than three to four years because of the considerable expense and time lost in converting existing computer programs to a new system. Lessees simply continued their contracts on a 90-day notification basis once they expired. Returned machines presented only minor marketing problems. If a returned computer was new enough so that the model was still in production, IBM would usually be able to place it with another lessee at the full rental rate enjoyed by a comparable piece of new equipment.

IBM's cash shortage in 1966

Although the ability to offer a one-year lease contract was a strong competitive advantage for IBM, customer acceptance of IBM's third generation System/360 line of computers was so great that in 1966 the company became a victim of its own success. The cash throw-off from operations, which amounted to $1.3 billion in 1966, was no longer sufficient to sustain IBM's growth rate. Whereas in 1964 (prior to the introduction of the System/360) IBM could boast of cash balances totaling nearly $1 billion, the situation had changed markedly by 1966, and the company found it necessary to raise money from external sources. In 1966 IBM's shareholders were called upon to supply the company with over $350 million in new equity capital. IBM's cash shortage in 1966 was probably unanticipated since in 1964 the company had *pre-paid* $160 million of loans bearing an interest rate of only 3½ percent.

System/360 was dramatically successful for IBM in terms of market acceptance, but the high percentage of shipments placed on a lease basis drained the corporation financially. Table 7–2 presents estimates of IBM's cash requirements arising solely from shipments of System/360 equipment placed on lease.

In September 1966, IBM's management moved to bring the firm's lease ratio down to a level consistent with the company's ability to finance its leases through internal cash generation. IBM reduced the sales price of its computers 3 percent and shortly thereafter raised its rental rates 3 percent. The expectation of trade sources was that this new pricing schedule would probably reverse the rising trend in IBM's lease ratio. When the new pricing decision was announced, the value of shipments made on a *lease basis* was estimated to exceed the value of shipments *sold outright* by almost 6 to 1. If the new pricing schedule could reduce the lease ratio from the estimated 85 percent[4] of shipments, the immediate cash inflow would be substantial, and the downward pressure on short-run corporate earnings implied by Table 7–1 would also be reduced. Since the heavy placements of leased systems were depressing earnings in 1966, this price change would also help the company maintain its historical uptrend in earnings per share.

TABLE 7–2

Estimated IBM cash flow arising solely from shipments of System/360 equipment placed on lease ($ millions)

	1966	1967	1968	1969	1970
Total lease revenue	518.3	1,130.7	1,800.3	2,510.7	3,272.5
Depreciation expense	348.4	673.0	933.2	1,108.2	1,198.3
Other costs	653.3	771.9	844.1	895.5	960.1
Pretax income	−483.4	−314.3	23.1	507.1	1,114.0
After-tax profit	−241.7	−157.1	11.5	253.5	557.0
Total inflow from operations	106.7	515.9	944.7	1,361.7	1,755.3
Total equipment investment	871.1	1,029.2	1,125.4	1,194.0	1,280.2
Cash inflow − outflow	−764.4	−513.3	−180.7	167.7	475.1

Assumptions:
1. Table 7–1 cost structure for equipment manufacture.
2. IBM shipments (at sale value) equal to $3.7 billion, $4.4 billion, $4.9 billion, $5.3 billion, and $5.8 billion in 1966 through 1970.
3. The fraction of total computer shipments placed on a lease basis equal 0.85, 0.86, 0.87, 0.88, and 0.89 in 1966 through 1970.

---

[4] Biggs, "Numbers Game."

The economics of independent computer leasing companies

The cash squeeze at IBM in 1966, coupled with the fact that an entirely new generation of computers was being introduced, created a potential profit opportunity for financial entrepreneurs. IBM had widened substantially the spread between the revenues available to computer lessors and the cost of purchasing computers to be placed on lease. Financial middlemen could purchase computers from IBM at standard prices and place them with lessees at rental rates 10 percent lower than those charged by IBM. If the machines were depreciated over ten years in contrast to the manufacturer's practice of using four years, reported profits could be substantial even during the first year that the equipment was placed in service. Since the System/360 represented an entirely new computer generation when it was introduced in late 1965, the economic life of these machines was expected to extend well into the 1970s, limiting an early buyer's risk of premature technological obsolescence. Experience showed that second generation equipment such as IBM's 1400 series was actively manufactured and marketed for as long as six years (1960–66), and the rental of equipment in this series was expected to continue for a number of years beyond 1966. The used market value of IBM's highly popular 1401 model had fallen from 70 percent of original purchase price to 40 percent of original purchase price within one year of the introduction of the IBM System/360 computer, however.[5]

Table 7–3 presents pro forma financial statements for a computer system costing $1 million that is placed on lease by a computer leasing company on January 1, 1966. The table assumes that the computer would be initially leased for two years at a rental rate 10 percent below the rate charged by IBM. After two years, the lease would be renewed annually at a discount that increases by two percentage points per year. At the end of a total of ten years, it is assumed that the machine would be sold for 40 percent of its original cost (that is, $400,000). The purchase price of the computer is assumed to be financed with a 2-to-1 debt-to-equity ratio, with the debt carrying an interest rate of nine percent.

The upper half of Table 7–3 (Lines 1–16) shows the annual federal income tax liability and the annual cash flow. The lower half of the table (Lines 17–31) shows the income statement and capital structure as they would appear in a leasing company's shareholder reports. Finally, Table 7–3 shows (in Lines 32 and 33) the anticipated profitability of a

---

[5] Equity Research Associates, "Data Processing Equipment Leasing," August 19, 1966, p. 6.

System/360 computer lease. The profitability measures are stated in terms of annual ROEs (Line 32) and in terms of the internal rate of return on the equity investment of $334,000 that was made in order to acquire the computer.[6]

Although Table 7–3 may at first appear complex, careful examination of a very few lines (those relating to depreciation expense and net profit) will show the importance of management accounting choices in the earnings reports of companies operating in this industry. Lines 9 and 22 project the annual pretax profit for tax and shareholder reports, respectively. It is important to note that except for the depreciation charge, all the revenue and expense items used to calculate pre-tax profit in the tax and shareholder reports are exactly the same each year. Only depreciation charges differ. This difference is enough to shift after-tax income in the first year from a $60,157 deficit (Line 12) to a $32,799 profit (Line 25). As the cumulative ten-year totals for these lines indicate, the *total* profit realized over the life of the computer system is not influenced by the assumed depreciable *life* or the *method* used for determining the annual depreciation charge. The total after-tax profit is $418,100 in each case. The *timing* of the recognition of that profit is dramatically influenced by the choice of depreciation life and method, however (Line 12 versus Line 25 of Table 7–3). Computer leasing firms generally chose a depreciation life and method designed to maximize near-term earnings.

One final factor is also clear from Table 7–3. Computer leasing could not be a highly profitable business. Given the assumptions of Table 7–3, the discounted cash flow rate of return on equity for a computer acquired in 1966 was projected at 12.9 percent. As shown in Table 7–4, the projected rate of return on equity ranged roughly between 10 percent and 15 percent when the assumptions were varied regarding:

a. the expected *technological life* of a machine placed on rent as of January 1, 1966, and
b. the expected *erosion rate* in the rental stream during the life of the equipment, and
c. the anticipated *sale value* of the equipment at the end of its technological life.

Given the risks to which computer lessors were exposed, these projected rates of return on equity do *not* suggest that computer lessors were likely to be earning a return significantly in excess of their equity

---

[6] Table 7–3 assumes that lenders were willing to advance debt in the ratio of $2 debt to $1 of equity. These were typical terms for the industry.

TABLE 7-3

Financial statements relating to a $1,000,000 computer placed under a two-year lease contract (cash flow and profitability as reported to shareholders for a typical computer leasing company; lines 1–31 in dollars)

Line		1966	1967	1968	1969	1970	1971	1972	1973	1974	1975	Cumulative totals
	Leasing company tax reports											
1	IBM rental rate	256,000	256,000	256,000	256,000	256,000	256,000	256,000	256,000	256,000	256,000	—
2	Discount allowed (See Note 1)	25,600	25,600	30,720	35,840	40,960	46,080	51,200	56,320	61,440	66,560	—
3	Overtime premium	7,680	7,680	7,680	7,680	7,680	7,680	7,680	7,680	7,680	7,680	—
4	Gross rentals	238,080	238,080	232,960	227,840	222,720	217,600	212,480	207,360	202,240	197,120	—
5	Maintenance expense (10% of Line 1)	25,600	25,600	25,600	25,600	25,600	25,600	25,600	25,600	25,600	25,600	—
6	Depreciation expense (Note 2)	188,889	165,278	141,667	118,056	94,444	70,833	47,222	23,611	—	—	—
7	Interest (9% of Line 30) (Note 3)	59,940	48,354	35,726	22,375	8,238	—	—	—	—	—	—
8	Selling, General, and Administrative	23,808	23,808	23,296	22,784	22,272	21,760	21,248	20,736	20,224	19,712	—
9	Pretax profit (loss)	(60,157)	(24,960)	6,672	39,025	72,166	99,407	118,410	137,413	156,416	151,808	696,200
10	Taxes (before investment credit)	—	—	—	—	16,373	49,703	59,204	68,706	78,208	75,904	348,100
11	Investment credit utilized (Note 4)	—	—	—	—	8,186	24,851	29,602	7,359	—	—	70,000
12	Net profit	(60,157)	(24,960)	6,672	39,025	63,979	74,555	88,807	76,066	78,208	75,904	418,100
13	Add depreciation	188,889	165,278	141,667	118,056	94,444	70,833	47,222	23,611	—	—	850,000
14	Total cash inflow	128,732	140,318	148,338	157,081	158,424	145,388	136,030	99,677	78,208	75,904	1,268,100
15	Remaining investment credit	70,000	70,000	70,000	70,000	61,813	36,962	7,359	—	—	—	—
16	Tax loss carryforward	60,157	85,117	78,445	39,420	—	—	—	—	—	—	—
	Leasing company shareholder reports											
17	Gross rentals	238,080	238,080	232,960	227,840	222,720	217,600	212,480	207,360	202,240	197,120	—
18	Depreciation (Note 2)	85,000	85,000	85,000	85,000	85,000	85,000	85,000	85,000	85,000	85,000	—
19	Maintenance	25,600	25,600	25,600	25,600	25,600	25,600	25,600	25,600	25,600	25,600	—
20	Interest (Note 3)	59,940	48,354	35,726	22,375	8,238	—	—	—	—	—	—
21	Selling, General, and Administrative	23,808	23,808	23,296	22,784	22,272	21,760	21,248	20,736	20,224	19,712	—
22	Pretax profit	43,732	55,318	63,338	72,081	81,610	85,240	80,632	76,024	71,416	66,808	696,200
23	Taxes (before investment credit)	21,866	27,659	31,669	36,040	40,805	42,620	40,316	38,012	35,708	33,404	348,100
24	Investment credit used (Note 4)	10,933	13,829	15,834	18,020	11,384	—	—	—	—	—	70,000
25	Net profit	32,799	41,488	47,503	54,061	52,189	42,620	40,316	38,012	35,708	33,404	418,100
26	Remaining investment credit	59,067	45,238	29,404	11,384	—	—	—	—	—	—	—
27	After-tax cash flow from liquidation (Note 5)	—	—	—	—	—	—	—	—	—	275,000	—
28	Debt repayment	128,732	140,318	148,338	157,081	91,531	0	0	0	0	0	666,000
29	Cash flow to equity	0	0	0	0	66,893	145,388	136,030	99,677	78,208	75,904	602,100
30	Debt outstanding (start of year)	666,000	537,268	396,950	248,612	91,531	0	0	0	0	0	0
31	Net worth (start of year)	334,000	366,799	408,287	455,790	509,851	495,147	392,379	296,665	235,000	192,500	—
32	Net profit/net worth	0.098	0.113	0.116	0.119	0.102	0.086	0.103	0.128	0.152	0.174	—
33	IRR on equity investment (1966–75)										0.129	—

Assumptions:

1. Discount: 10 percent of the IBM rate through 1967; increasing by two percentage points per year thereafter to 26 percent in 1975.
2. Depreciation: eight years sum-of-years-digits, 15 percent residual value for tax purposes; ten years, straight line, 15 percent residual for shareholders.
3. Interest: 9 percent rate on outstanding balance, which is reduced each year by the full cash flow.
4. Investment credit: 7 percent investment credit deducted from tax liability as fast as possible rather than evenly amortized over the life of asset.
5. Cash flow from liquidation: The computer is sold for 40 percent of original cost at end of 1975; taxes paid at the corporate rate (50 percent).

TABLE 7-4
Discounted-cash-flow rate of return on equity invested in a System/360 computer placed on lease January 1, 1966, (as a function of: (a) The technological life of the equipment; (b) The annual increase in the discount from IBM rates required to keep the computer on lease; and (c) The sale value of the computer versus original cost at the end of its technological life)

	Annual increase in discount from IBM rates (% points/year)	Technological life (years)		
		8	10	12
Assuming sale @ 40%	0	0.128	0.144	0.153
of original cost at end	2	0.116	0.129	0.136
of technological life	4	0.103	0.113	0.116
Assuming sale @ 70%	0	0.154	0.160	0.164
of original cost at end	2	0.143	0.147	0.149
of technological life	4	0.132	0.133	0.131

capital costs. Indeed this is hardly a surprising conclusion. It is unlikely to require enormous skill to persuade a lessee of IBM equipment to send his monthly rental check for computer equipment to a non-IBM address in exchange for a 10 percent discount! Absent the problem of capital availability, which we shall explore momentarily, the entry barriers associated with the computer leasing business are modest. In terms of the Chapter 1 valuation model, we would not expect rational investors to value the securities of computer leasing firms significantly in excess of book value.

Security valuation errors in the computer leasing industry

Basic economics notwithstanding, investors in the 1966-68 period perceived great future potential in the equity securities of computer leasing firms. The market value of the common stocks of three computer leasing firms noted in Table 7-5 averaged about *seven times* the book

TABLE 7-5
1967 fiscal year-end data for three of the largest independent computer leasing firms

	Net profit/ Average equity	Market value/ Book value	(Market price/share)/ (Earnings/share)
Data Processing Financial and General Corp.	0.174	7.9	52
Leasco Data Processing Equipment Corp.	0.132	9.1	105
Randolph Computer Corp. . .	0.111	3.8	54

value of their common stocks at the close of their 1967 fiscal years. The price/earnings ratios of each of their common stocks exceeded 50 in this same time frame. Given the unexceptional rates of return on equity earned by these firms (Table 7–5) and the modest level of profitability expected on System/360 leases that these firms would write in the future,[7] one naturally wonders why these securities were valued so highly.

> *The answer appears to rest with initial investor ignorance about the basic economics of the computer leasing business, and investors' use of a valuation model that was, in the short run, unrelated to the discounted value of future anticipated cash flows.*

Indeed, the valuation method utilized by investors appears to have involved little more than estimating next year's earnings per share for a firm, and multiplying that figure by a price/earnings ratio that was considered historically representative for the industry. The following comment from a brokerage report on the computer leasing industry was representative of the thinking and writing of securities analysts in 1968.

> The price/earnings ratio of stocks in this group possibly could be based on annualized earnings for the fourth quarter of the fiscal year ahead rather than the sum of the four quarters ahead. . . . If that is the case, a 30–40 times multiple for the full year ahead may become regarded as reasonable and not "fully valued" as determined by conventional practice.[8]

Investor ignorance regarding the basic economics of computer leasing

The 1966–68 era was a period of soaring investor enthusiasm for the equity securities of firms involved in the data processing industry. In late 1967, Merrill Lynch, the nation's largest retail brokerage firm, produced a multicolored brochure entitled "Investing in the Computer Industry." The brochure carried a brief business description along with share price charts for 25 firms involved in the data processing industry. Price charts for three of those firms are presented in Figure 7–1. The basic pattern of these charts, that of a fish hook, was an interesting harbinger of the course of future events.

In the Merrill Lynch brochure, as in other reports of that time, computer leasing firms were considered to be a major segment of the com-

---

[7] As we shall see later, in Table 7–9, the profitability of computers acquired later in the product-life cycle of the System/360 line of computers was expected to be lower than the profitability of machines acquired earlier.

[8] Market Letter, Hornblower & Weeks, Hemphill, Noyes, "Computer Leasing Industry," April 1, 1968.

FIGURE 7–1

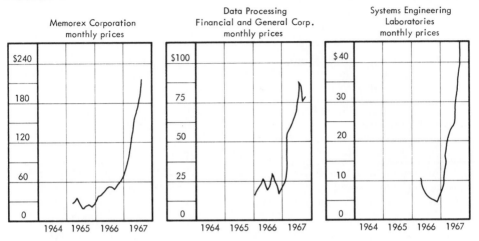

Memorex Corporation monthly prices	Data Processing Financial and General Corp. monthly prices	Systems Engineering Laboratories monthly prices

puter industry, which also included main frame manufacturers, peripheral equipment manufacturers, and software and service companies.[9]
As part of the computer industry, leasing firms were cloaked in all the
glamor associated with this industry. More specifically, the common
stocks of these firms enjoyed price/earnings ratios and market-value/
book-value ratios comparable to other data-processing oriented firms.
The fact that computer lessors had no proprietary products, no other
entry barriers, and no prospect for earning rates of return on equity
significantly in excess of their equity capital costs did not matter. These
firms all had the words "computer" or "data processing" in their names.
That was enough. The economics of the business were, at the time, less
important. Indeed, I have been unable to locate a *single* research report
aimed at investors (institutional or retail) in the late 1960s that ever
analyzed the rate of return (in the way presented in Table 7–3) that
a leasing firm could expect from its equity investment in computers.[10]

---

[9] It was not until early 1970 that computer leasing firms began to be viewed as
distinct from the rest of the computer industry. At that time one prominent Wall
Street research firm commented as follows: "Since computer leasing is basically a
financial proposition [we] will no longer view it as a part of our coverage on the
computer industry." (Equity Research Associates, "Computer Leasing—Rain, Rain,
Rain," January 21, 1970.)

[10] An abbreviated first-year income statement relating to a computer with a $1
million acquisition cost appeared in an article by Dick H. Brandon, "Latest Neurosis
—Computer Leasing," *Financial Analysts Journal,* May–June 1968, p. 89. Earlier,
another analyst had presented an eight-year forecast of annual income for a typical
computer lessor (Arthur D. Little, Inc., Service to Investors, "Data Processing Equipment Leasing," July 29, 1966). These reports, incomplete as they were, represent
the closest approximation to an economic analysis of the computer leasing industry
that I have encountered.

The valuation model used by computer leasing company investors

If investors were unaware (and perhaps uninterested) in the basic economics of computer leasing, what factors were important in helping investors to reach valuation decisions? The answer appears to be simply the *near-term anticipated growth rate in earnings per share.* In Chapter 2 we noted that high-ROE firms frequently produced rapid growth in earnings per share. This is simply the mathematical result produced when a high ROE and a high rate of earnings reinvestment are coupled together. We also noted in Chapter 2 (page 86) the five other avenues by which a firm might, over a short time interval, produce rapid growth in earnings per share. None of these other avenues required a high ROE, but the rapid growth in earnings per share produced in each case could not be sustained over a long time period. The last of these "other" methods noted in Chapter 2 was likened to a chain letter. The process works as outlined in the following hypothetical example. A firm with a net worth of $10 earns $1 and has one share outstanding. It thus earns a 10 percent rate of return on the book value of its equity. Given the risk inherent in its business, the cost of equity for our hypothetical firm is assumed to be 10 percent. Since the rate of return earned by the firm on its equity capital, and the cost of that equity capital, are equal, as noted in Chapter 1 the firm's common stock should sell for exactly its book value of $10 per share. Assume that for some reason not yet defined, investors have grossly overvalued the firm's common stock. Assume that investors have awarded the common stock a price of $30 per share and a price/earnings ratio of 30. The firm seizes upon the opportunity presented by its overvalued stock price, and sells one new share of stock for $30. It then invests the proceeds from the sale so as to earn a 10 percent return on equity. As shown in Table 7–6, the firm now earns $2 per share on the two shares outstanding. In one year it has *doubled* its earnings/share. Surely a firm with the proven ability to double its earnings per share in a year now *deserves* a price/earnings ratio of at least 30 even if the firm did not merit such a valuation initially!

TABLE 7–6
Chain letter earnings-per-share growth

Year	Number of shares at beginning of year	Earnings per share	Price	New shares sold	Amount realized from sale	Additional earnings at 10% accounting rate of return	Total earnings
1	1	$1	$ 30	1	$ 30	$ 3	$ 4
2	2	2	60	2	120	12	6
3	4	4	120	4	480	48	64
4	8	8	240	8	1,920	192	256

The cycle then ratchets ahead one year and is repeated. The tabulation shows that so long as (a) stock can be sold at a price/earnings ratio of 30 and (b) the proceeds can be invested at a 10 percent accounting rate of return (the equivalent of a price/earnings ratio of 10), earnings per share can be *doubled* in each year. The tabulation shows that to double earnings per share each year, however, the amount of equity capital raised each year must be increased by a factor of *four*.[11] The stakes in this game thus escalate quite rapidly. The process outlined above captures the essence of the computer leasing industry. The game included fast growth accompanied by a high price/earnings ratio and an ROE that was, at best, mediocre.

The early expansion of the capital bases of the firms involved in computer leasing was explosive, as was required by the chain letter example. Indeed, in the 1966–68 period it was not unusual to see a computer leasing firm complete three public security offerings in an 18-month period. Few *new* businesses have attracted such vast sums of money spread across so many firms in such a short period of time. Some relevant growth statistics for 11 of the major firms in the industry are presented in Lines 1–16 of Table 7–7.

The chain letter—The lull before the storm

As the computer portfolios of leasing companies grew between 1966 and 1968 (Lines 1–3, Table 7–7) so did their earnings per share (Lines 11–13, Table 7–7) and so did their stock prices (Lines 14–16, Table 7–7). By mid-1969, however, the expansion rate of these leasing companies' computer portfolios began to wind down (Lines 1–5, Table 7–7). There were several reasons for this phenomenon.

First, the annual doubling of System/360 computer purchases by computer lessors evidenced in Column 12 of Table 7–7 simply could not continue much beyond 1968 because of both *competitive* and *physical* limitations.

Second, as the industry matured, investors and the public accounting firms that audited the financial statements of computer lessors began to

---

[11] The chain-letter formula for calculating next year's stock price is a function of the firm's (a) price/earnings ratio, (b) return on equity, and (c) rate of equity capital expansion. The general equation follows below.

$$P_2 = \frac{[(EPS_1)(S_1) + (NS_1)(P_1)(R)]}{S_1 + NS_1} \left(\frac{P_1}{E_1}\right),$$

where

P = price per share,
S = shares outstanding at start of year,
NS = new shares issued in year,
R = accounting rate of return earned on equity.

TABLE 7-7

Growth in (a) the acquisition cost of leased computers; (b) the capital bases; (c) the reported earnings per share; and (d) the common stock prices of eleven major independent computer lessors during the late 1960s

Line	Date	(1) Boothe	(2) CIG	(3) Dearborn	(4) DCL	(5) DPF&G	(6) Granite†	(7) Greyhound	(8) Itel	(9) Randolph	(10) Reliance†	(11) Rockwood	(12) Total
	Gross value of computer equipment on lease ($ millions)												
1	Year end 1966	0	0	0	0	28.6	0.4	73.1	0	29.3	0	22.2	153.6
2	1967	12.7	14.3	7.8	12.7	121.9	17.1	127.7	0	73.6	17.0	92.1	496.9
3	1968	143.0	30.3	57.8	135.4	207.8	67.4	197.8	104.1	156.0	93.2	137.1	1,329.9
4	1969	158.5	45.5	74.8	166.0	227.9	80.9	217.6	195.5	167.0e	187.4	158.4	1,679.5
5	1970	204.8*	48.2	78.5	177.4	230.3	85.3	217.9	199.6	169.0e	253.2*	158.0	1,822.2*
	Total capital employed (borrowed money + net worth); ($ millions)												
6	Year end 1966	0	0	0	0	25.8	13.3	48.0	0	29.9	15.7	19.0	151.7
7	1967	32.1	20.0	5.7	18.6	119.1	46.8	86.7	0	77.1	61.3	99.8	567.2
8	1968	157.1	38.8	86.4	139.6	198.0	111.9	149.6	99.0	145.7	379.5	260.6	1,766.2
9	1969	163.2	47.1	109.2	154.2	193.9	159.2	170.4	187.1	145.7e	497.1	244.5	2,071.6
10	1970	191.5	43.7	106.5	150.3	172.0	159.1	153.7	221.9	145.7e	587.3	219.4	2,151.1
	Earnings per share as originally reported to shareholders‡ ($/share)												
11	Year end 1966	(0.15)	0.27	0.02	0.02	0.68	0.31	0.85	0.04	0.42	0.18	0.68	—
12	1967		0.30	1.50	0.28	1.16	0.80	1.09	0.17	0.99	0.26	2.24	—
13	1968	0.84				2.18	1.05	1.29		1.84	2.30	3.71	—
	Common stock price ($/share)												
14	12/31/66	—	—	—	—	11-7/8	6-7/8	9	—	8	6-7/8	8	—
15	12/31/67	—	23-1/4	23	20-1/4	64-3/4	40-1/8	35-3/8	—	53-7/8	27-1/2	49-1/2	—
16	12/31/68	45-1/2		46	58-1/8	58-1/8	43-3/4	36-1/8	32-1/4	40-1/4	49-3/4	53-1/4	—

Note: In Lines 1–13 in the table above, when a company's fiscal year ends on or before June 30, the data for that year are recorded under the prior year. The fiscal years of CIG, DPF&G, Granite, and Rockwood ended, respectively, on 3/31, 5/31, 2/28, and 3/31. Accordingly, these data are recorded under the prior year.

* Data for Boothe includes $50 million of equipment (at cost) acquired by Boothe from GAC Computer Leasing Corp.; data for Reliance include $55 million of equipment (at cost) acquired by Reliance in its European operations.

† Value shown for computer equipment includes operating leases only. Finance leases are not included.

‡ These data are not restated to reflect subsequent acquisitions, but are presented as the results were originally reported to shareholders, adjusted for stock splits.

Sources: Annual reports, 10K Reports, and *Bank and Quotation Record*.

understand more clearly the implications of the ten-year depreciation-life assumption associated with computers acquired late in the life-cycle of the System/360 generation. Attention began to focus on both the *accounting policies* and the *basic economics* of the computer leasing business.

Third, and finally, the actions taken by the managements of many computer leasing firms could lead to the inference that many of these managers were concerned in the late 1960s that the game in computer leasing was quickly drawing to a close. The management task thus shifted from one of rapidly building computer portfolios to one of finding some method for preserving, to the extent possible, the puffed-up equity values already generated. Preserving these values could involve continuing the chain letter by using some investment vehicle other than computer leasing. Each of the three factors noted above needs to be examined in turn.

The competitive and physical limitations on System/360 equipment purchases

According to the assumptions of Table 7–2 regarding IBM's shipments of System/360 computers, the computer leasing firms could not continue to more-than-double their purchases of equipment (as they had done in 1967 and 1968) much beyond 1968 without running into either a *competitive* or a *total-market* limitation. Indeed, the relationship between lease rates and sale price was critical to the economics of computer leasing. Since IBM determined both its lease rates and its equipment sale price, IBM could control, to some extent, the amount of equipment purchased by independent lessors by simply changing its sales prices or lease rates on System/360 equipment. IBM had utilized precisely this mechanism of economic incentives to *encourage* purchases in 1966. IBM's ability to influence the economic attractiveness of computer purchases might have placed a *competitive* ceiling on System/360 purchases. The fact that IBM was interested in the impact of computer leasing company purchases is reflected in an internal memo written in April of 1968. The memo sought

> . . . to examine the hypothesis that leasing company activity at some level of volume in relation to IBM total rental volume will reduce significantly IBM/360 program rental life and hence IBM program rental profits. If this hypothesis is valid, even in part, it poses an insidious, delayed action profit erosion problem which would not be readily apparent from the [data processing group] operating statements until serious erosion had begun to occur or had become imminent and irreversible.[12]

---

[12] *U.S.* v. *IBM*, Plaintiff Exhibit 3236, p. 1.

To illustrate the significance of computer leasing company purchase activity, the memo noted IBM's December 1966 placement projection for the System/360 Model 30.[13] The split between shipments made on a *rental* versus a *sale* basis is shown below. The contrast between projected and actual results demonstrates the substantial and *unanticipated* effect that computer leasing company purchases were having on IBM's operations.

	Unit placements through 1967		
	Projected (Dec. 1966)	Actual	Difference
Units rented	4,422	3,540	(882)
Units sold	417	1,231	814
Total placements	4,839	4,771	(68)

Even without any competitive response from IBM, however, it is clear from Table 7–8 that the independent computer lessors were also not far from a *market*-imposed ceiling on equipment purchases.

The accounting and economic constraints on System/360 purchases

In addition to competitive and physical limitations, both *accounting* and *economic* limitations to additional System/360 equipment purchases began to surface for the computer lessors after 1968. When the computer leasing firms began purchasing System/360 equipment in significant volume in 1966, it was clear that the useful life of these machines would not be determined by *physical* deterioration. The obsolescence would be

TABLE 7–8
Leasing company acquisition of IBM System/360 shipments required to maintain leasing company growth rates

Year	Projected total System/360 shipments by IBM ($ millions)	11 Major computer leasing companies' System/360 purchases ($ millions)	Leasing companies' purchases/IBM Shipments
1966	$3,700	$ 150	4%
1967	4,400	343	8%
1968	4,900	833	17%
1969	5,300	1,916*	36%e
1970	5,800	4,407*	76%e

*Represents estimated computer acquisitions required to maintain the 2.3 times annual growth factor in purchases established in 1967 and 1968.

[13] Ibid., p. 2.

technological rather than physical. Regardless of the date a System/360 machine was purchased, it would become obsolete at a *point* in time (following the introduction of a new computer generation) rather than after an elapsed *period* of time. This characteristic of a leasing company's principal asset caused accounting difficulties. The difficulty revolved around how long a public accounting firm could continue to accept a leasing company's ten-year depreciation-life assumption on all equipment, regardless of its acquisition date. The issue was critical, since if a computer lessor were forced to adopt, for example, an eight-year depreciation life on later equipment purchases, the first-year profits reported to shareholders from the acquisition of a new computer would drop by one third.[14] This eroded profitability would create havoc with the ability of a computer leasing firm to generate chain-letter growth in earnings per share. This problem extended into the realm of economics, as well as accounting. Computers purchased earliest in the life cycle of the System/360 were almost certain to earn the highest returns. As suggested by Table 7–3, a System/360 computer acquired on January 1, 1966, was expected to produce a discounted-cash-flow ROE of 12.9 percent. A System/360 computer acquired a year later would have a *shorter* technological life and, therefore, produce a lower rate of return. If we follow the assumptions of Table 7–3, we can generate a new table (Table 7–9) that shows in Column 1 the anticipated discounted-cash-flow internal rates of return on equity for System/360 computer purchases made at the beginning of each year after January 1, 1966. This table also shows the net present value of the cash flows streaming to the equity investment ($334,000) that would be required to purchase a $1 million computer. A net-present-value figure is calculated for both the 10 percent and 15 percent cost of equity capital assumptions in Columns 2 and 3 of Table 7–9. Given both the equity investment of $334,000 and the present value of the cash flows to the equity investment, we can immediately calculate the market-value/book-value ratio that a *rational* investor ought to place upon the equity investment required to purchase a computer for lease. This value would obviously be a function of the date the System/360 model was acquired and placed on lease, as Columns 4 and 5 of the table suggest.[15]

Table 7–9 confirms that the valuations placed on the equity securities

---

[14] Depreciation expense on a $1 million machine would increase from $850,000/10 = $85,000 per year to $850,000/8 = $106,250 per year. The added charge of $21,250 per year would reduce profit after taxes from $32,799 (Line 25, Table 7–3) to $22,174.

[15] A computer placed on lease as of January 1, 1966, for example, has a net present value of $74,000 at a 10 percent discount rate. The rational investor would thus value the equity investment of $334,000 at $\frac{\$74.000 + \$334.000}{\$334,000} = 1.2$ times book value.

TABLE 7-9

Summary statistics relating to the economic value of a System/360 computer acquired for $1 million and placed on a short-term lease at different dates in the life cycle of this computer generation

Line	Date equipment acquired and placed on lease	Discounted-cash-flow internal rate of return on equity*	Net present value ($000) of cash flow to equity discounted at an equity capital cost of:		Market-value/book-value ratio assuming an equity capital cost of:	
			10%	15%	10%	15%
1	1/1/66	12.9%	74.4	(45.2)	1.2	0.9
2	1/1/67	11.9%	46.0	(61.4)	1.1	0.8
3	1/1/68	10.5%	12.0	(82.2)	1.0	0.8
4	1/1/69	8.9%	(21.3)	(101.9)	0.9	0.7
5	1/1/70	7.0%	(51.3)	(117.5)	0.8	0.6
6	1/1/71	0.4%	(125.0)	(167.9)	0.6	0.5

*It is assumed that $334,000 of equity and $666,000 of debt carrying a 9 percent rate is used to acquire the $1 million system referred to in the table.

of computer leasing firms in 1967 (Table 7–5) were completely detached from economic reality. These securities probably did not even merit a market-value/book-value ratio of 1.0, let alone the average value of 7.0 that a number of them had achieved. Equally important, Columns 2 and 3 of Table 7–9 suggest that the acquisition of new System/360 equipment after January 1, 1968, was practically a guaranteed method for destroying the real *economic value* of a computer leasing firm's equity, since the returns to be earned on that equity were certainly less than any reasonable assumption regarding equity cost. Why, then, did computer lessors continue to buy computers beyond January 1, 1968, as suggested by Column 12, Lines 3–5 of Table 7–7?

Almost without exception, the senior managers of computer leasing firms in 1969 were also significant shareholders in these enterprises. It would not be unreasonable to assume that many of these managers were as concerned about the effect of continued computer purchases on the ultimate value of their *personal*-wealth position as they were about the impact of this decision on the wealth position of the corporation's shareholder group *overall*. Herein lies the critical dilemma that inevitably arises in situations involving economically irrational pricing of securities.

> *Decisions that benefit one group of shareholders do not necessarily benefit all groups of shareholders. Indeed the benefit to one group of shareholders can often come at the expense of another group of shareholders.*

The demonstration of the above point proceeds as follows. Imagine a computer leasing firm whose history roughly parallels that outlined in the chain-letter example of Table 7–6. Specifically the firm is presented with the opportunity to buy $10 million of System/360 computers on January 1, 1966. The purchase would be financed with $3.34 million of equity and $6.66 million of debt. Stock is sold at $10 per share to the firm's founder-managers and a group of private investors. Each year thereafter the firm faces the opportunity to double its computer purchases of the prior year, and if this is done, the firm's stock price is assumed to double each year, in keeping with the rapid growth in the firm's reported earnings per share. An example of this situation in which System/360 computers are purchased over periods ranging from one to five years is developed in Table 7–10. As this table shows, from an earnings-per-share standpoint it is attractive to sell stock and continue computer purchases for as long as (*a*) public accountants permit the utilization of a ten-year depreciation life and (*b*) investors continue to value the stock irrationally. If the valuation process utilized by investors simply involves applying a bloated price/earnings ratio to a growing stream of earnings per share, then the firm would serve the interests of its investors by forging ahead with additional System/360 purchases.

If investors were ultimately destined to adopt the *rational* valuation model presented in Chapter 1, however, a serious conflict of investor

TABLE 7-10

Calculation of the *cash flow* to a share of common stock and the *earnings per share* of a hypothetical computer leasing firm that stops acquiring System/360 computer equipment at various dates between January 1, 1966, 1967, and January 1, 1970

Line		1966	1967	1968	1969	1970	1971	1972	1973	1974	1975
1	Gross computer purchases in year ($ millions)	10	0	0	0	0	0	0	0	0	0
2	Cash flow to equity/share ($)	0	0	0	0	2.00	4.35	4.07	2.98	2.34	10.51
3	Reported earnings/share ($)	0.98	1.24	1.42	1.62	1.56	1.28	1.21	1.14	1.07	4.73
4	Gross computer purchases in year ($ millions)	10	20	0	0	0	0	0	0	0	0
5	Cash flow to equity/share ($)	0	0	0	0	0	4.93	6.29	5.83	3.87	15.76
6	Reported earnings/share ($)	0.98	1.60	1.96	2.13	2.42	2.10	1.81	1.71	1.60	5.84
7	Gross computer purchases in year ($ millions)	10	20	40	0	0	0	0	0	0	0
8	Cash flow to equity/share ($)	0	0	0	0	0	0	9.14	9.43	8.52	24.98
9	Reported earnings/share ($)	0.98	1.60	2.48	2.94	3.21	3.66	3.09	2.66	2.49	11.06
10	Gross computer purchases in year ($ millions)	10	20	40	80	0	0	0	0	0	0
11	Cash flow to equity/share ($)	0	0	0	0	0	0	0	15.33	14.67	44.96
12	Reported earnings/share ($)	0.98	1.60	2.48	3.76	4.46	4.89	5.59	4.89	4.01	6.97
13	Gross computer purchases in year ($ millions)	10	20	40	80	160	0	0	0	0	0
14	Cash flow to equity/share ($)	0	0	0	0	0	0	0	0	24.55	84.26
15	Reported earnings/share ($)	0.98	1.60	2.48	3.76	5.84	6.86	7.53	8.63	8.15	4.76

Assumptions:
1. Economic assumptions are the same as those made in Table 7–3.
2. Stock prices *double* each year (from $10 per share at January 1, 1966) as earnings per share expand. This doubling continues for as long as computer purchases also double in amount each year per Lines 1, 4, 7, 10, and 13.

interests emerges. This conflict is made apparent by Table 7–11. The issue is, "If we examine the problem in terms of *rational economics,* should our hypothetical company proceed with a common-stock offering on January 1, 1969, in order to acquire $80 million of additional System/ 360 computer systems?" According to Line 4, Column 1 of Table 7–9, the firm will earn a discounted-cash-flow return of 8.9 percent on its equity investment if the additional computers are purchased. The investor groups that have acquired (or will acquire) their shares on different dates and at different prices may fare quite differently as a result of our answer to this question. If we assume no further computer purchases (or common stock offerings) after January 1, 1969, then the original investors who purchased their shares at a price of $10 per share would (according to Line 4, Column 1 of Table 7–11) have acquired a share at that date with an *economic* value of $30.71.[16] This assumes that:

1. The investor would ignore all interim price gyrations in the stock market and hold his shares through December 31, 1975, and
2. The company would pay off its entire cash flow after debt amortization to its equity shareholders.

When should the firm stop selling new equity and cease investing in System/360 computers? Lines 1–5, Column 1 of Table 7–11 indicate that after three rounds of purchases, rational economics argue that the firm should stop buying new computers. Purchases made after January 1, 1968 simply *reduce* the net present value of the firm's total equity.[17]

---

[16] This $30.71 is derived from adding the acquisition cost of the share ($10) to the net present value of the share at that point, which (according to Line 4, Column 2 in Table 7–11) equaled $20.71.

[17] The net present value of the firm's total equity equals the discounted value of all cash flows to equity less the discounted value of all equity investments in the firm. The net present value of the firm would be zero if all of the firm's equity were invested at rates of return exactly equal to the cost of equity. The net present value of a firm's equity thus represents the *value created* as a result of the ability of a firm to invest in projects (the ownership of computers in this example) that produce returns that exceed capital costs.

IBM's analysts reached a similar conclusion regarding one time at which computer purchases would become economically unattractive. Using assumptions slightly different from those of Table 7–9, one IBM analyst calculated that the leasing companies would earn the following rates of return on equity via purchases of System/360 equipment made in the following years:

Date	Rate of return on equity
1965	12.2%
1966	11.2%
1967	9.5%
1968	7.0%
1969	4.6%

The IBM analyst concluded as follows: "There is an obvious trade-off in accepting a lower rate of return in order to maintain reported earnings for stockholders. In my opinion 6 percent is the minimum acceptable rate of return. Therefore I would stop buying IBM's System/360's [. . .] in 1969. . . ." (*U.S.* v. *IBM,* Plaintiff Exhibit 3095, p. 7.)

TABLE 7-11

Net present value of (1) The firm's total common equity and (2) A single share of common stock of a hypothetical computer leasing firm calculated as a function of the date and price at which the equity was acquired

Line	Firm stops acquiring new System/360 computers after:	(1) Net present value of the firm's total equity* ($ millions)	(2) on 1/1/66 @ $10 ($)	(3) on 1/1/67 @ $20 ($)	(4) on 1/1/68 @ $40 ($)	(5) on 1/1/69 @ $80 ($)	(6) on 1/1/70 @ $160 ($)
				Net present value† of a share purchased			
At 10% cost of equity							
1	1/1/66	0.7	2.22	—	—	—	—
2	1/1/67	1.6	6.44	(1.91)	—	—	—
3	1/1/68	1.9	12.33	4.56	(12.97)	—	—
4	1/1/69	0.5	20.71	13.77	(2.84)	(39.13)	—
5	1/1/70	(5.4)	32.90	27.18	11.91	(22.90)	(97.19)
At 15% cost of equity							
6	1/1/66	(0.5)	(1.05)	—	—	—	—
7	1/1/67	(1.5)	1.37	(6.89)	—	—	—
8	1/1/68	(4.1)	5.11	(2.62)	(20.01)	—	—
9	1/1/69	(9.7)	10.30	3.34	(13.16)	(49.13)	—
10	1/1/70	(20.9)	27.73	21.34	13.76	(37.71)	(111.37)

*The values in Column 1 equal the discounted value of all cash flows to equity less the discounted value of all equity investments in the firm.
†These values are equal to the discounted value of Lines 2, 4, 6, 8, and 10, respectively, of Table 7–10, less the acquisition cost of the share of stock in each instance.

Lines 1–5, Column 2 of Table 7–11 present quite a different answer, however. The founder-managers improve their net wealth position by continuing to buy computers right through January 1, 1970, so long as uninformed investors are willing to keep increasing the firm's share price each year in response to rapidly growing earnings per share (Lines 3, 6, 9, 12, and 15 in Table 7–10). The problem, as Table 7–11 shows, is that the last investors to acquire shares (before the chain letter stops) take a terrible beating when reality ultimately intrudes into the security-valuation process. Late investors get bailed out of their poor investments only when additional investors are brought into the game on economically even more disastrous terms. Ultimately this particular version of the chain-letter game must end, even if investors *never* wake up to reality. This is true because computer acquisitions after January 1, 1970, become so unprofitable that the cash flow from early, profitable computer acquisitions would ultimately have to be utilized to repay debt associated with later, unprofitable computer acquisitions that could not even cover their debt service charges.

Capitalizing on overvalued equities–The alternatives

It is, of course, difficult to know how well the managers of each computer leasing firm comprehended the dynamics of the game they were playing. Were these managers aware, for example, that by the late 1960s the opportunity to continue rapid growth of earnings per share via System/360 purchases would be over? Was it clear to these managers that the price of their firms' common stocks could not be sustained at the levels achieved in 1967 and 1968?

If the managers of computer leasing companies perceived a threat to the future profitability of their basic business, or to the sustainability of their stock prices, they could adopt a number of alternative strategies to deal with these problems.

First, the managers of computer leasing firms could sell a significant portion[18] of their own stock *before* the end of the chain letter was obvious to outside investors. This sale date would have to precede the point at which the prices of the equity securities of their firms returned to rational economic levels.

Second, the managers of computer leasing firms could have their firms be *acquired* for cash or for stock. Stock would be acceptable only if the acquiring firm were large enough so that when the value of computer leasing equities ultimately collapsed, the value of the common stock of

---

[18] It is unlikely that senior officers could sell all of their shares (except via strategy 2) without creating the very price collapse that they presumably hoped their stock sales would precede.

the firm into which they were merged would not be significantly depressed.

Third, the computer leasing firms could acquire the equity of *other* firms selling at lower price/earnings ratios so as to continue the chain letter a while longer. They could thus use *whole companies* rather than System/360 computers as their investment vehicle. By becoming conglomerates they would use the more traditional chain-letter method of achieving rapid earnings-per-share growth. Via conglomerate mergers they would layer-in significant additional earning power, and pay for it with overvalued computer leasing company common equity. When the collapse of the chain letter ultimately occurred, the position of shareholders who acquired their stock early (including the founder-managers) would be significantly improved (following the analogy of Table 7–11) over what would have been the case had the collapse occurred earlier.

Fourth, and finally, the managers of computer leasing firms could miss the value-transfer opportunity both personally and corporately. They could become, by choice or by accident, passive observers as the "puff" in the value of their firm's common stock ultimately disappeared.

As we will see shortly, all four of these alternative paths were followed by one or more of the management groups of the 11 computer lessors noted in Table 7–7.

The chain letter breaks and $1 billion disappears

Investors began to recognize the serious overvaluation of the common stocks of computer lessors in early 1969. Indeed, the value *erosion* in these stocks in 1969 and 1970 was practically the mirror image of the economically irrational value *explosion* that had taken place in 1966–67 (Figure 7–2). By the end of 1970, the market values of computer leasing common equities had fallen back to levels that could be explained more easily in terms of the rational economic model presented in Chapter 1.

The price changes from the month-end highs of 1968 to the year-end company values of 1970 swept away more than $1 billion in computer leasing equity values (Line 12, Columns 1 and 2 in Table 7–12) that had been generated between 1966 and 1968 (Figure 7–2). This erosion in value was no temporary phenomenon. Indeed, the aggregate value of the computer leasing company shares outstanding at the peak in 1968 was also more than $1 billion higher than it was at December 31, 1976 (Column 3, Table 7–12). This $1 billion value is an impressive figure, but the magnitude of the number is less important than one central fact:

> *If the economics of this industry had been correctly understood by investors in 1966 (utilizing data available at that time) a $1 billion value-transfer opportunity that spanned four years could never have existed.*

FIGURE 7-2

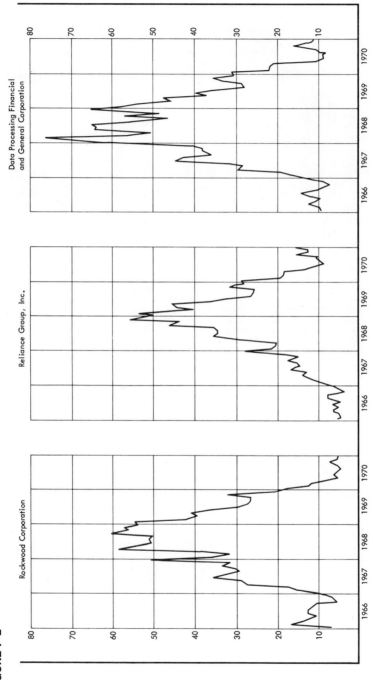

Market price of common stock (per share)

Rockwood Corporation

Reliance Group, Inc.

Data Processing Financial and General Corporation

Market price of common stock (per share)

TABLE 7–12

Peak month-end 1968 market value of the common shares outstanding for 11 computer lessors versus the market value of those same shares on December 31, 1970, and December 31, 1976

Line		(1) Market value ($ millions) 1968	(2) Market value ($ millions) 1970	(3) Market value ($ millions) 1976	(4) Market value ratio 1970/1968	(5) Market value ratio 1976/1968
1	Boothe Computer Corp. . . . . $	92	$ 21	$ 14‖	0.22	0.15
2	Computer Investors' Group . .	45	11	2	0.23	0.05
3	Dearborn Computer Corp.	72	38	86 §	0.52	1.20
4	Diebold Computer Leasing, Inc.	96	16	2	0.17	0.03
5	DPF&G	236	36	23	0.15	0.10
6	Granite Management Services Corp.	76	14	1	0.18	0.01
7	Greyhound Computer Corp. . .	157	31	33	0.20	0.21
8	Itel Corp.	119	59	47	0.50	0.40
9	Randolph Computer Corp. . . .	114	78‡	89‡	0.68	0.78
10	Reliance Group, Inc.*	452	124	155	0.27	0.34
11	Rockwood Corp.†	178	16	1	0.09	0.01
12	Total . . . . $	1,637	$444	$453	—	—

Note: The data of Columns 2 and 3 relate to the market value of the same number of shares outstanding as there were in 1968. This is not necessarily the same number of shares outstanding at December 31, 1970, or December 31, 1976.

*Previously known as Leasco Data Processing Equipment Corp.

†Previously known as Levin-Townsend Computer Corp.

‡Value of shares received in 1969 merger.

§Value of cash received in 1974 merger.

‖Value of shares received in 1976 merger.

Imperfections in the market mechanism for valuing securities clearly exist, and they occasionally occur on a fairly grand scale over rather long time periods. The computer leasing industry example demonstrates this fact quite clearly, as did the Avon Products example of Chapter 3. The computer leasing industry provided an extraordinary opportunity for the transfer of value. Leasing company managers capitalized on this opportunity in a number of ways.

Capitalizing on overvalued equities–Insider sales transactions

The senior managers of numerous computer leasing firms sold significant amounts of their own shareholdings in these firms in the 1967–70 period. As shown in Table 7–13, reports filed with the Securities and Exchange Commission indicate that during this period insiders[19] of at least four computer leasing firms individually divested shares in their

---

[19] The term "insider" is broadly defined to include officers, directors, and holders of 10 percent or more of any class of the firm's equity securities.

TABLE 7-13

Fraction of shares divested and estimated market value of shares divested by selected officers and directors of four computer lessors

	Percentage of ownership interest divested (January 1, 1967– June 30, 1970)*	Estimated market value of shares divested (January 1, 1967– June 30, 1967)† ($ millions)
Rockwood Computer Corp.		
President	27	4.7
Vice President	34	4.5
Granite		
Chairman	20	0.9
Director.	29	1.3
DPF		
Chairman	9	2.0
Reliance		
Chairman	21	1.7
Director.	32	2.9

*Equal to shares divested between January 1, 1967, and June 30, 1970, divided by the ownership interest at January 1, 1967.

†Equal to the shares divested (as reported monthly in the SEC publication "Official Summary of Securities Transactions and Holdings") multiplied by the month-end price of these shares. It should be noted that divested shares also include shares given to family members and charities. In addition, the divestiture data in the SEC "Summary" are sometimes incomplete, and for this reason the Line 2 data relating to the value of shares divested may be understated.

firms with market values exceeding $1 million. Since in most cases these shares were acquired as founder's stock, the shares had cost very little. Any cash proceeds received from the sale of such stock were thus almost entirely long-term capital gains. Interestingly, the managers of those firms who personally divested the greatest portion of their shareholdings in the 1967–70 period were also the managers of the firms (Rockwood and Granite) with the worst post-1970 stock performance records (Column 5, Table 7–12).

Capitalizing on overvalued equities–Diversification

By 1970 the opportunity for generating chain-letter growth in earnings per share was dead not only for System/360 purchases, but also for conglomerate mergers as well. Those computer lessors that had not already diversified by using their overvalued stock to acquire assets with solid earning power were simply out of luck by the end of 1970. The overvaluation spotlight has passed.

Five of the 11 independent computer lessors missed the opportunity to diversify significantly by 1970 (Column 1, Table 7–14). In the case of at least one of these firms, significant diversification via *major* acquisi-

TABLE 7-14

The value-transfer success of 11 computer leasing firms measured against their diversification success as of 1970

	(1)	(2) Firms undiversified by 1970	(3)	(4) Firms experiencing disastrous diversification by 1970	(5)	(6) Firms experiencing successful diversification and remaining independent	(7)	(8) Firms experiencing successful diversification and being ultimately acquired	(9)
	Percentage of 1970 revenue generated from businesses other than computer leasing*	Market value		Market value		Market value		Market value	
		1970/1968	1976/1968	1970/1968	1976/1968	1970/1968	1976/1968	1970/1968	1976/1968
Computer Investors' Group	0	0.23	0.05	—	—	—	—	—	—
Diebold Computer Leasing	0	0.17	0.03	—	—	—	—	—	—
DPF&G	0	0.15	0.10	—	—	—	—	—	—
Boothe Computer	11	0.22	0.15	—	—	—	—	—	—
Greyhound Computer	13	0.20	0.21	—	—	—	—	—	—
Itel	37†	—	—	—	—	0.50	0.40	—	—
Rockwood	43	—	—	0.09	0.01	—	—	—	—
Dearborn Computer	53	—	—	—	—	—	—	0.52	1.20
Granite Mangement	63	—	—	0.18	0.01	—	—	—	—
Reliance Group	88	—	—	—	—	0.27	0.34	—	—
Randolph Computer	99	—	—	—	—	—	—	0.78	0.78

Market value of a common share at 12/31/70 and 12/31/76 versus the value of that share at the month-end peak in 1968

*Data are for each firm's 1970 fiscal year.
†Includes acquisitions negotiated but not yet completed at December 31, 1970.
Source: Data drawn from Table 7–12.

tion was attempted, but the effort failed.[20] In a few other cases, the firms appear not to have tried to diversify at all. For the undiversified firms, the value of their common equities at December 31, 1970, was only about 20 percent of their 1968 month-end highs (Column 2, Table 7–14). Six years later, at December 31, 1976, the value of the common stocks of the five undiversified computer lessors ranged from 3 percent to 21 percent of the month-end highs that these stocks had reached in 1968 (Column 3, Table 7–14).

A substantial part of the continued erosion in the equity values of these firms between December 31, 1970, and December 31, 1976, can be explained in terms of the technological obsolescence that occurred when IBM introduced a new generation of computers. The first two models of System/370 were announced in mid-1970, with the first deliveries to occur in 1971. The new generation of computers significantly reduced the future revenue potential of System/360 equipment. Indeed, as Table 7–15 suggests, a number of computer lessors in 1972 wrote off a large enough fraction of the value of their computer portfolios to more than wipe out the cumulative pretax profits earned from computer leasing in the period 1966–72.[21]

Six of the independent computer lessors were significantly diversified by December 31, 1970. Two of the six (Rockwood and Granite) diversified with catastrophic results. In their haste to diversify, the managers of these firms had acquired businesses that were even *less* attractive

TABLE 7–15
Cumulative pretax profits of three computer lessors from 1966 to 1972 including the impact of equipment write-off in 1972 ($ millions)

	Cumulative pretax profits 1966–72 prior to 1972 write-off	1972 Write-off of computer equipment	Cumulative pretax profits 1966–72
Boothe Computer Corp.	8	34	(26)
DPF&G	24	42	(18)
Diebold Computer Leasing, Inc.	16	31	(15)

[20] In December 1967, DPF&G attempted to acquire the Railway Express Agency, Inc. The effort was unsuccessful. In July 1968, DPF&G attempted to acquire the Reliance Insurance Company. Another computer lessor, Leasco Data Processing, acquired Reliance and ultimately renamed itself The Reliance Group. DPF&G's effort failed. Finally, in December 1968, DPF&G attempted to acquire the one-third ownership of The Great Atlantic & Pacific Tea Co. owned by the John A. Hartford Foundation, Inc. The effort was unsuccessful. DPF&G always missed the big ones, and as a result wound up undiversified in 1970.

[21] Column 1 of Table 7–15 shows the cumulative pretax profit from all operations of these firms, not just computer leasing. Since Boothe and DPF&G both had significant losses on some diversification attempts, not all of the losses in Column 3 can be attributed solely to computer leasing.

than computer leasing.[22] One might argue that this was poetic justice were it not for the fact that the shareholders of these firms had, by 1976, lost essentially all of their investment (Column 5, Table 7–14).

Two others of the six diversified firms (Reliance and Itel) diversified on a large scale. When their computer leasing businesses ultimately collapsed in value, the *other* businesses owned by each firm sustained the market value of their common shares at 34 percent to 40 percent of the month-end highs achieved in 1968 (Column 7, Table 7–14). These firms diversified successfully, remained independent, and their senior managements survived throughout the rise and fall of the computer leasing industry.

Finally, two computer leasing firms managed the most brilliant diversifications and value transfers of all. Randolph Computer Corp. was acquired for stock in 1969 by a large insurance company. When its profitability collapsed, the event caused barely a ripple in the profits or the net worth of the insurance company. At December 31, 1976, the value of the insurance company shares for which Randolph shares were exchanged equaled 78 percent of the 1968 month-end high reached by Randolph's common stock (Column 9, Table 7–14).

The most successful computer lessor of all, Dearborn, diversified into the offshore oil service industry. Dearborn sold off its computer leasing division at a large loss in 1973. In 1974 Dearborn was acquired by another offshore oil service firm via a cash tender offer. The acquisition price equaled 1.2 times the month-end high price reached by Dearborn's common stock in 1968 (Column 9, Table 7–14).

The history of the computer leasing industry as a vehicle for the transfer of value has been chronicled in considerable detail in the preceding pages. It took an industry insider, however, to capture the essence of the industry in a few lines. The chairman of Itel described the computer leasing industry as follows:

> It was a vehicle to get us into other businesses. . . . It turns out to have been a break-even business, balancing the profits over the years against the write-offs. But we're here today on account of it.[23]

One final comment about the industry is worth noting. While functioning as public companies, the 11 computer leasing firms noted in Table 7–7 operated under a total of 25 different names.

---

[22] By 1970 Rockwood had acquired two land developers, a fast-food franchiser, and a Las Vegas hotel and casino. The firm also invested in Broadway musical shows and corporate art. Largely as a result of its acquisitions program, by March 31, 1972, Rockwood had managed to achieve a deficit net worth of $14 million. By March 31, 1977, the deficit net worth had grown to $46 million.

[23] *Business Week*, "Itel Rebuilds on Leasing's Ruins," February 23, 1974, p. 110.

VALUE
DESTRUCTION

The Great Atlantic & Pacific
Tea Company, Inc.

Chapter 8 introduces the last of the three major areas of value transformation. It presents an opportunity to observe managerial decisions
that had, as one effect, the *destruction* of shareholder value. The Great
Atlantic & Pacific Tea Company, Inc. (A&P), embarked on a program
of tonnage recovery in early 1972. Substantial product-price reductions
were a primary ingredient in this tonnage recovery program. An analysis
of A&P's price reduction strategy and its competitive impact represents
the principal focus of this chapter.

A&P originated in 1858. The company grew steadily from its founding,
but its most spectacular growth occurred during two relatively brief
periods. Between 1914 and 1916, the chain grew from 650 to 3,250 stores.[1]
Between 1920 and 1925, A&P grew from 4,600 to 14,000 stores.[2] The
growth of A&P's national market share mirrored the growth of the firm's
physical plant. A&P's share of total U.S. grocery store sales reached a
high of 16.4 percent in 1933.[3]

Beginning about 1920, A&P began a sequence of decade-long phases
of rapid sales growth followed by equally long periods of sales stagnation. As shown in Table 8-1, the company's volume quadrupled in the
decade between 1920 and 1930 as the firm expanded its geographic base.
Between 1930 and 1940, however, A&P failed to grow (Table 8-2). The
firm lost sales and market share as independent and chain supermarket
outlets began to challenge A&P's market position. A&P was slow in

---

[1] M. A. Adelman, *A&P: A Study in Price-Cost Behavior and Public Policy* (Cambridge, Mass.: Harvard University Press, 1959), p. 26.

[2] Ibid., p. 434.

[3] U.S. Federal Trade Commission, *Economic Report on the Structure and Competitive Behavior of Food Retailing*, January 1966, p. 304–6.

TABLE 8-1
A&P's sales growth, 1920-1970

Year	A&P sales ($ million)	Percentage increase in sales in decade
1920	240	—
1930	1,070	350
1940	1,120	5
1950	3,180	180
1960	5,250	65
1970	5,660	8

closing its outmoded small stores, and in opening the new, larger super-markets.

Once A&P began to open supermarket stores in the late 1930s and early 1940s, the company's sales volume once again expanded rapidly, almost tripling between 1940 and 1950. A&P's growth then slowed considerably as supermarket stores became the norm in the U.S. retail grocery industry (Table 4-4). By 1960 A&P entered a new decade of stagnation, with sales and net profits seemingly frozen at about $5.5 billion and $50 million per year, respectively (Table 8-3).

A&P's competitive position

A number of factors contributed to A&P's lackluster sales and profits in the 1960s. First, while A&P was the nation's largest grocery retailer, the firm lacked market share where it counted most. As noted in Chapter 4 (Table 4-9 and Figure 4-1), *city-market* share was extremely critical to a grocery retailer's profitability since important scale economies could be achieved at this level. A&P's market position in the firm's principal cities was often significantly below 10 percent (Column 3, Table 8-4). In

TABLE 8-2
A&P's sales growth and U.S. national market share, 1931-1939

Year	Number of stores Total	Supermarkets*	Total sales ($ millions)	Share of total U.S. grocery store sales (%)	Price index[†]
1931	15,600	0	1,008	n.a.[‡]	100
1933	15,100	0	820	16.4	84.8
1935	14,900	0	877	13.7	92.7
1937	13,300	282	882	n.a.	97.1
1939	9,100	1,127	990	12.8	94.2

*See Footnote 4, Chapter 4 for the definition of a supermarket.
[†]The index of prices relating to personal consumption expenditures; a general deflation in prices over the interval 1931-39 thus contributed significantly to A&P's volume decreases.
[‡]n.a. = not available.
Sources: M.A. Adelman, *A&P*, p. 434; U.S. Federal Trade Commission, *Economic Report on the Structure and Competitive Behavior of Food Retailing*, p. 306.

TABLE 8-3
A&P income statements, 1961–1971 (in millions)

Line		1961	1962	1963	1964	1965	1966	1967	1968	1969	1970	1971
1	Sales	$5,240.3	$5,310.5	$5,189.2	$5,079.6	$5,119.0	$5,475.3	$5,458.8	$5,436.3	$5,753.7	$5,664.0	$5,508.5
2	Cost of goods sold	4,373.0	4,368.3	4,248.4	4,141.4	4,168.9	4,449.0	4,412.4	4,383.2	4,622.3	4,523.3	4,416.9
3	Gross profit	867.3	942.3	940.8	938.2	950.0	1,026.2	1,046.4	1,053.1	1,131.4	1,140.7	1,091.6
4	Sales, general, and administrative	684.2	747.9	768.2	774.3	788.6	852.2	876.1	901.5	969.2	992.3	1,005.5
5	Pension and Retirement Expense	25.2	25.2	26.4	25.8	23.5	21.6	20.8	12.6	9.4	9.7	18.1
6	Depreciation and amortization	39.2	43.7	42.7	42.0	43.4	47.4	49.9	50.6	50.5	50.1	48.5
7	Operating income	118.7	125.5	103.5	96.1	94.5	105.0	99.6	88.4	102.3	88.6	19.5
8	Non-operating income	1.3	1.1	5.5	2.5	2.1	2.2	2.1	1.8	2.9	3.0	1.6
9	Profit before taxes	120.0	126.7	109.0	98.6	96.6	107.2	101.7	90.2	105.2	91.6	21.1
10	Income tax	62.5	66.4	51.5	46.5	44.2	51.0	45.8	45.0	51.9	41.5	6.5
11	Net income	$ 57.5	$ 60.2	$ 57.5	$ 52.1	$ 52.3	$ 56.2	$ 55.9	$ 45.3	$ 53.3	$ 50.1	$ 14.6
	Percentage of sales											
12	Gross margin	16.6	17.7	18.1	18.5	18.6	18.7	19.2	19.4	19.7	20.1	19.8
13	Pretax profit margin	2.29	2.39	2.10	1.94	1.89	1.96	1.86	1.66	1.83	1.62	.38
	Index of A&P's current- versus constant-dollar sales (1961=100)											
14	Sales index (current $s)	100.0	101.3	99.0	96.9	97.7	104.5	104.2	103.7	109.8	108.1	105.1
15	Sales index (constant $s)	100.0	100.2	96.8	93.4	92.6	96.3	93.4	89.2	89.6	83.3	77.6

Note: A&P's fiscal year ends in February. The data captioned 1971 are for the year ended February 28, 1972.
Source: A&P Annual Reports.

TABLE 8-4
Market structure of grocery retailing in the principal cities of A&P's operation, 1972

City-market area	(1) Number of A&P stores	(2) A&P's rank in city by share of market	(3) A&P's share of market in city (%)	(4) 1st	(5) 2d	(6) 3d	(7) 4th
				Percentage of city-market held by the grocery chain ranking			
New York	694	1	12.7	12.7	8.3	6.9	6.2
Chicago	201	5	6.5	30.0	18.0	13.5	7.0
Philadelphia	178	3	13.0	13.7	13.2	13.0	12.6
Detroit	120	4	11.5	17.4	16.2	12.7	11.5
Pittsburgh	96	3	11.6	16.0	12.1	11.6	10.9
Newark	75	3	15.0	30.0	25.0	15.0	10.0
Baltimore	60	n.a.*	n.a.	n.a.	n.a.	n.a.	n.a.
Syracuse	58	8	5.6	19.9	13.5	9.4	8.5
Cleveland	54	5	6.0	32.6	23.0	8.2	6.5
Washington	48	5	7.0	32.0	29.0	8.0	8.0
Boston	46	5	5.5	14.6	11.2	9.2	6.1
St. Louis	45	n.a.	n.a.	n.a.	n.a.	n.a.	n.a.
Atlanta	44	3	14.0	23.0	17.0	14.0	9.0
Dallas	39	6	5.0	30.0	18.0	10.0	10.0
Paterson	35	n.a.	n.a.	n.a.	n.a.	n.a.	n.a.
Milwaukee	30	4	6.4	39.0	16.6	10.4	6.4
Buffalo	30	3	7.7	15.6	12.6	7.7	7.6

*n.a. = not available.

Note: A&P's market share data are circled in cities where A&P ranks among the top four firms.

Source: *Supermarket News'* Distribution Study of Food Store Sales in 264 Cities—1973.

addition, the firm rarely achieved better than the number 3 market position in a city (Column 2, Table 8–4). Second, A&P's stores were generally small and rather inefficient. Of the ten largest grocery retailers in 1971, A&P had, by far, the smallest average store size, as noted in Table 8–5. The firm's productivity in terms of weekly sales volume per square foot of store area was extremely low (Table 8–5). A&P lacked many of the scale economies exploited by its competitors at the individual store level. Third, A&P stores were frequently located in the older sections of a city, away from the suburbs, which enjoyed better growth opportunities. Fourth, and finally, part of A&P's poor performance in the 1960s stemmed from the firm's desire to retain marketing and financial flexibility. Most of A&P's competitors were committed to fixed store locations since they usually signed 15- to 20-year leases. A&P stayed flexible in its ability to shift store locations quickly by avoiding such leases. A&P's preference for short-term leases is reflected in the fact that even as late as February 28, 1972, A&P's total lease commitments for all future periods amounted to only 6.4 times the firm's annual lease expense. Total lease commitments equal to twice that level were typical throughout the industry, as suggested in Table 8–6.

A&P's reluctance to sign long-term leases was a long-standing tradition. George L. Hartford, a former president of A&P,[4] "was implacably opposed"[5] to long-term leases up until the mid-1930s. The firm made a

TABLE 8–5
Average store size data of the ten largest U.S. grocery retailers, 1971

	Total sales ($ millions)	Average annual sales per store ($ 000s)	Average store size (square feet)	Average weekly sales of food stores* ($ per sq. ft.)
A&P	5,509	1,300	13,700	1.81
Safeway	5,359	2,300	18,700	2.40
Kroger	3,708	2,000	17,900	2.56
Food Fair . . ?	1,928	3,100	n.a.[†]	n.a.
American Stores . . .	1,861	2,200	17,800	2.30
Jewel	1,810	3,300	18,900	3.28
Lucky	1,794	4,000	25,400	3.38
National Tea	1,614	1,900	n.a.	n.a.
Winn-Dixie	1,609	1,900	n.a.	2.34
Grand Union	1,304	2,300	n.a.	n.a.

*A number of the top ten U.S. grocery retailers also operated nonfood retail stores. The data relating to sales per square foot of store area relate only to retail food operations.
[†]n.a. = not available.
Sources: Annual reports and 10K Reports to the SEC.

---

[4] George L. Hartford was president, and later chairman of A&P until 1956.
[5] M. A. Adelman, A&P, p. 56.

TABLE 8–6
Average minimum remaining life of store lease obligations for the ten largest U.S. grocery retailers, 1971 (years)

A&P	6.4
Safeway	14.7
Kroger	11.5
Food Fair	13.2
American Stores.	12.8
Jewel	12.8
Lucky	16.6
National Tea.	11.8
Winn-Dixie.	11.2
Grand Union.	9.0
Average (nine firms other than A&P)	12.6

Note: Average minimum remaining life equals the aggregate volume of total minimum future lease payment obligations divided by the current annual lease expense.
Sources: Annual reports and 10K Reports to the SEC.

major break with tradition in the late 1930s by allowing leases of up to five years. As late as 1949, however, more than 90 percent of A&P's stores were operated under one-year leases.[6] All during this period, "headquarters was reluctant to approve five-year leases, and choice locations were thereby lost."[7]

A&P's preference for short-term leases had a severe cost since it precluded A&P from securing many attractive large-store shopping center locations. In the decade of the 1960s, for example, leases on newly constructed supermarkets were generally signed for initial terms of 15 years (31 percent of all leases), 20 years (32 percent of all leases), or 25 years (13 percent of all leases).[8] New supermarket locations went to the chains that were willing to sign long-term leases since shopping centers were almost always financed and built on the borrowing power created by long-term lease commitments from prime commercial tenants.

A&P also had a policy of assuring its future financial flexibility by avoiding debt and holding a large pool of cash. At February 28, 1972, for example, A&P had no debt and over $100 million in cash (Table 8–7). Almost all grocery chains other than A&P utilized debt in their capital structure. In 1971, for example, the other grocery retailers among the top ten national firms had average borrowed money/equity ratios equal to 0.39, and total leverage ratios (including capitalized leases) equal to 1.38 versus 0.64 for A&P (Table 8–8). Some of these chains utilized debt quite aggressively. While A&P's competitors may have sacrificed financial flexibility as a result of their debt policies, the use of

[6] Blyth & Co., Inc., "Report on A&P," May 17, 1949.

[7] M. A. Adelman, *A&P*, p. 78.

[8] Super Market Institute, "The Supermarket Industry Speaks," 1961–70.

TABLE 8–7

A&P Balance Sheet
($ millions)

	As of February 28, 1967	1972
Assets		
Cash and marketable securities	121.6	102.5
Accounts receivable.	19.7	25.6
Inventory	387.5	442.9
Prepaid expenses	12.4	26.1
Current Assets.	541.2	597.0
Property	313.9	364.9
Deferred charges	12.5	15.8
Total Assets	867.6	977.7
Liabilities and Net Worth		
Accounts payable and accrued items	217.2	263.3
Taxes payable	19.3	7.2
Current Liabilities.	236.5	270.5
Deferred taxes and reserves	20.0	41.7
Net Worth	611.1	665.5
Total Liabilities and Net Worth	867.6	977.7

Source: A&P Annual Reports

this lower-cost source of funds made it possible for them to compete aggressively and successfully against A&P in A&P's traditional market areas. Indeed the "price-competition" model of Chapter 2 was utilized quite successfully by many of A&P's competitors to wrest market share from A&P. Greater operating efficiencies and more efficient capital structures allowed these competitors to offer customers a more attractive package of price and service than that delivered by A&P.

TABLE 8–8
Ratio of borrowed money and capitalized leases to net worth for the ten largest U.S. grocery retailers, 1971

	Borrowed money/ Net worth	Borrowed money and capitalized leases/ Net worth
A&P	0	0.64
Safeway	0.12	1.34
Kroger	0.27	1.25
Food Fair	1.01	2.45
American Stores.	0.28	1.11
Jewel	0.67	1.25
Lucky	0.68	1.85
National Tea.	0.44	1.65
Winn-Dixie.	0.04	0.77
Grand Union.	0.04	0.72
Average (nine firms other than A&P). .	0.39	1.38

Source: Annual reports.

In summary, by the early 1970s A&P was suffering from a competitive disadvantage (a) at the *city-market* level, owing to its small city-market share; (b) at the *individual store* level, because of the small average size and less desirable location of its stores; and (c) in its *capital structure* choice. The cumulative effects of these disadvantages were clearly taking their toll. A&P lost market share while its competition forged ahead (Table 4–2).

In 1971, A&Ps slowly eroding competitive position in grocery retailing took a dramatic downward plunge. A&P's costs were rising at a much faster rate than competitive conditions permitted the firm to increase its prices. While gross margins were near their peak in 1971 (Line 12, Table 8–3), net profits fell to less than $15 million (Line 11, Table 8–3). A&P's sales dropped almost 7 percent in *constant* dollars terms in 1971 (Line 15, Table 8–3). Even in *current*-dollar terms, the fall in sales was almost 3 percent. Clearly, some fairly drastic management response to A&P's problems was required.

Food discounting—The WEO response

Historically, A&P had built its public image around quality foods and low prices. During the 1960s, however, A&P had lost its low-price leadership position to rapidly growing food discount chains with significantly lower operating costs.

A&P moved slowly in responding to the food discounters. In 1969 A&P began experimenting with food discounting in its own stores. At first the firm converted 149 of its more than 4,000 stores to discount operations. In 1970, more than 200 additional stores were converted. In 1971 A&P converted a few stores to operations offering a significantly narrower selection of food products at even larger discounts. This discount retailing format, which became known as WEO,[9] was put in place in all of A&P's stores between January and September 1972.

The effect on industry profits of A&P's conversion to food discounting via the WEO campaign was impressive. In a 1975 report on food chain profits, the FTC examined the profitability of 30 food chains that had a *significant fraction* of their stores in local markets where A&P competed. The profitability of these 30 chains over the period 1965–73 was contrasted against the profitability of 15 chains operating in markets with *little* A&P competition. The results of this study are shown in Table 8–9. The differences are startling. Those 15 supermarket chains without significant A&P competition weathered the 1971–73 period with almost no reduction in their average ROEs. The 30 chains competing with A&P saw

---

[9] The initials WEO originally stood for "Warehouse Economy Outlet." In later public advertising campaigns the initials stood for "Where Economy Originates."

TABLE 8-9
Profits after taxes versus stockholders' equity and sales (for 45 supermarket chains classified by whether they compete with A&P, 1965-1973)

	1965	1966	1967	1968	1969	1970	1971	1972	1973
Profit as a percentage of stockholders' equity									
15 Chains with little A&P competition	15.8	15.6	14.0	14.1	13.8	13.9	14.8	14.9*	14.3*
30 Chains competitive with A&P	10.0	9.7	8.9	10.3	11.0*	9.9*	8.7	2.3	4.8
A&P	8.8	9.2	8.9	7.1	8.0	7.4	2.2	(8.6)	2.0
Profits as a percentage of sales									
15 Chains with little A&P competition	1.8	1.7	1.5	1.5	1.4	1.4	1.5	1.5	1.4*
30 Chains competitive with A&P	1.1	1.0	0.9	1.0	1.1*	0.9	0.8	0.2	0.4
A&P	1.0	1.0	1.0	0.8	0.9	0.9	0.3	(0.8)	0.2

*Numbers with asterisks exclude those chains with extremely low profits due to nonrecurring events. These are: Arden-Mayfair for 1972 and 1973; Allied Supermarkets for 1969 and 1970; and Thorofare for 1973.
Source: U.S. Federal Trade Commission, "Staff Economic Report on Food Chain Profits," July 1975, p. 19.

their ROEs reduced, on average, from around 10 percent to as low as 2 percent during the deepest WEO price cuts in 1972.

Table 8–9 shows the impact of A&P's WEO campaign and the price cutting by others that followed in the wake of WEO. The data of Table 8–9 are at a level that aggregates the operating results of many retail grocery chains. When the data are disaggregated, selected individual firm financial data are equally interesting.[10]

Quarterly pretax profits, profit margins, and sales volume trends for eight individual grocery chains are presented in Table 8–10. The first three chains (Lines 2–4, Table 8–10) chosen for comparison with A&P include Food Fair, National Tea, and Acme. These chains ranked 6, 9, and 4 respectively, in terms of national grocery sales in 1972.[11] From 54 percent to 65 percent of the stores[12] in these chains were located in counties where A&P operated competing stores. The next three firms chosen for comparison with A&P were smaller chains (Bohack, Foodarama, and Penn Fruit) that had almost all of their stores located in counties where A&P operated competing stores. Finally, data for Safeway Stores are presented since this chain met A&P in relatively few local markets. Only 19 percent of Safeway's units were located in counties where A&P operated competing stores.

The data presented in Table 8–10 indicate that:

1. A&P incurred a pretax loss of over $100 million in its price reduction program in 1972 (Line 1, Table 8–10).
2. All six of the A&P competitors in Table 8–10 showed losses in the six-month period spanning the second and third quarters of 1972.
3. The losses (as a percentage of sales) incurred by A&P's *large* competitors were significantly less than the losses incurred by A&P's *smaller* competitors (Lines 10–12 versus Lines 13–15, Table 8–10).
4. WEO price reductions were deepest in the second and third quarters of 1972. During this period A&P operated at about a −2.7 percent profit margin (Line 9, Table 8–10). Based on a normal pretax profit margin of 1.5 percent to 2.0 percent (Line 13, Table 8–3), it appears that during the first half of 1972 A&P lowered its pretax profit

---

[10] The firms chosen for comparison with A&P in Table 8–9 were not randomly selected from among A&P's major chain competitors. The chains selected for comparison with A&P were, for the most part, those firms with the greatest competitive overlap in city-markets served by A&P, and those with relatively low city-market penetration in these markets.

[11] *Progressive Grocer,* April 1973, p. 132.

[12] U.S. Federal Trade Commission, *Staff Economic Report on Food Chain Profits,* p. 31.

TABLE 8-10

Total pretax profits, profit margins, and an index of sales growth for A&P and Safeway and six of A&P's major U.S. grocery chain competitors (1st quarter 1971 through 4th quarter 1972)

Line		1971				1972			
		1st Qt.	2d Qt.	3d Qt.	4th Qt.	1st Qt.	2d Qt.	3d Qt.	4th Qt.
	Pretax profit ($ millions)								
1	A&P	20.9	20.5	9.6	(3.5)	(5.5)	(41.3)	(42.6)	(16.0)
	Large A&P competitors								
2	Food Fair	3.1	4.7	5.8	6.5	0.2	(9.2)	2.1	4.2
3	National Tea	7.4	3.7	3.5	2.7	6.5	0.1	(5.4)	(1.0)
4	Acme Markets	9.1	7.2	5.6	4.9	3.5	(1.2)	(2.9)	4.0
	Small A&P competitors								
5	Bohack	(3.4)	1.0	1.1	1.1	0.9	(0.6)	(0.2)	(0.4)
6	Foodarama	1.4	1.2	(1.1)	1.7	(4.6)	(1.3)	(4.7)	0
7	Penn Fruit	1.3	0.8	1.1	1.3	0.2	(2.5)	(1.4)	(0.9)
8	Safeway	29.6	37.4	39.7	48.4	33.1	38.4	37.8	59.1
	Pretax profit/Sales (%)								
9	A&P	1.46	1.50	0.70	(0.26)	(0.39)	(2.77)	(2.68)	(0.99)
	Large A&P competitors								
10	Food Fair	0.69	1.01	0.94	1.29	0.04	(1.89)	0.35	0.83
11	National Tea	1.84	1.00	0.72	0.71	1.74	0.03	(1.19)	(0.28)
12	Acme Markets	1.90	1.57	1.25	1.03	0.73	(0.25)	(0.59)	0.76
	Small A&P competitors								
13	Bohack	(5.08)	1.30	1.42	1.40	1.14	(0.72)	(0.23)	(0.48)
14	Foodarama	1.73	1.47	(1.35)	2.09	(5.73)	(1.57)	(5.80)	0
15	Penn Fruit	1.44	0.71	1.29	1.50	0.22	(2.39)	(1.85)	(1.14)
16	Safeway	2.52	3.07	3.15	2.83	2.50	2.79	2.66	3.05
	Sales/Sales in same quarter of 1970 (%)								
17	A&P	92	96	97	98	98	105	112	115
	Large A&P competitors								
18	Food Fair	109	115	111	111	114	120	108	111
19	National Tea	114	105	104	104	106	104	96*	96*
20	Acme Markets	112	107	103	104	112	110	113	116
	Small A&P competitors								
21	Bohack	98	113	112	109	115	121	123	116
22	Foodarama	108	105	107	105	107	107	106	87*
23	Penn Fruit	122	115	105	99	121	106	93	91*
24	Safeway	114	113	112	105	129	128	126	119

Note: The data of Table 8-10 relate to the nearest *calendar* quarters, not the *fiscal* quarters of the individual firms. Thus the fourth-quarter 1972 data presented for A&P in the table are for the quarter ended November 1972, not the company's fourth fiscal quarter, which ended February 1973.

*Significant store sales and/or closing contributed to the reduced index of sales volume of National Tea, Foodarama, and Penn Fruit by the fourth quarter of 1972.

Sources: Company quarterly reports to shareholders and company 10Q reports to the U.S. Securities and Exchange Commission.

margins,[13] its gross profit margins,[14] and its prices[15] by an amount ranging from four to five percentage points.

5. A&P's sales did not rise dramatically either *absolutely* or in *relation to its competitors* sales during the WEO campaign in 1972.[16] Indeed, A&P's sales were only 15 percent higher in the fourth quarter of 1972 than they were in the fourth quarter of 1970 (Line 17, Table 8–10).[17]

A&P's WEO campaign during 1972 does not appear to have produced exceptional *sales gains,* although it certainly produced *impressive losses.* These early results naturally raise questions about what A&P's management had hoped to accomplish with the WEO program. More specifically, A&P's WEO campaign raises the broader question of how one goes about evaluating an investment decision consisting of a price reduction strategy aimed at enhancing shareholder values over the long term.

The economics of value destruction—An appraisal of WEO

The sophistication of any economic analysis that A&P's management may have undertaken in evaluating the WEO program prior to its implementation will probably never be known outside the A&P firm. Never-

---

[13] This is simply the result of subtracting the new level of pretax profit margins from the old level of pretax profit margins i.e. $1.5\% - (-2.7\%) = 4.2\%$; and $2.0\% - (-2.7\%) = 4.7\%$.

[14] A&P does not publish quarterly gross-margin data, but these data can be estimated by combining quarterly pretax-profit-margin data with annual gross-margin data. A&P's gross-margin for all of fiscal 1972 (which ended February 28, 1973) amounted to 17.3 percent. This represented a decline of about 2.7 percentage points from the 20.0 percent average for 1970–71. Since 80 percent of A&P's 1972 pretax losses were concentrated in two quarters of 1972, this gross-margin information is consistent with the estimated reduction in gross margins of four to five percentage points at the height of the WEO price reductions.

[15] Changes in gross margins can, of course, occur without any change in prices as a result of a change in the mix of products (carrying different gross-margins) that are purchased by consumers. In the example above it is assumed that all of the shift in gross-margins resulted from price changes rather than product-mix changes. In fact, WEO incorporated a significant narrowing of the product line, which may have reduced the gross-margin potential of A&P's product offerings.

[16] It should be noted that the total square footage of all A&P stores declined by a little less than 2 percent between 1970 and 1972. It would be more appropriate to measure sales changes only for those units in operation during the entire 1970–72 time period. Since no major change in A&P's physical plant size took place during the period, any errors introduced by the use of data for *all* stores are probably minimal. It also should be noted that the consumer price index for "food at home" rose by a little over 9 percent between the fourth quarter of 1970 and the fourth quarter of 1972.

[17] It is certainly possible (indeed even highly likely, given the 1971 experience) that A&P's sales in 1972 (absent the WEO campaign) would have fallen significantly below the level of sales experienced in 1970. This would make the relative gain in sales resulting from the WEO campaign greater than 15 percent.

theless, it is possible to do an *independent* analysis of the economics of a general price reduction strategy for A&P. Table 8–11 represents the first step in this effort. Table 8–11 partitions A&P's costs in 1970 into fixed and variable components based on the author's understanding[18] of the cost characteristics of supermarket operations.

The table suggests that A&P's fixed costs amounted to roughly $480 million in 1970[19] and that the firm's variable costs were about 10.0 percent of sales based upon a price structure that produced a 20.1 percent gross margin.

TABLE 8–11
Estimated breakdown of fixed versus variable costs for A&P's operation in 1970

Line		$ millions	Percentage of sales
1	Sales.	5,644.0	100.0
2	Cost of sales	4,523.3	79.9
3	Gross margin	1,140.7	20.1
	Variable expenses:		
4	Store labor and fringe benefits	—	6.1*
5	Warehouse and delivery	—	2.2
6	Store supplies	—	0.9
7	Maintenance and repairs	—	0.3
8	All other store expenses	—	0.5
9	Total variable expenses	566.4	10.0
10	Contribution to fixed cost and profit	574.3	10.1
11	Fixed costs	482.7	—
12	Profit before taxes.	91.6	—

*Note that this is only the variable portion of store labor and fringe benefits. Total store labor and fringe benefits as a percentage of sales would be significantly higher.

Table 8–12 utilizes the cost breakdown developed in Table 8–11 in projecting the level of sales that A&P would require in order to achieve pretax profits comparable to the level achieved in 1970 (that is, $91.6 million) assuming the firm were to reduce its selling prices by an amount ranging from one to five percentage points. As Column D of Table 8–12 indicates, A&P would have to increase its sales by 38.5 percent in order to produce $91.6 million of pretax profits, assuming the firm implemented a permanent across-the-board 3 percent reduction in price levels. A&P's sales increase would have to reach 88.9 percent in order to accomplish

---

[18] Roughly comparable data on the split between fixed and variable costs for supermarket operations can be found in R. D. Buzzell, et al., "The Consumer and the Supermarket—1980," Family Circle, Inc. 1976, p. 20.

[19] Data for 1970 are utilized as the "base" year since A&P's operating results for 1971 may have been depressed somewhat by the firm's early experiments with food discounting prior to its across-the-board implementation of WEO, and because the firm was subject to price controls that froze gross-margins between August 15, 1971, and November 13, 1971.

TABLE 8–12

Calculation of the growth in sales required for A&P to maintain constant pretax profits at the 1970 level assuming a decline in prices ranging from 1 to 5 percentage points

Line		(A)	(B)	(C)	(D)	(E)	(F)	Derivation of data
				Percentage price decrease				
		0	*1*	*2*	*3*	*4*	*5*	
1	Sales ($ millions)	5,664.0	6,247.9	6,948.3	7,846.1	9,038.2	10,697.7	(Line 5)/(Line 17)
2	Cost of goods sold ($ millions)	4,523.3	5,042.5	5,665.0	6,462.9	7,522.4	8,997.3	(Line 1) X (Line 14)
3	Gross margin ($ millions)	1,140.7	1,205.4	1,283.3	1,383.2	1,515.8	1,700.4	(Line 1) X (Line 15)
4	Variable costs ($ millions)	566.4	631.1	709.0	808.9	941.5	1,126.1	(Line 1) X (Line 16)
5	Contribution to fixed costs and profit ($ millions)	574.3	574.3	574.3	574.3	574.3	574.3	Given
6	Fixed costs ($ millions)	482.7	482.7	482.7	482.7	482.7	482.7	Given
7	Pretax profit ($ millions)	91.6	91.6	91.6	91.6	91.6	91.6	Given
8	Percentage sales increase needed to maintain profits at $91.6 million	0	10.3	22.7	38.5	59.6	88.9	

Note: The data shown in Lines 1–8 are derived from the ratio relationships noted in Lines 9–17, which describe the behavior of cost of goods sold, gross margins, variable costs, and contribution margins as prices are reduced. It should be noted, for example, that variable costs *increase* as a percentage of sales in Line 16 because product prices have been reduced in order to achieve higher sales volume. Variable costs as a percentage of sales would have remained constant in this table if product prices had also been constant.

Line		(A)	(B)	(C)	(D)	(E)	(F)	
9	Sales ($)	100.0	99.0	98.0	97.0	96.0	95.0	
10	Cost of goods sold ($)	79.9	79.9	79.9	79.9	79.9	79.9	
11	Gross margin ($)	20.1	19.1	18.1	17.1	16.1	15.1	
12	Variable costs ($)	10.0	10.0	10.0	10.0	10.0	10.0	
13	Contribution to fixed costs and profit ($)	10.1	9.1	8.1	7.1	6.1	5.1	
14	Cost of goods sold (% of sales)	79.9	80.7	81.5	82.4	83.2	84.1	(Line 10)/(Line 9)
15	Gross margin (% of sales)	20.1	19.3	18.5	17.6	16.8	15.9	(Line 11)/(Line 9)
16	Variable costs (% of sales)	10.0	10.1	10.2	10.3	10.4	10.5	(Line 12)/(Line 9)
17	Contribution to fixed costs and profit (% of sales)	10.1	9.2	8.3	7.3	6.4	5.4	(Line 13)/(Line 9)

the same result assuming a permanent 5 percent reduction in price levels.[20]

The volume increases required in order to avoid reducing profit (assuming permanent price level reductions as indicated in Table 8–12) appear to be unrealizable in practice, particularly at the upper boundary. Indeed, A&P's actual experience in 1972 was that price cuts on the order of 4 percent to 5 percent were accompanied by volume gains that were probably closer to 15 percent. What one might have expected to happen did, in fact, happen. When A&P implemented its price cuts, A&P's competitors responded (to the extent required) with price cuts of their own to the degree that they felt such cuts were needed to preserve volume. Because of A&P's higher cost levels (given its existing physical plant), the firm was not well positioned to benefit from a permanent downward shift in product prices. Indeed, without a major transformation of its physical plant the only way A&P could ever *hope* to exceed the volume requirements needed to avoid reducing its profits in the face of permanent price-level reductions would be to cause a number of weaker competitors (that is, those with limited ability to absorb losses) actually to close down[21] all or a portion of their retail outlets. Even if competition did close down a large number of outlets, A&P was not equipped to pick up much of the volume previously handled by these outlets. The small size of A&P's stores, the limited checkout capacity at its stores, and the lack of available parking space at most stores combined to make a dramatic increase in A&P's sales almost a physical impossibility. Potential new customers would tend to gravitate to the larger, more attractive stores of A&P's remaining competition.

Table 8–12 suggests that a permanent price-reduction strategy appears to be economically unrealistic as a solution to A&P's cost structure, declining volume, and declining profitability problems. Across-the-board price reductions as a *short-term* strategy (to be followed by a return to higher price levels at a later date), however, might incorporate some economically defensible logic. Table 8–13 examines the economics of an "investment" in temporary price reductions.[22]

Line 1 of Table 8–13 assumes that A&P achieved a 15 percent volume

---

[20] Table 8–12 is predicated on the fixed versus variable cost assumptions shown in Table 8–11. If A&P's variable costs in 1970 were assumed to be only 8.0 percent of sales instead of 10.0 percent, then A&P's sales would have to have increased only about 62 percent in order to produce $91.6 million of pretax profits, assuming a permanent 5 percent reduction in price levels.

[21] In fact, for A&P to benefit permanently, these outlets would not only have to be closed, they would also have to be converted to nongrocery uses.

[22] An *instantaneous* return to the previous price level assumed in Table 8–13 would be competitively impractical. This problem is not particularly serious, however, since Table 8–13 is presented primarily to demonstrate an analytic approach for valuing an investment in temporary price reductions.

TABLE 8-13
Calculation of the net present value of the incremental cash flows to A&P from the WEO program

Line		1	2	3	4	5	6	Total
	No attrition							
1	Percent incremental growth in sales attributed to WEO (%)	15	15	15	15	15	15	—
2	Incremental growth in sales attributed to WEO* ($ millions)	850	850	850	850	850	850	—
3	Incremental net profits (and cash flow) realized† ($ millions)	44.6	44.6	44.6	44.6	44.6	44.6	—
4	Discount factor‡	0.894	0.799	0.715	0.639	0.571	0.511	—
5	Present value of cash inflows ($ millions)	39.9	36.6	31.9	28.5	25.5	22.8	$ 376
	Attrition over six years							
6	Percent incremental growth in sales attributed to WEO (%)	15	12.5	10.0	7.5	5.0	2.5	—
7	Incremental growth in sales attributed to WEO* ($ millions)	850	708	566	425	283	142	—
8	Incremental net profits (and cash flow) realized † ($ millions)	44.6	37.2	29.7	22.3	14.9	7.5	—
9	Discount factor ‡	0.894	0.799	0.715	0.639	0.571	0.511	—
10	Present value of cash inflows ($ millions)	39.9	29.7	21.2	14.2	8.5	3.8	117
	Attrition over four years							
11	Percent incremental growth in sales attributed to WEO (%)	15	11.3	7.5	3.8	—	—	—
12	Incremental growth in sales attributed to WEO* ($ millions)	850	640	425	215	—	—	—
13	Incremental net profits (and cash flow) realized† ($ millions)	44.6	33.6	22.3	11.3	—	—	—
14	Discount factor‡	0.894	0.799	0.715	0.639	—	—	—
15	Present value of cash inflows ($ millions)	39.9	26.8	15.9	7.2	—	—	90
	Attrition over two years							
16	Percent incremental growth in sales attributed to WEO (%)	15	7.5	—	—	—	—	—
17	Incremental growth in sales attributed to WEO* ($ millions)	850	425	—	—	—	—	—
18	Incremental net profits (and cash flow) realized† ($ millions)	44.6	22.3	—	—	—	—	—
19	Discount factor‡	0.894	0.799	—	—	—	—	—
20	Present value of cash inflows ($ millions)	39.9	17.8	—	—	—	—	58

*Equals A&P's assumed percentage level of sales growth attributable to WEO multiplied by the $5,664 million base level of sales achieved by A&P in 1970 (Line 1, Table 8-3).

†Equals the assumed level of incremental sales growth attributable to WEO multiplied by the pretax contribution margin on sales (Line 10, Table 8-11) multiplied by (1 − tax rate).

‡This discount factor utilizes A&P's estimated cost of equity capital in 1972 calculated according to the approach utilized in Chapter 1 assuming a Treasury bill rate of 4.3 percent and a β of 0.87 for A&P at the end of 1971. Since A&P's capital structure included no debt, the cost of capital for A&P is assumed to equal the firm's cost of equity capital.

§Data in Lines 1–5 are continued and present values are summed ad infinitum, since it is assumed that there is no attrition associated with the incremental sales volume.

The calculation assumes (1) the restoration of prices and gross margins to the pre-WEO level of 1970, and (2) the loss of the WEO-produced incremental sales over the time periods indicated.

increase between the fourth quarter of 1970 and the fourth quarter of 1972 (Line 17, Table 8–10) and that this volume increase was attributable to WEO. Line 2 of Table 8–13 translates the volume increase of 15 percent into its equivalent dollar value of $850 million. This latter figure is based on A&P's 1970 sales of $5.66 billion. Line 3 of Table 8–13 calculates the incremental after-tax profits (and cash flow)[23] that A&P would realize from the $850 million of incremental sales, assuming the contribution margin suggested in Table 8–11. Line 4 of Table 8–13 discounts the annual incremental cash flows attributed to WEO at A&P's estimated cost of capital. Line 5 of Table 8–13 then sums the discounted value of these cash flows to produce the total discounted value of the incremental cash flows produced by WEO.

As indicated, Line 5 of Table 8–13 assumes that the 15 percent sales gain attributed to WEO remains as a permanent addition to A&P's sales after prices and gross margins are returned to pre-WEO levels. Since a permanent retention of these incremental sales is undoubtedly an optimistic assessment, Lines 10, 15, and 20 assume that the benefits of WEO erode over various time periods ranging from as much as six years to as little as two years. The assumption here is that many of the new A&P customers drawn by WEO would probably switch their purchases back to the stores they previously patronized (if these stores were still in business) or would patronize new stores that might spring up near them after WEO had become a distant memory.

The data of Table 8–13 take into account only the *return* side of the WEO investment analysis. A&P's *investment* in WEO was, of course, the difference between the cash flows A&P would have realized with and without the WEO investment. This amount would presumably also equal the difference between A&P's after-tax profits with and without the WEO investment.[24]

A precise measure of A&P's investment in WEO is difficult to achieve, since A&P's profits, absent WEO, can only be estimated. The profits of A&P in 1970 and 1971 were $50 million and $15 million, respectively. A&P's operating results trended down sharply in the six-month period ending November 27, 1971, the period immediately preceding the intro-

---

[23] Incremental sales of $850 million would clearly add to A&P's inventory requirements (the cash-flow impact of which would be offset to some extent by additional accounts payable). If the historic relationship linking A&P's inventory, accounts payable, and sales level were continued, the $850 million addition to A&P's sales would create an increased capital requirement of about $35 million. This factor is not taken into account in the above analysis since the impact is not critical to the results of the analysis.

[24] If the tax credits generated from WEO losses in 1972 exceeded A&P's actual tax payments for the prior three years, then the differential between A&P's cash flow with and without WEO could be smaller than the differential between A&P's after-tax profit with and without WEO.

duction of WEO. In the firm's 1972 Annual Report, A&P management noted that they had "every reason to expect the declining trend [of 1971] to continue unless we took bold steps to turn our entire system around in the shortest possible time."[25] These facts indicate that A&P probably would have done well to earn $15 million in 1972 absent WEO. When this $15 million profit is compared with the $50 million after-tax loss that A&P sustained in 1972, A&P appears to have invested about $65 million in its WEO program in 1972. When this fact is combined with the results of Table 8–13, it is clear that if the WEO program were stopped at the end of 1972, and the WEO-generated incremental sales eroded in less than two years, the WEO campaign could probably be accurately described as an economic failure. As noted earlier, however, one way for A&P to make sure that the gains produced by WEO outlived the WEO program itself was to assure that some competing stores were no longer in operation when WEO was concluded. If the WEO-induced losses of competitors were large enough, this result might have been possible.

The competitive effect of value destruction

Some A&P competitors might be expected to shrink their operations as a result of unprofitable performance. Indeed, some of these competitors might be *forced* to cut back their operations by anxious lenders who desired to reduce their loan exposure to troubled supermarket operators. This is an area where A&P held a strong hand. The company was debt-free and had $100 million in cash. The firm also had an untouched $100 million revolving credit facility. By way of contrast, most of A&P's competitors had limited liquidity and far greater leverage (Table 8–14). A number of A&P's competitors (particularly the smaller ones) had bank term loans or privately placed long-term debt securities outstanding. If these firms suffered significant losses (as a result of the WEO program, for example) they could face the prospect of default under the terms of their loan agreements. Since the terms of these loan agreements were often a matter of public record,[26] one could project (within a few months) the date when a particular A&P competitor might be likely to breach the terms of its loan agreements. This projection would require, of course, a specific set of assumptions relating to the *level* and *duration* of the price reductions chosen by A&P in its WEO campaign. The process might op-

---

[25] Great Atlantic & Pacific Tea Company, Inc., 1972 Annual Report, p. 3.

[26] The SEC requires publicly held reporting companies to file Form 8K reports within ten days following the close of a month in which an unscheduled material event occurs that is of importance to shareholders. Increases and decreases in the amount of securities outstanding (such as would occur under a new loan agreement) are generally deemed to be material events. Copies of loan agreements of material importance to reporting firms are thus generally filed on Form 8K.

TABLE 8-14
Ratios of liabilities to net worth for A&P and Safeway and six of A&P's major U.S. grocery chain competitors, 1968-1972

Line		1968	1969	1970	1971	1972
1	A&P	0.4	0.4	0.4	0.5	0.7
	Large A&P competitors					
2	Food Fair.	1.5	1.6	1.8	1.9	2.2
3	National Tea	1.2	1.2	1.2	1.2	1.5
4	Acme Markets	0.8	0.9	0.9	0.9	1.1
	Small A&P competitors					
5	Bohack	2.2	1.8	1.8	2.4	3.0
6	Foodarama	1.3	1.5	1.2	1.2	2.6
7	Penn Fruit	0.8	0.9	1.0	1.0	1.3
8	Safeway.	0.6	0.7	0.8	0.8	0.9

Note: Liabilities are defined here as assets minus net worth.
Sources: Annual reports.

erate in the following way. At the end of October 1971, for example, Foodarama's net worth was about $2.4 million in excess of the level needed to avoid defaulting under a loan covenant restricting the ratio of liabilities and capitalized value of lease payments in relation to the firm's net worth. As shown in line 6 of Table 8–10, Foodarama suffered an $8.9 million pretax loss during the period extending from the fourth quarter of 1971 through the third quarter of 1972. Obviously, this created a default situation.

Foodarama's lenders temporarily waived compliance with the terms of their lending agreements in order to give the chain sufficient time to dispose of stores. Disposing of stores would produce enough cash to reduce significantly the balance of the loans outstanding. Foodarama sold the operating assets and inventory of 21 stores to eight different buyers. Eleven other Foodarama stores were closed (while four previously planned new stores were opened), thereby reducing the number of Foodarama's retail outlets from 60 to 41 in a period of less than 15 months. The process may appear to be somewhat merciless, but the most effective way to gain liquidity rapidly in grocery retailing is to shrink the scale of a firm's operations.[27]

The immediate reaction of A&P's competitors to the WEO campaign shows up in the shrinkage during 1972 of store outlets operated by a number of A&P's competitors (Table 8–15). All of the A&P competitors listed in Table 8–10 showed significant store reductions in 1972.

---

[27] Shrinking the number of retail outlets operated by a firm in order to improve its liquidity can, however, sometimes erode its long-run viability. This is particularly true for regional firms owning large warehouses (with attendant high fixed-costs) sized to the firm's volume requirements prior to its shrinkage.

TABLE 8-15

Percentage change in number of food stores in operation at year end for A&P, Safeway, and six of A&P's major U.S. grocery chain competitors (1968-1976)

Line		1968	1969	1970	1971	1972	1973	1974	1975	1976
1	A&P	0	(3)	(3)	(4)	(8)	(7)	(6)	(40)	(5)
	Large A&P competitors									
2	Food Fair	(1)	2	(2)	(2)	(12)	0	(2)	(2)	(3)
3	National Tea	(6)	19*	(3)	(6)	(35)	(7)	(8)	(7)	(52)
4	Acme Markets	(1)	(1)	(2)	(1)	(8)	3	4	2	(3)
	Small A&P competitors									
5	Bohack	19*	(10)	(3)	(6)	(4)	0	(54)	(11)	(8)
6	Foodarama	23*	4	157*	(4)	(41)	2	5	(2)	0
7	Penn Fruit	3	1	(1)	0	(10)	(3)	(9)	(5)	(65)
8	Safeway	0	1	2	(1)	2	1	3	1	(1)

*Indicates a merger.
Source: Annual reports and 10K Reports to the SEC.

The logical link between WEO and the store-reduction programs of A&P's competitors in 1972 is fairly easy to demonstrate. Any link between WEO and the later Chapter 11 bankruptcy petitions of Bohack (July 29, 1974) and Penn Fruit[28] (September 3, 1975) is more speculative, although WEO clearly contributed to the financial difficulties of these two smaller A&P competitors. Indeed, Mr. Joseph Binder, Bohack's president, was sufficiently exercised over A&P's WEO campaign to make the following statements at a press conference on September 14, 1972:

> Now, suddenly, the great Atlantic & Pacific giant—a sort of modern-day Rip Van Winkle—has awakened to the fact that it is no longer able to hold onto its number one food retailing position in America. A&P's only way to recapture this position was a desperation move—to try to buy sales and put its smaller competitors out of business. And if you keep buying items for 60 cents and selling them for 55 cents, this is not too difficult to do. Sooner or later, these predatory pricing practices will smother small competitors.
>
> I believe there are provisions in our anti-trust laws, such as Section 3 of the Robinson-Patman Act,[29] that make it unlawful "to sell . . . at

---

[28] An article entitled "How Penn Fruit Checked Out" appeared in *Philadelphia Magazine* in July 1977. The article was written by James Cooke, Penn Fruit's former president. In this article, Mr. Cooke lays most of the blame for Penn Fruits' collapse at the door of Acme Markets, rather than A&P. According to Mr. Cooke, Acme responded to the A&P WEO program in the Philadelphia area with price reductions that were deeper and of longer duration than those put in place by A&P. "A&P's strategy unlocked the door, permitting Acme to concentrate much of its firepower in Philadelphia without any qualms about government antitrust action. After all, Acme was ostensibly responding to a situation created by a giant rival. A&P, the original predator, became the victim of its own strategy and lost a portion of the Philadelphia market."

[29] Section 3 of the Robinson–Patman Act includes the following language: "It shall be unlawful for any person engaged in commerce, in the course of such com-

unreasonably low prices for the purpose of destroying competition or eliminating a competitor." These laws are designed to protect the small businessman from unfair competition and should be vigorously enforced.

The truth of the matter is this: the Great Atlantic and Pacific Tea Company didn't know how to run its own business, so it decided to run every one else out of business, using its gigantic financial and marketing muscle, plus a $100-million war chest of cash and marketable securities.

.   .   .

We are not afraid of the Great Atlantic & Pacific Tea Company. We may be only a David to their Goliath—and we all know who won that battle—but it is time someone called the public's attention to the disservice that is being done by this company, A&P, to our industry.[30]

As is obvious from the bankruptcy petitions noted earlier, Mr. Binder was somewhat optimistic in invoking the images of David and Goliath. In July 1977, 55 of Bohack's remaining retail grocery stores were liquidated. Penn Fruit closed 36 of its 55 supermarkets during 1976. The last 17 of Penn Fruit's retail grocery stores were sold to Food Fair in November 1976.

Mr. Binder's arguments of September 1972 were echoed by some lenders to A&P competitors. Reports emanating from a banking convention held in November 1972, included the following:

Now A&P's competitors have gained a powerful ally, the First National Bank of Chicago, which is calling on other bankers to take a more understanding position in making loans to help struggling supermarket chains ride out A&P's assault. Two weeks ago, Jay Doty, vice president of a

---

merce, . . . [ ] . . . to sell, or contract to sell, goods at unreasonably low prices for the purpose of destroying competition or eliminating a competitor."

Politically, the timing of A&P's WEO compaign could not have been better. The 1972 presidential election campaign was in full swing at the same time that the WEO price reductions were in effect. The Honorable John N. Mitchell was the U.S. Attorney General, and he also headed the Committee for the Reelection of the President. If the WEO price-cutting program had any Robinson–Patman Act implications, these implications were unlikely to be aggressively pursued (during a high-inflation election year) by an attorney general who also headed the president's re-election campaign.

The Federal Trade Commission shared antitrust responsibility with the Justice Department. To the extent WEO might have incorporated unfair trade practices, the FTC would thus have had a legal basis for action against A&P. The FTC began to study A&P's WEO pricing policies in October 1972, in response to complaints from A&P competitors. In February 1973, the FTC decided against initiating a formal investigation of WEO. A trade publication reported the event as follows: "The Commission decided there was no evidence to indicate the policy had resulted in prices being set deceptively low to drive small competition out of business. The Commission also did not want to put itself in the position of investigating a firm that is lowering food prices while the country is fighting inflation." (*Supermarket News*, February 5, 1973, p. 1).

[30] Bohack Corporation, *Report to Shareholders for the 13 Weeks Ended July 29, 1972.*

First National loan division, told a gathering of 700 bankers in Chicago that "this cutting of corporate throats is conceivably what A&P intended." Doty estimated that A&P began its drive with $60 million in cash reserves plus $100 million in bank credit lines, and that at its present rate of loss it could continue price paring for another year and a half without outside financing. To avoid a wipeout of some food chains, Doty urged bankers to help well-managed supermarket companies hold out.

Doty argued that if A&P becomes dominant east of the Mississippi, it will be able to raise its prices with relative impunity. First National is extending especially liberal credit terms to two national supermarket chains (it refuses to identify them). In Doty's view, bank-loan officers should take a lenient position with faltering food chains, assessing the firm's chances for survival, its record of profitability and the location and attractiveness of its stores. So long as the A&P offensive continues, Doty also urges, troubled supermarkets should "reduce overhead to an absolute minimum, postpone maintenance and modernization outlays, reduce or pass up dividends and improve inventory control."

Doty, who believes that even for A&P the WEO drive is misguided, says: "When all this is over, A&P will hardly be better off than it was before. Its market share will be greater, but it will not have updated its outmoded stores, it will not have moved to better locations. Thus in three or four years A&P will again see its share of market fall." For the moment, though, consumers paying steep prices for food can take some comfort in the knowledge that prices would be even higher without the battle of the supermarkets.[31]

WEO as one component of an overall competitive strategy

The previously noted information on the competitive impact of WEO (combined with the data of Table 8–13) suggests that A&P's WEO campaign might have made economic sense if it were part of a multistep corporate strategy with the following objectives:

1. WEO had to succeed in permanently closing a significant number of competing stores in the markets where A&P operated. If A&P failed to accomplish this task with WEO, then the incremental business attracted as a result of WEO would probably disappear as quickly as it had originally appeared once A&P returned its price structure to pre-WEO levels.

2. The WEO campaign had to educate lenders.[32] These financing sources

---

[31] Reprinted by permission from *Time*, The Weekly Newsmagazine; copyright Time Inc. 1972.

[32] The term "lenders" is broadly intended to include both the institutions providing dollar loans as well as real estate owners who provided physical facilities under long-term leases to retail supermarket chains.

needed to learn that loans (or leases) to retail grocery chains (particularly small but aggressive A&P competitors) could be a good deal riskier than these lenders had previously understood. Once this point was made, the borrowing power of A&P's smaller and more highly leveraged competitors might be curtailed. Ideally, lenders might be persuaded that at any specific time chosen by A&P, the risks in grocery retailing (particularly for A&P's smaller competitors) could be adjusted to A&P's particular taste.

3. For a substantial period after A&P had ended its WEO campaign, the company could hope to enjoy a hiatus during which few new stores would be opened by competitors. These firms (particularly the smaller ones) would be too busy trying to rebuild their equity bases and the confidence of their lenders to do much expanding. A&P could thus use this period to capture a significant portion of any attractive new store locations that might become available in city-markets served by A&P. This would help to remedy A&P's competitive disadvantage in the (a) store-location, (b) store-size, and (c) city-market share problem areas. Indeed, without this absolutely critical store-repositioning step, the WEO program could not be very effective in helping to solve A&P's long-run profit problem.[33]

4. The WEO campaign should have put A&P's competitors on notice that A&P was no longer willing to give up market share at the city-market level. Once A&P had demonstrated its resolve to hold on to (and rebuild) its individual city-market share, the incentive for A&P's competitors to "overstore"[34] an area to preempt the market growth of other competitors (including A&P) might be considerably reduced.

The achievement of all four of the items noted above was probably necessary if A&P's investment in WEO was to be economically successful.

The economic results of A&P's actions through the fourth quarter of 1972 have already been measured. WEO did not appear to be producing the volume increases needed to justify A&P's investment in WEO as of the fourth quarter of 1972. Measuring A&P success as of the end of the fourth quarter of 1972 may, however, be somewhat arbitrary, as A&P's price reductions were still in effect (albeit at a less intensive level) after the fourth quarter of 1972. Unfortunately for A&P, the WEO

---

[33] Implicit in the store repositioning step is the assumption that A&P would simultaneously deal with its merchandising and consumer-image problems. Changes in A&P's physical plant alone would probably not have been sufficient to reverse the chain's declining fortunes.

[34] "Overstoring" denotes the practice of building new store locations in advance of the demand growth needed to justify their opening.

price reduction program was halted in the first quarter of 1973, perhaps before it had run long enough to accomplish its intended result.[35]

A tender offer interrupts WEO

The end of A&P's WEO price reduction program coincided with the announcement of a tender offer to A&P's shareholders from Gulf & Western Industries. On February 1, 1973, Gulf & Western offered to acquire about 15 percent of A&P's common shares at a price of $20 per share. This was a 25 percent premium over A&P's pre–tender offer market price, although it represented only 83 percent of A&P's book value per share. Prior to the tender offer, Gulf & Western had acquired more than 4 percent of A&P's shares. This fact was not publicly known, however, until late in January, 1973.[36]

The Gulf & Western tender offer was undoubtedly encouraged by the low market-value/book-value ratios placed upon the common stocks of A&P and its competitors (Table 8–16). The stock prices of A&P and its competitors had been significantly reduced by WEO-induced profit erosion in 1972 and the impact of price controls in 1973. Indeed, Gulf & Western may well have concluded that A&P's common stock was undervalued as a result of the WEO profit pressure, and that the *value-transfer* potential inherent in the acquisition of A&P's stock was substantial.

As Table 8–16 demonstrates, A&P's WEO program destroyed shareholder values rather effectively. Indeed, WEO was almost certainly an important factor in restricting the access of A&P's small and thinly capitalized competitors to both the debt and equity capital markets in 1972 and 1973. Unfortunately for A&P, the WEO campaign destroyed the value of A&P's *own shares* almost as dramatically as it destroyed the value of the shares of A&P's major competitors (Column 3 versus Col-

---

[35] While the across-the-board WEO price reductions appear to have been reversed early in 1973, the WEO advertising campaign was not actually jettisoned until early in 1975.

It could be argued that A&P's sales growth and the rate of store closings among A&P's competitors might have accelerated over time if WEO had continued in effect for a longer period.

[36] According to testimony in a Federal court proceeding (as reported in *Supermarket News* on February 12, 1973), Gulf & Western's interest in A&P was known to A&P's management long before January 1973. On February 7, 1972, for example, A&P's management was contacted by an emissary of Gulf & Western, who attempted to arrange a meeting between the chief executives of the two firms. A&P declined the meeting, but was presumably forewarned to some extent of Gulf & Western's interest in A&P. On November 21, 1972, A&P's investment banker, Kuhn Loeb & Co., was contacted by Gulf & Western with regard to Gulf & Western's interest in acquiring shares of A&P held by the John A. Hartford Foundation. At that time the John A. Hartford Foundation owned about 33 percent of A&P's common stock.

TABLE 8-16
Market-value/Book-value ratios of the common stocks of the Dow Jones Industrial Average,
A&P, Safeway, and six of A&P's major U.S. grocery chain competitors (1971–1973)

Quarter	(1) Dow Jones Industrials	(2) Safeway	(3) A&P	(4) Large chain competitors*	(5) Small chain competitors†
1971					
1st 1.56		1.89	1.13	0.93	1.39
2d 1.51		1.74	0.95	0.94	1.21
3d 1.49		1.78	0.94	0.91	0.96
4th 1.47		1.68	0.79	0.81	0.89
1972					
1st 1.53		1.81	0.74	0.74	0.82
2d 1.49		1.57	0.66	0.65	0.61
3d 1.51		1.63	0.67	0.58	0.55
4th 1.59		1.83	0.68	0.47	0.54
1973					
1st 1.46		1.55	0.57	0.47	0.43
2d 1.34		1.20	0.54	0.41	0.34
3d 1.40		1.46	0.49	0.44	0.38
4th 1.23		1.45	0.36	0.35	0.26

*Includes Food Fair, National Tea, and Acme Markets.
†Includes Bohack, Foodarama, and Penn Fruit.
Sources: *Bank and Quotation Record* and 10Q Reports to the SEC.

umns 4 and 5 of Table 8–16). This fact made A&P vulnerable to a take-over threat such as that posed by Gulf & Western's tender offer.

A&P's WEO campaign may have been a casualty of the Gulf & Western tender offer. A&P's management may have felt compelled to improve gross margins and A&P's stock price in an effort to ward off the Gulf & Western bid.[37]

On the other hand, the Gulf & Western offer may have coincided quite accidentally with the point in time that A&P's management had planned to end WEO anyway.[38] If so, the Gulf & Western tender offer may have

---

[37] A&P's management informed its shareholders that Gulf & Western's $20 per share offer was inadequate, and that the acquisition of 20 percent of A&P's stock by Gulf & Western raised antitrust problems along several dimensions. A&P's management took umbrage at the fact that Gulf & Western's chairman personally owned 18 percent of Bohack's common stock prior to the tender offer, a situation that led some observers to wonder whether the Gulf & Western tender offer for A&P was designed, in part, to alleviate the profit pressure on Bohack caused by the WEO campaign. A federal court ultimately issued a preliminary injunction preventing G&W from completing its tender offer until the antitrust issues were determined in a trial. This preliminary injunction was upheld on appeal, and Gulf & Western subsequently withdrew its tender offer.

[38] On June 20, 1972, A&P held an annual shareholder meeting. In responding to a shareholder's question at that meeting, A&P's chairman stated that "perhaps a return to a profit will be seen [in the quarter ended February 28, 1973]." (*Supermarket News*, June 26, 1972, p. 4). In addition, A&P concluded a $100 million loan agree-

simply served as a convenient trigger point for terminating an investment (WEO) that would have been an abysmal failure anyway. The evidence favoring this latter interpretation comes in the form of data relating to A&P's new-store opening program *during* and immediately *after* the WEO program.

As noted earlier, unless WEO were followed by a significantly accelerated store opening program, A&P's price cutting was unlikely to provide a long-term solution to A&P's profit problems. As Table 8–17 shows, A&P's new-store opening and modernization program during and immediately following WEO was unimpressive. One could easily conclude from these data that the critical second step needed to permit WEO's success was either *never planned*[39] by A&P's management, or not effectively *implemented*. In any case, in the final analysis A&P's WEO investment was an economic failure.[40]

TABLE 8-17

Pre- and post-WEO data on A&P's store opening, store closing, and store remodeling history (1968–1976)

	(1) New stores opened	(2) Old stores closed	(3) Stores enlarged or remodeled	(4) Stores in operation at end of year
Pre-WEO data				
1968	169	180	466	4,713
1969	99	237	530	4,575
1970	70	218	37	4,427
1971	104	267	268	4,264
Post-WEO data				
1972	80	404	211	3,940
1973	89	349	153	3,680
1974	113	325	171	3,468
1975	91	1,485	189	2,074
1976	100	196	126	1,978

Sources: Annual Reports, 10K Reports to the SEC, and Prospectus dated June 29, 1976.

ment on September 1, 1972, that contained covenants restricting A&P's ability to sustain major losses indefinitely. The agreement limited the permitted erosion of A&P's net worth in the 12 months following the close of the agreement to $30 million. Additional net worth erosion in months 13 to 18 following the close of the agreement was limited to $10 million. These facts could be interpreted to mean that A&P had planned to reverse or significantly moderate the WEO price reductions at about the time of the Gulf & Western tender offer, even if the offer had never occurred.

[39] A&P's Annual Report for the year ending February 22, 1975 noted that the management consulting firm of Booz, Allen & Hamilton had been retained by A&P in January 1974, to undertake a comprehensive analysis of A&P's organization and operations. The fact that this strategy study was undertaken a year *after* the conclusion of the WEO price cuts may indicate that A&P's management really had no strategic plan for the critically important post-WEO period.

[40] A&P's Board of Directors elected a new chief executive officer who was brought in from outside the company in late 1974. Dramatic changes followed in both management and store operations. Within 18 months after the arrival of A&P's new

TABLE 8-18
A&P's current-dollar and constant-dollar sales versus the firm's gross margins (1970–1976)

	Gross margins (%)	Pretax profit margins (%)	Sales in current dollars ($ billions)	Sales in constant* 1974 dollars ($ billions)	Total area of all A&P stores (millions of sq. ft.)	Weekly sales per square foot in constant* 1974 dollars	
						A&P stores	All supermarket stores
1970	20.1	1.7	5.66	8.00	58.7	2.62	5.86
1971	19.8	0.4	5.51	7.60	58.6	2.49	6.28
1972	17.3	(1.7)	6.37	8.50	57.6	2.84	5.79
1973	18.3	0.3	6.75	7.87	56.4	2.68	5.49
1974	19.8	0.5†	6.87	6.87	55.8	2.37	5.09
1975	19.5	(0.1)	‡	‡	39.2	‡	4.98
1976	20.2	0.3	‡	‡	38.5	‡	4.93

*Equal to *current* dollar data for each year multiplied by the Bureau of Labor Statistics "food at home" price index for June 30, 1974 versus the index for June 30 of the year in question.
†Equal to (2.4) after special charge for the cost of closing facilities.
‡Data are not comparable to data for previous years because of the large reduction in store area caused by store closings.
Sources: A&P Annual Reports; The Supermarket Industry Speaks.

As A&P increased its gross margins in 1973 and 1974 (Column 1, Table 8–18), the company's sales grew very little in terms of current dollars (Column 3, Table 8–18). Sales actually *fell dramatically* in terms of constant dollars (Column 4, Table 8–18). The impact of the rise in A&P's prices (as reflected in the gross margin shifts) is clear. In the words of one A&P store manager, "Our prices got customers into the store, and got them right out again."[41] A&P's management thus dissipated a significant portion of the firm's principal resource, its financial strength, with minimal favorable long-term results.

---

chief executive, the number of A&P's executive officers rose from 12 to 23, and 7 of the original 12 executives were no longer officers of A&P. On the operating side, within a few months after the arrival of the new chief executive, A&P closed about 40 percent of its stores (Column 2, Table 8–17). Changes in profit levels have not yet been as dramatic as other changes in the firm, but it is obviously too early to tell whether A&P can reverse the downward slide of recent years.

[41] Mary Bralove, "Tough Turnaround," *The Wall Street Journal,* Sept. 19, 1974, p. 1.

9 | VALUE
CREATION,

The Levitz Furniture Corporation

TRANSFER,
AND
DESTRUCTION

Chapters 3–6 examined the actions of managers who had successfully *created value* for their shareholders. Chapter 7 surveyed an entire industry, computer leasing, where *value transfer* played an important role in the evolution of many firms. Chapter 8 showed how *value destruction* (generated in this instance by a price war) might play an important part in improving the competitive posture of a firm. The full range of value-transformation strategies noted in Chapter 2 has thus been reviewed. Chapter 9 will now examine how one firm, the Levitz Furniture Corporation, appears to have utilized *all three* of the broad areas through which shareholder value can be altered. The story is interesting in its own right. It was chosen for Chapter 9, however, because the actions of Levitz's management seem to fit neatly into the value-transformation models that form the basis of this book.

The evolution of Levitz Furniture over the last decade can be explained largely in terms of the history of the firm's common stock price (Figure 9–1). Levitz's stock price followed a pattern similar to that traced by many of the computer leasing firms examined in Chapter 7. Computer leasing industry stocks had collapsed by mid-1970 (Figure 7–2), however, just as Levitz's stock began the ascent portion of the now familiar bell-curve (Figure 9–1). Let us hope that investors did not flee the computer leasing industry in order to invest in Levitz. It would be patently unfair to have lightning strike the same investors twice!

As we will see later in the chapter, during most of Levitz's history as a public company[1] up until mid-1973, the market price of Levitz's common

---

[1] Levitz Furniture first issued stock publicly on July 9, 1968.

FIGURE 9–1
Levitz Furniture Corporation: Market-price history of a share of common stock

Common stock price ($ per share)

50 — 40 — 30 — 20 — 10

1968 1969 1970 1971 1972 1973 1974 1975 1976 1977

Source: *Bank and Quotation Record.*

stock was demonstrably detached from economic reality. During this period some members of the Levitz family sold, via three public offerings, common stock valued at $33 million. In these same public offerings the company issued $32 million of new common stock to finance its growth. *Value transfers* thus form an important part of the Levitz story.

The evolution of Levitz Furniture *prior* to 1972 is dramatically different from its evolution *after* 1972. Chapter 9 is partitioned accordingly. The first part of Chapter 9 focuses on *value creation* and *value transfer*, subjects that are most relevant in the period prior to the Levitz stock-price collapse of 1972–73. The last part of Chapter 9 deals with *value destruction*. It focuses on the events leading up to and following the collapse of Levitz's stock price.

The Levitz approach to furniture retailing

Levitz Furniture Corporation began in 1936 with a retail furniture store in Pottstown, Pennsylvania. The firm was successful as a one-store operation through 1963. In 1963, two sons of the Levitz founder opened stores in Allentown, Pennsylvania, and Phoenix, Arizona. These stores utilized what was, at the time, a new concept in furniture retailing. This was the "warehouse-showroom."

Levitz's stores combined a warehouse and furniture showrooms in one building. This arrangement forced the customer to walk through part of the warehouse to reach the showrooms. It created the image of Levitz as a furniture wholesaler. A standard Levitz warehouse-showroom covered 150,000 square feet. This was almost equivalent to the playing area contained in *four* football fields. Levitz's stores were obviously many times the size of a conventional furniture outlet. Roughly one third of the total floor space was devoted to displaying furniture in 260 model-room settings. The stores were large enough to accommodate $10 to $12 million in annual sales volume.

The consumer appeal of a Levitz warehouse-showroom was considerable. First, customers could view a large selection of nationally advertised brand-name furniture in a single location. Second, items displayed in a Levitz showroom could usually be purchased at prices somewhat below the prices charged for the same merchandise in a conventional store. Finally, furniture purchased at a Levitz outlet could usually be taken home immediately by the customer since any item displayed was inventoried in the attached warehouse.

Levitz's profitability versus that of the furniture retailing industry

Through 1971 Levitz operated with lower retail prices and lower gross margins, but higher net-profit margins than conventional furniture outlets (Table 9–1). A number of factors contributed to this result. Most signifi-

TABLE 9-1

Income statement ratio data for Levitz Furniture Corporation versus other large-store furniture retailers, 1968–1976

Year	(1) Gross-profit/Sales ratio Levitz*	(2) Industry†	(3) Difference	(4) All-other-expenses/Sales ratio Levitz	(5) Industry	(6) Difference	(7) Profit-before-taxes/Sales ratio Levitz	(8) Industry	(9) Difference
Period preceding stock price decline									
1968	0.347	0.392	(0.045)	0.259	0.336	(0.077)	0.088	0.056	0.032
1969	0.362	0.409	(0.047)	0.278	0.355	(0.077)	0.084	0.054	0.030
1970	0.381	0.400	(0.019)	0.291	0.359	(0.068)	0.090	0.041	0.049
1971	0.389	0.405	(0.016)	0.294	0.371	(0.077)	0.095	0.034	0.061
Period following stock price decline									
1972	0.392	0.400	(0.008)	0.322	0.358	(0.036)	0.070	0.042	0.028
1973	0.392	0.398	(0.006)	0.348	0.350	(0.002)	0.044	0.048	(0.004)
1974	0.407	0.416	(0.009)	0.387	0.382	0.005	0.020	0.034	(0.014)
1975	0.403	0.405	(0.002)	0.405	0.367	0.038	(0.002)	0.038	(0.040)
1976	0.415	0.412	0.003	0.384	0.369	0.015	0.031	0.043	(0.012)

*Levitz's fiscal year ends on January 31 of the following year. Thus, the data for 1968 shown above relate to Levitz's fiscal year ending January 31, 1969. This convention is followed throughout all of the tables in this chapter.

†Industry data relate only to those firms with annual sales volumes that exceed $1 million.

Sources: National Home Furniture Association Special Reports, *Operating Experiences, 1969–1976*; and Levitz Furniture Corporation Annual Reports.

cantly, the size of Levitz's individual stores produced scale economies in selling, handling, and transportation. Selling, handling, and transportation expenses are captured in the "all-other-expenses/sales" ratio of Table 9–1. Between 1968 and 1971 Levitz enjoyed, on average, a 7.5 percentage-point cost advantage against the average competitor falling into the $1 million, or above, category in annual sales volume.

Levitz saved on freight-in by purchasing furniture in rail-car and truckload lots. The firm saved on delivery expense by requiring customers to take their purchases with them, or by adding a service charge for delivery. Finally, Levitz's large size nationally gave the firm economies in the area of purchasing.[2] An amount equal to all of Levitz's purchasing savings plus some portion of the savings in "all other expenses" was passed on to the consumer in the form of lower prices.[3] This was a very significant ingredient in the Levitz strategy.

In terms of the Chapter 2 model, Levitz enjoyed a number of alternatives in dealing with the fruits of a superior cost structure. Levitz clearly chose to pass a portion of the benefits of its superior cost structure on to the consumer. Levitz did not give *all* of the benefits of its more efficient cost structure to the consumer, however. Indeed, the firm's margin of profits after taxes far exceeded that achieved by the average large furniture retailer. Equally important, Levitz's low prices attracted a heavy flow of customers who were willing to purchase furniture on a cash basis and also forgo home delivery in order to achieve purchase price savings. The unusually high inventory turnover and reduced investment in accounts receivable produced by this method of doing business generated for Levitz a significantly higher sales/assets ratio than that realized by most competitors. Levitz's higher asset turnover and higher margin of after-tax profit to sales combined to create for Levitz a very attractive rate of return on equity capital between 1967 and 1972 (Table 9–2). The mathematics of this phenomenon are as follows (page 243):

---

[2] In 1971, Levitz was the second largest furniture retailer in terms of national market share. Only Sears, Roebuck was larger.

[3] To the extent the mix of products sold by Levitz was similar to the mix sold by other furniture retailers, comparable gross margins would indicate comparable selling prices (assuming no differences in purchase prices among different retailers). If purchase prices were different among furniture retailers for products of comparable quality, however, such as might be the case for retailers who could purchase entire cuttings, then comparable gross margins would *not* be indicative of comparable selling prices. In the Levitz example, lower-than-average gross margins indicated that Levitz was passing along price reductions to the consumer in an amount equal to all purchase savings plus some portion of the operating-expense savings. The savings in operating expenses included the savings on delivery charges, which amounted to 3–4 percent of sales for the average retail furniture store.

TABLE 9-2

Data relating to the capital intensity, profit margins, leverage, and profitability of Levitz Furniture Corporation versus the furniture retailing industry, 1967–1976

Year	(1) (2) Sales/Assets ratio		(3) (4) Profit-after-taxes/Sales ratio		(5) (6) Assets/Net-worth ratio		(7) (8) Profit-after-taxes/Net-worth ratio	
	Levitz	Industry	Levitz	Industry	Levitz	Industry	Levitz	Industry
Period *preceding* stock price decline								
1967	3.57	1.58	0.033	0.022	2.60	2.20	0.308	0.076
1968	2.50	1.44	0.042	0.026	2.01	2.17	0.212	0.081
1969	2.35	1.56	0.042	0.026	1.53	2.19	0.153	0.089
1970	2.26	1.45	0.045	0.018	1.91	2.23	0.192	0.058
1971	1.89	1.54	0.050	0.017	1.79	2.16	0.169	0.058
Period *following* stock price decline								
1972	2.54	1.50	0.037	0.030	1.89	2.06	0.178	0.092
1973	2.74	1.33	0.023	0.031	1.79	2.33	0.112	0.095
1974	2.36	1.38	0.011	0.020	1.85	2.41	0.048	0.066
1975	2.29	1.46	(0.001)	0.014	1.75	2.17	(0.002)	0.043
1976	2.41	1.46	0.017	0.026	1.76	2.28	0.071	0.087

Note: The data in Columns 7 and 8 of Table 9–1 differ from the data in Columns 3 and 4 of Table 9–2 for two reasons. First, the profit data in Table 9–1 are pretax whereas the data in Table 9–2 are after taxes. In addition, the firms included in the NHFA data base used in Table 9–1 were not necessarily the same firms included in the Robert Morris Associates data base used in Table 9–2, although all of the industry data relate to firms with annual sales volume in excess of $1 million.

Sources: Robert Morris Associates, Annual Statement Studies, 1967–1977; and Levitz Furniture Corporation Annual Reports.

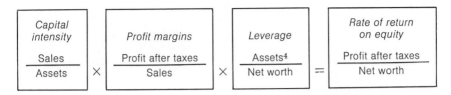

Levitz's capital structure included less leverage than the average firm in the industry.[5] The composition of Levitz's capital structure thus reduced the firm's ROE below the level that it would have reached if Levitz had been as highly leveraged as the average furniture retailer. At first glance this might suggest that Levitz should have further improved its ROE (and thus perhaps enhanced the spread between its ROE and its cost of equity capital) by increasing its leverage position. In fact, the low degree of leverage in Levitz's capital structure can be explained (and will be, later in this chapter) as a completely rational management response to a highly overvalued stock price.

> *Levitz may have been simply saving the value-enhancing benefits of added leverage until the value-transfer opportunities inherent in the firm's overvalued stock price had been exhausted.*

Figure 9–2 shows the factors contributing to Levitz's high profitability in relation to the profitability of the average furniture retailer.

FIGURE 9–2
Chart tracing the impact of operating scale economies on Levitz's return on equity

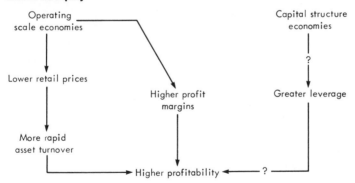

---

[4] Since assets are, by definition, equal to total liabilities plus net worth, the factor "assets/net worth" is equivalent to [total liabilities and net worth]/net worth. This latter ratio is nothing more than a measure of the intensity of a firm's utilization of nonequity financing.

[5] The calculation of Levitz's leverage does not include the capitalized value of leases. Since most furniture retailers lease rather than own their stores, the fact that leases are not capitalized should not significantly reduce the relevance of comparative industry data.

The rate of return on equity capital earned by Levitz prior to 1973 clearly exceeded the firm's cost of equity capital. We can show this fact in the following way. Levitz's rate of return on equity capital averaged slightly over 20 percent between 1967 and 1971. In early 1972, the 90-day Treasury bill rate was about 3.5 percent, and the beta coefficient of Levitz's common stock was roughly 1.5. According to the logic followed in Chapter 1, these data imply that Levitz had a nominal cost of equity capital in 1972 equal to about 16.6 percent.[6] Given the spread between Levitz's cost of equity capital and the returns achieved on that equity capital, Levitz had successfully *created value* for its stockholders as a result of the firm's innovations in furniture retailing. The actual extent of Levitz's value creation as defined in Chapter 1 will be explored later in this chapter, as we begin to zero in on Levitz's growth opportunities beyond 1971.

Before we can begin to assess the extent of Levitz's *value creation,* we need to return to the Chapter 1 valuation model. In Chapter 1 we determined that the rational economic value of a firm's common stock should be a function of three factors. These were:

1. The size of the percentage-point spread projected to be earned on common equity over the cost of the firm's common equity;
2. The volume of future capital-investment opportunities promising the above-average rates of return indicated in (1); and
3. The number of years during which the exceptional returns noted in (1) and (2) would continue to be attainable.

Since Levitz's growth opportunities (Item (2) above) appeared to be so spectacular in 1972, we ought to focus first on the extent of this growth potential. We can then attempt to establish an upper boundary for rationally valuing a Levitz common share in 1972. This upper boundary of rational economic value will then be compared to the *market value* and the *book value* of a Levitz share in 1972. This comparison will allow us to develop a richer understanding of Levitz's financing strategy in the early 1970s. It will also allow us to attempt to partition the Levitz stock price in early 1972 into that component that might (at the upper limit) be labeled *value creation* and that part that probably ought to be described as overvaluation or *value-transfer* potential.

Levitz's growth opportunities beyond 1971

The Levitz warehouse-showroom concept was a great success with consumers. As a result, the company rapidly expanded. Six stores were

---

[6] $K_e = R_f + \beta(K_m - R_f)$, where $R_f = 3.5\%$, $\beta = 1.5$, and K_m equals the *real* rate of return required on equity capital (8.8 percent) plus the anticipated rate of inflation (3.4 percent) embedded in the Treasury bill rate.

TABLE 9-3
Income statement, balance sheet, and other relevant nonfinancial operating data for Levitz Furniture Corporation, 1967–1976

Line		Period preceding stock price decline					Period following stock price decline				
		1967	1968	1969	1970	1971	1972	1973	1974	1975	1976
	Income statement data ($ millions)										
1	Sales	26.5	39.5	67.0	99.6	183.8	326.8	380.4	355.3	326.3	372.7
2	Cost of goods sold	17.7	25.8	42.7	61.7	112.3	198.9	231.3	210.8	194.7	218.2
3	Selling, general, and administrative	6.9	10.1	18.6	28.8	54.0	103.7	130.3	134.4	129.9	140.4
4	Interest expense (net of interest income)	0.2	0.1		0.2	0.1	1.2	2.0	3.1	2.4	2.4
5	Profit before taxes	1.7	3.5	5.7	8.9	17.4	23.0	16.8	7.0	(0.7)	11.7
6	Taxes	0.8	1.8	2.8	4.5	8.2	10.9	8.2	3.1	(0.6)	5.5
7	Profit after tax	0.9	1.7	2.8	4.4	9.2	12.1	8.6	3.9	(0.1)	6.2
	Balance sheet data ($ millions)										
8	Cash	0.5	3.2	2.0	1.6	9.3	6.8	7.3	6.6	7.2	8.5
9	Accounts receivable	1.3	1.6	3.1	6.4	9.5	11.4	10.5	12.7	8.8	10.0
10	Inventory	4.7	9.4	14.6	21.3	40.5	69.6	75.2	70.8	68.4	75.6
11	Other	0.1	0.3	1.1	2.4	14.1	10.8	9.0	21.9	3.6	2.8
12	Total current assets	6.6	14.5	20.8	31.7	73.4	98.6	102.0	112.0	88.0	96.9
13	Property and equipment	0.6	1.1	6.8	9.3	20.8	28.3	29.1	32.9	48.3	51.3
14	Other	0.2	0.2	0.9	3.1	3.2	1.8	7.8	5.7	6.4	6.6
15	Total Assets	7.4	15.8	28.5	44.1	97.4	128.7	138.9	150.6	142.7	154.8
16	Notes payable	0.9	1.8	0.8	—	4.3	4.5	10.4	22.2	4.0	8.0
17	Current Maturities of long-term debt	0.6	0.1	0.8	1.3	1.2	1.2	2.3	2.9	3.1	3.9
18	Accounts payable	1.1	3.8	2.3	7.8	18.5	17.2	16.3	15.4	17.8	16.8
19	Taxes payable	0.5	1.2	1.4	2.1	2.9	3.8	0.3	2.2	1.4	5.9
20	Accrued expenses	0.4	0.6	1.6	3.3	8.9	11.1	10.7	9.7	11.0	12.1
21	Total current liabilities	3.5	7.5	6.9	14.5	35.8	37.8	40.0	52.4	37.2	46.7
22	Long-term debt	1.1	0.4	3.0	6.1	5.4	19.2	16.9	11.5	18.7	14.8
23	Deferred taxes			—	0.4	1.9	3.6	4.5	5.1	5.3	5.5
24	Net worth	2.8	7.9	18.6	23.1	54.3	68.1	77.5	81.6	81.5	87.8
25	Total liabilities and net worth	7.4	15.8	28.5	44.1	97.4	128.7	138.9	150.6	142.7	154.8
	Nonfinancial operating data										
26	Number of stores in operation at year end	5	7	12	18	31	49	55	60	61	61
	Number of Levitz employees:										
27	Sales	n.a.*	221	n.a.	560	947	1,396	1,425	1,275	1,216	1,170
28	Advertising	n.a.	11	n.a.	30	60	104	84	72	59	66
29	Merchandising and display	n.a.	68	n.a.	240	447	678	759	503	497	508
30	Warehouse, maintenance, and delivery	n.a.	368	n.a.	860	1,245	1,861	1,872	1,471	1,395	1,386
31	Office and administration	n.a.	336	n.a.	540	1,055	1,489	1,871	1,667	1,578	1,540
32	Total employees	n.a.	1,004	n.a.	2,230	3,754	5,967	6,011	4,988	4,745	4,670
33	Advertising expenditures (% of sales)	n.a.	6	n.a.	7	7	7.6	7.5	7.8	8.7	9.2
34	Total purchases from 10 largest suppliers (%)	n.a.	65	n.a.	50	40	35	43	42	48	43
35	Total number of furniture suppliers	n.a.	300	n.a.	350	350	350	350	350	300	300
36	Sales for cash (%)	n.a.	67	n.a.	70	75	68	n.a.	64	66	65
37	Sales credit-financed (%)	n.a.	33	n.a.	30	25	32	n.a.	36	34	35

*n.a. = not available.

Sources: Levitz Furniture Corporation Annual Reports, 10K Reports to the SEC, and Registration Statements.

in operation by July 1968, when the company first sold common stock publicly. Once Levitz had access to the public equity market and both customers and investors were aware of the company's basic marketing strategy, Levitz's growth became explosive (Table 9–3, Line 1). Indeed, by the close of 1971, Levitz had 31 stores in operation (Table 9–3, Line 26) and had achieved annual sales of $184 million. Since selling stock publicly four years earlier, Levitz had enjoyed a 62 percent per year compound rate of growth in sales.

Levitz's growth history from 1968 through 1971 was nothing short of phenomenal. Levitz's success suggested that the furniture retailing industry in 1972 might be in the early stages of a transformation similar to that followed by the grocery retailing industry several decades earlier. As noted in Chapter 4, high-volume *grocery-store* outlets had moved their share of the grocery market from 12 percent in 1948 to 46 percent in 1958. This transformation took only a decade. By way of contrast, it was not until after 1963 that large-volume *furniture* outlets began to have a significant impact in the market (Table 9–4).

Even after 1963, however, the development rate of large retail-furniture outlets was relatively slow. Between 1963 and 1972, high-volume retail-furniture outlets had increased their national market share only from 14 percent to 27 percent (Table 9–4). Considerable additional room for growth in high-volume furniture outlets appeared to exist. In addition, furniture retailing was still an extremely fragmented industry in the United States in 1972. The 50 largest firms in furniture retailing held less than a 13 percent market share nationally, whereas the 50 largest grocery retailers held a 44 percent market share nationally (Table 9–5).

Finally, furniture retailing was primarily a business of local entrepreneurs in the United States. In 1967, single-store firms accounted for almost 75 percent of all furniture store sales. Firms with more than 25 stores constituted only about 5 percent of the national market (Table 9–6). By the end of 1972, retail furniture chains with more than 25 stores still had less than 8 percent of the national market. Most of the growth in

TABLE 9–4

Percentage of total industry sales made in stores with *over $1 Million* in annual sales volume

Year	Grocery stores	Furniture and home furnishings stores
1948	12%	10%
1954	33	13
1958	46	13
1963	53	14
1967	61	20
1972	72	27

Sources: U.S. Department of Commerce, Census of Business, *Retail Trade*, 1948, 1954, 1958, 1963, 1967, 1972.

TABLE 9-5
Share of U.S. national market held by the largest firms in grocery
retailing and furniture and home furnishings retailing, 1972

	Grocery retailers	Furniture and home furnishings retailers
4 Largest firms.	17.5%	4.4%
8 Largest firms.	24.5	6.2
20 Largest firms.	34.8	9.1
50 Largest firms.	43.9	12.7

the large chain segment between 1967 and 1972 could be attributed to
Levitz alone. All of this suggested enormous growth opportunity for
Levitz Furniture Corporation.

The capital requirements associated with Levitz's growth

Levitz's rapid growth could be sustained only by substantial infusions
of outside capital. As indicated earlier, to raise this capital the company
sold stock publicly in 1968, 1969, and 1971. The average capital committed by the company to a warehouse-showroom was slightly more than
$2.0 million.[7] Since Levitz's net income was less than $10 million in 1971
(Line 7, Table 9–3), the firm could finance only about five new stores in
1972 without external financing. How fast Levitz should grow and how
that growth should be financed were critical questions. Estimates of
Levitz's potential future market penetration were uncertain. The company's management and numerous securities analysts had made estimates,
however. At the end of 1969, with 12 stores in operation, Chairman Ralph

TABLE 9-6
Structure of the U.S. furniture retailing industry, 1967 and 1972

	Firms (number)		Share of market (%)	
	1967	1972	1967	1972
Single-store firms	49,736	58,936	74	69
2- to 5-store firms.	1,663	2,148	15	16
6- to 25-store firms	117	149	6	7
26- to 100-store firms	15	23	5	8
Total	51,531	61,256	100	100

Sources: U.S. Department of Commerce, Census of Business, *Retail Trade*,
1967, 1972.

---

[7] This figure did not include the $2.3 million average construction cost (includ-
ing land) associated with each new outlet. All outlets were planned to be financed
via long-term leases with outside investor groups.

Levitz had spoken of a total U.S. market potential of 50 Levitz stores. By the end of 1970, Levitz had 18 stores in operation, and the total market potential claimed by the Levitz chairman had grown to 80. On December 3, 1971, the company chairman stated that his firm would ultimately have 150 stores "covering every one of the 55 major marketing areas in the United States."[8]

If Levitz was to expand from a 31-store chain to a 150-store chain by the end of 1977,[9] it is a relatively straightforward task to project, at least broadly, how the firm's growth and financial performance might unfold. Levitz planned to open 20 stores in 1972,[10] for example. This represented a *percentage* growth rate in stores in operation of about 65 percent. Clearly this percentage growth rate in stores in operation had to decline, or Levitz would reach its 150-store goal well before the end of 1977. The decline in the percentage growth of stores in operation indicated in Column 3 of Table 9–7 produces an orderly progression toward the desired number of stores at year-end 1977.

Let us assume that with this pace of new store openings Levitz would maintain the sales/square-foot ratio of selling space and the profit-after-taxes/square-foot-of-selling-space ratio achieved during each quarter of 1971. The quarterly growth progression of Levitz's total selling space and the sales and profit yield from this selling space are presented in Table 9–8.

TABLE 9-7
Projection of the number of Levitz stores open at the end of each year, 1971–1977

Year	(1) Number of stores in operation	(2) Number of stores opened in year	(3) Percentage growth in number of stores in operation
1971—Actual	31		
1972—Pro forma	51	20	65
1973—Pro forma	76	25	50
1974—Pro forma	103	27	35
1975—Pro forma	124	21	20
1976—Pro forma	136	12	10
1977—Pro forma	150	14	10

---

[8] James H. Oliphant & Company, "Levitz Furniture Corporation: Progress Report," December 8, 1971, p. 2.

[9] In January 1972 a Levitz official stated that the firm would be operating out of 150 stores by 1978. Wight Martindale, *We Do It Every Day* (New York: Fairchild Publications, Inc., 1972), p. 53.

[10] In a report on Levitz Furniture, dated June 15, 1971, Oliphant Research Associates reported that Levitz planned to open 20 stores in 1972 and 26 stores in 1973. In addition Levitz reported in its 1971 10K report to the SEC that it had 20 store sites in various stages of investigation for acquisition. Finally, in Levitz's first-quarter report to shareholders in 1972, the firm announced that it planned to open at least 20 stores during the year.

TABLE 9-8

Actual and pro-forma data relating to the growth in selling area, and the sales and profit per square foot of selling space of Levitz Furniture Corporation, 1969-1977

Line		Actual data			Pro-forma data					
		1969	1970	1971	1972	1973	1974	1975	1976	1977
	Average square feet of selling space (000's)									
1	1st Quarter	445	725	1,060	1,961	3,192	4,614	6,114	7,267	7,959
2	2d Quarter	500	725	1,125	2,134	3,403	4,845	6,287	7,383	8,075
3	3d Quarter	610	780	1,340	2,538	3,864	5,364	6,691	7,613	8,363
4	4th Quarter	725	970	1,620	2,942	4,383	5,940	7,152	7,844	8,652
	Sales volume/Square foot of selling space ($)									
5	1st Quarter	27.02	28.33	31.10	(Same as 1971 data.)					
6	2d Quarter	29.61	30.57	34.30						
7	3d Quarter	28.05	32.14	36.55						
8	4th Quarter	31.81	32.86	39.04						
	Profit after taxes/Square foot of selling space ($)									
9	1st Quarter	0.86	0.96	1.17	(Same as 1971 data.)					
10	2d Quarter	0.96	1.07	1.43						
11	3d Quarter	1.38	1.63	1.92						
12	4th Quarter	1.57	1.75	2.32						

Sources: Levitz Furniture Corporation Annual Reports, Registration Statements, and 10K Reports to the SEC.

The rate of store openings forecasted in Table 9–7 can be combined with the volume and profitability projections of Table 9–8 to produce an estimate of Levitz's capital needs and/or capital surplus from 1972 through 1977. This is done in Table 9–9. According to Column 7 of Table 9–9, Levitz would require roughly $20 million in new capital annually for the three-year period covering 1972–74. Between 1975 and 1977, however, Levitz would greatly reduce its rate of new store openings and also enjoy a larger profit base with which to finance the new stores. As of 1975, the firm would begin to generate capital in excess of its needs to finance internally generated growth. The excess capital generated would approach $30 million per year by 1976 (Column 7, Table 9–9).

Financing Levitz's growth

The sharp shift in financing requirements implied by Table 9–9 between 1972 and 1977 created an interesting financing choice for Levitz in 1972. Levitz's external financing need would last for a relatively short period of time. For this reason debt might be a logical choice for filling all or at least a portion of Levitz's anticipated needs. Levitz's low leverage ratio in relation to the industry, coupled with the firm's exceptional profitability (Table 9–2), would suggest that additional debt was certainly *available* to Levitz. The cost advantage associated with debt utilization noted in Chapter 2 would seem to add further weight to the argument for using debt financing. In short, the weight of the traditional arguments generally put forth in favor of debt financing were practically overwhelming for Levitz in 1972.

Only one thing was left out of the analysis above. The omitted fact was that for several years Levitz's common stock had been greatly overvalued in the market.[11]

As we shall observe momentarily, in early 1972 Levitz's common stock was trading at a price many times the value that a rational investor should have been willing to pay for the stock. The sale of equity in early 1972 by Levitz thus promised to produce a significant value transfer benefiting the firm's existing shareholders at the expense of those shareholders who might acquire their shares in a new stock offering. In this regard, Levitz resembled the computer leasing industry example of Chapter 7. The process operated in the following way.

---

[11] The term "overvalued" is used here in the context described in Chapter 1. This is to say that Levitz's common stock was selling in early 1972 at a price in excess of the value that a rational investor could place on a Levitz share as a result of discounting the future cash inflows anticipated over the long run from owning a share of Levitz common stock.

TABLE 9-9

Calculation of the amount and timing of Levitz Furniture Corporation's external capital needs (assuming an expansion to 150 stores in the six years 1972 to 1977; $ millions)

Year	(1) Total selling area* (000 sq. ft.)	(2) Total sales[†]	(3) Profit after taxes[‡]	(4) Total capital required [§]	(5) New capital required during year	(6) Earnings retained	(7) Annual external financing needs
1971—Actual	1,620	183.8	9.2	62.6	—	9.2	—
1972—Pro forma	2,942	341.8	17.0	103.1	40.5	17.0	23.5
1973—Pro forma	4,383	528.3	26.2	153.6	50.5	26.2	24.3
1974—Pro forma	5,940	737.6	36.4	208.2	54.6	36.4	18.2
1975—Pro forma	7,152	929.6	45.6	250.6	42.4	45.6	(3.2)
1976—Pro forma	7,844	1,065.2	51.9	274.9	24.3	51.9	(27.6)
1977—Pro forma	8,652	1,167.9	57.0	303.2	28.3	57.0	(28.7)

*Table 9–8, Line 4 data.

[†]Calculated from data in Table 9–8 (Lines 1–8).

[‡]Calculated from data in Table 9–8 (Lines 1–4, 9–12).

[§]The derivation of these data assumes that the total capital required for each store is equal to $2.02 million. This figure for 1971 can be derived from Table 9–3 by adding Lines 16, 17, 22, 23, and 24, subtracting excess cash (that amount of cash exceeding 5 percent of noncash assets) equal to $4.45 million, and dividing this total by the 31 stores in operation at the end of 1971.

Setting the upper limit on the value of a Levitz share

Were Levitz to continue to finance itself without significant recourse to borrowed money,[12] all of its growth would be financed via profit retentions and the sale of new common stock. Table 9–10 shows how Levitz's earnings per share, ROE, and book value per share would ideally progress between 1971 and 1977, assuming all of the firm's external financing requirements were met via equity sales. The most significant year in this valuation analysis is 1977. In that year Levitz is assumed to have completed its store expansion program, having essentially saturated its market with 150 stores. Beyond 1977 Levitz could thus expect to grow no faster than the furniture retailing industry overall. Levitz would then ideally take its rightful place among the Hall of Fame firms identified in Chapter 1 that earned high ROEs, but that did not know quite what to do with all of their cash. These firms were sufficiently mature so that they generated cash much faster than they generated highly attractive investment alternatives.

If all went as projected in Tables 9–8 and 9–9, by 1977 Levitz would be earning a handsome ROE of about 20 percent (Line 7, Table 9–10), and the book value of a Levitz common share would have reached $16.76 (Line 8, Table 9–10). If the retail furniture industry were to grow at about 6 percent per year beyond 1977, Levitz would be able to reinvest no more than 6/20 or 30 percent of its profits in maintaining its market position.[13]

Calculating the extent of Levitz's value creation

According to the Chapter 1 valuation model, before we can calculate a rational value for a firm's common stock (and thereby determine the *value created*), we need to estimate three variables relating to the firm's future investment opportunities. These are (1) the percentage-point spread expected to be earned on common equity over and above the firm's cost of common equity; (2) the fraction of the firm's annual after-tax profits that can be reinvested in projects offering the extraordinary returns indicated in (1); and (3) the time period over which exceptional returns can be maintained. We have already assumed that Levitz would be able

---

[12] At the end of 1971, for example, Levitz had $9.3 million in cash which was offset by borrowings of $10.9 million. If we were to net excess cash against borrowings at the end of 1971, Levitz's borrowings would be insignificant.

[13] If a firm maintains a constant capital structure and capital intensity, it can increase sales without resort to external equity additions at a rate equal to its return on equity multiplied by the fraction of earnings retained in the business. Since Levitz was projected to earn a 20 percent return on equity, and grow at the rate of 6 percent annually, the firm could retain no more than 30 percent of its annual earnings without piling up redundant capital in the form of cash.

TABLE 9-10

Financial data for Levitz Furniture Corporation (assuming all of the firm's external financing needs from 1972–1974 were met via the sale of common stock, 1971–1977)

	Actual 1971	Pro forma					
		1972	1973	1974	1975	1976	1977
1 Profit after taxes ($ millions)	9.2	17.0	26.2	36.4	45.6	51.9	57.0
2 Financing need in year ($ millions)	—	23.5	24.3	18.2	(3.2)	(27.6)	(28.7)
3 Number of new common shares sold in year* (millions)	—	0.525	0.310	0.154	0	0	0
4 Common shares outstanding (year end) (millions)	16.779	17.304	17.614	17.768	17.768	17.768	17.768
5 Earnings/per share ($)	0.56	0.98	1.49	2.05	2.57	2.92	3.21
6 Dividends/per share ($)	0	0	0	0	0.18	1.55	1.62
7 Profit-after-taxes/Net-worth ratio	0.169	0.179	0.180	0.182	0.188	0.195	0.193
8 Book value/per share ($)	3.24	5.48	8.25	11.25	13.63	15.00	16.76
9 Borrowed money ($ millions)	0†	0	0	0	0	0	0
10 Net worth ($ millions)	54.3	94.8	145.3	199.9	243.3	266.6	294.9
11 Total capital ($ millions)	54.3	94.8	145.3	199.9	242.3	266.6	294.9

* Assumes stock is sold in 1972–74 at 80 times the earnings per share of the prior year. This was Levitz's price/earnings ratio as of the date that a common stock offering was planned in early 1972.

† At the end of 1971, Levitz had $9.3 million in cash and borrowings of $10.9 million. If Levitz's excess cash were netted against the firm's borrowings at the end of 1971, Levitz's borrowings would be insignificant.

to reinvest 30 percent of its profits at superior rates of return beyond 1977. Let us further assume that Levitz would be able to maintain its enviable profitability and market position for as long as *30 years* beyond 1977. What remains is a calculation of the spread to be earned by Levitz over its cost of equity capital.

As noted earlier in the chapter, if we calculate the cost of equity capital for Levitz as of early 1972, it is roughly 15 percent. The *spread* earned by Levitz over its equity-capital cost is thus estimated to be about five percentage points, since Levitz was expected to earn about a 20 percent return on equity after 1977 (Line 7, Table 9–10).[14]

According to the Chapter 1 valuation model (using the assumptions indicated above), Levitz's common stock at the end of 1977 would be rationally valued at 1.5[15] times the stock's book value at the end of 1977.[16]

This analysis suggests that if Levitz made no missteps in achieving its ambitious goal of opening 150 stores by 1977, and if the firm was able to maintain its profitability throughout its expansion phase and beyond, then the rationally determined value of a share of Levitz's common stock at the end of 1977 would equal $1.5 \times \$16.76 = \$25.14$. But what would this *1977* value suggest regarding a rational price for the Levitz share in early *1972*? Including the dividends projected in Line 6 of Table 9–10, the market price of a Levitz share in early 1972 (rationally determined according to the Chapter 1 model) should have been no higher than $12.43 as indicated in Table 9–11. Again, this value represents the *upper* rational price boundary assuming that all went as indicated in the Table 9–10 projection.[17]

---

[14] In fact, this is a somewhat generous estimate of the spread, since the calculation of Levitz's cost of equity capital produced a figure of 16.6 percent (Footnote 6), while Levitz's 1977 return on equity was projected at 19.3 percent (Line 7, Table 9–10).

[15] This value is slightly below the corresponding value of 1.7 that is shown in the 3,4 position of the first matrix in Table 1–3. This is true since the cost of equity capital assumed in the example above was 15 percent, whereas the cost of equity capital assumption utilized in Table 1–3 was 10 percent.

[16] With the larger and presumably more secure base of operations Levitz anticipated by 1977, the firm's business risk (and thus the beta coefficient of the firm's common stock) might be reduced, and/or the company's profit margins could conceivably expand beyond that achieved in 1971. Were Levitz to reduce its equity-capital cost from 15 percent to 10 percent by 1977, or increase its ROE by five percentage points, then the firm's stock would be rationally valued at roughly 2.7 times the firm's book value at the end of 1977, as indicated in Table 1–3.

The tabulation of market-value/book-value ratios shown in Table 1–3 covers only those situations in which the firm's growth rate has stabilized. For this reason we must "back into" the rational economic value of a Levitz share in 1972 by first valuing the share as of 1977, by which point the firm's growth rate is assumed to have stabilized at 6 percent.

[17] If we were to assume a *doubling* (to 10 percent) in the percentage-point spread earned by Levitz over its equity-capital cost, the rationally defined value of a Levitz share in early 1972 would rise to about $21.

TABLE 9-11

Discounted-cash-flow valuation of a share of Levitz common stock, as of early 1972

Based on: (1) the rationally determined value of a Levitz share on 12/31/77, (2) the value of the dividends anticipated between 1975 and 1977, and (3) the calculated 15 percent cost of equity capital.

Present value* (in early 1972) of Levitz's rationally determined $25.14 share value at 12/31/77	$10.86
Present value* (in early 1972) of dividend anticipated in:	
1975	.10
1976	.77
1977	.70
Total present value* (in early 1972) of a share of Levitz common stock.	$12.43

*All of these present value figures assume a 15 percent discount rate since this was Levitz's calculated cost of equity capital.

Calculating the potential for transferring value

On April 11, 1972, Levitz filed a registration statement covering the proposed sale of 600,000 shares of common stock. Levitz's stock traded at a price of $48⅜ per share at the time of the filing of this proposed offering. The size of the proposed offering indicated that Levitz intended to raise about $29 million of new equity capital in 1972. Based on a rational economic value of $12.43 for a Levitz share, the potential for *transferring value* from new shareholders to old shareholders amounted to about $36 for each new share of common stock sold.[18] Given this aberration in the capital markets, one could easily make the case that Levitz's *existing shareholders* would have been well served if the firms' management had concentrated its efforts on selling *stock* rather than selling *furniture*. Fortunately for those investors who might otherwise have acquired shares in the proposed 1972 Levitz offering, it was never completed.[19]

It should be quite clear at this point that Levitz's stock price was completely detached from economic reality in early 1972. This overvaluation was apparent even if one made the assumption that Levitz would be *completely successful* in reaching its ambitious 150-store goal by 1977. How such blatant valuation anomalies can occur in the securities markets is sometimes difficult to comprehend. As was the case in the computer

---

[18] This is simply equal to $48⅜ — $12.43.

[19] On June 2, 1972, the SEC filed a complaint for injunction against Levitz Furniture Corporation and three members of the Levitz family. The complaint alleged that statements made in preliminary prospectuses relating to the proposed offering were materially false and misleading in that they failed to disclose that the Teamsters Union intended to attempt to organize the company's employees, and that an executive of Levitz had informed the Teamsters that Levitz would not oppose the unionization effort if it were postponed until after the public offering. On June 9, 1972, the company consented to, among other things, a "stop order" that effectively precluded the proposed sale of stock.

leasing industry example of Chapter 7, however, we again find presumably sophisticated institutional securities analysts fixated on price/earnings ratios and relatively short-run growth in earnings per share. One highly regarded institutional analyst who covered Levitz quite closely wrote as follows, for example, in late 1971:

> We are continuing to recommend purchase of Levitz shares. As we have pointed out in the past, the stock has generally traded between 30 and 50 times 12-month horizon earnings. Our approach has been, and continues to be, that at 35 times 12-month horizon earnings the stock is a "screaming" buy; at 40 times earnings it is an outright buy; and at 45 times projected 12-month horizon earnings (while probably still capable of returning an attractive rate of appreciation), the shares are viewed as starting to get somewhat ahead of themselves and can probably be purchased instead at a more opportune moment.[20]

If one compares Levitz's early forecasts of the firm's market saturation point at various points in time against (1) the market-value/book-value ratio history of Levitz's common stock (Table 9–12) and (2) the rationally defined market-value/book-value ratios outlined in Table 1–3, one

TABLE 9–12

Market-value/Book-value ratios of Levitz Furniture Corporation's common stock at various dates, 1968–1977

Date	Market-value/Book-value ratio	Date	Market-value/Book-value ratio
July 1968	4.4*	Apr. 1973	2.7
Oct. 1968	3.6	July 1973	1.8
Jan. 1969	9.4	Oct. 1973	1.3
Apr. 1969	9.5*	Jan. 1974	1.0
July 1969	n.a.†	Apr. 1974	0.8
Oct. 1969	n.a.	July 1974	0.5
Jan. 1970	5.8	Oct. 1974	0.5
Apr. 1970	n.a.	Jan. 1975	0.6
July 1970	n.a.	Apr. 1975	0.8
Oct. 1970	n.a.	July 1975	1.1
Jan. 1971	8.3	Oct. 1975	0.9
Apr. 1971	6.5*	Jan. 1976	1.3
July 1971	7.8	Apr. 1976	1.3
Oct. 1971	10.2	July 1976	1.1
Jan. 1972	14.2	Oct. 1976	0.9
Apr. 1972	14.0‡	Jan. 1977	1.0
July 1972	13.0	Apr. 1977	0.9
Oct. 1972	5.7	July 1977	0.9
Jan. 1973	5.4	Oct. 1977	1.0

*Denotes that public offerings of Levitz common stock occurred around these dates that raised $5.3 million, $20.4 million, and $43.2 million, respectively.
†n.a. = not available.
‡Denotes an attempted public offering of common stock that was never completed.

---

[20] James H. Oliphant & Company, "Levitz Furniture Corporation: Progress Report," December 8, 1971, p. 9.

fact should be clear. During most of Levitz's history as a public company up until about mid-1973, the market price of Levitz's common stock was almost *always* irrationally high. This overvaluation covered the period during which Levitz grew from 6 stores to 54 stores.[21]

> In the period from 1968 to mid-1973, Levitz's expansion followed the chain-letter example of Chapter 7. Levitz used stores as its investment vehicle instead of computers, however. In addition, in contrast to the computer leasing example, Levitz's stores represented high-ROE investments (at least up until 1973), whereas computer leases never offered rates of return commensurate with equity-capital costs.

The required rate of return on equity capital

One other very interesting factor emerges from this example of a significant imperfection in the way securities are sometimes valued. Given the fact that the market value of a Levitz share was actually $48⅝ in early 1972, yet a share should not have been *rationally* valued above $12.43 at that time, one might ask the following question: What rate of return would Levitz have to have earned (between 1972 and 1977) on the proceeds of a 1972 stock sale in order to avoid *reducing* the rational economic value of a Levitz share outstanding in 1972? The answer is simply the internal rate of return associated with the cash flows shown in Table 9–13.

Table 9–13 suggests that a stock sale in 1972 would have been attractive to Levitz's existing shareholder group even if Levitz were to have earned a significant *negative return* between 1972 and 1977 on the capital raised in the offering. This is the epitome of low-priced capital. Indeed, in response to questions in early 1972 about his preference for equity

TABLE 9-13
Calculation of the rate of return (from 1972 to 1977) at which Levitz would have to invest the proceeds from a stock sale in early 1972 in order *not to reduce* the rationally determined value of a Levitz share

Year	Inflow to Levitz from the sale of a share in 1972	Outflow required to equal the dividend	Rational economic value of a Levitz share
1972	$48-5/8	–	$12.43
1973	–	–	–
1974	–	–	–
1975	–	$0.18	–
1976	–	1.55	–
1977	–	1.62	$25.14
Internal rate of return = –9%			

---

[21] In the years following the collapse in Levitz's stock price (from mid-1973 to early 1977) Levitz increased its number of stores by only seven.

financing, the chairman of Levitz Furniture, Ralph Levitz, made the following comments:

> The best kind of money is equity money. You have it forever. You don't pay it back. You don't pay interest on it.

. . . . .

> We are almost financing our key asset, inventories, for next to nothing.[22]

At the time these comments were made, some financial analysts undoubtedly thought the statements showed considerable financial naivete. Mr. Levitz was absolutely right, however. Levitz stock was so overvalued in 1972 that it carried a *negative* cost over the time period in question.

> *Levitz could have served its existing shareholders well in 1972 by selling stock, burying the sale proceeds in the ground, and digging up the money again in 1977.*

Such is the distorted logic of imperfect capital markets!

To summarize this first section of Chapter 9, in early 1972 Levitz's common stock had a *book* value of about $3.24 per share. It had a rational *economic* value of $12.43 per share assuming that the optimistic growth and profitability projections noted earlier were in fact realized. It had a *market* value of $48⅝ per share. Since Levitz had 16.8 million shares outstanding in early 1972, Levitz's management could entertain hopes of ultimately *creating value* equal to ($12.43 − $3.24) × 16.8 million = $154 million. This *created value* would, assuming all went as outlined in Table 9–10, emerge as a result of Levitz's superior profitability and operating skill. The bulk of Levitz's market value in 1972, however ($48⅝ − $12.43) × 16.8 million = $608 million, was ephemeral. It represented only *value-transfer potential* for those shareholders who were astute enough to sell their Levitz stock before economic reality ultimately intruded into the valuation process.

The destruction of shareholder value

To this point in the chapter we have looked only at *value creation* and *value transfer*. We have not yet examined any actions by Levitz's management that might have led to *value destruction*. This section of Chapter 9 will examine the competitive environment in furniture retailing, again during the period of the early 1970s, when Levitz's growth was most rapid. This segment of material will show Levitz discouraging warehouse-showroom competition through its decisions on pricing and on the location of stores. To some degree we will also find Levitz repeating the error

---

[22] *Forbes,* February 1, 1972, p. 17.

of those grocery retailers noted in Chapter 4 who drove for *national* market share while neglecting the more economically critical *city-market* share. While Levitz's preemptive strategy was modestly successful, it probably *accelerated* the collapse in Levitz's stock price. The value-destroying aspect of Levitz's actions may have been a key factor in cutting the firm off from its low-cost source of equity capital before the firm's 150-store physical plant was in place, and before its dominant national market position was assured.

Competition in furniture retailing

As noted earlier, competition in furniture retailing existed largely among local one-store entrepreneurs. Other broad categories of potential Levitz competitors were also identifiable, however. Levitz's principal competition fell into three broad categories. These included:

1. Local operators (usually with a single store) selling almost exclusively furniture and home furnishings;
2. Department store operators (such as Sears, Roebuck; Federated Department Stores; and Macy's) that operated numerous stores selling a broad line of goods (in which furniture usually occupied a relatively small position); and
3. Multi-unit warehouse-showroom operators (such as Wickes, Unicapital, and Mangurian's) who followed a selling format similar to that pioneered by Levitz.

The *local operators* posed little threat to Levitz's 150-store national marketing objective. This was true for several reasons. First, Levitz's market penetration objective rarely exceeded 20 percent in those cities large enough to support a warehouse-showroom.[23] Industry analysts, however, felt that the warehouse-showroom concept might ultimately penetrate between 40 percent and 60 percent of a city-market.[24] This meant that there would be room in each of Levitz's target cities for at least one enterprising local furniture retailer who could raise the $2 million needed to open a Levitz-type warehouse-showroom outlet. Second and more significantly, the one-store warehouse-showroom operator lacked both the purchasing efficiencies that Levitz had achieved nationally and the access to cheap equity capital that fueled Levitz's rapid expansion. For these reasons the one-store local operator was probably not a threat to Levitz's ultimate goal of dominating the retail furniture business in the United States.

---

[23] Robert Garrett & Sons, Inc., "Levitz Furniture Corporation," May, 1970, p. 4.

[24] Jas. H. Oliphant & Co., "Progress Report, Levitz Furniture Corporation," December 8, 1971, p. 3.

The *department store* operators posed a far more significant potential threat to Levitz. Even this threat was unlikely to become a serious problem for Levitz, however, for a number of reasons. Sears, Roebuck was probably the largest national retailer of furniture up until 1972, yet the average sales of furniture in a Sears store were probably only about $625,000.[25] For Sears to counterattack Levitz by building warehouse-showroom outlets would mean a partial abandonment of the full-service department store concept on which Sears was built. It would also involve constructing stores with target volumes of $8 to $10 million annually in order to preserve a market for furniture that probably averaged only $625,000 per Sears store. In short, while Sears certainly had access to capital (although it was not as cheap as Levitz's capital) and access to the purchasing savings that Levitz enjoyed nationally, Sears was unlikely to follow a "boutique" retailing strategy that would strike at the heart of its full-service department store image. Firms smaller than Sears, Roebuck (such as Federated Department Stores and Macy's) represented a slightly different problem for Levitz. Fortunately for Levitz, these firms moved rather cautiously in entering the warehouse-showroom field.[26] Levitz thus enjoyed a long lead in getting its planned 150 stores in place before these firms could test out and then duplicate the warehouse-showroom concept on a large scale.

The real threat to Levitz's 150 store growth plan came from warehouse-showroom operators with (1) significant national market-share ambitions, and (2) access to cheap equity capital resulting from overvalued stock prices. With regard to the two factors noted above, before its first warehouse-showroom opened in July 1971, for example, Wickes Corp. announced that it planned "to build 50 to 75 stores across the country."[27] At that time Wickes' only position in furniture retailing was the six warehouse-showrooms that it had under construction. These were scheduled to open in 1971. The firm did, however, have a net worth exceeding $100

---

[25] Sears, Roebuck had furniture sales estimated at $250 million in 1970 (Mitchell Hutchins & Co., Inc., "Levitz Furniture Corporation," May, 1970, p. 5). Somewhat less than 50 percent of Sears' 800 stores carried furniture, so the average furniture department in a Sears store sold roughly $250,000,000/400 = $625,000 in furniture annually.

[26] In July, 1971 Macy's announced that it planned to acquire a 50 percent interest in J. Homestock, Inc., a firm with one warehouse-showroom in Dedham, Mass. In announcing the proposed acquisition, Macy's suggested that the opening of two new warehouse-showrooms per year over the five years 1971–76 was a feasible objective (*Home Furnishings Daily*, July 29, 1971, p. 2). In early 1972 two firms in the Federated Department Stores group opened small experimental warehouse-showrooms in existing facilities in Dayton and Columbus, Ohio. In addition, Federated became directly involved in warehouse-showrooms through its Gold Key operation, which opened a warehouse showroom at Costa Mesa, California, in the spring of 1972, and planned to open two others in California in the fall of 1972.

[27] *Home Furnishings Daily*, June 4, 1971, p. 6.

TABLE 9–14

Financial data for warehouse-showroom furniture retailers with significant announced national share-of-market ambitions in the early 1970s

Line	Year	(1) Levitz	(2) Wickes	(3) Unicapital	(4) General Portland Cement
	Net worth ($ millions)				
1	1970	23.1	103.2	32.1	96.5
2	1971	54.3	165.0	36.6	115.6
3	1972	68.1	175.0	40.9	122.3
	Return on equity				
4	1970	0.192	0.073	0.118	0.091
5	1971	0.169	0.074	0.109	0.090
6	1972	0.178	0.097	0.120	0.092
	Market-value/Book-value* ratio				
7	1970	8.3	2.6	2.4	1.9
8	1971	14.2	2.4	2.8	1.8
9	1972	5.4	1.2	1.9	0.9

*Market-value/book-value ratio data as of January 31 of the following year.

million, an amount several times larger than that enjoyed by Levitz Furniture (Table 9–14).

Wickes' public offering of common stock in September 1971 was a more serious threat to Levitz's ambitions than Wickes' $100 million net worth. This stock sale gave Wickes a large pool of cash and boosted the firm's net worth by $55 million, an increase of 50 percent. The stock sale added financial credibility to Wickes' warehouse-showroom growth projections. The offering was sold at a price that equalled 3.2 times Wickes' book value at the time of the sale. Given Wickes' unimpressive ROE performance in its basic lines of business in the early 1970s (Lines 4–6, Column 2, Table 9–14) the Chapter 1 valuation model suggests that a 3.2 market-value/book-value ratio was probably significantly detached from economic reality. This valuation for Wickes represented a real threat to Levitz. If a number of warehouse-showroom competitors gained access to equity capital at a nominal cost (as a number of competitors had, for example, in the computer leasing industry) the race to open new outlets would be fierce indeed. Levitz's management clearly needed to find a way to close off its competitor's access to low-cost capital, while preserving its own access to this important competitive benefit.

Other furniture retailers were close behind Wickes in the attempt to capitalize on Levitz's market success. In July of 1971 Unicapital, Inc., announced (as the firm opened its first warehouse-showroom) that it planned "to open six [warehouse-showrooms] a year for six years, or one every 60 days."[28] At that time Unicapital had four warehouse-showrooms scheduled to open during 1971. Unicapital was *not* a newcomer to the

---

[28] *Home Furnishings Daily,* July 29, 1971, p. 5.

retail furniture business, as the firm already operated a chain of 68 smaller retail furniture stores. Unicapital also had a net worth of over $30 million (Table 9–14), an amount roughly comparable to Levitz. While Unicapital had no equity offering planned in 1971, the firm did enjoy a market-value/book-value ratio that was high in relation to the firm's historic ROE performance (Column 3, Table 9–14). It was less out of line than either Levitz or Wickes, however, and the Unicapital threat to Levitz was less serious in part for that reason.

Finally, in early 1972 Mangurian's announced that it planned "to continue expansion at the rate of about three new [warehouse-showroom] complexes annually in growth markets throughout the country."[29] By early 1972 Mangurian's had two self-contained warehouse-showrooms operating in Tampa and Dallas. The firm also had two large showrooms in Rochester, New York, which were served by a common warehouse, and four large showrooms located in south Florida (stretching from West Palm Beach to Miami), which were served by one common warehouse in Ft. Lauderdale.

Mangurian's had been acquired in late 1970 by the General Portland Cement Co. This acquisition boosted Mangurian's net worth (in consolidation with the parent company) from $10 million to $96.5 million (Table 9–14). While the acquisition increased Mangurian's immediate access to capital needed for growth, it may have had a negative impact on an equally important growth factor. The acquisition almost certainly reduced Mangurian's access to cheap equity capital. General Portland Cement acquired Mangurian's in 1970 at a price equal to 2.6 times Mangurian's book value. General Portland's stock, however, traded at less than two times book value (Line 8, Column 4, Table 9–14). This valuation undoubtedly reflected the firm's unexciting historic ROE and the unexciting future prospects for the cement business, balanced off in part by the more exciting prospects of Mangurian's warehouse-showroom furniture business. A potential investor in General Portland Cement had to acquire a large position in cement in order to gain access to Mangurian's possibly superior profitability prospects, however. This fact may well have prevented General Portland's common stock from achieving the irrational heights that would have been needed in order to assure the firm's access to cheap equity capital. Without such access the firm could not hope to compete effectively with Levitz.

To enhance the likelihood of success in achieving its 150-store objective, Levitz had to find a way to dissuade its emerging warehouse-showroom competitors from their aggressive expansion plans. One way for Levitz to accomplish this would be to enter every one of its planned city-markets with enough warehouse-showroom outlets to saturate each market before the arrival of national competition. A second way for Levitz to

---

[29] General Portland Cement Company, 1971 Annual Report, p. 8.

meet this objective would be to make sure that the first few stores opened by each major competitor were highly unprofitable. If the initial stores of Levitz's major potential competitors were unprofitable, Levitz might benefit in either of two ways. First, the managements of competitors might be persuaded to cut back on their expansion plans simply because of the *unprofitability* of their stores. Second, investors might be persuaded to be more realistic in valuing the common stocks of competing warehouse-showroom operators if these companies faced the prospect of sustained loss operations in their stores. Without access to cheap equity capital, Levitz's competitors might then be persuaded by the *capital markets* to cut back on their expansion plans. Either way, Levitz would win.

Levitz's early efforts to achieve rapid market penetration

A key element in Levitz's strategy was to get its 150-store physical plant in place as rapidly as possible. The pace of Levitz's new store openings was a critical concern of Levitz's management. The following comments from both industry analysts and Levitz's management were constantly repeated in the early 1970s.

> Levitz' strategy of rapid expansion is designed not only to preclude as many imitators as possible, but also to develop quickly the corporation's strength to enable it to compete effectively with those forms of competition, no matter how well financed, which are likely to appear in the future.[30]

✿ ✿ ✿ ✿ ✿

> Getting into a trading area first may be very important. Present Levitz stores are unique in their markets, and just how important this is will soon be discovered. But it may be vital. Therefore, the scramble for virgin territories for warehouse-showrooms becomes critical.[31]

✿ ✿ ✿ ✿ ✿

> Until this year, Levitz had the warehouse-showroom field virtually to itself. But no more. . . . To the rest of the industry, those profits look like the ice cream with the marshmallows and the cherries. . . . Literally hundreds of stores will be chasing the same rainbow.[32]

✿ ✿ ✿ ✿ ✿

> In addition, it is store openings which will receive the bulk of Levitz's attention during the coming years. Levitz is now gunning for 150 stores

---

[30] Mitchell, Hutchins & Co., "Levitz Furniture Corporation Report," May 1970, p. 13.

[31] *Home Furnishings Daily*, June 4, 1971, Section II, p. 8.

[32] *Business Week*, "Levitz: The Hot Name in Instant Furniture," December 4, 1971, p. 90.

covering 50 major markets. Sears, Roebuck has only 226 class "A" stores, and the chain has been building aggressively for decades. Levitz wants his stores up fast; they are his No. 1 priority.[33]

*****

. . . it is important to get into good markets early and to get the best store locations. Wouldn't it be better for the company in the long run to line up the stores we want now and get them open, and then wait for the big payoff in three or four years even if this did hurt our profitability for the next year?[34]

*****

The other guys [Levitz warehouse-showroom competitors] are going to try. But we've got a flying start. We're opening them [warehouse-show-rooms] faster than anybody else conceivably can do.[35]

The impact of Levitz's actions on competitors' expansion plans

Levitz obviously couldn't preempt its potential warehouse-showroom competitors by opening in *every* city *before* its competitors had become irreversibly committed to specific city-markets. Levitz could, however, open "fighting stores" on top of those warehouse-showroom competitors that had announced significant national market share aspirations. In several of the first few cities where Wickes and Unicapital announced their intention to open warehouse-showroom outlets, for example, the response by Levitz was dramatic (Table 9–15). In several of these early situations, it appears that once Levitz learned of a competitor's store-opening plans, Levitz simply pushed ahead the timetable of its long-range store-opening plans so as to arrive in the same cities where competition

TABLE 9–15
Store-opening dates in various cities (Levitz versus competing warehouse-showroom furniture retailers)

	Wickes		Levitz		Unicapital	
	Store*	Opening date	Store*	Opening date	Store*	Opening date
Minneapolis	1	July 1971	28	Dec. 1971	—	—
Houston	—	—	19	May 1971	1	July 1971
Cincinnati	2	Sep. 1971	20	Aug. 1971	—	—
St. Louis	3	Sep. 1971	24	Sep. 1971	2	Oct. 1971
Milwaukee	4	Nov. 1971	33	Apr. 1972	—	—

* Indicates order in sequence of new stores opened by each competitor.

---

[33] *Home Furnishings Daily,* "Retailer of the Year, Ralph Levitz," January 3, 1972, p. 5.

[34] Wight Martindale, Jr., *We Do It Every Day,* p. 142.

[35] *Forbes,* "Levit(z)ation," February 1, 1972, p. 17.

planned openings, but usually at an *earlier date* than that planned by its competitors. Reports regarding Levitz's competitiveness in the trade press at the time ran as follows:

The Houston market.

Levitz opened its first store this year on May 20, in Houston and we understand its first month volume has set new company records. The store was constructed, stocked, and opened within 75 days. Such a short lead-time enabled Levitz to begin its operations across the street from [Unicapital] over a month before this new competitor could open its warehouse-showroom.[36]

* * * * *

Houston may well be the toughest test the new [Unicapital] warehouse-showroom discount chain will face in any of the 36 cities it plans to enter in the next six years. [Unicapital's] nearest neighbors are less than one-half mile away on Houston's South Loop and they are its strongest competitors—Levitz and soon Mangurian's. Levitz opened its 19th store about June 1 in Houston, and [Unicapital] opened its first store July 1. The Mangurian's site directly adjoins Levitz and the store is to open late this fall. Levitz evidently pushed its opening ahead to squelch [Unicapital].[37]

* * * * *

Levitz is [. . . .] aggressive in beating competitors to the 55 major metropolitan markets it hopes to dominate in the coming years. In Houston . . . [Levitz] beat [Unicapital] by four weeks and set the stage for a full-scale furniture war. Within the same half-mile stretch, Mangurian's is building a unit to compete with the other two. Competition has become so fierce that David M. Cummings, Chairman of Furniture Outlets, complains that he was heaved bodily out of the Levitz store. "Normal hard competition is one thing," he says ruefully. "But with Levitz it's war."[38]

The Cincinnati market.

Then came the giants. Wickes announced its entry into the field and got its building underway. Levitz, not to be outdone, did what Cincinnati contractors thought was the impossible—rushed in with its own construction team, spent tons of money on day and night labor and built, racked, stacked, hired, advertised, and opened within some 45 days. One day there was a big empty field; the next, it seemed, there was Levitz.[39]

---

[36] Seidlitz and Company, Inc., "Levitz Furniture Special Report," July 7, 1971, p. 3.

[37] *Home Furnishings Daily,* July 29, 1971, p. 4.

[38] *Business Week,* "Levitz: The Hot Name in Instant Furniture," December 4, 1971, p. 91.

[39] *Home Furnishings Daily,* February 22, 1972, p. 13.

The St. Louis market.

Wickes Furniture may be winning a race with Levitz to be the first to open a warehouse-showroom operation in St. Louis. Levitz officials here decline to reveal a target date but competitors are expecting an early October opening. "If they could work eight days a week, they would" said a major competitor who does not believe Wickes has won the race yet.[40]

* * * * *

Levitz opened [in St. Louis] September 16, Wickes, September 30, and [Unicapital] October 11.[41]

The early profit performance of Levitz's principal national competitors in the warehouse-showroom derby was abysmal. Levitz's competitors lost heavily in establishing their market positions in 1971 (Table 9–16).

Over the following five years none of these firms were able to emerge from their loss positions. A weak economy in which consumer durables were particularly hard hit undoubtedly contributed substantially to the poor profit performance of these firms in the 1974–76 period. In the 1971–73 period, however, part of the credit for the poor performance of these firms belonged to Levitz.

The chronology of events as each Levitz competitor responded to Levitz's early competitive strategy is revealing.

Unicapital's response. One security analyst quoted Ralph Levitz as follows after a luncheon meeting discussion in the summer of 1971.

Our new policy of announcing store locations seems to have scared [Unicapital] away from the Ft. Lauderdale area.[42]

Another analyst reported on his discussions in December 1971 with the Levitz chairman.

Mr. Levitz answered several questions pertaining to competition. He noted that the Houston store is meeting its sales forecasts and that rumors have been circulating that [Unicapital] (his competitor in that market) had decided to stop building new units and may be looking to sell off its three existing warehouse-showrooms. . . . Levitz has cut prices somewhat to discourage competitors from becoming too aggressive in their expansion programs.[43]

As of the opening date of its first warehouse-showroom, the profit forecast for Unicapital's operations was as follows:

---

[40] *Home Furnishings Daily,* September 7, 1971, p. 12.

[41] *Home Furnishings Daily,* January 10, 1972, p. 8.

[42] Internal investment company memo dated August 6, 1971.

[43] Jas. H. Oliphant & Co., "Levitz Furniture Corporation," December 8, 1971, p. 4.

TABLE 9-16

Profitability data for the furniture retailing divisions of Levitz's principal national warehouse-showroom competitors

	(1)	(2)	(3)	(4)	(5)	(6)	(7)	(8)	(9)
		Unicapital* (warehouse-showroom operations)			Wickes† (warehouse-showroom operations)			General Portland Cement‡ (Mangurian's operations)	
	Sales ($000s)	Pretax profit ($000s)	Pretax profit/ Sales	Sales ($000s)	Pretax profit ($000s)	Pretax profit/ Sales	Sales ($000s)	Pretax profit ($000s)	Pretax profit/ Sales
1971	5,027	(1,760)	(0.35)	12,666	(2,650)	(0.21)	24,833	1,882	0.08
1972	13,698	(2,112)	(0.15)	52,931	(4,034)	(0.08)	41,283	1,694	0.04
1973	16,793	(864)	(0.05)	82,700	(2,622)	(0.03)	49,966	(760)	(0.02)
1974				91,404	(3,945)	(0.04)	23,095	(10,034)	(0.43)
1975	Data not broken out after 1973.			75,410	(5,382)	(0.07)	18,767	(2,950)	(0.16)
1976				84,292	(4,745)	(0.06)	14,587	(4,762)	(0.33)

*After 1973, Unicapital no longer specifically detailed the operating results of its warehouse-showroom operations. Unicapital reported only the *after*-tax profit contribution from its product lines, so the pretax profit figure in Column 2 is imputed assuming a 50 percent tax rate.

†Wickes reported only the operating income of its product lines *prior* to any allocation of corporate expenses and interest. The Column 5 data assume that the corporate expenses plus interest are allocated in proportion to sales. Prior to this allocation the operating losses of the warehouse-showroom operations were $2.5 million, $3.3 million, $.4 million, $1.0 million, $3.3 million and $2.4 million, respectively, in 1971-76.

‡General Portland Cement reported only the *after*-tax profit contribution from its divisions, so the pretax profit figure in Column 8 is imputed assuming a 50 percent tax rate. The results for 1974 include costs associated with closing the Denver and Houston warehouse-showroom outlets.

Sources: Annual reports and 10K Reports to the SEC.

During [1971] the initial [warehouse-showroom] units are scheduled to produce approximately $6 million in sales, and $200,000 in profits. The same initial three units are expected to have sales of $22 million and earnings of $900,000 during [1972]. A full 12-month operation by six [warehouse-showroom] stores should result in income of approximately $2 million.[44]

Obviously, Unicapital's initial profit forecasts were off rather dramatically. Unicapital's response to its profit shortfall was somewhat chaotic. The Houston store, for example, had three general managers within its first seven months of operation.[45] It was closed for six weeks in August, 1972 "in order to remodel, sell off old inventory, and institute new operating and control procedures."[46]

Unicapital opened a total of only three warehouse-showrooms before cancelling its future expansion plans. The Houston store was closed in the summer of 1976 and finally sold in early 1977. Unicapital's remaining stores in Cincinnati and St. Louis continued to perform unsatisfactorily.

Wickes' response. Unicapital caved in quickly. Wickes had greater financial strength and greater resolve, although its financial performance was only marginally better than Unicapital's (Column 6 versus Column 3, Table 9–16). Wickes maintained a relatively aggressive store opening program through 1973 (Table 9–17) in the face of some formidable losses. Comments by Wickes' management and the trade press summarizing Wickes' evolving strategy over time follow.

In response to an analyst's question in early 1973 as to whether Wickes planned to cut back its store openings, Wickes' President responded,

The answer is "No." We have 17 stores open. We will open an additional 12 in this year, which is pretty much on target; and as far as we can see we will continue that kind of expansion.[47]

TABLE 9–17
Warehouse-showroom opening history of Wickes Corporation

Year	Warehouse-showrooms opened in year	Total warehouse-showrooms
1971	6	6
1972	8	14
1973	7	21
1974	1	22
1975	0	22
1976	0	22

---

[44] *Home Furnishings Daily*, July 29, 1971, p. 5.

[45] *Home Furnishings Daily*, February 7, 1972, p. 20.

[46] Robinson–Humphrey Co., Inc., Unicapital Corp., Nov. 2, 1972.

[47] The Wickes Corporation, Transcript of Meeting Before the Los Angeles Society of Security Analysts, January 30, 1973, p. 15.

By mid-1973, Wickes' President was less optimistic.

> We started our furniture retailing business anticipating more immediate success than we received, and we met with some strong, emotional responses in the marketplace that required some increased expenditures and reduction in margins as we established ourselves.[48]

❀ ❀ ❀ ❀ ❀

> . . . in a few instances we have met a less stable kind of competition than anticipated with, in two or three locations, a great overspending in advertising and considerable price reduction taking place.[49]

Nonetheless, Wickes' President was reportedly

> . . . satisfied with the progress of the stores, except for those in Milwaukee, St. Louis, and Cincinnati.[50] . . . In the cities where Wickes and Levitz met in competition, the firm's were reportedly "waging a costly battle against each other."[51]

By early 1974, Wickes had ceased opening new outlets. It reported as follows in a financing prospectus:

> The company opened fewer new retail furniture stores in [1973] than had been planned as a result of a desire to conserve financial resources, to await the availability of a wider choice of satisfactory sites and to provide management with an opportunity to analyze the company's experience with a view to improving store profitability.[52]

Wickes opened no new outlets after March 1974. By the end of 1976 it had yet to report a profit from furniture retailing.

Mangurian's response. Mangurian's profitability began to collapse immediately after the firm was acquired by General Portland Cement and after it began opening self-contained warehouse-showrooms. At the end of 1973, General Portland announced its intention to sell its furniture operations. An agreement in principle to sell the bulk of Mangurian's stores to Wickes was announced in March 1974, but the sale was never consummated. By the end of 1974 General Portland had sold off Mangurian's operations in Rochester and Dallas, and had closed its warehouse-showrooms in Houston and Denver. After five years of effort aimed at selling Mangurian's as a going concern, in 1978 General Portland an-

---

[48] The Wickes Corporation, Transcript of Meeting Before the New York Society of Security Analysts, June 1, 1973, p. 9.

[49] Ibid., p. 26.

[50] *Business Week*, June 2, 1973, p. 71.

[51] Ibid., p. 71.

[52] Wickes Corporation Prospectus, May 30, 1974, p. 18.

nounced that it would liquidate the inventory and sell the real estate comprising the eight Mangurian's stores in Florida.

Value destruction reduces Levitz's value-transfer capability

If Levitz's management was attempting to moderate the store opening plans of warehouse-showroom competitors with national ambitions, the effort was reasonably successful. Unfortunately for Levitz, this strategy put considerable pressure on Levitz's *own* profit margins. This profit pressure, in turn, made it difficult for Levitz to continue to produce the rapid growth in earnings per share that kept Levitz's stock price inflated to such irrational levels. Table 9–18 points up the valuation issue quite clearly. Levitz's earnings per share stopped growing in the third quarter of 1972, and actually *declined* in the first quarter of 1973. This fact produced a shift in investor perceptions as to Levitz's future growth potential. The market-value/book-value ratio of Levitz's common stock declined from 13.0 to 2.7 (Table 9–18) within a nine-month period. Once the irrational valuation bubble at Levitz had been popped, the chain-letter game ended. Levitz's access to nominally priced equity capital vanished, and with it went Levitz's growth plans.

It is interesting to reflect on some "what if" questions regarding Levitz. But for a chance event (Footnote 19), Levitz would have successfully raised $29 million of new equity capital in April 1972. Had the firm been *less* aggressive in its competitive interactions in 1971–72, Levitz might have been able to raise (very cheaply in early 1973) the additional $37 million[53] in equity capital needed to carry the chain to its 150-store goal. Had Levitz concentrated early in the game on gaining *city-market dominance* via clustering its stores, rather than dissipating its strength in intercepting competitors harboring national ambitions, the valuation bubble might have lasted longer. Levitz might then have opened significantly more than 61 stores by 1977 (Line 26, Table 9–3). It could also have located these stores so as to have achieved greater market penetration (and presumably greater profitability) in those city-markets served. Under these circumstances, Levitz might have emerged from the 1973–75 profit collapse (Line 7, Table 9–3) in an extraordinarily powerful competitive posture. As maters stand in 1977, Levitz has announced that the firm will now place its primary expansion emphasis on gaining deeper penetration in its *existing* city-markets. At the 1977 annual meeting of shareholders, Levitz's president commented as follows:[54]

---

[53] This equals $23.5 + $24.3 + $18.2 millions of capital needed in 1972–74 (from Column 7, Table 9–9) less the $29 million that Levitz attempted to raise in April 1972.

[54] Levitz Furniture Corporation, Report to Shareholders on 1977 Annual Meeting, p. 5.

TABLE 9-18
Earnings and market-value data for the common stock of the Levitz Furniture Corporation, 1971-1977

Quarter	Four quarter moving average		Market-value/ Book-value ratio
	Earnings per share ($)	Profit-after-tax/ Net-worth ratio (%)	
1971			
1st	0.33	18.2	6.5
2d.	0.38	17.1	7.8
3d.	0.45	17.2	10.2
4th	0.56	18.8	14.2
1972			
1st	0.62	19.7	14.0
2d.	0.68	20.5	13.0
3d.	0.69	19.5	5.7
4th	0.72	19.6	5.4
1973			
1st	0.70	18.0	2.7
2d.	0.70	17.0	1.8
3d.	0.66	15.4	1.3
4th	0.51	11.6	1.0
1974			
1st	0.50	11.1	0.8
2d.	0.47	10.1	0.5
3d.	0.38	8.1	0.5
4th	0.23	4.9	0.6
1975			
1st	0.05	1.1	0.8
2d.	(0.09)	(1.7)	1.1
3d.	(0.11)	(2.4)	0.9
4th	(0.01)	(0.2)	1.3
1976			
1st	0.08	1.7	1.3
2d.	0.14	3.5	1.1
3d.	0.26	5.3	0.9
4th	0.37	7.4	1.0
1977			
1st	0.47	9.1	0.9
2d.	0.58	10.9	0.9
3d*	0.73	13.3	1.0

*In August 1977, Levitz's shareholders approved a 4-for-1 reverse stock split. None of the data in this chapter reflect the effects of this reverse stock split.
Sources: Quarterly Reports to Shareholders; *Bank and Quotation Record.*

Our plan is to resume with an expansion program of rounding out our current markets to maximize return on investment; and toward this end we closed our warehouse-showroom in Milwaukee, Wisconsin, which had not produced a satisfactory return, and will reinvest the capital in a new facility in South Miami. The Miami/Fort Lauderdale geographic area is one of the company's most successful markets, and the additional store [   ] will enable us to obtain a larger share of this market.

Several other existing markets are under consideration for either new warehouse-showrooms or satellite stores to supplement facilities which will enable us to increase volume in those markets at relatively little additional expense.

Levitz acquired the J. Homestock stores of R. H. Macy & Co.[55] in mid-1977, increasing Levitz's market penetration in three of its existing markets, and giving it significant penetration of the Boston market with three stores. By 1977 Levitz was pursuing city-market scale economies as a first priority. The strategy is hardly new. It was learned 25 years earlier by the most profitable grocery retailers as indicated in Chapter 4.

Summary

The creation, transfer, and destruction of shareholder value all followed from Levitz's corporate strategy during the period extending from the firm's initial public stock offering in 1968 through the collapse of Levitz's stock price in 1972.

Levitz *created value* for its shareholders by utilizing a marketing technique that gave the firm a more efficient cost structure than that of its traditional furniture-retailing competitors. This more efficient cost structure was parlayed into a return on equity capital that was higher than the cost of Levitz's equity capital.

Levitz *transferred value* during the period 1968–72 by raising large

TABLE 9-19

Estimated proceeds from publicly reported sales of Levitz Furniture Corporation common stock by member of the Levitz family

Year of sales	Estimated sale proceeds from stock sales by Levitz family members ($ millions)	Estimated average-sale-price-per-share/ Book-value-per-share ratio
1968	1.4	4.4
1969	11.1	9.4
1970	0	—
1971	20.5	11.3
1972	3.2	6.8
1973	0.4	1.7
1974	0.1	0.5
1975	1.2	1.0
1976	2.0	1.3
	$39.9	

Note: Includes only those sales made by four Levitz family members during those periods for which their ownership position was listed in registration statements, proxy material, or Form 4 reports to the SEC.

---

[55] As noted in Footnote 26, both Macy's and Federated Department Stores entered the warehouse-showroom market in 1971–72. Coincidentally, during the summer of 1977 these firms sold the operations that began in 1971–72. Homestock was sold to Levitz, and Federated's Gold Key chain of three stores was sold to an investor group that included the division's management.

amounts of equity capital for the firm during periods when the firm's stock price was inflated well beyond rational levels. Members of the Levitz family also capitalized on the value-transfer opportunity by selling significant amounts of their own personal stock holdings, particularly in those time periods during which the price of the firm's stock was most irrationally inflated (Table 9–19).

Finally, Levitz's actions aimed at enhancing the long-run value of its own common stock had the effect of *destroying* a portion of the market value of the common stocks of competing firms. That part of Levitz's strategy with *value-destruction* consequences backfired, however, since it affected the firm's options in the area of *value transfers*. A rapidly falling stock price cut Levitz's expansion plans short before the firm had completed its 150-store physical plant.

All of the value-enhancing options noted in Chapter 2 were available to Levitz's management in 1971–72. Most of the options were utilized brilliantly, either by conscious design or perhaps as a visceral response to fast-breaking events. Were it not for the value-transfer penalty additional Levitz investors would have to have paid, it is almost a shame that Levitz didn't achieve its 150-store corporate objective.

PART FOUR

Summary and conclusions

10

The scope and the ethics of value transformation opportunity

The primary objective of this book has been to demonstrate that thinking about methods for enhancing value can produce very significant benefits for shareholders. No check list designed to assure enhanced performance for every firm has emerged from the book. None was promised. Instead the book poses a challenge to managers to consider carefully how they might conduct a systematic review of value-enhancement opportunities.

Chapters 1 and 2 of the book were conceptual. These chapters provided a framework that made the management actions outlined in Chapters 3 to 9 more easily understood. Chapters 3 through 6 of the book indicated how the managements of various firms were able to *create value* for their shareholders. Chapter 3 showed, for example, that Avon Products' huge direct-marketing sales force gave the firm a dramatic advantage (in terms of cost structure and capital intensity) over its rivals in the cosmetics industry. This advantage permitted Avon to achieve rates of return on equity that translated into a remarkable record of value creation. In fact, at December 31, 1976, the amount of value created for Avon's shareholders (which could be explained in terms of the rational economic model outlined in Chapter 1) exceeded $1 billion (Column 6, Table 3–8).

Chapter 4 demonstrated that in the retail grocery industry, city-market share was one of the most critical variables influencing a firm's overall profitability. Firms that achieved both city-market and individual-store scale economies during the era of market consolidation in grocery retailing held a powerful weapon. A number of retail grocery chains in the 1950s and 1960s chose to forgo *national* market-share growth opportunities in favor of *regional* dominance. These firms effectively utilized their understanding of the evolving cost structure of grocery retailing. They reaped long-run rewards for their foresight in the form of greatly enhanced profitability. The four retail grocery chains singled out in Chapter 1 for their consistently high ROE performance were quite successful in creating value for their shareholders. At December 31, 1976, the total amount of value created for the shareholders of Winn-Dixie, Weis Markets, Lucky Stores, and the Dillon Companies exceeded $1 billion (Table 1–11).

Chapters 3 and 4 focused on methods for achieving superior profitability via management actions in the operating area. Chapter 5 (Freeport Minerals) examined a situation where shareholder value was created primarily through the lowering of a firm's financing costs. The financial design of Freeport's copper investment allowed this firm to add $25 million to $30 million in net-present-value benefits (Table 5–7) to its proposed Indonesian mining venture. Chapter 5 focused on the denominator rather than the numerator of the valuation equation first presented in Chapter 2 and repeated below.

$$\text{NPV} = \sum_{i=0}^{n} \frac{(\text{Revenues} - \text{Costs})_i}{(1 + k_0)^i}.$$

Chapter 6 (the last of the four clinical chapters addressing the issue of value creation) involved the response of a firm to its economically untenable market position in computer manufacturing. The 1970 combination of the GE and Honeywell computer divisions promised to produce operating scale economies with considerable value-creation potential. In both the timing and the design of its computer division divestiture, GE's management was able to generate a significant value enhancement for its own shareholders. The GE divestiture decision was specifically included in the book to make the point that you don't have to be *born* rich to *become* rich. It is sometimes possible to create substantial value from a very unattractive competitive position. GE was able to salvage about $300 million (Footnote 43, Chapter 6) for an operation that had essentially no "going concern" value.

In Chapter 7 our attention shifted from value *creation* to value *transfer*. Chapter 7 demonstrated that equity-market values occasionally become detached from economic reality for surprisingly long time periods. This fact made it possible for large amounts of shareholder wealth to be transferred between successive equity owners of computer leasing firms in the late 1960s. The fundamental economics of computer leasing were never particularly attractive, but investors lacked either a comprehension of or a concern over this basic and easily discernible fact. This lack of attention to basic economics cost some investors hundreds of millions of dollars in the form of shareholder wealth transferred by computer leasing company managers. Chapter 7 demonstrated that significant imperfections existed in the market mechanism for valuing relatively small-capitalization stocks. Chapter 3 (Avon Products) showed that this phenomenon also occurred in large-capitalization stocks with substantial ownership by sophisticated institutional investors.

Chapter 8 addressed the issue of *value destruction*. This chapter explored the link between price competition and value destruction not only for A&P's competitors, but also for A&P itself. A key issue in the chapter involved analyzing price competition as an investment decision.

Chapter 9 demonstrated that it is sometimes possible to utilize the full range of value-enhancing techniques all at one time. Value creation, value transfer, and value destruction all occurred during the early 1970s at Levitz Furniture, and the chapter chronicles the actions of Levitz's management in considerable detail during this period.

Finally, Table 10–1 presents a map of the clinical chapters of the book, and how these chapters relate to one of the overall objectives of the book. That objective was to focus attention on the broad areas of opportunity that need to be examined in a systematic fashion if managers are fully to exploit the value-enhancing potential of the decision choices they face on a regular basis.

The aggregate dollar significance of value creation, transfer, and destruction

The process of value *creation* received greater attention in this book than either value *transfer* or value *destruction*. In part, this stems from the fact that value creation appears to be the most important of the three phenomena in terms of a crudely defined measure of aggregate dollar impact. As suggested by Line 74 of Table 1–11, at December 31, 1976, nearly $68 billion of shareholder value was created by 72 firms with ROEs consistently in excess of 15 percent. It appears that value transfers accomplished by corporate managers over an extended time period have a much smaller aggregate dollar significance than $68 billion. Indeed the *total* of all new equity offerings, share repurchases, and acquisitions for stock or cash undertaken by manufacturing· and mining firms over the last decade have probably not amounted to much more than $68 billion.[1] Since equity offerings, share repurchases, and acquisi-

---

[1] Over the period 1967–76, U.S. manufacturing and mining firms issued $21 billion of equity securities and retired about $7 billion of equity securities. Over the same time period, large U.S. manufacturing and mining firms with assets of $61 billion were acquired. The $61 billion of assets acquired probably translated into about $70 billion of total consideration paid. Sources for the above data are (1) U.S. Securities and Exchange Commission, "Statistical Bulletin," April 1977; (2) U.S. Federal Trade Commission, "Statistical Report on Mergers and Acquisitions," November 1977; and (3) Belinda B. Brandon and Stephen J. Browne, "A Study of Large Mergers, 1965–1972," *Mergers and Acquisitions*, Fall 1975, p. 32.

TABLE 10-1
Matrix indicating chapters that detail clinical examples of managers utilizing the broad approaches to value enhancement described in chapter 2

	1(a) Ability to command premium product prices	1(b) Achievement of a reduced or lower-than-average cost structure	1(c) Achievement of a reduced or lower-than-average capital intensity	2(a) Ability to obtain debt at equity at lower-than-normal cost	2(b) Ability to obtain equity at lower-than-normal cost	2(c) Design of capital structure that is more efficient than that achieved by major competitors	2(d) Achievement of reduced level of business risk	3(a) Acquiring firms via the exchange of an overvalued equity	3(b) Selling overvalued equities	3(c) Repurchasing undervalued equities	(4) Actions with value-destruction consequences
Chapter 2 (Teledyne)										X	
Chapter 3 (Avon)	X*	X	X								
Chapter 4 (Grocery retailing)		X						X‡			
Chapter 5 (Freeport Minerals)		X		X		X	X				
Chapter 6 (GE—Honeywell)								X§	X‖		
Chapter 7 (Computer leasing)					X			X§	X		
Chapter 8 (A&P)		X†				X†					X
Chapter 9 (Levitz Furniture)		X	X		X				X		X

*In footnote 7 of Chapter 4 it was noted that considerable controversy surrounds the degree to which the superior profitability associated with high local market shares can be attributed to lower operating costs as opposed to higher product prices. That note of caution extends to Table 10–1.

†In the A&P chapter, it was A&P's *competitors* who achieved the lower operating costs and the more efficient capital structures, thus placing A&P at a competitive disadvantage.

‡In the Avon example, the attempted acquisition of Monarch Capital Corp. for Avon stock was unsuccessful.

§A firm that enjoys an overvalued equity security can also accomplish a value transfer by being acquired *itself* by a firm whose securities are priced in an economically more rational fashion. The acquisition of Scientific Data Systems, Inc., by Xerox (described in Chapter 6) and the acquisition of the Randolph Computer Corp. by a large insurer (described in Chapter 7) might be described as value transfers of this kind.

‖Given the price paid by Honeywell, GE's divestiture of its computer division to Honeywell could possibly be described as the sale of an overvalued equity, where the equity was GE's ownership interest in its computer division.

tions are the most important types of transactions that give rise to value transfers, the volume of value *transfers* accomplished by corporate managers on behalf of their shareholders is undoubtedly small in relation to the amount of value *created* by corporate managers. While the aggregate total of value transfers over some time interval like a decade may be small in comparison to $68 billion, for *individual firms* at specific points in time the magnitude of value-transfer opportunity can be quite impressive. Examples cited in the computer leasing industry, Levitz Furniture, and the Avon Products chapters make this point quite clearly.

As we proceed further down the hierarchy of valuation significance, value destruction appears to be a phenomenon with an aggregate valuation impact that is probably less significant than value transfer. For individual firms, however, value destruction can obviously have enormous importance. The liquidations of the retail grocery stores of the Bohack and Penn Fruit chains represent one extreme example of the economic consequences of value destruction at the individual firm level.

Some economic, social, and ethical implications of value enhancement

The three categories of value enhancement opportunity that are detailed in this book appear to fall into a fairly simple hierarchy of decreasing aggregate economic significance. The three categories also seem to fall into a comparable hierarchy of decreasing social and ethical acceptability.

Where value creation can be traced to either operating scale economies or the patent system, for example, value creation is generally regarded as a legitimate objective for corporate management in a capitalist system. Indeed, the proposed Industrial Reorganization Act noted in Chapter 1 specifically spared from attack those firms whose high rates of profitability could be traced to these protected origins.

Obviously not all areas of potential value creation are generally regarded as economically, socially, or legally acceptable. For example, strategies aimed at creating entry barriers that lead to highly profitable differentiated products (a once relatively unchallenged area of value-creation potential) are now under attack. Challenges in this area are in the early stages of litigation.[2]

---

[2] In April 1972, the U.S. Federal Trade Commission issued a complaint against the Kellogg Company, General Mills, Inc., General Foods Corp., and the Quaker Oats Company. The complaint alleged, among other things, that these firms utilized brand proliferation, product differentiation, and trademark promotion so as to "maintain a highly concentrated, noncompetitive market structure in the production and sale of [ready to eat] cereal." These actions were alleged to have permitted the respondent firms to obtain "profits and returns on investment substantially in excess of those that they would have obtained in a competitively structured market." While the case is not expected to be finally settled before the early 1980s, it clearly strikes at the heart of value creation that is generated largely through advertising-induced product differentiation.

Concern over some of the methods through which corporate managers can act to create value stems from the economically wasteful side effects associated with the creation of shareholder value that is accomplished through the exercise of monopoly power. Monopoly pricing, for example, produces a misallocation of economic resources. The magnitude of the loss to consumers caused by monopoly pricing can be estimated in dollar terms. The measuring scheme is somewhat complex, however. Economists measure this loss in terms of an erosion in "consumer surplus." The concept of consumer surplus can be explained most easily in terms of a graphical illustration. Figure 10–1, line D–D', shows a simplified and hypothetical level of consumer demand for a product at various levels of price. According to this figure, demand for the product would decline from 75 to 50 units if a unit were to rise in price from $5 to $10. At a $5 price, consumers who are quite prepared to pay a higher price (up to $20) for the product are receiving a substantial bargain. The size of the benefit collectively enjoyed by these consumers is measured by the area of the triangle DCP_C shown in Figure 10–2. The area of this triangle[3] is equal to $\frac{1}{2} \times (\$20 - \$5) \times 75 = \$562.50$, and it represents the "consumer surplus" created when this product is sold at a price ($5) that reflects a fully competitive market.[4]

If the product were sold at $10 per unit, however, perhaps because of monopoly-pricing power possessed by the producer, then the quantity of product demanded by consumers would fall. So would the size of the consumer surplus. Indeed, the total consumer surplus created under these new circumstances could be measured by the area of the triangle DBP_M shown in Figure 10–3. The area of this triangle is equal to $\frac{1}{2} \times (\$20 - \$10) \times 50 = \$250$. In this example the loss in consumer surplus is equal to the area of the trapezoid P_MBCP_C (Figure 10–4). This area is $\$562.50 - \$250 = \$312.50$. Not *all* of this $312.50 is lost to consumers, however. The area of the rectangle P_MDAP_C, which equals ($10 − $5) × 50 or $250, simply represents purchasing power *transferred* from one group of consumers to another. The area of this rectangle represents added profits earned by the producer (and thus its consumer-shareholders) as a result of the firm's monopoly-pricing power.[5] This

---

[3] The area of a triangle is equal to one half its length times its height.

[4] This $5 figure would thus equal the long-run cost of the product including a margin for profit based on a fully competitive market.

[5] The incremental revenue received by the monopolist as a result of his shift in price from $5 to $10 is equal to $125. The reduction in total costs enjoyed by the monopolist as a result of a production shift from 75 to 50 units (at a $5 cost per unit) equals $125. The added revenue and reduced costs thus add up to $250 in additional profits.

In the example of Figure 10–1 the monopolist would maximize his profits by charging $12.60 per unit and selling 37 units. This would produce monopoly profits of $281.20.

FIGURES 10–1 to 10–6
Hypothetical example showing (1) the erosion of consumer surplus due to monopoly pricing and (2) the cost of the misallocation of resources caused by monopoly pricing

FIGURE 10-1

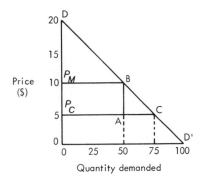

Quantity demanded

FIGURE 10-2
Consumer surplus under
competitive pricing = $562.50.

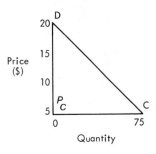

Quantity

FIGURE 10-3
Consumer surplus under
monopoly pricing = $250.00.

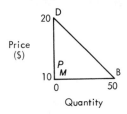

Quantity

FIGURE 10-4
Loss in consumer surplus due to
monopoly pricing = $312.50.

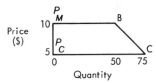

Quantity

FIGURE 10-5
Loss in consumer surplus transferred
to monopolist's shareholders = $250.00.

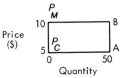

Quantity

FIGURE 10-6
Dead weight loss attributable to
monopoly pricing = $62.50.

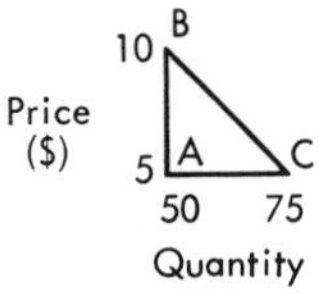

Quantity

added profitability would appear, of course, as a potential source of some of the value created in our Table 1–11 examples.

The loss to consumers collectively from monopoly pricing in this example is equal to the area of the triangle BCA. This is ½ × ($10 − $5) × (75 − 50) or $62.50. It represents value that has literally *disappeared* as a result of the misallocation of resources in this example. This value represents a real social loss. It is not simply a transfer from one group of consumers to another.

A number of economic studies have attempted to estimate the dead-weight loss to U.S. consumers caused by monopoly pricing. The resulting estimates have ranged from 0.5 percent to 2.0 percent of the U.S. gross national product.[6] While most of the studies concerning the dead-weight welfare loss throughout the U.S. economy have generated estimates of this loss that are not particularly alarming, it should be emphasized that these calculations relate only to the price-induced effects of monopoly power. They do not touch the question of cost-induced losses. Indeed, as noted in Chapter 2, there are a number of methods by which managers can reduce investment returns that promise to exceed capital costs. One of these was described as Option 4 in Chapter 2. It was called the "organizational slack" model. In this example, managers could simply bury potential monopoly returns through cost increases caused, for example, by (1) carrying excess production capacity or excess personnel or by (2) paying excessively high wages, salaries, or perquisites.[7] The economic loss to society in cases where corporate managements chose to absorb monopoly profits in this fashion could include the entire area of the *trapezoid* in Figure 10–4, not just the far smaller area of the *triangle* in Figure 10–6.

In my view, business managers have considerable latitude in the area of *value creation* without running afoul of present social norms regarding fair play and ethical business conduct. I am less sanguine about making a similar judgment in the area of *value transfers*. Economists might take comfort in the fact that value transfers usually involve only a reallocation of wealth. The phenomenon could thus be without major aggregate economic significance.[8] Regulatory authorities in the securities industry might view value transfers in a similar fashion. Perhaps the adequate disclosure of material facts is the most that a regulatory body

---

[6] F. M. Scherer, *Industrial Market Structure and Economic Performance* (Chicago: Rand McNally & Company, 1970), Chapter 17.

[7] A detailed discussion of cost-induced losses can be found in Chapters 3, 6, and 14 of Harvey Leibenstein, *Beyond Economic Man: A New Foundation for Microeconomics* (Cambridge, Mass.: Harvard University Press, 1976).

[8] This assumes that the marginal utility of a dollar is the same to both the transferee and the transferor of transferred wealth. This is probably a quite unrealistic assumption.

can hope to achieve. What investors do (or fail to do) in terms of analyzing these material facts is their own business. Caveat emptor! Some of the more egregious examples of value transfers raise difficult ethical questions. Nonetheless, such transfers are a fact of economic life. Indeed, the spectacularly large value transfers portrayed in Chapters 7 and 9 ought to serve as a warning to those who might someday be on the losing end of a value-transfer transaction. I like to think of this material as a warning to investors, as well as a prescription for managers as to how value transfers can be successfully accomplished.

The final area of value transformation involves *value destruction*. In its most violent form, value destruction can be used as a technique to eradicate a competitor or competition. Where the elimination of a competitor or competition is the *objective* of a firm's strategy, value destruction may be illegal in addition to being ethically objectionable.

Obviously, value destruction may sometimes result from the implementation of a quite laudable business strategy. For example, a firm might adopt a price-reduction strategy in order to become a market leader. These price reductions might be justified on the basis of cost reductions expected to flow from increased volume.

Indeed, in the 1930s the cost structure of A&P's supermarkets gave that firm a significant competitive advantage, an advantage that the firm had clearly lost by the 1960s. A&P used this advantage to cut its prices and build its volume in the 1930s. A&P's less efficient competitors found it difficult to follow A&P's price lead. As noted by Adelman,

> Competitive price cuts of any magnitude (1) typically involve the risk or expectation of "selling below cost" until and unless the market responds; and (2) invariably aim at larger profits (or smaller losses) through larger volume.[9]

> ○ ○ ○ ○ ○

> According to traditional economic analysis, unrestrained competition for additional business will drive firms in just this manner to reduce prices and costs, thereby passing on to society the benefits of more efficient operation.[10]

This type of business strategy ought to be applauded, even if it does force less efficient competitors out of the market. By way of contrast, the objectionable form of value destruction is the type that has as its *primary goal* the elimination of a competitor.

The fact that value destruction is presented as a technique through which major value transformations can be accomplished should not be

---

[9] M. A. Adelman, *A&P: A Study in Price-Cost Behavior and Public Policy* (Cambridge, Mass.: Harvard University Press, 1959), p. 336.

[10] Ibid., p. 335.

read as an endorsement of the technique. Again, one purpose of this book was to present a full analysis of the value-transformation possibilities, of which value destruction is clearly one. It may be hoped that the methods for enhancing shareholder value are sufficiently abundant as to make it unnecessary for managers to resort to objectionable extremes of the value-transformation art.

Bibliography

BOOKS

Adelman, M. A. *A&P: A Study in Price-Cost Behavior and Public Policy.* Cambridge, Mass.: Harvard University Press, 1959.

Bain, Joe S. *Barriers to New Competition.* Cambridge, Mass.: Harvard University Press, 1956.

Brock, Gerald W. *The U.S. Computer Industry, A Study of Market Power.* Cambridge, Mass.: Ballinger Publishing Co., 1975.

Clymer, Harold A. "The Changing Cost and Risks of Pharmaceutical Innovation." In J. Cooper, ed., *The Economics of Drug Innovation,* Washington, D.C.: The American University, 1970.

Cootner, Paul H. *The Random Character of Stock Market Prices.* Cambridge, Mass.: The MIT Press, 1964.

Cyert, R. M., and March J. G. *A Behavioral Theory of the Firm.* Englewood Cliffs, N.J.: Prentice-Hall, Inc., 1963.

Fama, Eugene F., and Miller, Merton H. *The Theory of Finance.* Hinsdale, Ill.: Dryden Press, 1972.

Haley, Charles W., and Schall, Lawrence P. *The Theory of Financial Decisions.* New York: McGraw-Hill, 1973.

Leibenstein, Harvey. *Beyond Economic Man: A New Foundation for Micro-Economics.* Cambridge, Mass.: Harvard University Press, 1976.

Lewellen, Wilbur G. *The Ownership Income of Management.* New York: National Bureau of Economic Research, 1971.

Lintner, John, and Glauber, Robert. "Higgledy Piggledy Growth in America." In J. Lorie and R. Brealey, eds., *Modern Developments in Investment Management.* New York: Frederick A. Praeger, Inc., 1972.

Lintner, John. "Bankruptcy Risk, Market Segmentation and Optimal Capital

Structure." In I. Friend and J. Bicksler, eds., *Risk and Return in Finance*. Cambridge, Mass.: Ballinger Publishing Company, 1977.

Lynch, Harry H. *Financial Performance of Conglomerates*. Cambridge, Mass.: Division of Research, Harvard University Graduate School of Business Administration, 1971.

Martindale, Wight, Jr. *We Do It Every Day*. New York: Fairchild Publications, Inc., 1972.

Mund, Vernon A. "The Return on Investment of the Innovative Pharmaceutical Firm." In J. Cooper, ed., *The Economics of Drug Innovation*. Washington, D.C.: The American University, 1970.

Porter, Michael E. *Interbrand Choice, Strategy, and Bilaterial Market Power*. Cambridge, Mass.: Harvard University Press, 1976.

Rayner, A. C., and Little, I. M. D. *Higgledy Piggledy Growth Again*. Oxford, England: Basil Blackwell, 1966.

Scherer, F. M. *Industrial Market Structure and Economic Performance*. Chicago: Rand McNally & Company, 1970.

Schulman, Rosalind, discussion of Forman, H. I. "Patents, Compulsory Licensing, Prices and Innovation." In J. D. Cooper, ed., *The Economics of Drug Innovation*. Washington, D.C.: The American University, 1970.

Solomon, Ezra. "Return on Investment: The Relation of Book Yield to True Yield." In Robert K. Jaedicke et al., eds., *Research in Accounting Measurement*. Madison, Wis.: American Accounting Association, 1966.

Stauffer, Thomas R. "Profitability Measures in the Pharmaceutical Industry." In Robert B. Helms, ed., *Drug Development and Marketing*. Washington, D.C.: American Enterprise Institute for Public Policy Research, 1975.

Vernon, John M. *Market Structure and Industrial Performance: A Review of Statistical Findings*. Boston: Allyn and Bacon, Inc., 1972.

ARTICLES AND GOVERNMENT DOCUMENTS

Areeda, P., and Turner, D. F. "Predatory Pricing and Related Practices Under Section 2 of the Sherman Act," *Harvard Law Review*, February 1975, pp. 697–733.

———— "Scherer on Predatory Pricing: A Reply," *Harvard Law Review*, March 1976, pp. 891–900.

"Avon Products, Inc.—A New Look," Boston, Mass.: Harvard Business School, 1977.

Biggs, Barton, M. "Numbers Game," *Barron's*, July 24, 1967.

Bloch, Harry "Advertising and Profitability: A Reappraisal," *Journal of Political Economy*, March/April 1974, pp. 267–86.

Blyth & Co., Inc. "Reports on A&P," May 17, 1949.

Bralove, Mary "Tough Turnaround," *The Wall Street Journal*, September 19, 1974.

Brandon, Belinda B., and Browne, Stephen J. "A Study of Larger Mergers, 1965–1972," *Mergers and Acquisitions*, Fall 1975, pp. 30–39.

Brandon, Dick H. "Latest Neurosis–Computer Leasing," *Financial Analysts Journal*, May–June 1968, pp. 85–90.

Brown, Philip, and Niederhoffer, Victor "The Predictive Content of Quarterly Earnings," *Journal of Business*, October 1968, pp. 488–97.

Business Week, September 19, 1970, p. 83.

——— "Levitz: The Hot Name in Instant Furniture," December 4, 1971, p. 90.

——— June 2, 1973, p. 71.

——— "Itel Rebuilds on Leasing's Ruins," February 23, 1974, p. 110.

Buzzell, Robert D., et al. "The Consumer and the Supermarket–1980," A study sponsored by *Family Circle* and the National Association of Food Chains, 1976.

California Computer Products, Inc. v. *International Business Machines Corporation*, 77-1563, U.S. Court of Appeals, Ninth Circuit, "Brief of Appellee International Business Machines Corporation," September 26, 1977.

Cook, James "How Penn Fruit Checked Out," *Philadelphia Magazine*, July 1977.

Datamation, April 1976, p. 100.

Davidson, S., and Weil, R. L. "Inflation Accounting: The SEC Proposal for Replacement Cost Disclosures," *Financial Analysts Journal*, March/April 1976, pp. 57–66.

Donaldson, Gordon "The Management of Risk and Return in the Individual Business Firm" (mimeo), May 1977.

Economic Report of the President, Washington, D.C.: U.S. Government Printing Office, January 1977.

Equity Research Associates "Computer Leasing–Rain, Rain, Rain," December 21, 1970

——— "Data Processing Equipment Leasing," August 19, 1966.

Fama, Eugene F.; Fisher, Lawrence; Jensen, Michael C.; and Roll, Richard "The Adjustment of Stock Prices to New Information," *International Economic Review*, February 1969, pp. 1–21.

Fama, Eugene F. "Efficient Capital Markets: A Review of Theory and Empirical Work," *Journal of Finance*, May 1970, pp. 383–423.

Fama, Eugene F., and MacBeth, J. D. "Tests of the Multiperiod Two-Parameter Model," *Journal of Financial Economics*, May 1974, p. 43–66.

Farrar, Donald E., and Selwyn, Lee L. "Taxes, Corporate Financial Policy, and Return to Investors," *National Tax Journal*, December 1967, pp. 444–54.

Feldstein, Martin, and Summers, Lawrence "Is the Rate of Profit Falling?" paper presented at the Brookings Panel on Economic Activity, April 1977.

Financial Accounting Standards Board "Statement of Financial Accounting

Standards No. 2—Accounting for Research and Development Costs," October 1974.

Forbes, April 1, 1967, p. 22.

———— "Levit(z)ation," February 1, 1972, p. 17.

Fortune, June 1, 1967, p. 92.

———— October 1970, p. 156.

Franklin, J. Thomas "An Overwhelming Antitrust Case Against IBM," *Computers and People,* February 1977, p. 18.

Garrett, Robert, & Sons, Inc. "Levitz Furniture Corporation," May 1970.

Hart, Philip A., Senator "The Industrial Reorganization Act, S. 1167," *Congressional Record,* vol. 119, no. 38, March 12, 1973.

Holland, D. M., and Myers, S. C. "Trends in Corporate Profitability and Capital Costs," (mimeo), August 1977.

Home Furnishings Daily "Retailer of the Year, Ralph Levitz," January 3, 1972.

———— June 4, 1971, p. 6.

———— July 29, 1971, p. 2.

———— September 7, 1971, p. 12.

———— January 10, 1972, p. 8.

———— February 7, 1972, p. 20.

———— February 22, 1972, p. 13.

Hornblower & Weeks, Hemphill, Noyes, Market Letter "Computer Leasing Industry," April 1, 1968.

Hutchins, Mitchell, & Co., Inc. "Levitz Furniture Corporation," May 1970.

Ibbotson, R. G., and Sinquefeld, R. A. "Stocks, Bonds, Bills, and Inflation: Year-by-Year Historical Returns (1929–1974)," *Journal of Business,* January 1976, pp. 11–47.

Jaffe, Jeffrey F. "Special Information and Insider Trading," *Journal of Business,* July 1974, pp. 410–28.

Jensen, Michael C. "The Performance of Mutual Funds in the Period 1945–1964," *Journal of Finance,* May 1968, pp. 389–416.

———— "Capital Markets: Theory and Evidence," *Bell Journal of Economics and Management Science,* Autumn 1972, pp. 357–98.

Jensen, Michael C., and Meckling, William H. "Theory of the Firm: Managerial Behavior, Agency Costs and Ownership Structure," *Journal of Financial Economics,* October 1976, pp. 305–60.

Koller, Roland H. "The Myth of Predatory Pricing: an Empirical Study," *Antitrust Law and Economics Review,* Summer 1971, pp. 105–23.

Lintner, John "Inflation and Security Returns," *Journal of Finance,* May 1975, pp. 259–80.

Little, Arthur D., Inc. Service to Investors "Data Processing Equipment Leasing," July 29, 1966.

Malkiel, Burton G. "Equity Yields, Growth, and the Structure of Share Prices," *The American Economic Review,* December 1963, pp. 1004–31.

Mandelker, Gershon   "Risk and Return: The Case of Merging Firms," *Journal of Financial Economics,* December 1974, pp. 303–35.

Marks, Kenneth R.   "The Stock Price Performance of Firms Repurchasing Their Own Shares," *The Bulletin,* New York University Graduate School of Business Administration, 1976–1.

May, Marvin M.   "The Earnings Per Share Trap: The Chain Letter Revisited," *Financial Analysts Journal,* May–June 1968, pp. 113–17.

Merrill Lynch, Pierce, Fenner & Smith, Inc.   "Investing in the Computer Industry," 1967.

Miller, Merton H., and Modigliani, Franco   "Dividend Policy, Growth, and the Valuation of Shares," *The Journal of Business,* October 1961, pp. 411–33.

Modigliani, Franco, and Miller, Merton H.   "The Cost of Capital, Corporation Finance, and the Theory of Investment," *American Economic Review,* June 1958, pp. 261–97.

———   "Corporate Income Taxes and the Cost of Capital: A Correction," *American Economic Review,* June 1963, pp. 433–43.

Modigliani, F., and Pogue, G. A.   "An Introduction to Risk and Return," *Financial Analysts Journal,* March–April 1974, pp. 69–80; and May–June 1974, pp. 69–86.

Mullins, David Wiley, Jr.   "Product Market Inefficiency, Capital Market Inefficiency, and a Managerial Theory of the Firm." Unpublished manuscript, Harvard Business School, July 1978.

Myers, Stewart C.   "Determinants of Corporate Borrowing," *Journal of Financial Economics,* November 1977, pp. 147–75.

New York Times, The, October 15, 1970, p. 79.

Niederhoffer, Victor, and Osborne, M. F. M.   "Market Making and Reversal on the Stock Exchange," *Journal of the American Statistical Association,* December 1966, pp. 897–916.

Niederhoffer, Victor   "The Predictive Content of First Quarter Earnings Reports," *Journal of Business,* January 1970, pp. 60–62.

Oliphant, James H. & Company   "Levitz Furniture Corporation—Progress Report," June 15, 1971.

———   "Levitz Furniture Corporation: Progress Report," December 8, 1971.

Peles, Yoram   "Amortization of Advertising Expenditures in the Financial Statements," *Journal of Accounting Research,* Spring 1970, pp. 128–37.

Progressive Grocer, April 1973, p. 32.

———   April 1976, p. 76.

———   April 1977, pp. 126–30.

Robinson-Humphrey Co., Inc.   "Unicapital Corp.," November 2, 1972.

Rubinstein, Mark E.   "A Mean-Variance Synthesis of Corporate Financial Theory," *Journal of Finance,* March 1973, pp. 167–81.

Scherer, F. M.   "Predatory Pricing and the Sherman Act: A Comment," *Harvard Law Review,* March 1976, pp. 869–90.

———   "Some Last Words on Predatory Pricing," *Harvard Law Review,* March 1976, pp. 901–3.

Scholes, Myron S. "The Market for Securities: Substitution versus Price Pressure and the Effects of Information on Share Prices," *Journal of Business*, April 1972, pp. 179–211.

Seidlitz and Company, Inc. "Levitz Furniture Special Report," July 7, 1971.

Shapiro, Alan C. "Capital Budgeting for the Multinational Corporation," *Financial Management*, Spring 1978, pp. 7–16.

"Spectrum 3" and "Spectrum 1," Computer Directions Advisors, Inc., December 1976.

Stauffer, Thomas R. "The Measurement of Corporate Rates of Return: A Generalized Formulation," *Bell Journal of Economics and Management Science*, Autumn 1971, pp. 434–69.

Stiglitz, Joseph E. "Taxation, Corporate Financial Policy, and the Cost of Capital," *Journal of Public Economics*, January 1973, pp. 1–34.

Supermarket News, June 26, 1972, p. 4.

———— February 5, 1973, p. 1.

———— February 12, 1973.

Time Magazine, "Banking Against A&P," December 11, 1972, p. 106.

United States of America v. *International Business Machines Corporation*, 69 CV 200, U.S. District Court, Southern District of New York, "An Economic Analysis of the Market for General Purpose Digital Computer Systems," December 10, 1974.

———— Deposition of Fred J. Borch, June 20, 1974.

———— Pretrial Brief for Defendant International Business Machines Corp., January 15, 1975.

———— Deposition of C. Peter McColough, Exhibit 5305-002, March 12, 1976.

———— Plaintiff Exhibit 322.

———— Plaintiff Exhibit 331A.

———— Plaintiff Exhibit 350A.

———— Plaintiff Exhibit 353.

———— Plaintiff Exhibit 362.

———— Plaintiff Exhibit 371A.

———— Plaintiff Exhibit 380.

———— Plaintiff Exhibit 402.

———— Plaintiff Exhibit 405A.

———— Plaintiff Exhibit 3095.

———— Plaintiff Exhibit 3236.

———— Testimony by Reginald H. Jones, Trial Transcript, December 9, 1975, pp. 8751–892.

United States v. *International Business Machines Corporation*, 1956 Trade Cas. 71, 117 (S.D.N.Y. 1956).

United States Congress, Joint Economic Committee, Testimony before the Joint Economic Committee on March 20, 1977, *Statement of Dr. Ray A. Goldberg.*

———— Testimony before the Joint Economic Committee on December 17, 1974.

———— *The Profit and Price Performance of Leading Food Chains, 1970–1974,* March 1977.

United States Department of Commerce, Bureau of the Census *Census of Retail Trade,* 1948, 1954, 1958, 1967, and 1972.

United States Federal Trade Commission *Economic Report on the Structure and Competitive Behavior of Food Retailing,* January 1966.

———— In the Matter of National Tea Company, Docket 7453, Findings as to the Facts, Conclusions and Order, March 4, 1966.

———— In the Matter of Kellogg Company, General Mills, Inc., General Foods Corp., and the Quaker Oats Company, Docket 8883, April 26, 1972.

———— "Staff Economic Report of Food Chain Profits," July 1975.

———— "Statistical Report on Mergers and Acquisitions," November 1977.

United States Internal Revenue Service *Statistics of Income, Corporation Income Tax Returns.* Washington, D.C.: U.S. Government Printing Office.

United States Securities and Exchange Commission, *Accounting Series Release No. 190,* March 23, 1976.

———— "Official Summary of Securities Transactions and Holdings."

———— "Statistical Bulletin," April 1977.

Vancil, Richard F. "Inflation Accounting—The Great Controversy," *Harvard Business Review,* March–April 1976, pp. 58–67.

Wall Street Journal, The, July 22, 1975, p. 2.

———— December 12, 1975, p. 16.

Weiss, Leonard W. "Advertising, Profits, and Corporate Taxes," *The Review of Economics and Statistics,* November 1969, pp. 421–30.

Welles, Chris "Xerox: Whatever Happened to Act II," *Corporate Financing,* July/August 1971.

Wickes Corporation, The "Transcript of Meeting Before the Los Angeles Society of Security Analysts," January 30, 1973.

———— "Transcript of Meeting Before the New York Society of Security Analysts," June 1, 1973.

CORPORATE REPORTS AND STATISTICAL SOURCES

Acme Markets, Inc., Annual Reports.

———— Quarterly Reports to Shareholders.

———— 10K Reports to the Securities and Exchange Commission.

———— 10Q Reports to the Securities and Exchange Commission.

American Stores Company, Annual Reports.

———— 10K Reports to the Securities and Exchange Commission.

Avon Products, Inc., Annual Reports.

———— 10K Reports to the Securities and Exchange Commission.

Bank & Quotation Record, National News Services Inc., New York.

Barron's, Dow Jones & Company, Inc., New York.

Bohack Corporation, Annual Reports.

——— Quarterly Reports to Shareholders.

——— 10Q Reports to the Securities and Exchange Commission.

——— 10K Reports to the Securities and Exchange Commission.

Boothe Computer Corp., Annual Reports.

——— 10K Reports to the Securities and Exchange Commission.

Burroughs Corporation, Annual Reports.

Computer Investors Group, Inc., Annual Reports.

——— 10K Reports to the Securities and Exchange Commission.

Control Data Corporation, Annual Reports.

Data Processing Financial and General Corp., Annual Reports.

——— 10K Reports to the Securities and Exchange Commission.

Dearborn Computer Corp., Annual Reports.

——— 10K Reports to the Securities and Exchange Commission.

Diebold Computer Leasing, Inc., Annual Reports.

—— —— 10K Reports to the Securities and Exchange Commission.

Digital Equipment Corp., Annual Report, 1967.

Distribution Study of Grocery Store Sales in 264 Cities (1973, 1977), Fairchild Publications, Inc., New York.

Foodarama Supermarkets, Inc., Annual Reports.

——— Quarterly Reports to Shareholders.

——— 10K Reports to the Securities and Exchange Commission.

——— 10Q Reports to the Securities and Exchange Commission.

Food Fair Stores, Inc., Annual Reports.

——— Quarterly Reports to Shareholders.

——— 10K Reports to the Securities and Exchange Commission.

——— 10Q Reports to the Securities and Exchange Commission.

Freeport Minerals Company, Annual Reports.

——— 10K Reports to the Securities and Exchange Commission.

General Electric Company, Annual Reports.

General Portland Cement Company, Annual Reports.

——— 10K Reports to the Securities and Exchange Commission.

Grand Union Company, Annual Reports.

——— 10K Reports to the Securities and Exchange Commission.

Granite Management Services Corp., Annual Reports.

——— 10K Reports to the Securities and Exchange Commission.

Great Atlantic & Pacific Tea Company, Inc., The, Annual Reports.

——— Prospectus, June 29, 1976.

——— Quarterly Reports to Shareholders.

———— 10K Reports to the Securities and Exchange Commission.

———— 10Q Reports to the Securities and Exchange Commission.

Greyhound Computer Corp., Annual Reports.

———— 10K Reports to the Securities and Exchange Commission.

Honeywell, Inc., Annual Reports.

———— Proxy Statement, August 21, 1970.

International Business Machines Corporation, Annual Reports.

Itel Corp., Annual Reports.

———— 10K Reports to the Securities and Exchange Commission.

Jewel Companies, Inc., Annual Reports.

———— 10K Reports to the Securities and Exchange Commission.

Kroger Company, Annual Reports.

———— 10K Reports to the Securities and Exchange Commission.

Levitz Furniture Corporation, Annual Reports.

———— Quarterly Reports to Shareholders.

———— Registration Statements.

———— Report to Shareholders on 1977 Annual Meeting.

———— 10K Reports to the Securities and Exchange Commission.

Lucky Stores, Inc., Annual Reports.

———— 10K Reports to the Securities and Exchange Commission.

Merrill Lynch, Pierce, Fenner & Smith, Inc., "Security Risk Evaluation," January 1976.

Moody's Industrial Manual, Moody's Investors Service, Inc., New York.

National Cash Register Company, Annual Reports.

National Home Furniture Association, Special Report, "Operating Experiences" (1969–76).

National Tea Company, Annual Reports.

———— Quarterly Reports to Shareholders.

———— 10K Reports to the Securities and Exchange Commission.

Penn Fruit Co., Inc., Annual Reports.

———— Quarterly Reports to Shareholders.

———— 10K Reports to the Securities and Exchange Commission.

———— 10Q Reports to the Securities and Exchange Commission.

RCA Corporation, Annual Reports.

Randolph Computer Corp., Annual Reports.

———— 10K Reports to the Securities and Exchange Commission.

Reliance Group, Inc., Annual Reports.

———— 10K Reports to the Securities and Exchange Commission.

Revlon, Inc., Annual Reports.

———— 10K Reports to the Securities and Exchange Commission.

Robert Morris Associates, "Annual Statement Studies," (1967–77), Philadelphia.

Rockwood Corp., Annual Reports.

—————— 10K Reports to the Securities and Exchange Commission.

Safeway Stores, Inc., Annual Reports.

—————— Quarterly Reports to Shareholders.

—————— 10K Reports to the Securities and Exchange Commission.

—————— 10Q Reports to the Securities and Exchange Commission.

Scientific Data Systems, Inc., Annual Report, 1968.

Sperry Rand Corporation, Annual Reports.

Standard and Poor's Corporation, Investment Management Sciences, Inc., "Compustat Primary, Supplementary, and Tertiary Industrial Files," Denver, Colo.

—————— "Standard and Poor's Trade and Securities Statistics, Security Price Index Record," New York, 1976.

The Super Market Institute, Inc., "Facts about New Supermarkets Opened in [1953, 1958, 1963, 1967, 1972, 1976]," Chicago.

—————— "The Supermarket Industry Speaks," (1961–70), Chicago.

—————— *1975 Annual Financial Review*, Chicago.

Unicapital Corp., Annual Reports.

—————— 10K Reports to the Securities and Exchange Commission.

Value Line Investment Survey, Arnold Bernhard & Co., Inc., New York.

Wickes Corporation, The, Annual Reports.

—————— Prospectus, May 30, 1974.

—————— 10K Reports to the Securities and Exchange Commission.

Wilshire Associates, Incorporated, "Capital Market Equilibrium Statistics," December 31, 1975.

Winn-Dixie Stores, Inc., Annual Reports.

—————— 10K Reports to the Securities and Exchange Commission.

Xerox Corporation, Annual Reports.

—————— 10K Reports to the Securities and Exchange Commission.

Yearbook of the American Bureau of Metal Statistics, American Bureau of Metal Statistics, New York, 1970.

Index

A

A&P; *see* Great Atlantic & Pacific Tea Co., Inc.
Acme Markets, Inc., 218–21, 226–33
Advertising expenses
  Avon Products Inc., 99–101
  economic versus GAAP accounting, 35–39, 55–58
  scale economies, 120–21
Alberto-Culver Co., 94
Albertson's, Inc., 127
Allied Supermarkets, Inc., 123, 127
American Home Products Corp., 30–31, 36–37, 44–45, 52–53
American Stores Co., 213–15
Atlas Consolidated Mining & Development Corp., 30–31, 36–37, 44–45
Avon Products, Inc., 3, 30–31, 34–37, 39, 44–45, 50, 52–53, 55–62, 83–84, 93–114, 280

B

Bechtel Corp., 132
Block, H & R, Inc., 30–31, 36–37, 44–45
Bohack Corp., 218–22, 226–33
Boothe Computer Corp., 192, 204, 206–7
Borch, Fred, 153, 155, 160
Bristol-Meyers Co., 30–31, 36–37, 44–45, 52–53
Burroughs Corp., 151, 162, 164
Business risk, 71, 145

C

Caldor, Inc., 30–31, 36–37, 44–45
Campbell Red Lake Mines, Ltd., 30–31, 36–37, 44–45
Capital asset pricing model, 33, 77–78
Capital intensity, 94–95, 97–99
Capital productivity, U.S. NFCs, 22

Capital structure, 68–71
  A&P competitors, 215–16
  determination of optimal, 69
Chain letter EPS growth, 79, 86, 190–92, 201–2, 257
Champion Spark Plug Co., 30–31, 36–37, 44–45, 52–53
Chesebrough-Pond's Inc., 30–31, 36–37, 44–45, 52–53, 94
Coca-Cola Co., 30–31, 36–37, 44–45, 52–53
Computer Investors Group, Inc., 192, 204, 206
Computer leasing industry, 4, 180–208
  economics of, 184–89
Consumer surplus, 282–83
Consumer wealth model, 72–75
  A&P Co., Inc., 215
  numerical example, 73
Control Data Corp., 151, 162, 164
Cordiner, Ralph, 160
Cost of capital
  definition, 67
  equation, 67, 71
  Freeport Indonesia, Inc., 144
Cost of equity capital
  A&P Co., Inc., 224
  Avon Products, Inc., 103
  formula for calculating, 33–34
  formula incorporating leverage changes, 113–14
  Freeport Indonesia, Inc., 132
  Levitz Furniture Corp., 244, 257
  nominal cost (sample calculation), 34
  real cost (sample calculation), 35

D

Data Processing Financial and General Corp., 187, 192, 204–7
Dead-weight welfare loss, 282–84
Dearborn Computer Corp., 192, 204, 206

Diebold Computer Leasing, Inc., 192, 204, 206, 207
Dillon Companies, 3, 30–31, 36–37, 44–45, 115, 127
Discretionary cash flow, 161, 165
Dover Corp., 30–31, 36–37, 44–45, 52–53
Dow Jones & Co., Inc., 30–31, 36–37, 44–45, 52–53
Dr. Pepper Co., 30–31, 36–37, 44–45
Dun & Bradstreet, Inc., 30–31, 36–37, 44–45, 52–53

E

Eastman Kodak Co., 30–31, 36–37, 44–45, 52–53
Eckerd (Jack) Corp., 30–31, 36–37, 44–45
Economic value
    compared to historic NFC market value, 23–25
    defined, 19
    equation, 66, 90
Economic value/book value
    calculation for computer leasing industry, 196
    formula, 12–13
    sample calculations, 8–11
    table, 12–13
Efficient capital markets
    semi-strong form, 77–78
    strong form, 78
    sufficient conditions, 77
    weak form, 77
Eli Lilly & Co., 30–31, 36–37, 44–45, 52–53
Emerson Electric Co., 30–31, 36–37, 44–45
Emery Air Freight Corp., 30–31, 36–37, 44–45
Entry barriers, 42–43, 46, 66–67, 102
Export-Import Bank, 137, 139
Export-Import Bank of Japan, 136, 139
Expropriation, 135, 145

F

Federal Republic of Germany, 137, 139
Federal Trade Commission, 87, 122–25, 216, 229, 281
Financing risk, 71
First National Stores, Inc., 123
Fisher Foods, Inc., 127
Focused product lines, 46–47, 150
Food Fair Stores, Inc., 213–15, 218–21, 226–33

Foodarama Supermarkets, Inc., 218–21, 226–33
Freeport Indonesia, Inc., 136–48
Freeport Minerals Co., 4, 129–48, 280

G

General Electric Co., 4, 80, 149–79, 280
    Ventures Task Force, 115, 160, 165–68
General Portland Cement Co., 259–70
Genuine Parts Co., 30–31, 36–37, 44–45, 52–53
Giant Foods, Inc., 127
Gillette Co., 30–31, 36–37, 44–45, 52–53, 94
Grand Union Co., 123, 127, 213–15
Granite Management Services Corp., 192, 204, 205
Great Atlantic & Pacific Tea Co., Inc., 4, 116–17, 120, 127, 209–36, 280
Greyhound Computer Corp., 192, 204, 206
Grocery retailing industry, 115–28
Growth of common equity versus profits
    adjustment required for excess cash, 110–14
    calculation of average value, 15
Gulf & Western Industries, Inc., 232–34

H

Hall of Fame firms
    criteria for inclusion
        broadly defined, 29
        narrowly defined, 41
    firms included
        broadly defined, 30–31
        narrowly defined, 36
Hart, Philip A., Senator, 32
Hartford, George L., 213
Heublein, Inc., 30–31, 36–37, 44–45
Honeywell, Inc., 80, 149–79, 280

I

Industrial Reorganization Act S. 1167, 32, 281
Insider securities transactions, 78
    Avon Products, Inc., 108
    Computer Leasing Industry, 204–5
    Levitz Furniture Corp., 239, 272
International Business Machines Corp., 30–31, 36–37, 44–45, 48, 50, 52–53, 87–89, 149–79, 180–208
Investment opportunity profile, historic for U.S. NFCs, 15
Itel Corp., 192, 204, 206

J

Jaffe, Jeffrey F., 78
Jewel Companies, Inc., 127, 213–15
Jones, Reginald H., 160
Jostens, Inc., 30–31, 36–37, 44–45

K

Kaneb Services, Inc., 30–31, 36–37, 44–45
Kellogg Co., 30–31, 36–37, 44–45, 52–53
Kroger Co., 123, 127, 213–15

L

Leasco Data Processing Equipment Corp., 187
Levitz Furniture Corp., 4, 125, 237–73
Loehmann's, Inc., 30–31, 36–37, 44–45
Longs Drug Stores, Inc., 30–31, 36–37, 44–45
Louisiana Land & Exploration Co., 30–31, 36–37, 44–45, 52–53
Lubrizol Corp., 30–31, 36–37, 44–45, 52–53
Lucky Stores, Inc., 3, 30–31, 36–37, 44–45, 52–53, 115, 127, 213–15

M

McDonald's Corp., 30–31, 36–37, 44–45, 52–53
Malone & Hyde, Inc., 30–31, 36–37, 44–45
Marion Laboratories, Inc., 30–31, 36–37, 44–45
Market value/book value
    aggregate historic ratio for NFCs
        unadjusted, 20
        adjusted, 20
    calculated for
        A&P Co., Inc., and competitors, 233
        Avon Products, Inc., 109
        computer leasing companies, 187
        computer manufacturers, 164
        Freeport Minerals Co., 130
        grocery retailers, 127
        Levitz Furniture Corp., 256, 271–72
        specific firms, 44–45
    historic profile for NFCs, 24
Marketing competition model, 72–73, 75
    numerical example, 73
Marsh & McLennan Companies, Inc., 30–31, 36–37, 44–45, 52–53
Mary Kay Cosmetics, Inc., 94

MASCO Corp., 30–31, 36–37, 44–45, 52–53
Melville Corp., 30–31, 36–37, 44–45, 52–53
Merchants, Inc., 30–31, 36–37, 44–45
Merck & Co., Inc., 30–31, 36–37, 44–45, 52–53
Modern portfolio theory; see Capital asset pricing model and Efficient capital markets
Moore Corp., 30–31, 36–37, 44–45

N

Nalco Chemical Co., 30–31, 36–37, 44–45, 52–53
National Cash Register Co., 151, 162, 164
National Chemsearch Corp., 30–31, 36–37, 44–45
National Tea Co., 122–25, 127, 213–15, 218–21, 226–33
Neiderhoffer, Victor, 78
New Process Co., 30–31, 36–37, 44–45
NFCs (non-financial corporations)
    characteristics, 16–17
    historic profitability and reinvestment profile, 15

O

Organizational slack
    model, 72–73, 75–76, 284
    numerical example, 73
Overseas Private Investment Corp., 138–39
Overvaluation, 51–55, 77, 79–80, 83–86
    Avon Products, Inc., 103–10
    definition, 3
    individual firm examples, 52–53, 83–84
    Levitz Furniture Corp., 257–58
    methods for achieving, 85–86

P

Panhandle Eastern Pipe Line Co., 30–31, 36–37, 44–45, 52–53
Penn Fruit Co., Inc., 218–21, 226–33
PepCom Industries, Inc., 30–31, 36–37, 44–45
PepsiCo Inc., 30–31, 36–37, 44–45, 52–53
Prentice-Hall, Inc., 30–31, 36–37, 44–45
Procter & Gamble Co., 30–31, 36–37, 44–45
Purolator, Inc., 30–31, 36–37, 44–45, 52–53

Q–R

Quaker State Oil Refining Corp., 30–31, 36–37, 44–45, 52–53
Randolph Computer Corp., 187, 192, 204, 206
RCA Corp., 151–52, 162, 164, 173–74, 176
Redundant cash
  defined, 47
  high ROE firms, 47–51
  impact on ROE
    for Avon Products, Inc., 50, 103–6, 111–14
    for IBM Corp., 50
  persistence in high ROE firms, 48–49
  significance to specific firms, 52–53
Reinvestment rate; see Growth of common equity versus profits
Reliance Group, Inc., 192, 204–6
Replacement cost accounting, 39–40, 61–62
Research and development expenses, economic versus GAAP accounting, 35–39, 55–58
Return on equity
  adjustments for advertising and R&D expenditures, 35–39
  adjustments for replacement cost accounting, 39–41, 44–45
  calculation of average value, 15
  nominal return, 35–39
  real return, 39–41, 44–45
Revlon, Inc., 30–31, 36–37, 44–45, 52–53, 94–102
R. J. Reynolds Industries, Inc., 30–31, 36–37, 44–45, 52–53
Roadway Express, Inc., 30–31, 36–37, 44–45
Robins, A. H., Co., 30–31, 36–37, 44–45, 52–53
Robinson-Patman Act, 87, 228–29
Rockower Brothers, Inc., 30–31, 36–37, 44–45
Rockwood Corp., 192, 204–6
Rollins, Inc., 30–31, 36–37, 44–45
Rorer-Amchem, Inc., 30–31, 36–37, 44–45
Russell Stover Candies, Inc., 30–31, 36–37, 44–45

S

Safeway Stores, Inc., 127, 213–15, 218–21, 226–33
Scale economies, 43
  A&P Co., Inc., 213

Scale economies—Cont.
  computer manufacturers, 150, 152–53, 168–69
  grocery retailing, 118–21
Schering-Plough Corp., 30–31, 36–37, 44–45, 52–53
Scholes, Myron S., 78
Scientific Data Systems, Inc., 174–76
Searle, G. D., & Co., 30–31, 36–37, 44–45, 52–53
Share repurchases, 80–83
Shareholder wealth model, 72–74
  numerical example, 73
Sherman Act, 87
Smithkline Corp., 30–31, 36–37, 44–45, 52–53
Sovereign risk, 143, 145
Sperry Rand Corp., 151, 162, 164
Square D Co., 30–31, 36–37, 44–45, 52–53
Sterling Drug Inc., 30–31, 36–37, 44–45, 52–53
Stone & Webster, Inc., 30–31, 36–37, 44–45
Stop & Shop Companies, Inc., 127
Supermarkets General Corp., 127

T

Tampax, Inc., 30–31, 36–37, 44–45
Teledyne, Inc., 73, 81–83, 280
Thomas & Betts Corp., 30–31, 36–37, 44–45

U–V

Unicapital Corp., 259–70
Value creation
  aggregate potential, 42–45
  calculated for specific firms, 44–45
    Avon Products, Inc., 102–10
    Freeport Minerals Co., 140
    General Electric Co., 171, 173
    grocery retailing industry, 127
    Levitz Furniture Corp., 252–54, 258
  critical variables in determining magnitude, 11, 14, 17–18
  methods for accomplishing, 2, 65–76
  sample hypothetical calculations, 8–11
Value destruction, 209
  competitive effect of, 226–30
  defined, 1
  economics of, 220–26
  Levitz Furniture Corp., 259–72
  methods for accomplishing, 3, 86–89

Value transfer
   aggregate potential, 279, 281
   methods for accomplishing, 2–3, 76–
      86, 180, 201–8
   potential estimated
      for Avon Products, Inc., 105, 107
      for computer leasing industry, 202–4
      for Levitz Furniture Corp., 255–58
   unrealized opportunity, 108–10

W

Wackenhut Corp., 30–31, 36–37, 44–45
Weis Markets, Inc., 3, 30–31, 36–37,
   44–45, 115, 127

WEO
   competitive effects, 226–30
   economic appraisal, 220–26, 230–35
   the program, 216–20
Wickes Corp., 259–70
Winn-Dixie Stores, Inc., 3, 30–31, 36–37,
   44–45, 115, 122–25, 127, 213–15

X–Y

Xerox Corp., 30–31, 36–37, 44–45, 52–
   53, 151, 162, 164, 175–76
   loss in computer manufacturing, 174–
      76
Yellow Freight Systems, Inc., 30–31, 36–
   37, 44–45

*This book has been set linotype and IBM in
10 and 9 point Caledonia, leaded 2 points. Part
numbers are 24 point Weiss Roman and part
titles are 18 point Weiss Roman. Chapter numbers are 30 point Weiss Roman and chapter
titles are 16 point Weiss Roman. The size of
the type page is 27 by 45½ picas.*